T0402608

OXFORD MONOGRAPHS IN
INTERNATIONAL LAW

General Editors

PROFESSOR CATHERINE REDGWELL

*Chichele Professor of Public International Law at the University
of Oxford and Fellow of All Souls College, Oxford*

PROFESSOR ROGER O'KEEFE

Professor of International Law at Bocconi University, Milan

Access to Courts for Asylum Seekers and Refugees

OXFORD MONOGRAPHS IN
INTERNATIONAL LAW

The aim of this series is to publish important and original pieces of research on all aspects of international law. Topics that are given particular prominence are those which, while of interest to the academic lawyer, also have important bearing on issues which touch the actual conduct of international relations. Nonetheless the series is wide in scope and includes monographs on the history and philosophical foundations of international law.

Access to Courts for Asylum Seekers and Refugees

State Obligations under the 1951 Refugee Convention

EMMA DUNLOP

OXFORD
UNIVERSITY PRESS

Great Clarendon Street, Oxford, OX2 6DP,
United Kingdom

Oxford University Press is a department of the University of Oxford.
It furthers the University's objective of excellence in research, scholarship,
and education by publishing worldwide. Oxford is a registered trade mark of
Oxford University Press in the UK and in certain other countries

© Emma Dunlop, 2024

The moral rights of the author have been asserted

First Edition published in 2024

Public sector information reproduced under Open Government Licence v3.0
(http://www.nationalarchives.gov.uk/doc/open-government-licence/open-government-licence.htm)

Published in the United States of America by Oxford University Press
198 Madison Avenue, New York, NY 10016, United States of America

British Library Cataloguing in Publication Data
Data available

Library of Congress Control Number: 2023948179

ISBN 978–0–19–888559–7

DOI: 10.1093/oso/9780198885597.001.0001

Printed and bound by
CPI Group (UK) Ltd, Croydon, CR0 4YY

General Editors' Preface

An increasingly significant element of refugee protection is the obligation of States parties to guarantee refugees and asylum seekers access to domestic courts under article 16 of the 1951 Convention relating to the Status of Refugees. In the politicised context of asylum claims, denial of this critical gateway domestic right for asylum seekers and refugees effectively forecloses their ability to defend other rights under domestic law. Yet, notwithstanding its importance, article 16 has received little scholarly attention to date. This gap in the literature is now filled by this original and insightful work, which explores the extent of the protections afforded by article 16, concluding that it has a key role to play despite the presence of access-to-court provisions in relevant human rights instruments. This carefully crafted and nuanced reading of article 16 is a welcome addition to studies on the accountability and litigation strategies available in the context of human rights violations experienced by refugees and migrants. It makes a significant contribution to the existing literature on refugee law of benefit to both academics and practitioners in the field. It also offers the generalist international lawyer rich pickings from a meticulous analysis grounded squarely in the international rules on treaty interpretation and on the identification of customary international law. It makes a most welcome addition to the Oxford Monographs on International Law series.

CR and ROK
August 2023

Acknowledgements

This book is based on my PhD thesis, completed at UNSW Sydney. I am grateful for the vibrant academic community I found there, and particularly to Professors Jane McAdam and Melissa Crouch. Professor Guy Goodwin-Gill, as always, provided invaluable advice and a critical eye. I am also grateful for the insights of Daniel Joyce, Sarah Williams, Rosemary Rayfuse, Jonathan Bonnitcha, and Brooke Marshall, and the unwavering support of Jenny Jarrett. The Lauterpacht Centre for International Law welcomed me into its community in early 2019, for what was a very fruitful period of research. I have learnt much from my fellow refugee law PhD students—Khanh, Luke, Tristan, Riona, Regina, Brian, Ashraf, Aidan, and Natasha—over coffees, during hikes, and in the wonderful Rely group. My time at UNSW was indelibly shaped by my involvement with the Kaldor Centre. I am so thankful to Madeline, Claire, Frances and Frances, Lauren, Sangeetha, and of course Jane and Guy, for welcoming me into the life of the Centre, and for all the doors that that has opened. I also gratefully acknowledge my support through an Australian Government Research Training Program Scholarship.

This book could not have come together without the help of my family and friends. In particular, I must thank Hugh, for his unwavering support, humour, perspective, kindness, and cooking. And Will and Leigh, the light of our lives.

Contents

List of Cases, Opinions, Awards, and Communications

INTERNATIONAL COURT OF JUSTICE

INTERNATIONAL CRIMINAL COURT

AFRICAN COURT ON HUMAN AND PEOPLES' RIGHTS

AFRICAN COMMISSION ON HUMAN AND PEOPLES' RIGHTS

COURT OF JUSTICE OF THE EUROPEAN UNION

EUROPEAN COURT OF HUMAN RIGHTS/ EUROPEAN
COMMISSION OF HUMAN RIGHTS

HUMAN RIGHTS COUNCIL

AUSTRALIA

UNITED KINGDOM

UNITED STATES OF AMERICA

ARBITRAL AWARDS

List of Instruments

List of Abbreviations

ACmHPR	African Commission on Human and Peoples' Rights
ACtHPR	African Court on Human and Peoples' Rights
ADHR	American Declaration of the Rights and Duties of Man
AJIL	American Journal of International Law
BYIL	British Yearbook of International Law
CEAS	Common European Asylum System
CFR	Charter of Fundamental Rights of the European Union
CJEU	Court of Justice of the European Union
CRPD	Convention on the Rights of Persons with Disabilities
CRPD Cttee	Committee on the Rights of Persons with Disabilities
CUP	Cambridge University Press
ECHR	European Convention on Human Rights
ECOSOC	United Nations Economic and Social Council
ECtHR	European Court of Human Rights
EJIL	European Journal of International Law
EOIR	Executive Office for Immigration Review
ExCom	UNHCR Executive Committee
HRC	Human Rights Committee
IACmHR	Inter-American Commission on Human Rights
IACtHR	Inter-American Court of Human Rights
ICCPR	International Covenant on Civil and Political Rights
ICJ	International Court of Justice
ICLQ	International & Comparative Law Quarterly
IHL	International Humanitarian Law
IJRC	International Justice Resource Center
IJRL	International Journal of Refugee Law
ILC	International Law Commission
ILR	International Law Reports
IRO	International Refugee Organization
JRS	Journal of Refugee Studies
NYIL	Netherlands Yearbook of International Law
OAS	Organization of American States
OUP	Oxford University Press
RSD	Refugee Status Determination
RSQ	Refugee Survey Quarterly
UDHR	Universal Declaration of Human Rights
UK	United Kingdom

UN	United Nations
UNDP	United Nations Development Programme
UNGA	UN General Assembly
UNHCR	United Nations High Commissioner for Refugees
US	United States

1

Introduction

1. Framing the Issue

This book focuses on the scope and content of article 16 of the 1951 Convention relating to the Status of Refugees.[1] Article 16 reads:

ACCESS TO COURTS

1. *A refugee shall have free access to the courts of law on the territory of all Contracting States.*
2. *A refugee shall enjoy in the Contracting State in which he has his habitual residence the same treatment as a national in matters pertaining to access to the Courts, including legal assistance and exemption from* cautio judicatum solvi.
3. *A refugee shall be accorded in the matters referred to in paragraph 2 in countries other than that in which he has his habitual residence the treatment granted to a national of the country of his habitual residence.*

This provision has not been the subject of extensive academic discussion or case law.[2] In the decades after the 1951 Convention's adoption, it was characterised as uncontroversial, a vestige of a time where aliens were not guaranteed access to courts as a matter of course. More recently, some scholars have dismissed it as being subsumed by international human rights law. Yet others interpret article 16 as enshrining more substantive protections for those seeking asylum that are relevant to contemporary challenges. In light of these different approaches, surveyed in Chapter 2, the book examines the obligations that bind Contracting States

---

[1] Convention relating to the Status of Refugees, 189 UNTS 137 (adopted 28 July 1951, entered into force 22 Apr 1954) ('1951 Convention'), read in conjunction with the Protocol relating to the Status of Refugees, 606 UNTS 267 (adopted 31 Jan 1967, entered into force 4 Oct 1967) ('1967 Protocol'). The 1967 Protocol removed the temporal restriction in the 1951 Convention, which originally applied only to those persons who became refugees as a result of events occurring before 1 January 1951. In addition, the 1967 Protocol removed the option available to States to limit the geographic scope of the 1951 Convention to events occurring in Europe, save for those States that had already made a declaration exercising that option in accordance with the 1951 Convention. See 1951 Convention, art 1(A)2; art 1(B)1–2; and 1967 Protocol, art I(1)–(3).

[2] For analysis of scholarship, see Chapter 2.

Access to Courts for Asylum Seekers and Refugees. Emma Dunlop, Oxford University Press. © Emma Dunlop, 2024.
DOI: 10.1093/oso/9780198885597.003.0001

to provide asylum seekers and refugees with access to courts under article 16 of the 1951 Convention, and whether these obligations extend beyond those that otherwise bind States under international human rights treaties, customary international law, and general principles of law. It argues that despite developments in international human rights law since its adoption, article 16 of the 1951 Convention remains a relevant and robust source of protection. Article 16 requires Contracting States to the 1951 Convention to ensure access to courts, not merely for the recognised refugee, but also for the asylum seeker. In line with the 1951 Convention's object and purpose, this obligation entails a requirement to ensure 'effective' access, which may call for specific accommodations to be made to ameliorate vulnerabilities in the individual case (where, for example, a person does not speak the language of the court; is detained and lacks easy access to a lawyer; or lacks the funds to secure a lawyer and the interests of justice would call for legal representation). Furthermore, article 16 guarantees additional rights to those asylum seekers or refugees who have attained 'habitual residence' in the host country, a threshold which is dependent neither on recognition as a refugee nor on lawful presence. This interpretation positions article 16—which binds the 149 Contracting States to the 1951 Convention or its Protocol[3]—as a central bulwark of protection for refugees and asylum seekers. It is complemented by a rich, but uneven, patchwork of fair trial and due process rights under international, regional, and specialised human rights treaties.[4]

This introduction frames the analysis by establishing the importance of access to courts for asylum seekers and refugees (Section 1.1) and the practical and legal hindrances that they may face when attempting to access courts (Section 1.2). Section 1.3 addresses practical challenges for States. Section 2 then sets out the structure of the book and the key conclusions reached in each chapter and highlights issues that fall outside the book's scope. A note on methodology is included in Section 3. Section 4 concludes.

---

[3] At the time of writing, there were 146 parties to the Refugee Convention and 147 parties to the 1967 Protocol (the most recent accession to each instrument being that of South Sudan, in December 2018): See 'Convention relating to the Status of Refugees' (UNTC) <https://treaties.un.org/pages/ViewDetailsII.aspx?src=TREATY&mtdsg_no=V-2&chapter=5&Temp=mtdsg2&clang=_en>; 'Protocol relating to the Status of Refugees' (UNTC) <https://treaties.un.org/pages/ViewDetails.aspx?src=TREATY&mtdsg_no=V-5&chapter=5>. Before the accession of South Sudan, 148 States were parties to either the Convention, its Protocol or both instruments: see UNHCR, 'States Parties to the 1951 Convention relating to the Status of Refugees and the 1967 Protocol' (as of Apr 2015) <http://www.unhcr.org/en-au/protection/basic/3b73b0d63/states-parties-1951-convention-its-1967-protocol.html>. No reservation can be made to article 16(1), per article 42. Only three States have sought reservations under Article 16(2)–(3): Timor Leste (with respect to art 16(2)); China (with respect to art 16(3)); and Uganda (with respect to obligations of legal assistance under both sub-provisions).

[4] Surveyed in Chapter 5.

1.1 Access to Courts—General and Particular

The right of access to courts is not only of concern to refugees. It is a well-recognised requirement of an effective judicial system, central to modern characterisations of the rule of law,[5] and essential to the full integration of an individual in civic life. In Paulsson's words, '[t]he right of access to courts is fundamental and uncontroversial'.[6] Although there are limitations on the right of access to courts—for example, the use of civil restraint orders to prevent a litigant from commencing targeted litigation,[7] or the effect of State and official immunities against suit,[8] it is generally recognised that such carve-outs must be carefully circumscribed. The right of access to courts has been recognised as an inherent element of the International Covenant on Civil and Political Rights (ICCPR)[9] and the European Convention on Human Rights (ECHR).[10] However, as discussed in Chapter 5, both instruments have been interpreted so as to exclude the review of failed asylum claims from the scope of their protection.

While of general importance, the right of access to courts is particularly significant for asylum seekers and refugees for three reasons. First, the ability to access the courts in a country of refuge is intrinsically linked to recognition as a person before the law, who is capable of possessing both obligations and rights. Without access to domestic courts, a person is effectively foreclosed from seeking to uphold any other rights that he or she may possess under domestic law.[11] Early work on the drafting of the 1951 Convention shows a concern to avoid a position of legal

---

[5] Lord Bingham proposes that the 'core of the existing principle', while not comprehensive, is that 'all persons and authorities within the state, whether public or private, should be bound by and entitled to the benefit of laws publicly made, taking effect (generally) in the future and publicly administered in the courts.': Tom Bingham, *The Rule of Law* (Allen Lane, Penguin Books 2010) 8. In cases where parties are unable to settle a dispute and 'the clear need is for a public and authoritative ruling of the court', he considers that 'the rule of law requires that there should be access to a court': 86. In *Golder v United Kingdom,* App no 4451/70 (ECtHR, Court (Plenary), 21 Feb 1975), the European Court of Human Rights stated 'in civil matters one can scarcely conceive of the rule of law without there being a possibility of having access to the courts': para 34.

[6] Jan Paulsson, *Denial of Justice in International Law* (CUP 2005) 134.

[7] See, eg, *Melville* [2006] EWCA Civ 1894, paras 6, 8 (Neuberger LJ).

[8] Paulsson (n 6) 138. See, eg, *Jones and Others v United Kingdom*, App nos 34356/06 and 40528/06 (ECtHR, 4th Section, 14 January 2014), paras 186–189, 198, 215.

[9] 999 UNTS 171 (signed 16 Dec 1966, entered into force 23 Mar 1976) (ICCPR). See also its Optional Protocol, 999 UNTS 171 (adopted 16 Dec 1966, entered into force 23 Mar 1976).

[10] Convention for the Protection of Human Rights and Fundamental Freedoms, 213 UNTS 221 (opened for signature 4 Nov 1950, entered into force 3 Sept 1953), as amended by Protocols No 11, ETS No 155 (entered into force 1 Nov 1998), No 14, CETS No 194 (entered into force 1 June 2010) and No 15, CETS No 213 (entered into force 1 August 2021) (ECHR). See further Chapter 5, Section 2.3.1.

[11] Or rights under the 1951 Convention, to the extent that they are incorporated into domestic law. See 'Written submissions on behalf of the Office of the United Nations High Commissioner for Refugees, Intervener' and 'Further Written Submissions on behalf of the Intervener (UNHCR)' in Guy S Goodwin-Gill, '*The Queen (Al-Rawi and others) v Secretary of State for Foreign and Commonwealth Affairs and another* (United Nations High Commissioner for Refugees intervening)' (2008) 20 International Journal of Refugee Law 675, 681.

ostracism in the host country.[12] The preamble to the 'preliminary draft Convention relating to the Status of Refugees (and stateless persons)', which was submitted to the Ad Hoc Committee by the Secretary-General as a basis for discussion, included in its first paragraph a reference to the right to 'recognition everywhere as a person before the law' under article 6 of the Universal Declaration of Human Rights (UDHR).[13] It also noted that 'a refugee whose juridical status has not been determined does not possess a guarantee of the right to recognition everywhere as a person before the law', and that until the point of repatriation or obtaining a new nationality, a refugee 'must be granted juridical status that will enable him to lead a normal and self-respecting life'.[14] Comments on the preamble laid out the practicalities underlying this concern, noting that refugees 'run the risk of not being recognised in every place as persons before the law, owing to the difficulty of submitting the documents issued to them in their country of origin which constitute evidence of their identity and status'.[15] The Secretary-General affirmed that 'it is essential in the interests both of the refugee and of the country which has received him that he should enjoy a status defining his rights and obligations'.[16] Although these references did not make their way into the final text,[17] they do reflect the general concern, to adopt Justice Sachs' words, 'that refugees would not end up as pariahs at the margins of host societies'.[18]

Second, the significance of ensuing that asylum seekers and refugees have access to courts is heightened by the challenges inherent in enforcing their rights at the international level. Although there are arguments that the international legal system is undergoing a recalibration towards an 'individual-centred, humanized system',[19] States remain the central actors on the international plane. While the ECHR offers accessible remedies to individuals within its jurisdictional scope,[20]

---

[12] On this material see Guy S Goodwin-Gill and Jane McAdam, with Emma Dunlop, *The Refugee in International Law* (4th edn, OUP 2021) 55, fn 1, noting 'today, although "refugee status" is understood more as the formal confirmation of entitlement to international protection or asylum in the sense of solution, than as a particular civil quality, its absence or denial may well entail the marginalization of substantial numbers of individuals otherwise in need of refuge'.

[13] UN Economic and Social Council (ECOSOC), 'Ad Hoc Committee on Statelessness and Related Problems: Status of refugees and stateless persons—Memorandum by the Secretary-General', E/AC.32/2 (3 Jan 1950), Annex, 13 ('Secretary-General Memorandum'); Universal Declaration of Human Rights, UNGA Res 217 A(III) (10 Dec 1948), art 6 (UDHR).

[14] Secretary-General Memorandum (n 13) Annex 1, 13.

[15] ibid Annex 1, 14.

[16] ibid.

[17] As noted by Goodwin-Gill and McAdam (4th edn) (n 12) 55, fn 1.

[18] Justice Albie Sachs, 'From refugee to judge of refugee law' in James C Simeon (ed), *Critical Issues in International Refugee Law: Strategies Toward Interpretative Harmony* (CUP 2010) 51, citing his judgment in *Union of Refugee Women and Others v Director, Private Security Industry Regulatory Authority and Others* (CCT 39/06) [2006] ZACC 23, para 134.

[19] Anne Peters, 'Humanity as the A and Ω of Sovereignty' (2009) 20 European Journal of International Law 513, 514.

[20] Obligations under the ECHR are enforced by the European Court of Human Rights, which has jurisdiction over 'all matters concerning the interpretation and application of the Convention and the Protocols thereto': ECHR, arts 19, 32. Article 34 provides that the Court may receive applications from, inter alia, individuals claiming a violation of their rights under the Convention by a State Party. For the

the protections offered by human rights treaties are often illusory, even for individuals who retain the protection of their State of nationality. In Hathaway's words, the implementation structures of international human rights law 'are generally sluggish and only occasionally effective'.[21] In the field of international refugee law, these implementation structures are not merely ineffective, but non-existent. The 1951 Convention contains no mechanism through which refugees themselves can seek redress for a breach of their Convention rights. While article 38 of the 1951 Convention provides that States may refer a dispute on its appropriate interpretation or application to the International Court of Justice (ICJ),[22] no such avenue exists for individuals. In this procedural respect, the 1951 Convention provides less protection than either the ECHR, which is enforced through individual applications to the European Court of Human Rights (ECtHR),[23] or the ICCPR, which is supported by the Human Rights Committee's (HRC's) individual complaints mechanism.[24]

This second challenge is compounded by the fact that the classical method of seeking remedies for failures to uphold an alien's rights in a foreign State— diplomatic protection—is also generally closed to asylum seekers and refugees.[25] Aliens have typically called upon their State of nationality to pursue a claim on their behalf on the international level, a process that recasts the harm to the alien as harm to the State itself.[26] For asylum seekers and refugees who by definition are

right to a remedy at the domestic level, see ECHR, art 19. See also International Law Commission (ILC), 'First Report on diplomatic protection, by Mr. John R. Dugard. Special Rapporteur', A/CN.4/506 and Add 1 (52nd sess, 2000), para 25, cited in Paulsson (n 6) 9.

[21] James Hathaway, 'Reconceiving Refugee Law as Human Rights Protection' (1991) 4 Journal of Refugee Studies 113, cited in part in Jane McAdam, 'The Refugee Convention as a Rights Blueprint' in Jane McAdam (ed), *Forced Migration and Global Security* (Hart Publishing 2008) 269.

[22] 1951 Convention, art 38; Jane McAdam, 'Interpretation of the 1951 Convention' in Andreas Zimmermann (ed), *The 1951 Convention Relating to the Status of Refugees and its 1967 Protocol* (OUP 2011), 77, fn 2. This avenue has never been used. See also the Summary Conclusions of the 'Roundtable on the Future of Refugee Convention Supervision' (2013) 26 Journal of Refugee Studies 327, 328 (concluding that there is 'real value in considering' the establishment of a committee of experts within UNHCR to issue Advisory Opinions on the interpretation and application of the 1951 Convention); and Anthony M North and Joyce Chia, 'Towards Convergence in the Interpretation of the Refugee Convention: A Proposal for the Establishment of an International Judicial Commission for Refugees' in Jane McAdam (ed), *Forced Migration, Human Rights and Security* (Hart Publishing 2008), 226.

[23] See fn 20.

[24] States parties to the ICCPR Optional Protocol recognise the HRC's competence to receive and consider communications from individuals who are subject to its jurisdiction who claim that the State in question has violated of their rights: Optional Protocol to the International Covenant on Civil and Political Rights, 999 UNTS 171 (adopted 16 Dec 1966, entered into force 23 Mar 1976), art 1.

[25] James C Hathaway, *The Rights of Refugees under International Law* (2nd edn, CUP 2021) 779.

[26] This method of pursuing claims has its own weaknesses: See Rosalyn Higgins, *Problems & Process: International Law and How We Use it* (Clarendon Press 1994, reprinted 2010), 52 (noting '[a]ll too often his national government is not at all interested in pursuing his claim (or in rectifying the harm allegedly done to itself, to rephrase it in the classic formula). It has broader interests to concern itself with, and the instigation of litigation may not fit with these broader considerations. The individual is thus left with no effective remedy' (footnotes omitted)).

unable or unwilling to avail themselves of the protection of their State of nationality, this is hardly a viable option. In addition, as the International Law Commission (ILC) noted in the commentaries to its Draft Articles on Diplomatic Protection, a refugee who seeks the protection of the State from which he or she initially fled would 'run the risk of losing refugee status in the State of residence'.[27] Although the ILC accepts that a State of refuge may, in its discretion, exercise diplomatic protection on behalf of a refugee who is lawfully and habitually resident in its territory,[28] there are few options available if the State of refuge is itself the offender.

Third, guaranteeing asylum seekers and refugees access to courts is significant for the broader institutional purpose that it can serve in the field of refugee law. As McAdam notes, there is 'no uniform international practice or single interpretation' of the 1951 Convention due to the absence of an international refugee court that could rule on its appropriate interpretation, and the one avenue in the Convention for seeking a definitive interpretation (recourse to the ICJ) has never been engaged.[29] The United Nations High Commissioner for Refugees (UNHCR) lacks an authoritative role in interpreting the 1951 Convention—its work is limited to a supervisory capacity[30] and 'does not extend to a mandate to provide authoritative rulings or opinions on the meaning of particular treaty terms'.[31] In this environment, the elaboration of refugee-specific rights by courts can assist in building judicial consensus on the scope and content of rights under the 1951 Convention. Two caveats should be made to this claim. First, refugee-specific rights will only ever be a small section of the claims litigated on the national level, and in some States, the rights in the Convention may not be incorporated into domestic law at all. Second, the focus of the 'judicial dialogue' regarding the 1951 Convention has historically been on the refugee definition rather than on the rights under the Convention.[32] Nonetheless, domestic courts do have a role to play in interpreting the parameters of rights under the 1951 Convention, and it is only by ensuring that refugees have access to the courts that this dialogue can be preserved.

---

[27] See ILC, Draft articles on diplomatic protection' in *Report of the International Law Commission*, Vol II, A/61/10 (58th sess, 2006), Commentary, 49.

[28] ibid draft art 8(2), providing that a State *may* exercise diplomatic protection in respect of a recognised refugee who was lawfully and habitually resident in that State both at the time of the injury and the making of the claim. The commentary makes it clear that this is a discretionary right. See also *R (on the application of Al-Rawi) v Secretary of State for Foreign and Commonwealth Affairs and Another* [2006] EWCA Civ 1279.

[29] See McAdam, 'Interpretation' (n 22) 77.

[30] See 1951 Convention, art 35(1); Statute of the Office of the United Nations High Commissioner for Refugees, annexed to UNGA Res 428(V) (14 Dec 1950), paragraph 8(a); Chapter 3.

[31] McAdam, 'Interpretation' (n 22) 79.

[32] See Hathaway, *Rights* (2nd edn) (n 25) 1. See also discussion of this 'transnational judicial dialog' on the refugee definition in James C Hathaway and Michelle Foster, *The Law of Refugee Status* (2nd edn, CUP 2014) 4–5; and, generally, Guy S Goodwin-Gill and Hélène Lambert (eds), *The Limits of Transnational Law: Refugee Law, Policy Harmonization and Judicial Dialogue in the European Union* (CUP 2010).

1.2 Practical and Legal Hindrances to Accessing Courts

This section maps the ways and means in which that access may be practically hindered during flight, refugee status determination (RSD), and settlement in a host society. The approach is broad, encompassing measures that aim to limit an asylum seeker's relationship to the host State by, for example, restricting access to territory or to administrative decision-making. This foreshadows discussions outlined in Chapter 2 on the geographic scope of article 16 and whether it applies to administrative agencies conducting RSD, while also emphasising that access to courts can be circumvented in indirect ways. The 'subject-matter jurisdiction' question— namely, whether article 16 could require a State to create jurisdiction to vindicate an internationally protected right that is not recognised under domestic law—is also addressed in Chapter 2.

Rights of access to courts may be hindered in a several ways. Most fundamentally, asylum seekers may be denied access to a State's territory entirely through a suite of measures designed to prevent any legal relationship from forming between the State and an individual seeking protection.[33] Arrangements between transit and destination States can hinder onward movement.[34] Maritime interceptions and turn-backs are carried out on the high seas,[35] while visa requirements and carrier sanctions can prevent asylum seekers from boarding a plane to a potential host country.[36] States may also post immigration officials abroad to prevent onward movement—UK officials have staffed foreign airports to stop asylum seekers from boarding planes, a measure that the House of Lords found to be consistent with the 1951 Refugee Convention but in breach of anti-discrimination law.[37]

Countries also restrict access to the asylum process by limiting the number of people who can cross the border or enter transit zones. In the US, the policy of

---

[33] Much has been written on these developments. See eg Hathaway, *Rights* (2nd edn) (n 25) 313–21, 329–36; Thomas Gammeltoft-Hansen and James C Hathaway, '*Non-refoulement* in a World of Cooperative Deterrence' (2015) 53 Columbia Journal of Transnational Law 235; Thomas Gammeltoft-Hansen, *Access to Asylum: International Refugee Law and the Globalisation of Migration Control* (CUP 2011) (who recalls that '[a]ccess to legal aid, counselling and national complaint mechanisms may be severely impaired for a refugee who never sets foot on European soil': at 5); Goodwin-Gill and McAdam (4th edn) (n 12) 415–28. See also discussion of externalisation—conceptualised as 'the process of shifting functions that are normally undertaken by a State within its own territory so that they take place, in part or in whole, outside its territory' (at 122)—in David Cantor et al, 'Externalisation, Access to Territorial Asylum, and International Law' (2022) 34 International Journal of Refugee Law 120. The authors note that externalisation 'often involves attempts to shift responsibility for the externalised measures to other entities': at 123.

[34] See Gammeltoft-Hansen and Hathaway (n 33) 248–57, also discussing more direct operations and the use of international agencies in interception operations.

[35] Though these are not always successful in insulating a State from legal responsibility: see *Hirsi Jamaa and Others v Italy*, App no 27765/09 (ECtHR, Grand Chamber, 23 Feb 2012).

[36] See eg Hathaway, *Rights* (2nd edn) (n 25) 483–84.

[37] *R v Immigration Officer at Prague Airport and another, ex parte European Roma Rights Centre and Others,* [2004] UKHL 55. See further Hathaway, *Rights* (2nd edn) (n 25) 321; and Goodwin-Gill and McAdam (4th edn) (n 12) 425–27 (noting that 'many States' post immigration officials abroad: at 423).

'metering' has prevented asylum seekers from crossing the US land border at ports of entry, limited the number of asylum applications that could be made at a port of entry per day, and sent those added to a waitlist back to a precarious existence in Mexico.[38] In Hungary, a policy of requiring all asylum applications to be made in transit zones while simultaneously limiting the number of applicants authorised to enter those zones was found to be a breach of EU asylum law.[39] Extraterritorial processing also complicates the picture;[40] it has the effect of 'deliberately bur[ying] any potential litigation in *any* court under an avalanche of complex jurisdictional issues'.[41]

If an asylum seeker succeeds in reaching a State's territory or jurisdiction, he or she may nonetheless face difficulties accessing the domestic RSD process. This may be a result of practical or legal hindrances, or a combination of the two. An asylum seeker intercepted by State officials at sea may be afforded only a brief interview (if any) that is not conducive to fully articulating an asylum claim.[42] Border officials may systematically fail to detect or register asylum claims, misrepresent the substance of their claim in official reporting,[43] or deny an applicant the right to make a

---

[38] Andrew I Schoenholtz, Jaya Ramji-Nogales, and Philip G Schrag, *The End of Asylum* (Georgetown University Press 2021) 57–59; 'Fact Sheet: Metering and Pushbacks' (American Immigration Council, 8 Mar 2021) <https://www.americanimmigrationcouncil.org/research/metering-and-asylum-turnbacks>.

[39] Case C-808/18, *Commission v Hungary (Accueil des demandeurs de protection internationale)* (CJEU, Grand Chamber, 17 Dec 2020), paras 128, 315. UNHCR reports considered by the Court showed that 'the number of daily authorised entries into those transit zones decreased gradually and steadily, such that, in 2018, only two persons per day were authorised to enter each': at para 115.

[40] Gammeltoft-Hansen notes that '[t]o some extent, refugees encountering the state outside its territory or by proxy are ... likely to keep on experiencing additional barriers in claiming their legal entitlements': Gammeltoft-Hansen (n 33) 235–36. See also Azadeh Dastyari, *United States Migrant Interdiction and the Detention of Refugees in Guantánamo Bay* (CUP 2015), 188–89 (noting that 'members of the protected population [i.e. refugees and migrants who may be tortured if returned to their country of origin] in Guantánamo Bay have no right to have their detention reviewed'); and Ben Doherty and Saba Vasefi, 'Asylum Seeker Boy on Nauru Pleads for Medical Help for his Mother' (The Guardian, 26 Apr 2018) <https://www.theguardian.com/australia-news/2018/apr/25/asylum-seeker-boy-on-nauru-pleads-for-medical-help-for-his-mother> (citing the Australian Border Force's practice of flying offshore refugees to Taiwan for medical care rather than bringing them to Australia, 'because refugees taken there cannot access Australia's courts, where refugees often win injunctions preventing their return to Nauru'). A number of successful cases have however been brought in Australia enabling offshore asylum seekers and refugees to access medical care in Australia: see 'Medical Transfer Proceedings' (Kaldor Centre, undated) <https://www.kaldorcentre.unsw.edu.au/medical-transfer-proceedings>.

[41] Angus Francis, 'Bringing Protection Home: Healing the Schism Between International Obligations and National Safeguards Created by Extraterritorial Processing' (2008) 20 International Journal of Refugee Law 273, 309. See also Björn Elberling, 'Article 16' in Andreas Zimmermann (ed), *The 1951 Convention Relating to the Status of Refugees and its 1967 Protocol* (OUP 2011) 945, citing Francis.

[42] See eg *Hirsi* (n 35); Maria O'Sullivan, 'Interdiction and Screening of Asylum Seekers at Sea: Implications for Asylum Justice' in Maria O'Sullivan and Dallal Stevens (eds), *States, the Law and Access to Refugee Protection: Fortresses and Fairness* (Hart Publishing 2017) 93–112. UNHCR considers that processing international protection claims at sea is 'generally not appropriate, unless reception arrangements (including for vulnerable persons), eligibility screening processes, and procedural safeguards in line with international standards can be guaranteed': UNHCR, 'Legal considerations on the roles and responsibilities of States in relation to rescue at sea, non-refoulement, and access to asylum' (1 December 2022) para 4.4 (footnotes omitted).

[43] See *MK and others v Poland*, App nos 40503/17, 42902/17 and 43643/17 (ECtHR, 1st Section, 23 July 2020) paras 174–175; HRC, *AB and PD v Poland*, Comm No 3017/2017, CCPR/C/135/D/

claim outright.[44] The practical effect of consigning an asylum seeker to a designated frontier zone or detention centre may be to prevent their access to a lawyer or limit information on how to lodge an asylum claim.[45] Of course, barriers can also be intentionally constructed by a State through the removal of funding for legal aid for asylum seekers[46] or other, more creative methods. In 2021, the Grand Chamber of the Court of Justice of the European Union (CJEU) found Hungary's new criminal offence of 'facilitating illegal immigration', which extends to '[a]nyone' conducting 'organising activities with a view to ... enabling asylum proceedings to be brought' by a person who is not a refugee to be in breach of its obligations under EU law.[47] Domestic law may also prevent protection applications from being lodged at all. In Australia, different procedures for lodging an asylum claim apply to those who arrive 'legally' and 'illegally', with the latter barred from making a claim unless special dispensation is granted by the Minister.[48]

Even if an asylum seeker succeeds in lodging a protection claim, the RSD process itself may involve procedural rules or bars that have the effect of winnowing down the total number of successful applications. Procedures implemented to streamline RSD process include fast tracking of status determination claims[49] and safe country schemes.[50] While these processes would not be problematic were

---

3017/2017 (3 February 2023) paras 9.2; 9.5–9.7. See also allegations and recommendations in HRC, 'Concluding observations on the fourth periodic report of the Plurinational State of Bolivia', CCPR/C/BOL/CO/4 (2 June 2022), paras 28 and 29(b).

[44]   See eg Schoenholtz, Ramji-Nogales and Schrag (n 38) 57 (on informal pushbacks at the US border); Hathaway, *Rights* (2nd edn) (n 25) 326; and Delphine Rodrik, 'Rights Not Recognized: Applying the Right to Recognition as a Person before the Law to Pushbacks at International Borders' (2021) 33 International Journal of Refugee Law 541 (arguing that pushbacks should be characterised as a violation of article 16 ICCPR—recognition as a person before the law).

[45]   See eg Júlia Iván, 'Where do State Responsibilities Begin and End: Border Exclusions and State Responsibility' in O'Sullivan and Stevens (n 42) 63–64 (on Hungary's border practices).

[46]   In 2014, the Australian government abolished funded legal aid for most asylum seekers arriving without a visa: see Kaldor Centre, 'Factsheet: Do People Seeking Asylum Receive Legal Assistance?' (updated May 2020), available via <https://www.kaldorcentre.unsw.edu.au/publication/legal-assistance-asylum-seekers>. The 2022 Note on International Protection states that effective access to asylum is enhanced through measures including 'the participation of legal aid providers ... from the onset of the asylum procedure': UNGA, 'Note on International Protection', A/AC.96.1222 (19 July 2022), para 26.

[47]   Case C-821/19, *European Commission v Hungary* (CJEU, Grand Chamber, 16 Nov 2021), para 144; discussed in Chapter 6, Section 2.2.1.

[48]   See Migration Act 1958 (Cth), s 46A (Visa applications by unauthorised maritime arrivals).

[49]   See eg Directive 2013/32/EU of the European Parliament and of the Council of 26 June 2013 on common procedures for granting and withdrawing international protection (recast), OJ L 180/60 (recast Procedures Directive), art 31(8); Kaldor Centre, 'Research Brief: "Fast track" Refugee Status Determination' (updated June 2022) 5 (comparing the Australian fast track system to the earlier UK Detained Fast Track System). In the Australian Federal Court case *BSQ16 v Minister for Immigration and Border Protection* [2018] FCA 469, [32], Wigney J stated: 'While some may consider that the provisions of Part 7AA [Migration Act] and the procedures to be adopted by the [Immigration Assessment] Authority are anything but fair to an applicant, those are the procedures that Parliament has provided for applicants who are unlucky enough to be "fast track review applicants"'.

[50]   See Goodwin-Gill and McAdam (n 12) 436–60 (covering safe country of origin and safe third country schemes).

they simply to hasten the rejection of unmeritorious claims, there is a risk that applicants—particularly those that are vulnerable or lack the benefit of advice—may be rejected without appropriate consideration of their claim. Appeal rights may be available to administrative bodies and/or courts, on the merits or on questions of law.[51] However, practical and legal hurdles can limit asylum seekers' ability to access these processes. Elberling and other commentators have identified certain practices—either specific to a single State or generally—that may be in breach of article 16.[52] Examples include: the application of shorter time limits for seeking judicial review of unsuccessful asylum applications as compared to other administrative appeals;[53] the adoption of procedural requirements that 'effectively make it impossible ... to initiate proceedings';[54] and 'severely restricting' legal aid, as compared to what is available to nationals.[55]

Beyond the RSD process, asylum seekers and refugees may face difficulties accessing the courts to vindicate general rights under domestic law.[56] Asylum seekers and refugees may be deterred from accessing the court system to defend their rights by impecuniosity, lack of familiarity with the judicial system or legal assistance, fear of authorities, and/or communication barriers. The difficulties for asylum seekers can be particularly acute. Detention raises its own set of hurdles—in Australia, the Refugee Advice & Casework Service (RACS) has reported that assisting detained clients is 'consistently frustrated' by inconsistent access to the internet or telephone, and 'regular client transfers without notice'.[57]

---

[51] ibid (n 12) 629–31.

[52] Note however that Elberling is wary of 'sweeping statements' on domestic regimes' compatibility with the obligations in article 16: (n 41) 945. All examples attributed to Elberling are subject to his proviso that 'the State in question has courts which can generally be seised of disputes concerning administrative law questions': at 945, fn 109.

[53] Dana Baldinger, *Vertical Judicial Dialogues in Asylum Cases: Standards on Judicial Scrutiny and Evidence in International and European Asylum Law* (Brill Nijhoff 2015) 29 (noting that '[s]uch shorter time limits are, in fact, more stringent admissibility conditions which do not apply to nationals in administrative court proceedings'). See also Elberling (n 41) 945.

[54] Elberling (n 41) 945, giving as examples 'overly stringent procedural requirements as to time and form of filings ... especially where not paralleled in other administrative proceedings', and citing Hathaway's reference to *Sahak v Minister of Immigration and Multicultural Affairs* [2002] FCAFC 215: James C Hathaway, *The Rights of Refugees under International Law* (1st edn, CUP 2005) 631–32.

[55] Elberling (n 41) 945–46, citing this as an example of '*general* procedural differences in treatment between [RSD] proceedings and other administrative law proceedings' that are 'suspect' under article 16(2), and noting that an 'in-depth examination of the national court system and the precise nature and scope of the differences in treatment' would be necessary to any such analysis. See also Baldinger (n 53) 29 (referring to 'obstacles to obtaining legal aid').

[56] In Australia, RACS notes that asylum seekers 'present with a range of legal problems beyond their migration status': consultation cited in Law Council of Australia, 'The Justice Project: Final Report—Part 1: Asylum Seekers' (August 2018) 11. More broadly, victims of crime may face difficulties in seeing perpetrators brought to justice: see eg Oghenerioborue Esther Eberechi, 'A Comparative Analysis of the Application of the 1951 Refugee Convention to Victims of Sexual Violence in South Africa, Tanzania and Uganda' (2020) 23 PER/PELJ <https://perjournal.co.za/article/view/6225/10396>, 18–20 (conclusions on South Africa) and 18, 21 (Uganda). While also noting issues in Tanzania, the author considered that poor and absent documentation made it impossible to draw firm conclusions: 18, 20–21.

[57] Law Council of Australia (n 56) 18, summarising RACS, 'Submission no 108' (9 Oct 2017) 11, available via <https://www.lawcouncil.asn.au/justice-project/justice-project-submissions>.

Parliaments may also simply remove certain causes of action from the purview of the courts or curtail rights of appeal. On 20 July 2023, the Illegal Migration Act 2023 (UK) received royal assent.[58] The Act renders inadmissible 'protection claims and certain human rights claims made by persons who meet the conditions for removal [under the Act]'.[59] Section 5(4) of the Act states that a declaration of inadmissibility is not a decision to refuse the claim, and consequently, no right of appeal under s 82(1)(a)–(b) of the Nationality, Immigration and Asylum Act 2002 (UK) arises.[60] The Illegal Migration Act 2023 does provide for two 'suspensive claims'—the first challenging a removal notice on the basis that a person does not meet the removal conditions, and the second challenging removal to a specified third country on the basis that a person would there face 'a real, imminent and foreseeable risk of serious and irreversible harm'.[61] However, UNHCR considers that the suspensive claim procedure is unlikely to prevent refoulement, due, amongst other concerns, to the fact that 'normal rights of appeal are made unavailable, and the new rights of appeal ... are subject to a series of significant procedural and substantive limitations'.[62]

In Australia, the Migration Act 1958 bars 'unauthorised maritime arrivals' from instituting or continuing any legal proceedings related to the lawfulness of their detention as an 'unlawful non-citizen'.[63] Considering this provision, the Federal Court noted a 'recurring theme in this legislative scheme of curtailment of the jurisdiction and the powers of courts',[64] and a legislative intention 'to restrict access to Australian courts, and to make it as difficult as constitutionally possible for individuals to litigate over the subject matter categories'.[65]

---

[58] Illegal Migration Act 2023 (UK), accessed via <https://www.legislation.gov.uk/ukpga/2023/37/enacted>. On commencement, see s 68.

[59] ibid, s 1(2)(b). See also s 2(1) (duty to make arrangements for removal if four conditions in s 2 are met); s 5(2) (obligation on Secretary of State to declare a protection or human rights claim inadmissible if a person meets the four conditions), and s 4 (exceptions).

[60] Under s 82(1)(a)–(b) of the Nationality, Immigration and Asylum Act 2002 (UK), a person may appeal a decision by the Secretary of State to refuse a protection claim or a human rights claim to the Tribunal: Nationality, Immigration and Asylum Act 2002 (UK), available via <https://www.legislation.gov.uk/ukpga/2002/41/section/82>.

The Illegal Migration Act 2023 (UK) also provides that the duty of removal in s 2(1) will apply to a person who meets the four conditions in s 2 regardless of whether he or she makes an application for judicial review in relation to removal: s 5(1)(d). See also s 54 (restricting interim remedies in court proceedings relating to a decision to remove a person under the Act) and s 55.

[61] See Illegal Migration Act 2023 (UK), ss 38–53.

[62] See UNHCR, 'UNHCR Recommendations on the Implementation of the Illegal Migration Act 2023' (6 Oct 2023), para 31 and fn 48.

[63] See s 494AA(1)(c) Migration Act. In 2019, the Federal Court of Australia found that, by virtue of this provision, it had no jurisdiction to consider a claim for damages for unlawful imprisonment brought by a 5-year-old applicant on behalf of a class of people who sought asylum in Australia and were, for the most part, subsequently granted visas: see *DBE17 v Commonwealth of Australia* [2018] FCA 1307.

[64] ibid para 75.

[65] ibid para 128. This particular comment related to the fact that judicial recourse to the High Court (which possesses original jurisdiction under s 75(iii) of the Australian Constitution to consider 'all matters' in which the Commonwealth is a party) remained unaffected, such that litigants were 'compell[ed]' to issue proceedings in that Court. The applicant subsequently commenced an action in the High

These efforts are not always successful, as domestic courts may exercise 'judicial ingenuity' to circumvent parliamentary attempts to oust their jurisdiction.[66] In other cases, however, courts may show deference to parliamentary efforts to restrict the rights of asylum seekers and refugees. In 2020, the US Supreme Court upheld the constitutionality of a bar on habeas corpus review under the Illegal Immigration Reform and Immigrant Responsibility Act (IIRIRA) in relation to an asylum seeker.[67] The court argued that the respondent was seeking a use of the writ which would have been 'unrecognizable' at the time of the Constitution's drafting, namely to 'obtain additional administrative review of his asylum claim'.[68] In a dissenting opinion, Justice Sotomayor (joined by Justice Kagan) castigated the majority for 'declar[ing] that the Executive Branch's denial of asylum claims in expedited removal proceedings shall be functionally unreviewable through the writ of habeas corpus, no matter whether the denial is arbitrary or irrational or contrary to governing law'.[69]

Paradoxically, many of the examples discussed here were revealed through legal proceedings. However, the cases that do reach court often demonstrate the difficulties associated in bringing actions in the first place. One basic example is the challenge of maintaining regular contact between lawyers and clients living in precarious circumstances.[70] In *Hirsi*, the ECtHR found Italy to have violated the rights of the 24 applicants, who were among 200 people who attempted a voyage from Libya to Italy before being intercepted by the Italian navy and returned to Tripoli.[71] Between the application and the judgment, the applicants' lawyers had lost contact with all but six of the applicants.[72] In another case, one judge considered that the matter should have been struck out due to lawyers' poor reporting of the applicants' location.[73] A series of cases for injunctive relief has been brought in the

---

Court, which the High Court then remitted to the Federal Court: see *DBE17 (by his litigation guardian Marie Theresa Arthur) v Commonwealth of Australia* [2020] FCA 958, paras 3–4. Leave to discontinue was granted in *DBE17v Commonwealth (No 3)* [2021] FCA 1584.

[66] See Emma Dunlop, Jane McAdam and Greg Weeks, 'A Search for Rights: Judicial and Administrative Responses to Migration and Refugee Cases', in Matthew Groves, Janina Boughey and Dan Meagher (eds), *The Legal Protection of Rights in Australia* (Hart Publishing 2019) 349.

[67] *Department of Homeland Security v Thuraissigiam* 591 U.S. ___ (2020). The Court considered §1252(e)(2) IIRIRA, which limited the habeas corpus review available to asylum seekers (amongst others) to a determination of (i) whether the petitioner is an alien; (ii) whether the petitioner was ordered removed; and (iii) whether the petitioner can prove that he or she holds permanent residence or has been granted asylum or refugee status. The Supreme Court reversed a decision by the Ninth Circuit that had found that IIRIRA unconstitutionally suspended the writ of habeas corpus and violated an asylum seeker's right to due process.

[68] ibid 2.

[69] *Thuraissigiam* (n 67) (Sotomayor, joined by Kagan J, dissenting) 1.

[70] On this issue see also Marie-Bénédicte Dembour, *When Humans Become Migrants: Study of the European Court of Human Rights with an Inter-American Counterpoint* (OUP 2015) 418.

[71] *Hirsi* (n 35) para 179; see also *ND and NT v Spain,* App nos 8675/15 and 8697/15 (ECtHR, Grand Chamber, 13 Feb 2020) paras 9–11, 207.

[72] ibid para 17. Two applicants had died in unknown circumstances before the application was lodged: para 15.

[73] *ND and NT* (n 71), Concurring Opinion of Judge Pejchal 106–07.

Australian courts in relation to asylum seekers subjected to offshore processing in Nauru and Papua New Guinea. Commenting on the evidence provided in one case, Justice Mortimer noted that it had not been possible for medical experts to consult directly with the applicant, 'even by a method such as Skype or telephone', as the Nauruan government had passed regulations 'which prohibited such consultations'.[74] The cases that do reach court are likely to represent a thin tranche of actionable claims. And while judicial proceedings do shed light on many practical barriers to justice, the most successful barriers may evade judicial scrutiny entirely.

1.3 Practical Challenges for States

Finally, a note is called for on the practical impact of claims by asylum seekers and refugees on States. At the end of 2021, UNHCR estimated that 89.3 million people were forcibly displaced worldwide, including over 31 million refugees and asylum seekers.[75] The context of asylum claims—in sheer numbers of applicants—is often adverted to by decision-makers and raises real questions for the smooth operation of immigration system[76] and the courts.[77] These pressures, in combination with domestic political imperatives, have driven legislative attempts to restrict judicial review in asylum cases.[78] In *R (Cart) v Upper Tribunal*, Lady Hale discussed the political context to the introduction of statutory review alternative to judicial review in immigration matters, noting:[79]

> [i]n most tribunal cases, a claimant will have little to gain by pressing ahead with
> a well-nigh hopeless case ... But in immigration and asylum cases, the claimant

---

[74] *CEU19 v Minister for Immigration, Citizenship and Multicultural Affairs* [2019] FCA 1050, para 22, citing the Health Practitioners (Telemedicine Prohibition) Regulations 2019 (Nr). The experts were confined to preparing their reports on the basis of the applicant's medical records, as retained by the Commonwealth-contracted medical treatment provider in Nauru.

[75] UNHCR, 'Global Trends: Forced Displacement in 2021' (UNHCR 2022) 2. The total number of forcibly displaced people includes 53.2 million internally displaced people, and 5.8 million Palestinian refugees who fall under the mandate of the UN Relief and Works Agency (UNRWA).

[76] See eg discussion in Geoffrey Care, *Migrants and the Courts: A Century of Trial and Error?* (Routledge Ashgate 2013) 62.

[77] Between 2016 and 2020, migration matters accounted for over 70% of all appeals in the Australian Federal Court, reaching a height of 80% from 2017–18 and 2018–19. By 2020–2021 the proportion dropped to 67%. These figures are however not disaggregated into asylum and other applications: see figures in Federal Court of Australia, *Annual Report 2020–2021*, Appendix 5, 133, available via <https://www.fedcourt.gov.au/digital-law-library/annual-reports/2020-21>. In 2021–2022, the Federal Court reported that the number of migration appellate filings have decreased by 33% since the last reporting year: Federal Court of Australia, *Annual Report 2021–2022*, 28, available via <https://www.fedcourt.gov.au/digital-law-library/annual-reports/2021-22>.

[78] See eg on Australian efforts, Justice Ronald Sackville, 'Some Thoughts on Access to Justice' (FCA) [2003] Federal Judicial Scholarship 22; Stephen Gageler SC, 'Impact of Migration Law on the Development of Australian Administrative Law' (2010) 17 Australian Journal of Administrative Law 92, 98ff. On UK efforts, see eg Richard Rawlings, 'Review, Revenge and Retreat' (2005) 68 Modern Law Review 378.

[79] [2011] UKSC 28. On the nature of statutory review and how it differed from the standard judicial review process, see paras 21, 46 (Lady Hale).

may well have to leave the country if he comes to the end of the road. There is every incentive to make the road as long as possible, to take every possible point, and to make every possible application. This is not a criticism. People who perceive their situation to be desperate are scarcely to be blamed for taking full advantage of the legal claims available to them. But the courts' resources are not unlimited and it is well known that the High Court and Court of Appeal were overwhelmed with judicial review applications in immigration and asylum case until the introduction of statutory reviews.[80]

Consider also comments by Gillian Triggs, the UNHCR Assistant High Commissioner for Protection in a 2021 Executive Committee debate:

Accusations had been made that judicial procedures were abused in order to avoid deportation. Government officials complained of the difficulties of executing legally sanctioned returns to countries of origin. UNHCR took seriously the concerns expressed about the integrity of the asylum system. Technical support was provided to front-line and host countries to develop processes for identifying persons in need of protection; a fast, fair system with a right to appeal to an independent court could be more effective in identifying those who could return home in safety ... [81]

These arguments may still be adverted to when judicial protections are guaranteed by a domestic constitution. In *Department of Homeland Security v Thuraissigiam*, Justice Alito began his opinion of the Court by recalling the 'hundreds of thousands of aliens ... apprehended at or near the border', many of whom ask for asylum,[82] while also noting that in the first quarter of 2020, there were 1,066,563 pending removal proceedings,[83] and that '[t]he average civil appeal takes approximately one year'.[84] Justice Sotomayor criticised these references in her dissenting opinion, noting:

---

[80]   ibid para 47. See also para 51 (Lady Hale) ('The real question, as all agree, is what level of independent scrutiny outside the tribunal structure is required by the rule of law ... the fact that the courts have hitherto found it difficult to deter repeated or unmeritorious applications in immigration and asylum cases does not mean that such applications should become virtually impossible. There must be a principled but proportionate approach'); and paras 124 and 126 (Lord Dyson) (referring to the 'huge problems' in the justice system caused by immigration and asylum cases, and the courts having been 'overwhelmed with unmeritorious judicial review claims' before the introduction of statutory review in 2002).

[81]   UNGA, 'Executive Committee of the Programme of the United Nations High Commissioner for Refugees', 72nd sess, summary record of the 742nd meeting, A/AC.96/SR.742 (15 October 2021), para 24.

[82]   *Thuraissigiam* (n 67) 1.

[83]   ibid 3.

[84]   ibid.

[t]he Court appears to justify its decision by adverting to the burdens of affording robust judicial review of asylum decisions. But our constitutional protections should not hinge on the vicissitudes of the political climate or bend to accommodate burdens on the Judiciary.[85]

The ECtHR has taken a similar line to the dissentients in *Thuraissigiam* when faced with government arguments based on the heavy caseload of asylum appeals.[86] In *Hirsi*, it stated that 'problems with managing migratory flows cannot justify having recourse to practices which are not compatible with the State's obligations under the Convention.'[87] However, as will be seen, the Court does exclude the judicial review of negative RSD decisions from its jurisprudence on article 6 ECHR.

Although this political context is not legally relevant to the scope of protection under article 16 of the 1951 Convention, it is important for understanding State efforts to insulate administrative decision-making from judicial review, and to impede asylum seekers' ability to access domestic courts where remedies are available.

2. Book Structure

This book consists of seven chapters. Chapter 2 sets the scene by surveying the literature on the scope and content of article 16. It argues that while early commentators on the 1951 Convention gave little attention to the provision, more creative approaches have been taken in recent analyses. The chapter identifies eight issues on which scholars' views have evolved and sets out the range of views on each. These are (i) whether the term 'refugee' in article 16 encompasses the unrecognised asylum seeker; (ii) the scope of the term 'courts', and the provision's application to RSD proceedings; (iii) the geographic scope of the provision; (iv) whether 'free' access implies a guarantee of 'effective' access; (v) the appropriate definition of 'habitual residence', and whether legal residence is a pre-requisite; (vi) the scope of the term 'matters pertaining to access to the Courts'; (vii) the appropriate comparator for whether a 'refugee' is afforded 'the same treatment as a national'; and (viii) whether article 16 obliges the Contracting State to create jurisdiction to hear

---

[85] *Thuraissigiam* (n 67) (Sotomayor J, joined by Kagan J, dissenting) 2.

[86] See *Čonka v Belgium*, App no 51564/99 (ECtHR, 3rd Section, 5 Feb 2002), paras 74, 84 (referring to 'the duty to organise [a State's] judicial systems in such a way that their courts can meet its requirements ...'). More generally, see *M.S.S. v Belgium and Greece*, App no 30696/09 (ECtHR, Grand Chamber, 21 Jan 2011), paras 223–224 (stressing the absolute nature of State obligations under article 3 of the ECHR, while also recognizing the 'difficulties' posed by 'the increasing influx of migrants and asylum-seekers ...') and *Khlaifia and others v Italy*, App no 16483/12 (ECtHR, Grand Chamber, 15 Dec 2016) paras 178–185.

[87] *Hirsi* (n 35) para 179; see also *ND and NT* (n 71) para 170.

a dispute where a court otherwise lacks competence. The chapter also reviews the limited guidance by UNHCR and the UNHCR Executive Committee (ExCom) on the interpretation of article 16.

Chapter 3 turns to the rule of treaty interpretation as it applies to the 1951 Convention. After introducing the principles in articles 31–32 of the Vienna Convention on the Law of Treaties,[88] the chapter focuses on the evidentiary weight that can be attributed to three sets of materials that are relevant to the 1951 Convention's interpretation: first, domestic and regional court decisions; second, the UNHCR *Handbook on Procedures and Criteria for Determining Refugee Status* ('the Handbook'),[89] UNHCR Guidelines, and other interpretative materials, and, finally, ExCom Conclusions. It finds that a grey zone exists in interpretation of the 1951 Convention in which materials that do not fall neatly within the parameters of articles 31–32 are nonetheless relied upon when interpreting the 1951 Convention. Drawing on Venzke's work,[90] the chapter argues that while courts are at liberty to draw on materials that they find persuasive (since, in so doing, they can cause 'soft' principles to harden into State practice), a scholar should adopt a cautious approach and not place undue reliance on soft law instruments or treat case law which has not reached the standard of 'subsequent practice' as declarative of the scope of a given provision. This approach will ensure that refugee law scholarship remains a useful tool for courts and practitioners, and an accurate reflection of the current state of the law. Finally, the chapter argues for an evolutionary, teleological approach to the interpretation of the 1951 Convention, finding support in the treaty's object and purpose.

With this groundwork in place, Chapter 4 investigates the origins of article 16, situating it in its historical context. Through a survey of access to courts clauses in early commercial treaties and refugee instruments, the chapter concludes that these clauses were traditionally understood to have a narrow scope and that article 16 was drafted deliberately to grant refugees more protections than were afforded under commercial treaties. The chapter then analyses the *travaux préparatoires* of the 1951 Convention in order to better understand the drafters' own views on the scope and content of article 16.

Chapter 5 takes a broader view to examine the extent to which access to courts is protected under international human rights law, customary international law, and general principles of law. This survey draws on the work of Cantor and others, supplemented by a survey of recent jurisprudence and guidance from human rights

---

[88]   Vienna Convention on the Law of Treaties, 1155 UNTS 331 (concluded 23 May 1969, entered into force 27 Jan 1980) (Vienna Convention).

[89]   UNHCR, *Handbook on Procedures and Criteria for Determining Refugee Status and Guidelines on International Protection under the 1951 Convention and the 1967 Protocol relating to the Status of Refugees* (1979, reissued Feb 2019), HCR/1P/4/ENG/REV.4.

[90]   Ingo Venzke, *How Interpretation Makes International Law: On Semantic Change and Normative Twists* (OUP 2012).

bodies.[91] While it might be thought that article 16 has no role to play in this crowded field, the chapter argues that international human rights law consists of an uneven patchwork of rights. The HRC and ECtHR have concluded that core rights under the ICCPR and ECHR, respectively, are not engaged by RSD decision-making. Robust rights are available under certain regional instruments and specialised treaties for vulnerable groups, but many people will fall outside the protection of these regimes. As regards customary international law, the high threshold for acceptance means that only a limited tranche of rights are recognised, while 'general principles' are a relatively fragile basis on which to build concrete protections. The chapter concludes that gaps remain in the protective framework of international human rights law, which leave space for the operation of article 16 of the 1951 Convention. It is also argued that the interpretative approach taken by courts and treaty bodies to these treaties—particularly on the principle of effectiveness—can be applied when interpreting article 16.

Chapter 6 builds on the analysis in earlier chapters to provide a reasoned interpretation of article 16. Addressing the provision clause by clause, it reaches several conclusions on its scope and content, which respond to the key issues discussed in Chapter 2. First, the term 'refugee' in article 16 encompasses asylum seekers, bringing it within a select group of Convention provisions that are engaged prior to RSD. Second, the reference to 'courts' cannot be extended to encompass decisions by administrative agencies, with the consequence that article 16 is not engaged in administrative RSD proceedings. It is also concluded that the provision entails no inherent right of judicial review of an administrative decision to deny refugee status. Third, article 16(1) should be interpreted in a manner that ensures that 'effective' access to courts is available, which may require the State to take positive measures on a case-by-case basis, such as the provision of legal aid or interpreters. Fourth, article 16(1) applies wherever a jurisdictional link with a Contracting State exists, including on the high seas or in other States. Fifth, the 'habitual residence' standard in article 16(2) should be interpreted autonomously, through a flexible, fact-based approach, and may be satisfied by an asylum seeker whose residence status is precarious or whose presence is unlawful under domestic law. Sixth, the term 'matters pertaining to access to the Courts' has a wide scope that is not limited to the two examples expressly provided (namely legal assistance and the exemption from security for costs). It is proposed that two classes of matters be covered: (i) practical matters, such as the availability of translation or legal aid; and (ii) procedural matters that pertain to access to the courts. Seventh, the most appropriate comparator for determining whether an asylum seeker or refugee has received 'the same treatment as a national' is Spijkerboer's standard of 'substantively equal'

---

[91] David James Cantor, 'Reframing Relationships: Revisiting the Procedural Standards for Refugee Status Determination in Light of Recent Human Rights Treaty Body Jurisprudence' (2015) 34 Refugee Survey Quarterly 79. See further Chapter 5, Section 2.

procedural treatment.[92] Finally, article 16 does not require a Contracting State to 'create' jurisdiction to hear a dispute, as it is necessary to show a jurisdictional basis under domestic law to bring a claim. However, where an asylum seeker or refugee has reached the threshold of habitual residence, a discriminatory bar on bringing a claim may breach the article 16(2)–(3) obligation to guarantee the 'same treatment as a national'. Chapter 7 concludes.

Finally, two points on the scope of this book—and issues that are not addressed—should be mentioned. First, the focus is squarely international. While it is recognised that rights of access to courts may also be expressly or impliedly guaranteed under domestic law, it is beyond the scope of this book to give a comprehensive account of domestic rights protection. Where domestic materials are analysed, it is through the lens of international law. Domestic cases are examined primarily for their insights into the interpretation of treaty provisions, for their weight as evidence of State practice, and for the factual record they provide, for example, of legislative attempts to oust access by asylum seekers and refugees to the courts. This focus is not to discount the fact that domestic legal remedies may in many cases provide asylum seekers and refugees with a more immediate, and satisfactory, remedy than reliance on international law. However, the complex comparative exercise of mapping the domestic sources of rights protections and indicia of whether courts are likely to defer to restrictive legislative moves, or engage in judicial creativity to circumvent them, is beyond the scope of this work. What is at issue here is simply an effort to establish the obligations that bind all Contracting States to the 1951 Convention.

Second, the book is limited to a doctrinal study of article 16 of the 1951 Convention and does not assess the extent to which States comply with its terms, as interpreted here. As already noted, the obligations in article 16(2) are framed by reference to the rights enjoyed by nationals and hence will vary in their application from State to State. Undertaking comparative case studies would enable more nuanced conclusions to be drawn on whether specific State migration management tools are compatible with article 16.

3. A Note on Methodology

The analysis in the chapters that follow is centred on doctrinal research and a critical review of academic scholarship.[93] In Chapter 3, discussion of the interpretation of the 1951 Convention draws on general commentaries on articles 31 and

---

[92] Thomas Spijkerboer, 'Higher Judicial Remedies for Asylum Seekers—An International Legal Perspective' in Geoffrey Care and Hugo Storey (eds), *Asylum Law: First International Judicial Conference, London, 1995* (The Steering Committee of the Judicial Conference on Asylum Law 1995), 224.
[93] Searched consistently to 1 January 2023. Certain cases and documents after this date have also been included.

32 of the Vienna Convention on the Law of Treaties; specific scholarship on the interpretation of the 1951 Convention; and case law. Chapter 4, on the origins of article 16, provides a contextual account of the genesis of 'access to courts' provisions in early commercial and refugee treaties and the drafting process of the 1951 Convention. This account draws, in particular, on a survey of the *travaux préparatoires* of the 1951 Convention, as well as some desk-based archival research on 'access to courts' provisions in early refugee conventions.[94] Although under the rules of treaty interpretation, the *travaux préparatoires* have a supplementary role, an account of the development of the relevant provisions of the 1951 Convention is useful from an academic perspective;[95] it situates obligations in their historical context and allows a greater understanding of why the *travaux préparatoires* were silent on certain issues.

Chapter 5 surveys relevant obligations under international human rights law. This analysis draws on General Comments and various other committee documents issued with respect to the ICCPR, the Convention on the Rights of the Child (CRC),[96] and the Convention on the Rights of Persons with Disabilities (CRPD), amongst others.[97] Regional instruments and case law are also considered, along with obligations deriving from customary international law and general principles of law.

Building on these foundations, Chapter 6 then interprets article 16 of the 1951 Convention, drawing on domestic and regional case law. A comprehensive survey of judicial decisions throughout the 149 Contracting States to the 1951 Convention or its Protocol is not feasible for a sole researcher,[98] and is even a challenge for UNHCR.[99] Accordingly, cases were gathered through a three-step process. First,

---

[94] Namely the Convention relating to the International Status of Refugees, No 3663 [1935] LNTSer 91; 159 LNTS 199 (signed 28 Oct 1933, entered into force 13 June 1935) (1933 Convention); and the Convention concerning the Status of Refugees coming from Germany, with Annex. Signed at Geneva, February 10th 1938, No 4461 [1938] LNTSer 61 (1938 Convention).

[95] Gardiner, for example, gives a brief introductory account of the development of interpretative rules in his book on articles 31–33 of the Vienna Convention: see Richard K Gardiner, *Treaty Interpretation* (2nd edn, OUP 2015) 57–80. His analysis of various terms in Part II commences with a brief examination of history and preparatory work: see eg on 'good faith' (168–70); 'ordinary meaning' (182); and 'object and purpose' (212).

[96] 1577 UNTS 3 (adopted 20 Nov 1989, entered into force 2 Sept 1990).

[97] Convention on the Rights of Persons with Disabilities, 2515 UNTS 3 (adopted 13 Dec 2006, entered into force 3 May 2008); see also its Optional Protocol, 2518 UNTS 283 (adopted 3 May 2008, entered into force 3 May 2008).

[98] There are basic challenges to uncovering such cases in a systematic, multi-state manner. A researcher will be limited by language and accessibility of translation, familiarity in using foreign databases, and the very availability of case law in certain jurisdictions. Using institutional databases will not always correct for these issues, since they may also privilege materials from certain countries or in certain languages. Finally, on a more basic level, some jurisdictions will simply more generate case law on the 1951 Convention than others. Where article 16 is given 'direct effect' in the domestic legal order, for example, it is more likely that it will be relied on in argument and interpreted in judgments.

[99] See discussion and proposals in Cecilia M Baillet, 'National Case Law as a Generator of International Refugee Law: Rectifying an Imbalance within UNHCR Guidelines on International Protection' (2015) Emory International Law Journal 2059, 2080.

cases on article 16 cited by other scholars were collected.[100] Second, three collections of international cases were consulted—the International Law Reports, UNHCR's 'Refworld' database,[101] and the collection of case summaries prepared by the European Database of Asylum Law (EDAL).[102] Third, specific national databases and/or reports were consulted for eight countries: Austria[103], Australia,[104] New Zealand,[105] Belgium,[106] Netherlands,[107] the United Kingdom,[108] Canada,[109] and the United States.[110] These States were chosen for practical reasons. The initial two steps of the survey suggested that domestic jurisprudence in these States directly addressed article 16, and databases were available that were readily searchable online. The scope of the survey was limited by the author's language skills.[111] In certain cases, a summary of the judgment in international reports was relied on.[112] While the dataset includes both common law and civil law cases, it is weighted towards anglophone and francophone jurisprudence from the Global North.[113] This geographic bias, which is identified as an issue elsewhere,[114] undercuts the ability to reach definitive conclusions on the consistency of State practice, in so far as it is drawn from domestic judicial decisions. It is recognised that 'case law on article 16' is not a perfect proxy for State practice. First, it does not capture relevant case law

---

[100] I rely on Carlier and Boeles' discussion of certain Belgian cases, and one Dutch case, that were not found independently. Austrian cases were available in German summary only (via RIS). Accordingly, discussion of these cases is limited and relies on other scholars' summaries. I also rely on Elberling's discussion of one German case.

[101] Via the search terms 'free access to courts', 'free access to the courts', 'same treatment as a national', '16 & access to courts', 'libre et facile accès', and 'jouira du même traitement'.

[102] <https://www.asylumlawdatabase.eu/en>.

[103] Via <https://www.ris.bka.gv.at/Jus/>.

[104] Via Lexis Advance.

[105] ibid.

[106] Via a search of recent editions of the *Tijdschrift voor Vreemdelingenrecht* (2012–2021) and the *Revue Belge Droit International*.

[107] Via the Netherlands Yearbook of International Law, checking the index to volumes 1–51.

[108] Via Westlaw, LexisNexis Pacific (UK), and LexisAdvance, and a search through the British Yearbook of International Law to 1973 and from 1996 to 2017 (those volumes available via databases at the time of writing).

[109] Via CanLii.

[110] Via Westlaw US.

[111] All judgments surveyed are available in English or French with the exceptions of those from Austria and one German decision referred to by Elberling.

[112] These include, for example, cases reported in the ILR, the NYIL, and the IJRL.

[113] On this tendency in refugee law more broadly, see Chapter 3.

[114] See discussion in Anthea Roberts, *Is International Law International?* (OUP 2017) 166–67 noting that a reliance on national court decisions as evidence of State practice 'results in a primary focus on the practices of Western states in general and core English-speaking common law states in particular in a way that obscures or downplays the importance of non-Western, non-English-speaking, noncommon law states': at 166. She notes that textbooks from Russia, China, the United Kingdom, the United States, and France each 'turn primarily to the case law of Western states, regardless of whether those states are geographically, linguistically, or culturally proximate to the state in which the book is being used': at 167. See also, in relation to UNHCR's Guidelines, Cecilia M Bailliet, 'National Case Law as a Generator of International Refugee Law: Rectifying an Imbalance within UNHCR Guidelines on International Protection' (2015) Emory International Law Journal 2059, 2064 (finding, in her review of the Guidelines, 'a clear bias in favor of citation of common law jurisdictions over civil law jurisdictions, and no citations from the developing world whatsoever').

in situations where a state has incorporated its international obligations directly into a domestic law that is then the subject of the litigation. Second, it does not cover other forms of State practice, such as legislation or public statements by State officials, that directly address article 16. Third, it does not cover practice (whether case law, legislation, or public statements) that, while not engaging with article 16, conflicts with one or more possible interpretations of the provision. As one basic example, a hypothetical recalcitrant State that offered no access to its courts what-soever might generate no case law at all. Only those asylum seekers and refugees with some access to courts will have the opportunity to litigate their rights on the domestic level. These limitations foreclose bald statements on the 'consistency' of case law between Contracting States to the 1951 Convention.

4. Conclusion

The discussion here has sought to contextualise the research that follows, while also providing a sense of the issues at stake in ensuring asylum seeker and refugee access to courts. This book argues that article 16 of the 1951 Convention plays an important role in safeguarding that access, and that greater attention should be paid to it in the framing of domestic measures and the regulation of State policies. The chapters that follow seek to support this conclusion through a rigorous and reasoned analysis which builds on existing literature to develop a principled ap-proach to the interpretation of article 16.

2

Mapping the Field: New Interest in an Overlooked Provision

1. Introduction

Article 16 of the 1951 Convention is a core, yet under-theorised, obligation in international refugee law.[1] As discussed in Chapter 1, access to courts is a fundamental element of the judicial system which is of particular importance for refugees and asylum seekers. The scope of article 16—and whether it provides any protection over and above that afforded under international human rights law and general principles of law—is therefore an important question when interpreting the Convention.

Despite this, article 16 has not received extensive attention from academic commentators. Early commentaries were particularly brief, often simply reiterating key points from a relatively anodyne discussion in the *travaux préparatoires*. There has, however, been a renewed (or perhaps simply new) interest in article 16 in recent scholarship. Some scholars are now taking creative approaches to the provision, investigating its application to reviews of negative refugee status determination (RSD) decisions and arguing that it affords more comprehensive protection than previously recognised. This appears to be partly driven by the exigencies of RSD decision-making, on the one hand, and the adoption by States of restrictive procedural mechanisms to manage asylum caseloads, on the other. As Hyndman recognised over two decades ago, onerous procedural requirements are one of the many 'forms of discouragement' adopted by States in the face of rising asylum claims.[2] To take a recent example, UNHCR referred in its 2021 Note on International Protection to practices during the Covid-19 pandemic including 'the suspension of asylum procedures and registration; border closures restricting access to asylum … and limits on legal representation in asylum procedures'.[3] More

---

[1] O'Sullivan and Stevens note that 'this provision has rarely been utilised in litigation and is often overlooked in academic commentary' (footnotes omitted): Maria O'Sullivan and Dallal Stevens, 'Access to Refugee Protection: Key Concepts and Contemporary Challenges' in Maria O'Sullivan and Dallal Stevens (eds), *States, the Law and Access to Refugee Protection* (Hart Publishing 2017) 20.

[2] Patricia Hyndman, 'The 1951 Convention and Its Implications for Procedural Questions' (1994) 6 International Journal of Refugee Law 245, 245.

[3] UNGA, 'Note on International Protection', A/AC.96/1211/Rev.1 (1 Oct 2021) para 19. See also UNGA, 'Note on International Protection: Report of the High Commissioner', A/AC.96/1156 (12 July 2016), para 17.

Access to Courts for Asylum Seekers and Refugees. Emma Dunlop, Oxford University Press. © Emma Dunlop, 2024.
DOI: 10.1093/oso/9780198885597.003.0002

broadly, Hathaway and Gammeltoft-Hansen note the rise of 'the politics of *non-entrée*', namely those policies designed to prevent asylum seekers from entering a State's jurisdiction, including carrier sanctions, the creation of non-territorial zones (eg in airports), maritime pushbacks, and entry into memoranda of understanding (MOUs) and other arrangements 'designed to conscript countries of origin and transit to effect migration control on behalf of the developed world'.[4] These developments inform attempts to read more robust protections into article 16 in recent literature, as questions that were ignored by early scholars take on a greater significance.

Section 2.1 examines the evolution of scholars' views on eight key issues relating to article 16. These are: (i) whether the term 'refugee' in article 16 encompasses the unrecognised asylum seeker; (ii) the scope of the term 'courts', and the provision's application to RSD proceedings; (iii) the geographic scope of the provision; (iv) whether 'free' access implies a guarantee of 'effective' access; (v) the appropriate definition of 'habitual residence', and whether legal residence is a pre-requisite; (vi) the scope of the term 'matters pertaining to access to the Courts'; (vii) the appropriate comparator for whether a 'refugee' is afforded 'the same treatment as a national'; and (viii) whether article 16 obliges the Contracting State to create jurisdiction to hear a dispute where a court otherwise lacks competence.

Section 2.2 surveys UNHCR and ExCom guidance on the interpretation of article 16. UNHCR has not articulated a comprehensive interpretation of article 16, although scattered references to the provision are found across its various outputs. ExCom Conclusions provide some guidance on the scope of the provision, while ExCom discussions are virtually silent on the issue. This survey provides the basis for the analysis in the chapters that follow.

2. Key Questions on the Scope and Content of Article 16 of the 1951 Convention

2.1 Literature on the Scope and Content of Article 16

Literature on the article 16 obligation to provide refugees with access to courts is quite limited. The early commentators—Grahl-Madsen, writing in the early 1960s;[5] Weis, a participant in the 1951 Convention's drafting process whose unfinished commentary was posthumously published in 1995;[6] and Robinson, whose

---

[4] See Thomas Gammeltoft-Hansen and James C Hathaway, '*Non-Refoulement* in a World of Cooperative Deterrence' (2015) 53 Columbia Journal of Transnational Law 235, 241–43 (quote at 243).

[5] See Atle Grahl-Madsen, *Commentary on the Refugee Convention 1951, Articles 2–11, 13–37* (Republished by the Division of International Protection of the United Nations High Commissioner for Refugees, 1997), foreword.

[6] Paul Weis (ed), *The Refugee Convention, 1951* (CUP 1995). See also 'Editorial: Paul Weis 1907–1991' (1991) 3 International Journal of Refugee Law 183; Joan Fitzpatrick, 'Book reviews and notes: *The*

commentary was published in 1953[7]—took a narrow, technical view of article 16. Recent analyses tend towards a more creative approach which is responsive to contemporary challenges faced by asylum seekers and refugees. Scholarly approaches to eight key questions on the scope and content of article 16 are set out in Sections 2.1.1 to 2.1.8.

2.1.1 Interpreting the term 'refugee'—does protection extend to the unrecognised asylum seeker?

A fundamental question is whether the obligations in article 16 are engaged only in relation to the recognised refugee, or if they are also owed to an asylum seeker prior to any formal recognition of status by a host State. If article 16 obligations do extend to the asylum seeker, he or she would be entitled to 'free access to the courts of law', under article 16(1), and to the additional protections in article 16(2)–(3) if the threshold of 'habitual residence' is met. This question has implications for a second question, discussed in Section 2.1.2—namely, whether the provision is engaged in RSD procedures, and if so, how.

Early commentators were not particularly animated by this question, perhaps due to the more flexible approach taken to status determination in the early days of the Convention. Grahl-Madsen noted that article 16(1) applied to any refugee 'subject only to the rule underlying the Convention that each Contracting State must determine for its own purposes whether a person is to be considered a refugee or not'.[8] Weis accepted the application of article 16(1) to an unlawfully resident refugee, without specifying whether it would also apply to the unlawfully resident asylum seeker.[9] Robinson recalled discussion in the Ad Hoc Committee that article 16(1) applied 'to such persons as had only recently become refugees and therefore had no habitual residence anywhere', without specifying whether that process of 'becoming' was due to their objective circumstances or recognition by a Contracting State.[10]

Refugee Convention, 1951, The Travaux Préparatoires Analysed with a Commentary. Edited by Paul Weis. New York: Cambridge University Press, 1995' (1996) 90 American Journal of International Law 175. There is some question as to the reliability of this Commentary: see Guy S Goodwin-Gill, 'Book Review, The Refugee Convention, 1951. The *Travaux Préparatoires* analysed, with a Commentary by the late Dr Paul Weis' (1996) 9 Journal of Refugee Studies 103.

[7] Nehemiah Robinson, *Convention Relating to the Status of Refugee: History, Contents and Interpretation: A Commentary* (Institute of Jewish Affairs, World Jewish Congress 1953).

[8] Grahl-Madsen (n 5) Article 16, II. In his other writings, Grahl-Madsen has however taken a 'declaratory' approach to refugee status. See Grahl-Madsen, *The Status of Refugees in International Law* (AW Sijthoff 1972), Vol II, 223–24 ('A person who sets foot on foreign territory in order to escape persecution becomes thereby a refugee—at the very moment when he has effected his entry . . . the refugee is, from the very moment of his entry, entitled to treatment in accordance with the Refugee Convention'). He recognises, however, that certain guarantees under the Convention hinge on recognition: at 224.

[9] Weis (n 6) 134.

[10] Robinson (n 7) 112, citing E/AC.32/SR.25, para 19 (Mr Henkin, USA). This question is also left open by Mr Henkin's comments.

In recent scholarship, there is support for the view that State obligations under article 16 extend to the asylum seeker, based either on the declaratory theory or on other grounds. The declaratory theory treats the refugee definition as 'objective', crystallising as soon as an individual meets the definition rather than upon recognition by a host State.[11] Hathaway, a proponent of the theory,[12] argues that 'refugees are entitled to assert their rights before the courts of any state party, including prior to being admitted to a status determination procedure'.[13] Elberling reaches the same conclusion, again referring to the declaratory theory.[14] Moreno-Lax's acceptance that article 16 applies to the asylum seeker draws on the declaratory theory,[15] principles of effectiveness and good faith,[16] and articles 3 and 31 of the 1951 Convention.[17] Boeles would extend the protection of article 16 to any asylum seeker 'whose claim to refugee status is *not entirely groundless*', on the basis of the principle of effectiveness.[18] Carlier also recognises the potential applicability of article 16 to the asylum seeker,[19] as, implicitly, do all other commentators who consider article 16 to be engaged in judicial reviews of RSD decisions.[20] Goodwin-Gill, however, seems to favour a more restrictive reading of the provision, noting that while 'the right of recognised refugees to access the courts is expressly stated in Article 16 of the 1951 Convention ... those seeking protection whose status is not yet determined may need to rely on the general

---

[11]   See UNHCR, *Handbook on Procedures and Criteria for Determining Refugee Status and Guidelines on International Protection under the 1951 Convention and the 1967 Protocol relating to the Status of Refugees* (1979, reissued Feb 2019), HCR/1P/4/ENG/REV.4, para 28; UNHCR, 'Note on Determination of Refugee Status under International Instruments', EC/SCP/5 (24 Aug 1977), available via <http://www.refworld.org/docid/3ae68cc04.html>, para 5; James C Hathaway and Michelle Foster, *The Law of Refugee Status* (2nd edn, CUP 2014) 1; and Björn Elberling, 'Article 16' in Andreas Zimmermann (ed), *The 1951 Convention Relating to the Status of Refugees and its 1967 Protocol* (OUP 2011) 938, 940. See also Guy S Goodwin-Gill and Jane McAdam, with Emma Dunlop, *The Refugee in International Law* (4th edn, OUP 2021) 307, 596.

[12]   James C Hathaway, *The Rights of Refugees under International Law* (2nd edn, CUP 2021) 178–81.

[13]   ibid 915 (footnotes omitted); see also 924, n 665.

[14]   Elberling (n 11) 938.

[15]   Violeta Moreno-Lax, *Accessing Asylum in Europe: Extraterritorial Border Controls and Refugee Rights under EU Law* (OUP 2017) 400, 402.

[16]   ibid.

[17]   ibid 400–01.

[18]   Pieter Boeles, 'Effective Legal Remedies for Asylum Seekers according to the Convention of Geneva 1951' (1996) 43 Netherlands International Law Review 291, 303 (emphasis added) (noting that this interpretation is necessary 'in order to avoid a situation where *ex post* it turns out that the protection intended by the Convention was withheld from a refugee').

[19]   Jean-Yves Carlier, *Droit d'asile et des réfugiés: de la protection aux droits (Vol. 332)*, Collected Courses of the Hague Academy of International Law (Brill Nijhoff 2008) 323, 333–34.

[20]   See, eg, Dana Baldinger, *Vertical Judicial Dialogues in Asylum Cases: Standards on Judicial Scrutiny and Evidence in International and European Asylum Law* (Brill Nijhoff 2015) 27 (concluding that article 16 applies to 'contemporary judicial asylum proceedings'); Thomas Spijkerboer, 'Higher Judicial Remedies for Asylum Seekers—An International Legal Perspective' in Geoffrey Care and Hugo Storey (eds), *Asylum Law: First International Judicial Conference, London, 1995* (The Steering Committee of the Judicial Conference on Asylum Law, London, 1995) 221, 224 (concluding that 'matters pertaining to access' encompasses the asylum procedure and that '[r]efugees have the right to substantively equal procedural possibilities in their asylum procedure as nationals of the state of their habitual residence'.)

principle [of access to courts, as a source of law under article 38(1)(d) of the ICJ Statute]'.[21]

2.1.2. Interpreting the term 'court'—scope of article 16 and its application to refugee status determination procedures

For Grahl-Madsen and Weis, it was uncontroversial that the obligations in article 16 applied only to courts of law and did not extend to administrative bodies. The only exception to this principle was if another article of the 1951 Convention providing for access to administrative authorities was engaged (Weis used the example of article 32 expulsion decisions).[22] There is no discussion in Weis, Grahl-Madsen, or Robinson on the potential application of article 16 to RSD proceedings, whether in administrative proceedings or judicial appeals.

Since these early commentaries were written, RSD decision-making has evolved significantly. Gibney notes a trend in European countries over the past decades to move RSD 'gradually out of the realm of state discretion to independent, quasi-judicial bodies'.[23] The term 'quasi-' is key—a vast tranche of RSD decision-making globally has now been shifted to domestic administrative agencies.[24] Hamlin's study of modern RSD regimes in the US, Canada, and Australia illustrates the complex institutional relationships in RSD decision-making, and the 'frontline' role played by administrative agencies.[25] The issue of whether the obligations in article 16 can be extended to apply to administrative agencies—or indeed to judicial review of negative administrative RSD decisions—takes on greater significance as a result of these developments.

Hathaway and Elberling agree with the early commentators that the term 'courts' cannot be extended to encompass administrative agencies.[26] However, Boeles takes a different view. He considers that a 'reasonable interpretation' of article 16 would also afford refugees equal treatment to nationals 'in cases in which forms of legal remedies are available to ... nationals which do not have a judicial character, such

---

[21] Guy S Goodwin-Gill, 'The Office of the United Nations High Commissioner for Refugees and the Sources of International Refugee Law' (2020) 69 International and Comparative Law Quarterly 1, 28.

[22] Weis (n 6) 134; Grahl-Madsen (n 5) Article 16, VI. Robinson does not address this issue expressly but gives no indication that the right would extend beyond courts: (n 7) 112–13.

[23] Matthew J Gibney, 'The State of Asylum: Democratisation, Judicialisation and Evolution of Refugee Policy' in Susan Kneebone (ed) *The Refugee Convention 50 years on: Globalisation and International Law* (Ashgate Publishing Limited 2003) 36.

[24] This trend is reflected in the EU in Directive 2013/32/EU of the European Parliament and of the Council of 26 June 2013 on common procedures for granting and withdrawing international protection (recast) (recast Procedures Directive). Art 2(f) defines 'determining authority' as 'any quasi-judicial or administrative body in a Member State responsible for examining applications for international protection competent to take decisions at first instance in such cases'.

[25] Rebecca Hamlin, *Let Me Be a Refugee: Administrative Justice and the Politics of Asylum in the United States, Canada and Australia* (OUP 2014) 9.

[26] Elberling (n 11) 939; Hathaway, *Rights* (2nd edn) (n 12) 923, fn 659. Although not directly addressing the point, other scholars also seem to accept this view: see, eg, Baldinger (n 20); Carlier (n 19).

as administrative appeal to a higher administrative body'.[27] This interpretation has not been accepted by other scholars.

Even if the term 'courts' is interpreted to exclude administrative agencies, a question remains as to whether, and to what extent, article 16 is engaged in judicial RSD decision-making, such as judicial review of a negative administrative decision on asylum. This question is premised on acceptance that the term 'refugee' extends to asylum seekers.

The division between scholars on this question in contemporary debates can be sharp. To Battjes, article 16 'has no implications for asylum procedures',[28] while to Boeles, its role is 'of paramount importance'.[29] As Carlier notes, the *travaux préparatoires* to the 1951 Convention do not discuss the application of article 16 to RSD.[30] Like other commentators, he concludes, however, that there is nothing to indicate that the '*droit d'ester en justice*' [access to courts] should not be interpreted broadly.[31] Baldinger's survey of commentators leads her to conclude that article 16 applies 'to contemporary judicial asylum proceedings',[32] such as judicial review of RSD and expulsion appeals.[33] In reaching this result, she relies in part on the application of a 'living instrument' or 'dynamic' approach to the interpretation of human rights treaties.[34] She notes that the silence of the *travaux préparatoires* on this question is not determinative since modern practice on RSD procedures has largely developed since the Convention was drafted.[35]

Elberling reflects on this question at length, concluding that 'even if not intended that way, the article does indeed affect status determination procedures'.[36] He considers article 16 to apply 'at least in principle' to judicial appeals of negative RSD decisions.[37] However, he takes the view that States are not required to

---

[27] Boeles (n 18) 310.
[28] Hemme Battjes, *European Asylum Law and International Law* (Martinus Nijhoff Publishers 2006) 319 (noting that 'the provision merely addresses the issue of access to the court, not the content of proceedings').
[29] Boeles (n 18) 303.
[30] Carlier (n 19) 320.
[31] ibid 320–21 ('Rien n'indique toutefois que le "droit d'ester en justice" ne doive pas être interprété largement'). See also Spijkerboer (n 20) 221; Violeta Moreno-Lax, 'Seeking Asylum in the Mediterranean: Against a Fragmentary Reading of EU Member States' Obligations Accruing at Sea' (2011) 23 International Journal of Refugee Law 174, 212, citing Carlier, ibid 320ff and citations therein; and more generally, Elberling (n 11) 939 (noting that article 16(1) applies 'principally to any type of legal proceeding); and Hathaway, *Rights* (2nd edn) (n 12) 800 (noting that 'the right of access to the courts is framed as a general right, in no sense limited to access for purposes of launching or defending a civil suit' and that it '[i]n principle' applies 'when refugees seek to litigate their Convention or any other rights before domestic courts' (footnotes omitted)).
[32] Baldinger (n 20) 27.
[33] ibid 25.
[34] ibid 27–28; fn 46.
[35] ibid 25–26 (noting that '[a]t that time, national asylum court proceedings as we know them nowadays were practically non-existent in many States parties to the Convention': 25).
[36] Elberling (n 11) 944.
[37] ibid (footnotes omitted). See also comments at 936 ('As far as it has an impact on the refugee status determination procedure, Art. 16, again, is only concerned with the possibility of judicial remedies against negative status decisions').

vest courts with the jurisdiction to hear such claims, which may 'severely limit' the protection article 16 affords (see further Section 2.1.8).[38] This is a narrower form of protection than that argued for by Moreno-Lax, who considers that article 16 must provide a means by which asylum seekers can 'vindicate their condition as Convention refugees'.[39]

Hathaway also sees article 16 as engaged 'in the context of judicial review or another form of appeal or reassessment conducted by a court of either general or subject-matter-specific jurisdiction'.[40] Like Elberling, he argues that article 16(1) only guarantees access to existing domestic remedies,[41] but, subject to this limitation, considers efforts by States to deny judicial review of negative RSD decisions to be 'prima facie incompatible' with article 16(1).[42] This approach suggests that a State in which courts are currently vested with powers of judicial review of RSD decisions would be unable to withdraw that jurisdiction in favour, for example, of a second level of administrative review.[43]

Cantor, who takes the general view that international refugee law offers a 'relatively fragile legal basis for the elaboration of [RSD] procedural standards',[44] agrees with this assessment. He concludes that 'the most that can be said is that [a]rticle 16(1) may require that States not withdraw existing rights of access to the courts by putative refugees to challenge negative administrative decisions on refugee status'.[45]

This discussion reveals that there are two issues on which scholarly views differ and which warrant further consideration. The first is whether 'courts' should be defined in an expansive manner, such that the protections in article 16 are extended to administrative RSD proceedings. The second is whether, and to what extent, article 16 is engaged in judicial RSD decision-making. If is accepted that article 16 can apply to such decisions, does it create an inherent right to judicial review of a negative RSD assessment? Or do its protections only become operational when a State affords a right of review under its domestic law?

2.1.3 Geographic scope of article 16

A third question relates to the geographic scope of article 16. Article 16(1) provides that a refugee is entitled to free access to the courts 'on the territory of all

---

[38] ibid.

[39] Moreno-Lax, *Accessing Asylum in Europe* (n 15) 402.

[40] Hathaway, *Rights* (2nd edn) (n 12) 923, referring specifically to art 16(2).

[41] ibid 800.

[42] ibid 798.

[43] See also Hathaway's suggestion that Canada's 'refusal ... to allow appeals by claimants from "designated" countries' would breach article 16(1): ibid.

[44] David James Cantor, 'Reframing Relationships: Revisiting the Procedural Standards for Refugee Status Determination in Light of Recent Human Rights Treaty Body Jurisprudence' (2015) 34 Refugee Survey Quarterly 79, 85.

[45] ibid.

Contracting States'. Modern practices of offshore detention,[46] interceptions, and push-backs at sea,[47] among others,[48] raise important questions on whether a State Party is obliged to extend access to its courts to a 'refugee', as defined under article 16, who is not physically present. Clearly, the extraterritorial application of article 16 is more significant if it applies to asylum seekers.

The early commentaries pre-date these developments, so it is unsurprising that the geographic scope of article 16 was not addressed by Weis and Robertson. Grahl-Madsen, however, noted that article 16(1) applied 'to any refugee with regard to the law courts in the territory of any Contracting State, that is to say the State in which he lives as well as any other Contracting States'.[49] However, this was subject to the condition that 'each Contracting State must determine for its own purposes where a person is to be considered a refugee or not'.[50]

Scholars now uniformly accept that physical presence within a State is not a prerequisite for the engagement of obligation under article 16(1).[51] There must however be some jurisdictional link that enlivens the court's jurisdiction under domestic law.[52] In this respect, its relevance to offshore processing has also been recognised.[53]

2.1.4 Interpreting the term 'free access'—does article 16(1) guarantee 'effective' access?

The *travaux préparatoires* show that the drafters did not intend refugees to be exempt from the costs of bringing legal proceedings.[54] However, in accordance with article 29(1) of the 1951 Convention, such costs must correspond to the costs borne by citizens.[55] Grahl-Madsen and Weis both noted that 'free' does not imply a

---

[46] See, eg, Madeline Gleeson, *Offshore: Behind the Wire on Manus and Nauru* (NewSouth Publishing 2016).

[47] Consider, eg, the facts in *Hirsi Jamaa and others v Italy*, App no 27765/09 (ECtHR, Grand Chamber, 23 Feb 2012).

[48] See Gammeltoft-Hansen and Hathaway (n 4).

[49] Grahl-Madsen (n 5) Article 16, VI.

[50] ibid Article 16, II.

[51] Moreno-Lax, *Accessing Asylum in Europe* (n 15) 401; Hathaway, *Rights* (2nd edn) (n 12) 797; Carlier (n 19) 323; Elberling (n 11) 938, 945; Thomas Gammeltoft-Hansen, *Access to Asylum: International Refugee Law and the Globalisation of Migration Control* (CUP 2011) 101–02.

[52] Moreno-Lax, *Accessing Asylum in Europe* (n 15) 401; Carlier (n 19) 323; Gammeltoft-Hansen (n 51) 101–02 (noting that 'access to courts (Art. 16)' is one of the few rights held by a refugee 'who is presumed to be within a state's jurisdiction, yet still outside its territory').

[53] See Angus Francis, 'Bringing Protection Home: Healing the Schism Between International Obligations and National Safeguards Created by Extraterritorial Processing' (2008) 20 International Journal of Refugee Law 273, 278–79 (arguing that obligations in relation to extraterritorial processing include art 16(1)); Elberling (n 11) 945 (noting that '[a]rt 16, para. 1 does not allow States to deny refugees all access to the courts simply by channelling them into "international" or "transit" zones defined as not being part of the State territory or by immediately removing them to neighbouring countries' (footnotes omitted)).

[54] See Ad Hoc Committee on Statelessness and Related Problems, First Session, Summary Record of the 11th Meeting, E/AC.32/SR.11 (3 Feb 1950), 7, paras 32–33. This exchange is discussed in Weis (n 6) 131–32.

[55] See Grahl-Madsen (n 5) Article 16, III, and Weis (n 6) 134, each reading art 16 in conjunction with art 29 of the 1951 Convention. See also Elberling (n 11) 936. Article 29(1) provides that any

freedom from fees.[56] Grahl-Madsen noted that 'free access' meant only that 'there should not be any additional obstacles for refugees'.[57]

More recent scholars have questioned whether 'free access' should be given a more expansive definition. Boeles and Elberling propose an interpretation of 'free' based on 'effective' access.[58] To Elberling, 'where access to court is formally granted, but in fact made impossible by, *e.g.*, overly stringent formal requirements, it cannot be considered 'free' in the sense of [article 16(1)]'.[59] This position is also supported by Hathaway.[60] The focus on effectiveness raises the question whether a formal requirement that was non-discriminatory between refugees and nationals could nonetheless be breach article 16(1) in practice, in light of the particular vulnerabilities faced by refugee claimants.

2.1.5 Interpreting the term 'habitual residence'—questions of duration and legal status

The guarantees in article 16(2)–(3) are conditioned on the refugee holding 'habitual residence' in the host State. An obvious question, therefore, is the length and quality of residence required to meet the 'habitual' standard. This question takes on particular importance if the guarantees in article 16 extend to asylum seekers. Years may elapse before a final decision is taken on an asylum seeker's protection application, during which time he or she may be on a temporary visa or even unlawfully present in the territory of the State Party.

Early commentators draw on discussion in the *travaux préparatoires* in their interpretation of the scope of habitual residence in articles 14 and 16, a source that gives indications of the drafters' intent but no clear answer as to when the threshold will be met.[61] Weis notes that the term 'habitual residence' was introduced as a distinction from 'purely temporary residence',[62] while Robinson defines habitual residence as 'residence of a certain duration, but it implies much less than permanent residence'.[63] It was generally accepted that a refugee may be without habitual

---

'duties, charges or taxes, of any description whatsoever' payable by refugees cannot be 'higher than those . . . levied on their nationals in similar situations'.

[56] See Grahl-Madsen (n 5) Article 16, VI; Weis (n 6) 134. Robinson does not expressly address the scope of the term 'free access': (n 7) 112–13. See further Chapter 4, Section 4.2.2.1.
[57] Grahl-Madsen (n 5) Article 16, VI. See also Baldinger (n 20) 29: '[a]rticle 16, therefore, requires that obstacles which are particularly felt by refugees are to be removed so that they have real, and not illusive, access to courts, just like nationals'.
[58] See Boeles (n 18) 303 and Elberling (n 11) 939, 945. See also Moreno-Lax's discussion of the principle of effectiveness and its application to art 16: Moreno-Lax, *Accessing Asylum in Europe* (n 15) 401–02.
[59] Elberling (n 11) 939.
[60] Hathaway, *Rights* (2nd edn) (n 12) 799, citing ibid.
[61] See further discussion in Chapter 4.
[62] Weis (n 6) 123.
[63] Robinson (n 7) 107 (on Article 14), citing A/CONF.2/SR.23, 26 (Mr Hoare (UK)).

residence in any country.[64] Grahl-Madsen referred to 'new refugees' as potentially lacking a habitual residence.[65] Weis and Robinson considered that an illegally present refugee would not be entitled to the guarantees in article 16(2)–(3).[66]

More recent analysis has been affected by Hathaway's theory of attachment under the 1951 Convention. In his seminal 2005 book, *The Rights of Refugees under International Law*, Hathaway argued that the 1951 Convention creates 'an expanding array of rights as [an asylum seeker or refugee's] relationship with the asylum state deepens.'[67] He set out five levels of attachment, which were, from lowest to highest: falling within a State's jurisdiction; physical presence in a State's territory; lawful presence within a State; lawfully staying within a State; and durable residence.[68] Within this hierarchy, habitual residence was equated with durable residence, the highest level of attachment.[69] Accordingly, Hathaway concluded that the guarantees in article 16(2)–(3) did not preclude a decision to restrict legal assistance or apply *cautio judicatum solvi* (security for costs) to an asylum seeker until such time as his or her refugee status was formally recognised.[70]

In the second edition of this work, published in 2021, Hathaway realigns the levels of attachment, placing habitual residence squarely in the middle of the hierarchy. Under the new model, the five levels of attachment are: falling within a State's jurisdiction; physical presence within a State's territory; *lawful or habitual presence*; lawfully staying within a State; and durable residence.[71] This has implications for the scope of habitual residence. Under Hathaway's 2005 model, habitual residence necessarily required something more than lawful presence, and likely recognition of refugee status.[72] However, under the 2021 model, habitual residence is treated as

---

[64] Grahl-Madsen (n 5) Article 16, VII, and Robinson (n 7) 112 (noting that the drafters considered art 16(1) to apply to a refugee with 'no habitual residence anywhere' (footnotes omitted)). Robinson also notes that a refugee may have a habitual residence in more than one State: at 107 (on art 14). Weis is internally inconsistent on this point: compare (n 6) 123 ('It was felt that every refugee would have a country of habitual residence'); and 134 ('Refugees who have not yet established habitual residence in any country will not benefit from the provisions in [art 16(2)–(3)]').

[65] Grahl-Madsen (n 5) Article 14, I.A.1(c).

[66] See Weis (n 6) 123; Robinson (n 7) 108. In footnote 155, Robinson appears to refer to the question posed to the Australian delegate by Mr Rochefort (France) in A/CONF.2/SR.5, 16, noting that 'this question was raised in connection with access to courts but no decision was taken thereon'. See further discussion of this point in the travaux in Chapter 4, Section 4.2.2.2.

[67] James C Hathaway, *The Rights of Refugees under International Law* (1st edn, CUP 2005) 156. Hathaway refers to the asylum seeker as a refugee in this discussion, reflecting the declaratory theory.

[68] ibid 156. See further discussion of each level at 160–92.

[69] ibid 190. The first line of his discussion of 'durable residence' reads: 'Only a few rights are reserved for refugees who are habitually resident'. The guarantees in art 16(2)–(3) are expressly mentioned as examples of rights conditioned on 'durable residence'.

[70] Hathaway, *Rights* (1st edn) (n 67) 909 (noting that this outcome is due to the fact that 'mere lawful presence is insufficient to give rise to entitlement under Art. 16(2)').

[71] Hathaway, *Rights* (2nd edn) (n 12) 176–77. See further discussion of each of these levels of attachment at 181–219.

[72] See Hathaway, *Rights* (1st edn) (n 67) 909 and the examples cited therein. Hathaway did however recognise that 'the stage between "irregular" presence and the recognition or denial of refugee status, including the time required for exhaustion or any appeals or reviews, is also a form of "lawful presence"': Hathaway, *Rights* (1st edn) (n 67) 175 (footnotes omitted). For discussion in the 2nd edition of jurisprudence in favour of this position, and a critique of the UK Supreme Court's contrary position in

'a standard borrowed from private international law, the meaning of which is both fungible and evolving':

> [t]his standard might be thought both more and less demanding than the notion of 'lawful presence'. On the one hand, while 'residence' ('résidence') is based on a factual inquiry to identify the place which is the center of one's interests, the qualifier 'habitual' may be said to require 'residence of some standing or duration'—thus opening the door to a subjective assessment that could delay the acquisition of rights. On the other hand, ... residence can in principle be habitual without also being lawful—meaning that rights might be acquired earlier than under the lawful presence benchmark.[73]

Hathaway recognises that '[d]espite the flexibility' of the standard, 'there will clearly be some refugees who—especially shortly after arrival to seek asylum—will not yet be habitually present in the asylum country'.[74] He concludes that habitual residence defines 'a middle ground between simply having arrived in an asylum country and having been formally authorized to stay there on an ongoing basis'.[75]

This recalibration of the scope of habitual residence emphasises the unsettled nature of key questions on article 16. Yet the shift also brings Hathaway into closer alignment with other commentators. Spijkerboer and Elberling, for example, consider that lawful presence is not a pre-requisite for habitual residence.[76] Spijkerboer treats habitual residence as a 'contextual' standard', according to which the country with which the refugee has the 'most bonds' must be found. He writes: '[o]nly if [the refugee] has been in that country for just a few days [will he have] no "habitual residence" in any country'.[77] Elberling also considers that 'habitual residence' does not require that an asylum seeker's claim has been accepted, but instead rests on 'something more than mere presence, namely some form of "willed connection" between refugee and State'.[78] Carlier does not rule out that an asylum seeker may meet the threshold of habitual residence, but argues that it connotes a 'rather strong' connection, which will not always be met at the outset of RSD

R (ST) v Secretary of State for the Home Department [2012] UKSC 12, [2012] 2 AC 135, see Hathaway, *Rights* (2nd edn) (n 12) 198, 200–08.

[73] Hathaway, *Rights* (2nd edn) (n 12) 211 (footnotes omitted). Hathaway continues, however, to note that illegality of presence may weigh against a finding of habitual residence: at 211–12.

[74] ibid 920.

[75] ibid. Hathaway notes that admission to an asylum procedure is 'generally agreed to be an indicator of the required connection, though it is neither mandatory nor sufficient': 919–20 (footnotes omitted).

[76] See, eg, Spijkerboer (n 20) 221 ('from the fact that lawfulness of the presence of a refugee is not required, we can conclude that it is not necessary that the authorities of the country consented to his presence'); Elberling (n 11) 940 (noting that the term habitual residence 'contains no reference to legality or acceptance of status, but rather implies a factual element' (footnotes omitted)).

[77] Spijkerboer (n 20) 222.

[78] Elberling (n 11) 940 (footnotes omitted) and discussion at 941.

proceedings.[79] To Boeles, habitual residence is simply a mechanism by which to choose the most appropriate judicial system against which to measure equal treatment.[80] Article 16(2)–(3) should thus be interpreted in a manner which treats all asylum seekers as having a habitual residence. In the case of asylum seekers 'sent from country to country' (ie 'refugees in orbit'), the State where the person '*de facto* sojourns' should be treated as the State of habitual residence.[81]

2.1.6 Scope of the term 'matters pertaining to access to the Courts'

A sixth issue is the appropriate interpretation of the phrase 'matters pertaining to access to the Courts' in article 16(2). This subsection guarantees a refugee 'the same treatment as a national' in relation to such matters, 'including legal assistance and exemption from *cautio judicatum solvi*'. The use of the word 'including' suggests that the two 'matters' cited do not exhaust a State's obligations and are instead indicative of a broader class.

The early commentators gave little attention to whether 'matters pertaining to access' included 'matters' beyond the two expressly cited. Grahl-Madsen does not address the broader implications of the phrase, noting simply that the rule 'mostly' bears 'on [refugees'] eligibility for legal assistance and exemption from cautio judicatum solvi'.[82] Robinson and Weis ignore the broader implications entirely, with Robinson simply noting that article 16(2) 'assimilates refugees, habitual residents of the country where the court is located, to nationals insofar as access to court in general and the requirement of cautio judicatum solvi and free legal assistance in particular are concerned'.[83]

More recent scholarship accepts that the phrase 'matters pertaining to access to the Courts' has a broader meaning than the two examples given.[84] Spijkerboer, for example, addresses the question in the context of article 16's application to asylum procedures. He considers that the words 'matters pertaining to' indicate that 'the provision goes even beyond access to the courts in the strict sense of the term' and

---

[79] Carlier (n 19) 324 (referring to 'une proximité assez forte'). See also his discussion of the *Aung Maw Zin et al v Total* cases at 334–35.

[80] Boeles (n 18) 300–01. See also on this concept Battjes (n 28) 468–69: '[t]he terms "habitual residence" and "domicile" do not define lawfulness or length of sojourn, but rather serve to distinguish between several states with which the refugee may have ties'.

[81] Boeles (n 18) 302. Following Boeles, Elberling also calls for the State in which the refugee is currently present to be treated as the State of habitual residence: Elberling (n 11) 940.

[82] Grahl-Madsen (n 5) Article 16, VII. He also notes that the legal assistance guarantee will not apply in cases where legal aid is granted by bar associations, rather than by the State—a point also made by Weis: (n 6) 134.

[83] Robinson (n 7) 113. It is presumed that the reference 'access to court in general' recalls obligations in art 16(1). See also Weis (n 6) 134.

[84] See, eg, Carlier (n 19) 321–22 ('*Parmi* les droits relatifs au libre accès aux tribunaux, sont expressément visées l'assistance judiciaire et l'exemption de caution *judicatum solvi*'—expressly referred to *amongst* the rights relating to free access to the courts are legal assistance and exemption from *cautio judiatum solvi*—author's translation, first emphasis added in both French and English texts); Elberling (n 11) 942, drawing on Dutch, German, and Austrian case law; Hathaway, *Rights* (2nd edn) (n 12) 921; Boeles (n 18) 311.

must be interpreted 'without any restriction'.[85] Both Boeles and Hathaway highlight the right to an interpreter as a 'matter' falling within the scope of article 16(2).[86]

2.1.7 The appropriate comparator—how best to compare the rights afforded to refugees and nationals

The seventh question is which 'comparator' should be used in determining whether a refugee is granted 'the same treatment as a national' in 'matters pertaining to access to the Courts'. Boeles proposes that the right of nationals to appeal against administrative decisions is the appropriate comparator.[87] However, in cases where States allow nationals to appeal some administrative decisions but not others, this type of comparator could be difficult to apply. Spijkerboer addresses this issue directly and argues that the comparator should be treatment that is 'substantively equal' procedurally to that granted to nationals.[88] He recalls an example of the Dutch Minister of Justice arguing in favour of removing a 'second appeal in immigration cases' on the basis that 'in some cases Dutch citizens only have one instance' of review.[89] Rejecting this approach, Spijkerboer argues that it is not appropriate to use 'an exotic category' as a comparator in determining what 'same treatment' would entail: 'The general rule in Dutch administrative law is that there are two judicial tiers. Therefore, "the same treatment as a national" means two judicial tiers for asylum seekers as well.'[90] As Elberling indicates, there is also a risk that if too narrow an approach is taken, refugee-specific proceedings will not fall within the scope of article 16(2) at all—such actions will not be applicable to national citizens.[91] He tentatively proposes an interpretation that echoes Spijkerboer's solution—a requirement of '"procedurally" equal treatment', despite the differences of substantive law.[92] The implications of this approach are not, however, fully elaborated.

Elberling notes that while 'general procedural differences in treatment between status determination proceedings and other administrative law proceedings' are suspect under article 16(2),[93] the 'peculiarities of the [domestic] legal system' may be significant in determining the scope of protection.[94] Hathaway proposes

---

[85] Spijkerboer (n 20) 221.

[86] Boeles (n 18) 311, noting it to be 'indispensable for the realization of "free access to the courts"'; Hathaway, *Rights* (2nd edn) (n 12) 921, noting that the provision of an interpreter is required 'to the extent necessary to ensure real access to judicial proceedings'.

[87] Boeles (n 18) 308. Baldinger adopts a similar comparator, arguing that that 'shorter time limits for bringing an appeal against a negative administrative decision on an asylum application to court (compared to other administrative appeals)' could breach art 16: Baldinger (n 20) 29.

[88] Spijkerboer (n 20) 224.

[89] ibid 222 (footnotes omitted).

[90] ibid (footnotes omitted).

[91] Elberling (n 11) 944–45. This point is also made by Hathaway: *Rights* (2nd edn) (n 12) 924.

[92] Elberling (n 11) 945.

[93] ibid.

[94] ibid. See also 926 (noting that 'such cases require an in-depth examination of the national court system and the precise nature and scope of the differences in treatment').

a solution that on its face appears more tailored. Using the example of legal assist-ance, he argues that the appropriate course is:

> to identify the underlying factual predicate for the provision of legal aid in a given jurisdiction—for example, whether it is limited only to certain types of cases (e.g. criminal or family law), or whether it is instead provided to citizens more broadly in situations where there is a significant risk of loss of liberty—and then to apply that premise in a non-discriminatory way to the situation of someone seeking the review or appeal of a negative refugee status assessment before the courts. If na-tionals would receive legal aid when faced with a risk of comparable gravity, then so too should habitually present refugees.[95]

Although this test seems more responsive to jurisdictions that lack a uniform ap-proach, it also invites debate on a different comparator, that of the 'risk of compar-able gravity'.

2.1.8 The subject-matter jurisdiction question—access to courts in the absence of competence to hear a dispute

Finally, recent commentators have grappled with the question whether article 16 could require States to '*create*'[96] access to courts in certain circumstances. If a do-mestic court is not competent to adjudicate a given dispute, or to vindicate a certain right, must a Contracting State expand the court's jurisdiction? Battjes dismisses such an implication, arguing that article 16 'merely addresses the issue of access to the court, not the content of proceedings'.[97] Hathaway likewise considers that art-icle 16 'does not provide a remedy' if a court lacks jurisdiction to hear a refugee's claim.[98] In his earlier work, Hathaway had argued that guarantees in article 14 of the ICCPR[99] could fill this gap in protection.[100] However, developments in Human Rights Committee (HRC) jurisprudence have largely foreclosed this possibility. Article 14(1) entitles '[a]ll persons' to 'a fair and public hearing by a competent, independent and impartial tribunal established by law' in 'the determination ... of his rights and obligations in a suit at law'.[101] The HRC considers that proceedings

---

[95] Hathaway, *Rights* (2nd edn) (n 12) 924 (footnotes omitted).
[96] See Boeles (n 18) 301 (emphasis in original).
[97] Battjes (n 28) 319.
[98] Hathaway, *Rights* (2nd edn) (n 12) 800 (footnotes omitted). See also Moreno-Lax, *Accessing Asylum in Europe* (n 15) 402, citing Hathaway's first edition.
[99] 999 UNTS 171 (signed 16 Dec 1966, entered into force 23 Mar 1976) (ICCPR).
[100] Hathaway, *Rights* (1st edn) (n 67) 647–56. This prospect was also discussed by Francis, who, fol-lowing Hathaway, read the two provisions together in other to argue that asylum seekers were guaran-teed 'a right of judicial appeal to challenge the legality of a decision determining their entitlement to protection': (n 53) 279; and Elberling, who at the time of writing noted that it was an 'open question' whether RSD proceedings were encompassed by article 14(1) ICCPR: (n 11) 946 (footnotes omitted).
[101] For analysis of art 14 ICCPR in criminal proceedings, see Amal Clooney and Philippa Webb, *The Right to a Fair Trial in International Law* (OUP 2020).

relating to the expulsion of aliens—a category into which failed asylum applications have been subsumed[102]—do not constitute either the determination of 'rights and obligations in a suit at law'[103] (or indeed the determination of a criminal charge[104]) under article 14(1). Such proceedings are instead said to fall under the specific 'expulsion' guarantees in article 13 of the Covenant.[105] Hathaway refers to this construction of article 14(1) as 'unfortunate',[106] and recognises that it is now unlikely that first-instance or appellate judicial decisions on RSD will fall within its scope.[107] He nonetheless notes that 'suit at law' under article 14(1) may encompass actions brought by asylum seekers on the basis of unlawful detention.[108]

Cantor notes that, despite these jurisprudential developments, 'certain procedural parameters' may apply to RSD proceedings if ICCPR protections of the right to life (article 6) or freedom from torture or cruel, inhuman, or degrading punishment (article 7) are engaged.[109] The HRC has determined that States parties may not deport an individual if:

> there are substantial grounds for believing that there is a real risk of irreparable harm, such as that contemplated by articles 6 and 7 of the Covenant, either in the country to which removal is to be effected or in any country to which the person may subsequently be removed.[110]

Cantor concludes that 'the Committee's jurisprudence combining Articles 2(3), 6, 7 and 13 strongly suggests that in respect of access to—and due process in—asylum procedures, this difference is much less pronounced'.[111]

Like Hathaway, Elberling takes the view that article 16 'only requires that the State allow refugees to bring their claims to the courts, but not that it should provide the courts with subject-matter jurisdiction or enact substantive law provisions

---

[102] See further Chapter 5, Section 2.1.1 and Cantor (n 44) 86–89, 104.

[103] HRC, *A v Denmark*, Comm no 2357/2014, CCPR/C/116/D/2357/2014 (4 Aug 2016), para 7.6; HRC, *X v Denmark*, Comm no 2007/2010, CCPR/C/110/D/2007/2010 (26 Mar 2014), para 8.5; HRC, *Arusjak Chadzjian v Netherlands*, Comm no 1494/2006, CCPR/C/93/D/1494/2006 (22 July 2008), para 8.4; HRC, *PK v Canada*, Comm no 1234/2003, CCPR/C/89/D/1234/2003 (22 May 2007), para 7.5. See discussion in Cantor (n 44) 87.

[104] *PK v Canada* (n 103) para 7.4. Cantor notes that '[t]he exception may be where deportation constitutes a sanction as a result of criminal proceedings and thus may involve the "determination of a criminal charge" in the meaning of Art. 14(1) ICCPR': (n 44) 87, fn 59. This possibility appears to have been left open by the HRC in *Arusjak Chadzjian v Netherlands* (n 103) para 8.4, and *PK v Canada*, para 7.4.

[105] *A v Denmark* (n 103) para 7.6; *Arusjak Chadzjian v Netherlands* (n 103) para 8.4; *X v Denmark* (n 103) para 8.5; *PK v Canada* (n 103) para 7.5.

[106] Hathaway, *Rights* (2nd edn) (n 12) 804.

[107] ibid 801–05, 808.

[108] ibid 808.

[109] Cantor (n 44) 87.

[110] HRC, 'General Comment No. 31', CCPR/C/21/Rev.1/Add.13 (26 May 2004), para 12. See also discussion in Goodwin-Gill and McAdam (4th edn) (n 11) 351, 369.

[111] Cantor (n 44) 89 (footnotes omitted).

which would allow these claims to be successful.[112] However, his analysis suggests that there is room for further work in deciding whether restrictive measures fall on the side of impermissible restrictions to 'access' or permissible restrictions based on 'substantive law'. Elberling writes:

> [w]ith many ... measures, elaborate interpretation may be required to decide whether they fall on the 'access to courts' or the 'substantive law' side of the mentioned distinction. To give one example: where State law provides that rejected refugee claims from nationals of certain countries be treated as 'clearly unfounded' and thus without appeal, such provisions can be interpreted as restricting access to existing remedies in the context of administrative/asylum law, and thus being in violation of Art. 16. However, they can also be interpreted as restricting the subject-matter jurisdiction of the courts to claims that are not 'clearly unfounded', which would render them compatible with Art. 16.[113]

Boeles proposes an even more expansive view of State obligations. He suggests that article 16 guarantees refugees 'a right of access to the courts for appeal against administrative decisions in disputes *about questions of law raised by the Convention*, in those cases where the national law of the State of habitual residence provides for its own nationals *an appeal to the courts against administrative decisions*'.[114] In reaching this conclusion, Boeles relies on the principle of effectiveness and article 33 of the 1951 Convention (the prohibition on *refoulement*),[115] as well as the framing of article 16 in the Convention's chapter on 'juridical status'.[116] Boeles' interpretation of article 16 has a surprising result: it would appear to require Contracting States that take a dualist approach to international law to legislate in order to ensure that disputes on questions of law raised under the 1951 Convention can be heard by domestic courts. Such an outcome appears to go much further than the general requirements of *pacta sunt servanda*.[117]

---

[112] Elberling (n 11) 944 (footnotes omitted).

[113] ibid.

[114] Boeles (n 18) 308 (emphasis added). Boeles considers that State actions subject to review include 'at least those administrative decisions which involve answering questions of law raised by the [1951 Convention]': 309. Moreno-Lax implies a similar scope in her statement that '[t]o be able to enforce the rights they derived from the Convention, refugees were to be granted unimpeded access to judicial protection', but does not expound on this further: Moreno-Lax, *Accessing Asylum in Europe* (n 15) 400.

[115] Boeles (n 18) 303.

[116] Boeles argues that the inclusion of art 16 in the chapter 'Juridical Status' of the Convention gives 'the implicit message ... that disputes concerning juridical status must be able to be brought before the courts': Boeles (n 18) 300. This argument is less convincing in light of the decision, included in the Final Act of the Conference of Plenipotentiaries, that 'the titles of the chapters [of the 1951 Convention] and of the articles of the Convention are included for practical purposes and do not constitute an element of interpretation': *Final Act of the United Nations Conference of Plenipotentiaries on the Status of Refugees and Stateless Persons*, II, available via <http://www.unhcr.org/protect/PROTECTION/3b6 6c2aa10.pdf>.

[117] Vienna Convention on the Law of Treaties, 1155 UNTS 331 (concluded 23 May 1969, entered into force 27 Jan 1980), art 26 (Vienna Convention).

2.2 UNHCR and ExCom Guidance on Article 16

UNHCR is not empowered to issue binding interpretations of the 1951 Convention.[118] It does, however, provide 'guidance' on its interpretation.[119] This role is a delicate one—Goodwin-Gill notes that UNHCR 'does not claim to be, and is not accepted as, the final authority on the meaning of words',[120] while emphasising its extensive experience and acknowledged expertise on protection issues.[121] Guidance on the scope of article 16 is, however, quite limited. The UNHCR Handbook does not directly address the provision but suggests that it may be irrelevant to RSD. A smattering of statements in UNHCR's annual Notes on International Protection, Guidelines, and other materials suggest that article 16 provides more robust protection, which extends to asylum seekers and encompasses legal aid even for those who have not reached the threshold of habitual residence. However, the persuasive value of these statements is limited by a lack of supporting analysis and, at times, an apparent conflation of the obligations in article 16(1) and (2). Three sets of documents—a 1978 Note, an amicus intervention, and commentary on the Illegal Migration Act 2023 (UK)—provide more sustained analysis of article 16 and some insight into the principle of effectiveness. Finally, some guidance can be gleaned from ExCom Conclusions, which is particularly valuable given that ExCom is made up of State representatives.[122] ExCom discussions, however, were virtually silent on article 16.

2.2.1 UNHCR guidance

As discussed in Section 2.1.2, some scholars consider that article 16 is engaged in RSD procedures, either because it is directly applicable to administrative decision-making, or because article 16(1)–(2) is capable of guaranteeing a right of judicial review in certain circumstances. The UNHCR *Handbook on Procedures and Criteria for Determining Refugee Status* ('the Handbook'),[123] which, despite its non-binding

---

[118] UNHCR's duty is framed rather as 'supervising the application of the provisions' of the 1951 Convention, per art 35(1). See also Jane McAdam, 'Interpretation of the 1951 Convention' in Zimmermann (n 11) 79.

[119] ibid.

[120] Guy S Goodwin-Gill, 'The Search for the One, True Meaning …' in Guy S Goodwin-Gill and Hélène Lambert (eds), *The Limits of Transnational Law: Refugee Law, Policy Harmonization and Judicial Dialogue in the European Union* (CUP 2010) 219.

[121] ibid. See also North and Chia, arguing that UNHCR has limited capacity to promote 'convergence' in interpretation of the 1951 Convention: Anthony M North and Joyce Chia, 'Towards Convergence in the Interpretation of the Refugee Convention: A Proposal for the Establishment of an International Judicial Commission for Refugees' in Jane McAdam (ed), *Forced Migration, Human Rights and Security* (Hart Publishing 2008) 235–38, cited in ibid 219 and McAdam, 'Interpretation' (n 118) 79.

[122] ExCom was established by the UN Economic and Social Council (ECOSOC), Resolution 672 (XXV), 'Establishment of the Executive Committee of the Programme of the United Nations High Commissioner for Refugees' E/RES/672 (30 Apr 1958). See 'The Executive Committee's origins and mandate' (UNHCR, undated) < https://www.unhcr.org/executive-committee>.

[123] UNHCR, *Handbook* (n 11).

nature, is widely relied upon as guidance in interpreting the 1951 Convention,[124] states that '[p]rovisions [of the 1951 Convention] that define the *legal status* of refugees ... have no influence on the process of determination of refugee status'.[125] It further notes that RSD 'is not specifically regulated by the 1951 Convention', and that the Convention 'does not indicate what type of [RSD] procedures are to be adopted'.[126] These statements suggest that UNHCR does not consider article 16 to play a role in the RSD process, but are not conclusive of the question.

A broader search of UNHCR materials reveals scattered references to article 16 that are generally unsupported by critical analysis. A survey of UNHCR Notes on International Protection from 1965 to 2022 undertaken for this chapter uncovered only three express references to article 16 of the 1951 Convention.[127] Two of these references (in the 1994 and 2008 Notes) are not particularly helpful in providing guidance.[128] The third, in 2001, reads:

> [t]here is an obligation on refugees imposed by the Convention to respect law and order in the country of asylum. This is mirrored by their right of access to courts

---

[124] See Goodwin-Gill and McAdam (4th edn) (n 11) 57, fn 19 (reflecting that '[t]he *Handbook* has been widely circulated and approved by governments and is frequently referred to in refugee status proceedings throughout the world; however, courts citing it, even with approval, commonly note that it is not binding'); and Jeremy Hill, *Aust's Modern Treaty Law and Practice* (4th edn, CUP 2023), 246 (noting that the Handbook 'is generally treated as an authoritative commentary' on the 1951 Convention (footnotes omitted)).

[125] UNHCR, *Handbook* (n 11) para 12 (ii), cited in Elberling (n 11) 944. Hathaway considers that UNHCR's position is 'overly broad' and 'at odds with the general ambit of Art. 16(1) of the Convention': Hathaway, *Rights* (2nd edn) (n 12) 800, fn 2816.

[126] UNHCR, *Handbook* (n 11) para 189. Accordingly, the Handbook concludes that it is 'left to each Contracting State to establish the procedure that it considers most appropriate, having regard to its particular constitutional and administrative structure': ibid. See also UNGA, 'Report of the United Nations High Commissioner for Refugees', A/32/12 (2 Sept 1977), para 37, noting that procedures should nonetheless 'contain certain common features and guarantees that are necessary to protect the legitimate interests and concerns of the individual applicant'. At the time of the 1977 Report, RSD procedures had only been established 'on a formal basis' in seventeen countries: ibid para 38. The 1976 Report of the High Commissioner noted that, in light of the asylum seeker's 'exceptional situation', it was 'essential for his application to be examined swiftly and in full knowledge of the facts by qualified personnel, *within the framework of special procedures which provide the asylum-seeker with adequate legal guarantees and, in case of refusal, possibility of appeal*': UNGA, 'Report of the United Nations High Commissioner for Refugees', A/31/12 (1 Jan 1976), para 24 (emphasis added).

[127] See UNGA, 'Note on International Protection: Report of the High Commissioner', A/AC.96/1053 (30 June 2008), para 34; UNGA, 'Note on International Protection', A/AC.96/951 (13 Sept 2001), para 53, fn 21; UNGA, 'Note on International Protection (submitted by the High Commissioner)', A/AC.96/830 (7 Sept 1994), para 29.

[128] The 1994 Note mentions art 16(2) in passing in a discussion of the rights that accrue at each stage of a refugees' residence in a host State: (n 127) para 29. The 2008 Note cites article 16 of the 1951 Convention and arts 6–8 and 10 of the Universal Declaration of Human Rights (UDHR) in a statement on challenges in 'securing recognition as a person before the law, equal protection of the law, an effective remedy for violations of ... rights and/or full equality in a fair and public hearing by an independent and impartial tribunal'. It also refers to issues of distance from domestic courts and denial of access; gender discrimination within 'traditional justice mechanisms' operating in refugee camps; and weaknesses in the rule of law upon repatriation: see (n 127) para 34. One might argue that this list of challenges suggests UNHCR is open to a broad conception of 'access' that encompasses practical as well as formal hindrances. However, the Note makes no express statement to this effect and does not distinguish between challenges related to the (binding) obligations under art 16 of the 1951 Convention rights and those related to the (non-binding) UDHR principles.

on the same basis as nationals. Such access is an essential element of the inclusion of refugees in a functioning system of freedom and justice and is a provision of the Convention to which no reservations are permitted. It *encompasses many aspects including access to legal representation, interpretation and translation facilities, costs and fees, as well as broader concepts of due process and fair trial*. Although the Convention does not expressly mention the latter, they are inherent to the right of access to courts and exist under general human rights standards.[129]

This statement appears to conflate the non-derogable right of 'free access to courts' in article 16(1) with the rights of access on the same basis as nationals in article 16(2), which are only available to refugees who have their 'habitual residence' in a Contracting State. It is therefore unclear whether UNHCR considers 'access to legal representation, interpretation and translation' to fall within the non-derogable right in article 16(1), or whether these rights are only engaged when the threshold of habitual residence (under article 16(2)) is met.

Article 16 is also mentioned in UNHCR's Detention Guidelines[130] and its Guidelines on Decent Work.[131] The Detention Guidelines reference article 16(2) in a discussion of asylum seekers' rights regarding detention. This suggests that UNHCR considers the sub-provision to extend to asylum seekers, and that asylum seekers can meet the threshold of habitual residence. The Guidelines on Decent Work refer to refugees, rather than asylum seekers. The right of 'free access to courts' in article 16 is said to 'encompasses many aspects', citing the language of the 2001 Note on International Protection.[132] The Guidelines therefore suggest that these aspects (of legal representation, interpretation, etc) are inherent in article 16(1), rather than contingent on meeting the habitual residence threshold under article 16(2).

There are also mentions of article 16 in more targeted documents prepared by UNHCR. Again, these materials generally do not engage in analysis of article 16. In two documents, UNHCR argues that article 16 is engaged during the RSD process.[133] A third, the Guide for Parliamentarians prepared jointly by the

---

[129] See the 2001 Note (n 127) para 53, citing '1951 Convention, Article 16; UDHR, Article 10; ICCPR, Article 14' (emphasis added).

[130] See UNHCR, 'Detention Guidelines: Guidelines on the Applicable Criteria and Standards relating to the Detention of Asylum-Seekers and Alternatives to Detention' (2012) available via <http://www.unhcr.org/en-au/publications/legal/505b10ee9/unhcr-detention-guidelines.html> 27; fn 80.

[131] UNHCR, 'UNHCR Guidelines on International Legal Standards Relating to Decent Work for Refugees' (July 2021) <https://www.refworld.org/docid/60e5cfd74.html> 25.

[132] 2001 Note (n 127) para 53.

[133] See UNHCR, 'Comments of the United Nations High Commissioner for Refugees on Proposed Rules from U.S. Citizenship and Immigration Services (U.S. Department of Homeland Security): "Procedures for Asylum and Bars to Asylum Eligibility", "Fee Schedule and Changes to Certain Other Immigration Benefit Request Requirements", and "Asylum Application, Interview, and Employment Authorization for Applicants"' (21 Feb 2020) available via <https://www.refworld.org/docid/60f845f14.html> 7–8; UNHCR, *Options Paper 1: Options for governments on care arrangements and alternatives to detention for children and families* (revised 2019), available via <https://www.refworld.org/docid/5523e8d94.html> 7.

Inter-Parliamentary Union and UNHCR, also expressly accepts the extension of article 16 to asylum seekers, but appears to conflate the protections in article 16(1) and (2).[134] The Guide refers to '[r]ights of all asylum-seekers and refugees, regardless of status or length of stay' as including '[a]ccess to courts and to legal assistance (Article 16, no reservations permitted, treatment as nationals)'.[135]

None of the Notes, Guidelines or targeted documents discussed engage in sustained analysis of article 16, which weakens their persuasive value as guidance. The possible conflation of article 16(1) and 16(2) in certain documents only compounds this view. In all, these materials seem an apt example of Hathaway's critique regarding 'the sheer volume of less-than-fully-consistent advice now emanating from UNHCR'.[136]

However, there are exceptions from the conclusory approach generally taken to article 16 of the 1951 Convention by UNHCR. One is in a 1978 Note on the extraterritorial effect of RSD.[137] A second is an amicus curiae intervention in the case of *Al-Rawi*.[138] A third is UNHCR's observations on the Illegal Migration Bill and Illegal Migration Act 2023 (UK).[139]

The 1978 Note is helpful in resolving the question of whether one Contracting State to the 1951 Convention is obliged to recognise refugee status afforded by another Contracting State. Such a situation may arise when an individual attempts to exercise rights under article 16(3). Directly discussing article 16, the Note considers it to be 'only reasonable' that a refugee seeking to exercise rights in a country other than that in which he is normally resident may rely on his status in the host

---

[134] See IPU/UNHCR, 'A guide to international refugee protection and building state asylum systems Handbook for Parliamentarians N° 27, 2017' (2017) available via <https://www.refworld.org/docid/5a9d57554.html> 97, 202.

[135] ibid 202. See also 62 and 213. The reference to access to courts obligations at 62 is also cited in UNHCR, 'Analytical Report: On the Legislation and Practice of the Republic of Uzbekistan in the Context of Prospects for the Accession to the 1951 Convention relating to the Status of Refugees and its 1967 Protocol' (2022), 173 ('The following rights should be granted in accordance with the standards applicable to nationals ... Access to courts and legal assistance (no reservations permitted)').

[136] Hathaway, *Rights* (2nd edn) (n 12) 66.

[137] UNHCR, 'Note on the Extraterritorial Effect of the Determination of Refugee Status under the 1951 Convention and the 1967 Protocol Relating to the Status of Refugees' EC/SCP/9 (24 Aug 1978), available via <https://www.refworld.org/docid/3ae68cccc.html>.

[138] A search of UNHCR's amicus curiae interventions found only two references to art 16. The first intervention, in the *Roma Rights* case, merely referenced art 16(1)'s non-derogable nature. The second, a pair of interventions in the Court of Appeal case of *Al-Rawi*, engaged more directly with the provision. See UNHCR, 'UNHCR intervention before the Court of Appeal of England and Wales in the case of the European Roma Rights Center and Others (Appellants) v. (1) The Immigration Officer at Prague Airport, (2) The Secretary of State for the Home Department (Respondents)' (30 Jan 2003), available via <https://www.refworld.org/docid/3e5ba6d45.html>, paras 91, 101; 'Written submissions on behalf of the Office of the United Nations High Commissioner for Refugees, Intervener' and 'Further Written Submissions on behalf of the Intervener (UNHCR)' in Guy S Goodwin-Gill, '*The Queen (Al-Rawi and others) v Secretary of State for Foreign and Commonwealth Affairs and another* (United Nations High Commissioner for Refugees intervening)' (2008) 20 IJRL 675 at 677 and 698 respectively.

[139] See UNHCR, 'UNHCR Legal Observations on the Illegal Migration Bill' (2 May 2023 (updated)); UNHCR, 'UNHCR Recommendations on the Implementation of the Illegal Migration Act 2023' (6 Oct 2023).

State. Requiring a 'fresh determination' would 'give rise to a number of technical difficulties, which could seriously impede the effective exercise of these various rights'.[140] This position is supported by reference to State practice and discussion in the *travaux préparatoires*.[141]

The amicus curiae intervention, in the case of *Al-Rawi*,[142] also adverts to 'effectiveness' in the context of article 16. In *Al-Rawi*, the Court of Appeal was called on to decide whether the British government was obliged to exercise diplomatic protection on behalf of two recognised refugees, amongst others,[143] who had indefinite leave to remain in the United Kingdom and were detained in Guantánamo Bay by US authorities. The United Kingdom had declined to intervene on behalf of the two appellants to secure their release.[144] In the lower court, it was accepted that the US's conduct in denying the refugee appellants access to the courts was inconsistent with article 16(1) of the 1951 Convention,[145] although it was ultimately determined that the argument that diplomatic protection was necessary to ensure the effective exercise of that right was unsustainable.[146] Granted permission to intervene in proceedings before the Court of Appeal, UNHCR argued that:

> in failing to provide the Appellants ... with [effective][147] access to a court under Article 16 of the 1951 Convention relating to the Status of Refugees, the United States is ... in breach of its treaty obligations to the United Kingdom ...[148]

The reference to 'effective' access to a court in this citation was inserted in UNHCR's further written submissions in response to information that habeas corpus applications filed by each applicant had been stayed by the US District Court.[149] This addition reflects UNHCR's position that the obligation in article 16 may be breached where access to the courts is rendered nugatory. The *Al-Rawi* interventions show that UNHCR is open to an implication of effective protection when determining whether access is practically available. The depth of analysis supports giving this position greater weight than the materials surveyed here. However, the Court of

---

[140] UNHCR, 'Extraterritorial Effect' (n 137) para 15.

[141] ibid paras 16–17.

[142] *R (on the application of Al-Rawi) v Secretary of State for Foreign and Commonwealth Affairs and Another* [2006] EWCA Civ 1279 (UK).

[143] ibid para 1 (Laws LJ), noting that two of the appellants had been granted asylum and the others were members of their families. All had been granted indefinite leave to remain.

[144] See 'Written submissions' (n 138) 679, para 15.

[145] *R on the Application of Bisher Al Rawi & Others v SS for Foreign and Commonwealth Affairs and the SS for the Home Department* [2006] EWHC 972 (Supreme Court of Judicature, Queen's Bench Division Divisional Court), para 61 ('It follows that in relation to the second and third [refugee] claimants, they are being denied access to the courts of the United States in contravention of [the 1951 Convention], the United States being one of the Contracting States.')

[146] ibid paras 62–65.

[147] This amendment was noted in 'Further Written Submissions' (n 138) 700, para 9.

[148] 'Written submissions' (n 138) 681, para 21, as amended by the Further Written Submissions: ibid.

[149] 'Further Written Submissions' (n 138) 700, paras 7–9.

Appeal ultimately declined to determine whether the United States had breached its obligations under the Convention, noting simply that '[a] violation by the Americans of Article 16(1) carries no consequence that the first respondent should make representations of the kind sought by the appellants'.[150] In reaching this finding the court declined to engage with UNHCR's 'effectiveness' argument.[151]

UNHCR's comments on the Illegal Migration Bill and Illegal Migration Act 2023 (UK) indicate a view that article 16 applies both to asylum seekers and to recognised refugees.[152] In its observations on the Bill, UNHCR considers draft provisions characterised as excluding refugees from laws of general application and notes:

> [w]here the Bill bars access to the courts that would otherwise be available or limits the ability of courts to take into account the human rights of those falling within its scope in the usual way, it is also arguably in direct violation of Article 16(1) of ... the Refugee Convention ... [153]

In its recommendations on the implementation of the Illegal Migration Act 2023 (UK), UNHCR sets out history and jurisprudence on art 16(2), indicating that habitual residence may not be dependent on lawful status.[154]

UNHCR's comments are also relevant to article 16 of the 1954 Convention relating to the Status of Stateless Persons ('1954 Convention'),[155] which is framed in similar terms to article 16 of the 1951 Convention.[156] While a full survey has not been undertaken for the purposes of this chapter, there is also discussion of article 16 of the 1954 Convention in UNHCR statelessness reports.[157] In the 2021 Republic of Korea Report, UNHCR noted that while stateless persons were entitled to 'judiciary services' as a matter of law, an obligation on public officials to notify the immigration office if they became aware of a person subject to deportation posed a 'significant obstacle' to implementation of the right of free access to the courts.[158]

---

[150] *Al-Rawi* (Court of Appeal) (n 142) para 129 (Laws LJ).
[151] ibid paras 121–29. The Court noted that even if the United Kingdom were considered to have standing to challenge the US's conduct as a fellow Party to the 1951 Convention, that standing would merely entitle the United Kingdom to argue that the US should provide the appellants with the benefit of art 16, not that they should be released entirely: at para 124.
[152] See UNHCR, 'Bill' (n 139) paras 74, fn 77 and 79 (on art 16(1)); UNHCR, 'Act' (n 139) paras 8 and 12(ix), fn 24 (on art 16(1)-(2)).
[153] UNHCR, 'Bill' (n 139) para 79.
[154] UNHCR, 'Act' (n 139) 12(ix), fn 24.
[155] Convention relating to the Status of Stateless Persons, 360 UNTS 117 (adopted 28 September 1954, entered into force 6 June 1960).
[156] UNHCR, 'Bill' (n 139) para 77.
[157] See, eg, UNHCR, 'Mapping Statelessness in the Republic of Korea' (December 2021), 86–87; UNHCR, 'Mapping Statelessness in Slovakia' (2022) 29 and conclusions on access to courts at 35.
[158] UNHCR, 'Mapping Statelessness in the Republic of Korea' (n 157), 86-87 (noting that this obligation has some exceptions: at 87).

2.2.2 ExCom guidance

Some guidance on the scope of article 16 of the 1951 Convention can be gleaned from ExCom Conclusions. Goodwin-Gill and McAdam note that while ExCom Conclusions 'do not have force of law', they may 'contribute ... to the formulation of *opinio juris*',[159] one of the two core elements for the formation of customary law.[160] While ExCom has proposed procedural guarantees that should be applied to RSD, these are generally framed in hortatory language and are not linked back to the obligations in the 1951 Convention.[161] For example, ExCom Conclusion No 8 on the Determination of Refugee Status[162] sets out 'basic requirements' that such procedures should follow.[163] These 'requirements' are, in fact, recommendations—the Conclusion expresses 'the hope' that Contracting States yet to adopt formal RSD procedures 'would take steps to establish such procedures'.[164] The repeated use of 'should' in each sub-clause shows an intention that the purported 'requirements' be non-binding.[165]

In light of the discussion here, it is relevant that ExCom considers that the authority charged with conducting—or reviewing—the RSD decision need not be a court.[166] This demonstrates a view by States that there is no requirement for judicial review of an administrative decision under the 1951 Convention. While an avenue for appeal is recommended, it could be 'either to the same or to a different authority, whether administrative or judicial, according to the prevailing [system]'.[167] ExCom Conclusion No 30 on the Problem of Manifestly Unfounded or Abusive Applications for Refugee Status or Asylum[168] accepted that 'expeditious' procedures could be adopted to handle applications 'so obviously without foundation as not to merit full examination at every level of the procedure'.[169] While the Conclusion recognised the need for 'appropriate procedural guarantees'

---

[159] Goodwin-Gill and McAdam (4th edn) (n 11) 256.

[160] On the formation of customary international law see further ILC, 'Draft conclusions on identification of customary international law, with commentaries' (2018).

[161] Though see ExCom, 'General Conclusion on International Protection', Conclusion No 81 (XLVIII) (17 Oct 1997), para (h) (noting that 'a comprehensive approach to refugee protection comprises, *inter alia* ... access, consistent with the 1951 Convention and the 1967 Protocol, of all asylum-seekers to fair and effective procedures for determining status and protection needs').

[162] ExCom, 'Determination of Refugee Status', Conclusion No 8 (XXVIII) (12 Oct 1977) <http://www.unhcr.org/excom/exconc/3ae68c6e4/determination-refugee-status.html> (ExCom Conclusion No 8). See also discussion in Boeles (n 18) 304.

[163] ExCom Conclusion No 8 (n 162) para (e); UNHCR, *Handbook* (n 11) para 192.

[164] ExCom Conclusion No 8 (n 162) para (d).

[165] ibid para (e)(i)–(vii).

[166] See ibid para (e)(vi).

[167] ibid para (e)(vi). See also para (e)(vii), noting that an unsuccessful applicant 'should ... be permitted to remain in the country while an appeal to a higher administrative authority or to the courts is pending'.

[168] ExCom, 'The Problem of Manifestly Unfounded or Abusive Applications for Refugee Status or Asylum', Conclusion No 30 (XXXIV) (20 Oct 1983), also cited in Boeles (n 18) 304.

[169] ExCom Conclusion No 30 (n 168) para (d).

in such cases, it is not framed in the language of obligation[170] and again no reference is made to article 16 of the 1951 Convention.[171] ExCom Conclusion No 44 on the Detention of Refugees and Asylum-Seekers also appears to support the 'subject-matter' limitation discussed in the literature by implying that there is no requirement that detention necessarily be reviewed by a court. ExCom accepted that review of the detention of refugees and asylum seekers may be conducted by the Executive, 'recommending' that decisions to detain be 'subject to judicial *or* administrative review'.[172] This position is inconsistent with the guarantee of habeas corpus enshrined in article 9(4) of the ICCPR.[173]

One intriguing reference to refugee protection in relation to access to courts appeared in ExCom Conclusion No 22 on Protection of Asylum-Seekers in Situations of Large-Scale Influx. The Conclusion provided that asylum seekers who have been 'temporarily admitted pending arrangements for a durable solution' should be provided with minimum guarantees, including 'free access to courts of law *and other competent administrative authorities*'.[174] Although on the face of it, this statement implies that asylum seekers hold broader rights than those potentially available under article 16 of the 1951 Convention (or, indeed, supports an argument bolstering a broader interpretation of article 16 that encompasses a right of access to administrative agencies), the better view is that this Conclusion drew on a wider range of human rights standards under international law and that, accordingly, its scope was formulated more broadly than the traditional elements of article 16.

Finally, a survey of ExCom summary records between 1979–2022 undertaken for this chapter shows that States have been virtually silent on the scope of article 16.[175] The survey uncovered only two references to article 16, both by delegates representing India, which is not a Party to the Convention.[176] A search for discussion

---

[170]   ibid. See, eg, para (i): 'as in the case of all requests for the determination of refugee status or the grant of asylum, the applicant *should* be given a complete personal interview by a fully qualified official and, *whenever possible*, by an official of the authority competent to determine refugee status' (emphasis added).

[171]   ibid para (e)(iii).

[172]   ExCom, 'Detention of Refugees and Asylum-Seekers', Conclusion No 44 (XXXVII) (13 Oct 1986), para (e) (emphasis added), also cited in Boeles (n 18) 304. See also the UNHCR Detention Guidelines, which note that asylum seekers who are detained or facing detention are entitled to 'be brought promptly before a judicial *or other independent authority* to have the detention decision reviewed': (n 130) 27 (emphasis added).

[173]   The HRC expressly notes that this right extends to asylum seekers: see HRC, 'General Comment No. 35: Article 9 (Liberty and security of person)' CCPR/C/GC/35 (16 Dec 2014) paras 3 (referring to asylum seekers) and 40 (referring to immigration detention). See further discussion in Chapter 5, Section 2.3.4.2.

[174]   ExCom, 'Protection of Asylum-Seekers in Situations of Large-Scale Influx', Conclusion No 22 (XXXII) (21 Oct 1981), para II.2(f) (emphasis added).

[175]   Documents A/AC.96/SR.304—A/AC.96/SR.754. The summary records were searched for references to the terms 'access to courts'; 'access to the courts'; 'article 16'; 'art 16'; 'art. 16'; 'same treatment as a national'; 'no reservation'; 'non-derogable'; and 'article 42'.

[176]   See UNGA, ExCom, Summary Record of the 621st meeting on 7 October 2008, A/AC.96/SR.621, 9 (India (Ms Mahawar)); UNGA, ExCom, Summary Record of the 558th meeting on 4 October 2001, A/AC.96/SR.558, 2 (India (Mr Prasad)). Delegates noted measures taken by national courts 'with

of non-derogable obligations—given that article 16(1) is an obligation to which no reservation can be made—drew only one additional reference: an interpretative statement by Germany in 1989.[177] The ExCom discussions do not, therefore, shed particular light on States' understanding of the provision and seem to underscore the general lack of attention paid to article 16.

A survey of these materials demonstrates that there is no one definitive analysis of article 16. Instead, one is faced with a series of scattered references of varying persuasive value. The question of the ultimate scope and content of article 16 is therefore yet to be comprehensively resolved.

3. Conclusion

The environment in which refugee protection is afforded has changed significantly since the adoption of the 1951 Convention seventy years ago. New protection challenges, unanticipated by the Convention's early commentators, are now exercising the minds of scholars engaging with article 16. This brief account of academic, UNHCR, and ExCom guidance on article 16 shows that there is room for further enquiry on the provision's scope and application. Guidance from UNHCR is developing, and academic scholarship shows an evolving, but not always consistent, approach to key questions on the provision's scope and content. Does the word 'refugee' in article 16 encompass the unrecognised asylum seeker? When, if at all, and how, does article 16 apply to RSD procedures? What is the appropriate comparator when determining if refugees are given 'the same treatment as a national' under article 16(2)? And, consequently, when will procedural hindrances to accessing courts constitute a breach of article 16? This book seeks to build on the existing scholarship and guidance by developing a reasoned interpretation of article 16. The principles governing that interpretative exercise are addressed in Chapter 3.

---

regard to refugees' access to courts' (Mr Prasad), and affirmed India's respect for the 'principle' of free access (Ms Mahawar).

[177] Namely that that a reference to 'recognized basic human standards' in ExCom's conclusion on irregular movement should not be interpreted as going further than those obligations that are non-derogable under article 42: see UNGA, ExCom, Summary Record of the 442nd meeting held on 9 October 1989, A/AC.96/SR.442, 24; ExCom, 'Problem of Refugees and Asylum-Seekers Who Move in an Irregular Manner from a Country in Which They Had Already Found Protection', Conclusion No 58 (XL) (13 Oct 1989), para (f).

3

Applying the Rule of Treaty Interpretation to the 1951 Convention

1. Introduction

As noted in Chapter 1, the 1951 Convention lacks an authoritative interpreter of its terms or an 'in-built monitoring system'[1] and UNHCR's duty of supervising the application of the Convention under article 35 'does not extend to a mandate to provide authoritative rulings or opinions on the meaning of particular treaty terms'.[2] In this environment, scholars play an important role in synthesising evidence of State practice and arguing for greater attention to human rights developments.[3] However, a rigorous approach to treaty interpretation is needed if this endeavour is to provide useful guidance on the scope of the 1951 Convention.

Section 2 of this chapter analyses the general rule of treaty interpretation, before turning to the evidentiary weight that can be attributed to three sets of materials: (i) domestic and regional court decisions; (ii) the UNHCR Handbook, Guidelines, and other interpretative materials; and (iii) ExCom Conclusions. This discussion highlights that the key sources of international refugee law fit uncomfortably within the parameters of the general rule in the Vienna Convention on the Law of Treaties (Vienna Convention).[4] A 'grey zone' exists in which instruments

---

[1] See Jane McAdam, 'Interpretation of the 1951 Convention' in Andreas Zimmermann (ed), *The 1951 Convention Relating to the Status of Refugees and its 1967 Protocol* (OUP 2011) 77; Guy S Goodwin-Gill, 'The Search for the One, True Meaning …' in Guy S Goodwin-Gill and Hélène Lambert (eds), *The Limits of Transnational Law: Refugee Law, Policy Harmonization and Judicial Dialogue in the European Union* (CUP 2010) 207.

[2] McAdam, 'Interpretation' (n 1) 79; see also Goodwin-Gill, 'Search' (n 1) 218–19 (noting that UNHCR 'does not claim to be, and is not accepted as, the final authority on the meaning of words', although in light of its extensive experience, '[t]he exact nature of UNHCR's role in relation to interpretation of the law is somewhat uncertain').

[3] Although Venzke argues that 'any individual scholar's semantic authority is at best marginal', scholars have played a central role in the development of international refugee law and are frequently cited in judicial decisions. However, that in itself is a means of increasing scholars' semantic authority, securing 'recognition for interpretative claims': See Ingo Venzke, *How Interpretation Makes International Law: On Semantic Change and Normative Twists* (OUP 2012), 65, 110. See also, on the role of scholars, Guy S Goodwin-Gill, 'The Office of the United Nations High Commissioner for Refugees and the Sources of International Refugee Law' (2020) 69 International and Comparative Law Quarterly 1, 31.

[4] Vienna Convention on the Law of Treaties, 1155 UNTS 331 (concluded 23 May 1969, entered into force 27 Jan 1980) (Vienna Convention). On this point see Goodwin-Gill noting that UNHCR's role

Access to Courts for Asylum Seekers and Refugees. Emma Dunlop, Oxford University Press. © Emma Dunlop, 2024.
DOI: 10.1093/oso/9780198885597.003.0003

that do not constitute interpretative tools under the Vienna Convention rule are nonetheless relied on as 'persuasive' in the interpretation of the Convention. While consideration of such materials by courts will cause 'soft' principles to harden into State practice, the scholar must be particularly cautious not to place undue reliance on such instruments in the process of interpretation, or to overstate their legal effects.

Section 3 then assesses whether a human rights approach to interpreting the 1951 Convention is justified. It argues that the 1951 Convention warrants a dynamic or evolutionary approach to interpretation that allows the development of human rights law more broadly to be considered in the interpretative process. Support for a teleological approach is found in the object and purpose of the 1951 Convention. However, the chapter ultimately cautions against arguing for interpretations that stretch the treaty beyond what its terms can bear.[5] That which is normatively preferable should not be conflated with that which is possible as a matter of interpretation.[6] Section 4 concludes.

2. The General Rule in the Vienna Convention on the Law of Treaties

The interpretation of treaties in general, and the 1951 Convention in particular, has already received significant attention. Rather than giving a comprehensive account of the applicable rules of interpretation, this section focuses on key issues that arise in the context of interpreting the 1951 Convention. Section 2.1 sets out the rule of interpretation established in the Vienna Convention. Section 2.2 looks at the particular issue of 'subsequent practice' under article 31(3)(b) in the context of the 1951 Convention, examining what level of consistency in judicial decisions is required to reach the level of State practice, whether documents prepared by UNHCR fall within the scope of the provision, and what weight can be afforded to ExCom Conclusions.

---

raises 'questions about the adequacy of traditional "sources" doctrine to account for "other" factors, such as international organisation "practice" and municipal judgments, even when they clearly influence the interpretation, application and development of international law.': Goodwin-Gill, 'Sources' (n 3) 2.

[5] As McAdam notes in the context of complementary protection regimes, 'soft law' should not be used 'to fudge standards or replace treaty based obligations': Jane McAdam, 'The Refugee Convention as a Rights Blueprint for Persons in Need of International Protection' in Jane McAdam (ed), *Forced Migration and Global Security* (Hart Publishing 2008) 281.

[6] Goodwin-Gill's encouragement to UNHCR to 'distinguish carefully between positions which deal with matters of interpretation ... and those which are more in the form of recommendations for amendment' applies equally to the academic interpreter: see Goodwin-Gill, 'Search' (n 1) 240–41.

2.1 Vienna Convention on the Law of Treaties—The General Rule

The principles for the interpretation of treaties are well-established. The precise scope and application of those principles remain, however, the subject of much debate.[7] In keeping with the dictum that interpretation is more an art than a science,[8] Hill has stated that '[g]ood interpretation is often no more than the application of common sense'.[9] While refreshing in its simplicity, what may appear common sense to one is hardly common to all, and the Vienna Convention is framed in such a way as to allow for multiple possible interpretations to coexist. The relevant rules are set out in articles 31 and 32 of the Vienna Convention:

Article 31. GENERAL RULE OF INTERPRETATION

1. *A treaty shall be interpreted in good faith in accordance with the ordinary meaning to be given to the terms of the treaty in their context and in the light of its object and purpose.*
2. *The context for the purpose of the interpretation of a treaty shall comprise, in addition to the text, including its preamble and annexes:*
   (a) *any agreement relating to the treaty which was made between all the parties in connexion with the conclusion of the treaty;*
   (b) *any instrument which was made by one or more parties in connexion with the conclusion of the treaty and accepted by the other parties as an instrument related to the treaty.*

---

[7] See Ian Sinclair, *The Vienna Convention on the Law of Treaties* (2nd edn, Manchester University Press 1984) 114. As Sinclair notes, 'much in the way of discretion and appreciation is left to the tribunal called upon to interpret a particular treaty provision', and 'widely differing results can still be achieved even if a conscious effort is being made to apply the Convention rules': at 153. See similarly Ulf Linderfalk, *On the Interpretation of Treaties: The Modern International Law as Expressed in the 1969 Vienna Convention on the Law of Treaties* (Springer 2007) 3–5.

[8] Drawing from ILC, 'Third report on the law of treaties by Sir Humphrey Waldock, Special Rapporteur', in *Yearbook of the International Law Commission 1964*, Vol II, 54 (Commentary to articles 70–73), cited in ILC, 'Fragmentation of International Law: Difficulties arising from the Diversification and Expansion of International Law: Report of the Study Group of the International Law Commission, Finalized by Martti Koskenniemi', A/CN.4/L.682 (13 Apr 2006), 234. Keith references this dictum in his discussion of interpretative codes on the domestic and international level, noting that '[w]hile the codes may and do in practice increase the science of the process of interpretation, many cases ... show that in hard cases the art, even if reduced somewhat, will remain': KJ Keith, 'Interpreting Treaties, Statutes and Contracts', New Zealand Centre for Public Law, Occasional Paper No 19 (May 2009), 55.

[9] Jeremy Hill, *Aust's Modern Treaty Law and Practice* (4th edn, CUP 2023), 262.

3. *There shall be taken into account, together with the context:*

   (a) *any subsequent agreement between the parties regarding the interpretation of the treaty or the application of its provisions;*

   (b) *any subsequent practice in the application of the treaty which establishes the agreement of the parties regarding its interpretation;*

   (c) *any relevant rules of international law applicable in the relations between the parties.*

4. *A special meaning shall be given to a term if it is established that the parties so intended.*

Article 32. SUPPLEMENTARY MEANS OF INTERPRETATION

Recourse may be had to supplementary means of interpretation, including the preparatory work of the treaty and the circumstances of its conclusion, in order to confirm the meaning resulting from the application of article 31, or to determine the meaning when the interpretation according to article 31:

   (a) *leaves the meaning ambiguous or obscure; or*

   (b) *leads to a result which is manifestly absurd or unreasonable.*

The Vienna Convention expressly states that it does not apply to treaties adopted prior to its entry into force, in 1980.[10] This is not, however, a bar to applying its principles to the interpretation of the earlier 1951 Convention, as it is well established that the interpretative principles in the Vienna Convention reflect customary international law.[11] The International Court of Justice (ICJ) has recognised this development,[12] and duly applies the Vienna Convention rules both to treaties pre-dating the entry into force of the Vienna Convention,[13]

---

[10] See Vienna Convention, article 4.

[11] See ILC, 'Draft Conclusions on Subsequent Agreements and Subsequent Practice in Relation to the Interpretation of Treaties' in Report of the International Law Commission, A/73/10 (70th sess, 2018), draft conclusion 2(1) ('Draft conclusions on subsequent agreements and subsequent practice'). The UN General Assembly welcomed the adoption of the draft conclusions and commentaries and took note of them: 'Resolution adopted by the General Assembly on 20 December 2018', A/RES/73/202, paras 1, 4. See also Richard K Gardiner, *Treaty Interpretation* (2nd edn, OUP 2015) 14ff; Hill (n 9) 14–15; 239–40; Sinclair (n 7) 153; Linderfalk (n 7) 7; Michelle Foster, *International Refugee Law and Socio-Economic Rights: Refuge from Deprivation* (CUP 2007) 40–41; ILC, 'Fragmentation' (n 8) 215. See however the more equivocal position taken by Villiger in his commentary: Mark E Villiger, *Commentary on the 1969 Vienna Convention on the Law of Treaties* (Martinus Nijhoff Publishers 2009) 440. Goodwin-Gill considers that the Vienna Convention encapsulates recognised 'general principles of international law': see Goodwin-Gill, 'Search' (n 1) 206–07.

[12] See *Maritime Delimitation in the Indian Ocean (Somalia v. Kenya), Preliminary Objections, Judgment* [2017] ICJ Rep 3, 29. See further discussion in Gardiner (n 11) 13–20.

[13] See, eg, *Case concerning Kasikili/Sedudu Island (Botswana/Namibia), Judgment* [1999] ICJ Rep 1045, 1060, applying the Vienna Convention rules to an 1890 treaty, cited in Gardiner (n 11) 16, fn 37.

and to disputes in which one of the parties is not bound by the Vienna Convention.[14]

The general rule in article 31 is a unitary rule of interpretation, not a hierarchy of considerations.[15] The International Law Commission (ILC) stated in its commentary to the draft articles that the act of interpretation is 'a single combined operation … the provisions of the article form a single, closely integrated rule'.[16]

The rule brings together a textual approach ('ordinary meaning'),[17] and a teleological approach (through reference to 'good faith' and 'object and purpose'), with due attention to the context in which the treaty was adopted and subsequent practice by its parties.[18] It therefore establishes a balance between competing schools of interpretation, while avoiding an absolute statement on which approach has dominance.[19] Paragraph 2 elaborates on the meaning of 'context' in paragraph 1, establishing that it covers agreements between all the parties related to the conclusion of the treaty, and such instruments made by a smaller group of parties that have nonetheless been accepted by other parties as 'an instrument related to the treaty'. The ILC refers to context as items that 'form part of or are intimately related to the text'.[20] Sinclair considers this category to be 'deliberately narrow, in the sense that it is confined to documents drawn up in connection with the conclusion of a treaty'.[21]

Paragraph 3 addresses agreements and practice made since the adoption of the treaty. These elements were considered by the ILC to be 'extrinsic to the text'[22] but nonetheless relevant to interpretation. Since paragraphs 2 and 3 are focused on the parties' collective agreements and practice, they open the door for quite significant

---

[14] See *Sovereignty over Pulau Ligitan and Pulau Sipadan (Indonesia/Malaysia), Judgment* [2002] ICJ Rep 625, 645 (applying the principles in articles 31 and 32 of the Vienna Convention to Indonesia (a non-Party) on the basis that those articles reflect customary international law), cited in Gardiner (n 11) 17.

[15] See 'Report of the International Law Commission on the work of its eighteenth session' in *Yearbook of the International Law Commission 1966,* Volume II, 219–20 (Commentary on draft articles 27–28); Hill (n 9) 243; Villiger (n 11) 435–36; McAdam, 'Interpretation' (n 1) 83.

[16] 'Report of the International Law Commission' (n 15) 219–20 (Commentary on draft articles 27–28). See now also ILC, 'Draft conclusions on subsequent agreements and subsequent practice' (n 11) draft conclusion 2(5) ('The interpretation of a treaty consists of a single combined operation, which places appropriate emphasis on the various means of interpretation indicated, respectively, in articles 31 and 32'), and its commentary at paras 11–13.

[17] The text 'must be presumed to be the authentic expression of the intentions of parties', but its interpretation is not a substitute for 'an investigation *ab initio* into [their] intentions': see 'Report of the International Law Commission' (n 15) 220, 223 (Commentary on draft articles 27–28).

[18] See, further, discussion in McAdam, 'Interpretation' (n 1) 81–82 (noting that the Vienna Convention rules encompass the subjective approach; the objective approach; and the teleological approach to treaty interpretation).

[19] See discussion in ILC, 'Fragmentation' (n 8) 215 ('[i]t is in fact hard to think of any approach to interpretation that would be excluded from articles 31–32').

[20] 'Report of the International Law Commission' (n 15) 220.

[21] Sinclair (n 7) 119.

[22] 'Report of the International Law Commission' (n 15) 218 (commentary on articles 27 and 28), as noted by Gardiner (n 11) 224; Sinclair (n 7) 119.

changes to the text of the treaty itself.[23] Villiger considers that 'Article 31, paras. 2 and 3 … envisage a uniform interpretation of the treaty by the parties and for the parties'.[24] He sees the parties, under paragraphs 2 and 3, as being able to amend or revise a treaty in a manner which goes beyond the scope of 'interpretation' under article 31(1).[25] This approach has not, however, been 'generally recognized'.[26]

The relegation of the *travaux préparatoires* to a supplementary role is clear in article 32. The ILC justified this approach by noting that preparatory work lacks the 'same authentic character' of the elements in article 31, which 'all relate to the agreement between the parties *at the time when or after it received authentic expression in the text*'.[27] While certain commentators draw heavily on the *travaux préparatoires* when interpreting the 1951 Convention,[28] Goodwin-Gill notes that an academic focus on the *travaux* is generally not echoed in the courtroom, where judges tend to find these materials less useful.[29] A cautious approach that does not over-emphasise the role of the *travaux* in the interpretative process is preferable, in that the ultimate conclusions reached will be more easily accepted by other interpreters of the Convention.

2.2 The Limits of Subsequent Practice—Sources and Principles

The question of what falls within the scope of 'subsequent practice' under article 31(3)(b) of the Vienna Convention rules is particularly relevant to the interpretation of the 1951 Convention. This section examines three key examples of 'practice' to determine if they meet the threshold of 'subsequent practice … establish[ing] the agreement of the parties regarding … interpretation' under article 31(3)(b): domestic and regional court decisions; UNHCR's various interpretative materials; and the Executive Committee (ExCom) Conclusions on international protection.

---

[23] A commonly cited example of this principle is article 27(3) of the UN Charter, in which the reference to the 'concurring' votes of the P5 in the Security Council has been interpreted through subsequent practice as being satisfied by either an affirmative vote or an abstention: see *Legal Consequences for States of the Continued Presence of South Africa in Namibia (South West Africa) notwithstanding Security Council Resolution 276 (1970), Advisory Opinion* [1971] ICJ Rep 16, 22 (*South West Africa* Opinion) and discussion in Hill (n 9) 251–52; Gardiner (n 11) 277–78; and John Dugard, 'The Opinion on South-West Africa (Namibia): The Teleologists Triumph' (1971) 88 The South African Law Journal 460, 474.

[24] Villiger (n 11) 429.

[25] ibid. See also Hill (n 9) 247, on subsequent agreement.

[26] See ILC, 'Draft conclusions on subsequent agreements and subsequent practice' (n 11) draft conclusion 7(3).

[27] 'Report of the International Law Commission' (n 15) 220 (emphasis in original). This report meets the ILC's characterisation of preparatory work.

[28] See, eg, Hathaway's approach to discerning a treaty's object and purpose: James C Hathaway, *The Rights of Refugees under International Law* (2nd edn, CUP 2021) 148.

[29] Goodwin-Gill, 'Sources' (n 3) 33–34, fn 185. Goodwin-Gill argues that 'the value of the travaux at the international level is somewhat moot, given that only 26 of the [then] 146 States currently party to the Convention actually participated in the drafting': at fn 185.

2.2.1 Domestic and regional judgments

As noted in Chapter 1, the 1951 Convention lacks an 'authoritative interpreter' in practice. No State Party has yet taken advantage of the opportunity provided in article 38 of the Convention to bring a dispute 'relating to [the Convention's] interpretation or application' before the ICJ. Given that the Convention is less concerned with the relations between States than it is with the protection afforded by individual States to a third party (namely refugees),[30] this is not unexpected. The lack of an authoritative interpreter does, however, have the effect of turning attention to the many domestic (and, to a lesser extent, regional) court decisions on the interpretation and application of the 1951 Convention.[31] Domestic decisions fall within the ambit of 'practice in the application of the treaty' for the purposes of article 31(3)(b) of the Vienna Convention rules.[32] Regional decisions do not meet this threshold, but may nonetheless 'be relevant when assessing the subsequent practice of parties to a treaty'.[33]

While it is clear that domestic judicial decisions can constitute 'subsequent practice', establishing that this practice shows 'agreement of the parties' is more complex. At the time of writing, 149 States were Party either to the Convention or its 1967 Protocol. The sheer number of Contracting States (and the differences in their legal systems and judicial capacity) make inconsistencies in practice inevitable.[34] There are also practical hurdles in surveying that practice (including language, familiarity in legal research across jurisdictions, and judicial publication rates) that will naturally lead to blind spots in any effort to comprehensively survey judicial decisions to demonstrate 'agreement'. Goodwin-Gill and Lambert's edited study of judicial dialogue between nine EU Member States on refugee matters[35] shows the difficulties of finding coherence even amongst States in the same regional grouping: Goodwin-Gill concludes that the study demonstrated 'how great are the obstacles in the way of developing a coherent, harmonized, case-based approach to the Refugee Convention'.[36]

In these circumstances, what level of uniformity and consistency is necessary to reach the standard of 'subsequent practice ... establish[ing] the agreement of

---

[30] Though see discussion of the 'object and purpose' of the Convention in Section 3.2.2. The themes of international cooperation and responsibility sharing are also apparent in the treaty's preamble.

[31] McAdam argues that case law on the interpretation of a treaty may be particularly persuasive in the absence of an international supervisory tribunal: McAdam, 'Interpretation' (n 1) 108.

[32] See ILC, 'Draft conclusions on subsequent agreements and subsequent practice' (n 11) commentary to draft conclusion 4, para 18. See also Goodwin-Gill, 'Search' (n 1) 209, 214.

[33] ibid draft conclusion 5(2). Regional decisions are not expressly mentioned in the commentary, but see discussion of arguably analogous forms of conduct in para 11.

[34] See Goodwin-Gill, 'Search' (n 1) 209, fn 18, concluding that 'judicial decisions are unlikely ever to present a picture of uniform and consistent interpretation common to all or most of the parties'. See also Goodwin-Gill, 'Sources' (n 3) 16, 29–31.

[35] Belgium, Denmark, France, Germany, Ireland, Italy, Spain, Sweden, and the UK. The UK has since left the EU.

[36] Goodwin-Gill, 'Search' (n 1) 204.

the parties regarding [the Refugee Convention's] interpretation' under article 31(3)
(b) of the Vienna Convention rules? Goodwin-Gill considers that the required
standard for domestic judicial practice to 'give rise to a new, binding interpretation'
of the 1951 Convention under article 31(3)(b) is 'severe', requiring such practice to
be 'common to/and or accepted by all the parties'.[37] This view is shared by several
commentators on the Vienna Convention. Sinclair notes that the 'value and significance of subsequent practice will naturally depend on the extent to which it is
concordant, common and consistent'—and 'common to all the parties',[38] though
Hill considers it sufficient to show that each party has 'accepted' a practice, even if
'tacitly'.[39] The ILC notes that the practice of 'judicial dialogue' may also 'add to the
development of a subsequent practice'.[40] However, from the text of article 31(3)
(b), it is clear that subsequent practice is intended to capture those compilations of
practice which confirm the agreement of the parties.

A stringent test for the establishment of 'subsequent practice' under article 31(3)
(b) appears uncontroversial in relation to most treaties. However, some modifica-
tion may be called for in the case of multilateral treaties with a broad (and sometimes almost universal) membership that evince an intention to be applied in an
evolutionary manner over an extended period.[41] In these cases, too rigid an application of the 'subsequent practice' rule could run counter to the principle of effectiveness. The changes in the composition of the international community over time
(with the number of Member States to the United Nations almost quadrupling
since its formation in 1945)[42] also lends support to a more flexible approach.
Clearly, an approach that ignores the will of States Parties would not be acceptable.
But a softening of the 'severe' standard, perhaps to accept the formation of subsequent practice without clear proof of tacit acceptance or wholly uniform application could better meet the objects and purposes of this category of treaties.

One argument in favour diminishing the weight given to 'subsequent practice'
rests on the nature of the 1951 Convention as a treaty agreed to by States for the
benefit of a third party—refugees themselves. To Hathaway, allowing State practice to constrict the interpretation of a refugee or human rights-orientated treaty
could hinder its ultimate purpose.[43] Similarly, Hathaway and Foster contend that

---

[37] ibid 209, citing Sinclair (n 7) 138 and Aust, *Modern Treaty Law and Practice* (2nd edn, CUP 2007)
241–43. Goodwin-Gill considers the likelihood of such practice giving rise 'to a new, binding interpretation' to be 'extremely remote': Goodwin-Gill, 'Sources' (n 3) 38 (footnotes omitted).

[38] Sinclair (n 7) 137–38 (footnotes omitted).

[39] Hill (n 9) 252. See also Villiger, who considers that subsequent practice 'must establish the agreement of the parties regarding its interpretation … it will have been acquiesced in by the other parties;
and no other party will have raised an objection': Villiger (n 11) 431 (footnotes omitted).

[40] ILC, 'Draft conclusions on subsequent agreements and subsequent practice' (n 11), commentary
to draft conclusion 7, para 19 (footnotes omitted).

[41] See Section 3.1.2, concluding that the 1951 Refugee Convention falls within this category.

[42] The number of Member States in the United Nations has grown from 51 (in 1945) to 193 (as of
2021): see 'Growth in United Nations membership, 1945–present' (United Nations, undated) <https://
www.un.org/en/about-us/growth-in-un-membership>.

[43] Hathaway, *Rights* (2nd edn) (n 28) 162.

a 'narrow view of the interpretative relevance of State practice' is called for when interpreting the 1951 Convention and other international human rights instruments.[44] While this argument has its merits, it is at odds with the fundamental role of States as the arbiters of their own obligations (at least absent an authoritative ruling by the ICJ). In any event, if evidence demonstrates a consistent practice involving a strained interpretation of a treaty (contrary to its 'ordinary meaning', perhaps), which also seemed at odds with its object and purpose as an instrument to further the promotion of human rights, the appropriate interpretation may well be ascertained through the application of the general rule in article 31 of the Vienna Convention, without recourse to any specialised approach.

Subsequent practice that does not meet the high standard of article 31(3)(b) may still constitute a supplementary means of interpretation under article 32.[45] It is therefore possible for a court to consider a single domestic judgment in the course of its interpretation, although this will carry less weight than subsequent practice that meets the article 31(3)(b) threshold.[46] As the ILC notes, 'one must … always remain conscious of the fact that "the view of one State does not make international law"'.[47] Under this supplementary route, domestic judicial decisions are capable of 'contribut[ing] to the clarification of the meaning of a treaty'.[48] However article 32 is an imperfect home for the work that domestic decisions are called on to do in the interpretative process, as Goodwin-Gill notes:

> '[p]rogressive development' does not appear to be what 'supplementary means' are intended to achieve. Where obscurity, ambiguity, likely absurdity or unreasonable results are not the issue, then the relevance and normative force of jurisprudence (and doctrine) will need a different entry point if international refugee law is to ensure that protection is effective and in accord with changing times and circumstances.[49]

Goodwin-Gill argues for a third way of accounting for the interpretative value of domestic decisions—that of 'subsidiary means', under article 38(1)(d) of the ICJ Statute.[50] Under this route, decisions could be considered as 'material which demonstrates the existence of applicable rules in practice, and their acceptance as

---

[44] Hathaway and Foster (n 55) 11.
[45] See ILC, 'Draft conclusions on subsequent agreements and subsequent practice' (n 11) draft conclusion 2(4) and its commentary, paras 8–9, draft conclusion 4(3) and its commentary, paras 16, 23–35; also Villiger (n 11) 432 (footnotes omitted); Goodwin-Gill, 'Search' (n 1) 210, citing Sinclair (n 7) 138, amongst others.
[46] See ILC, 'Draft conclusions on subsequent agreements and subsequent practice' (n 11) commentary to draft conclusion 4, paras 33–35.
[47] ibid para 33 (footnotes omitted).
[48] See ILC, 'Draft conclusions on subsequent agreements and subsequent practice' (n 11), conclusion 7(2).
[49] Goodwin-Gill, 'Sources' (n 3) 39.
[50] ibid.

binding by States' without the need to demonstrate consistency across jurisdictions.[51] Although this avenue has the clear benefit of a legally sanctioned means of considering domestic decisions without the high threshold imposed by article 31(3)(b) of the Vienna Convention, the subsidiary purpose to which those decisions could be put does not seem to reflect the rich judicial dialogue that occurs in practice in the interpretation of the 1951 Convention. The reliance on judgments by courts and the academic interpreter alike in the interpretative process seems to eschew the strict parameters of the Vienna Convention's general rule.

In practice, certain judgments carry greater weight than others in the interpretation of the 1951 Convention. Goodwin-Gill argues that 'persuasive force' will be afforded to those judgments that 'stand out by reason of their rigorous analysis and use of materials'.[52] Although weighing judgments on this basis seems uncontentious, in practice it tends to privilege decisions from common law jurisdictions.[53] The fact that a judgment is published in English is also a factor in its diffusion as a persuasive interpretation of the Convention. As an example, Foster's study of international refugee law and socio-economic rights focuses on anglophone, common law case law on the basis that the most 'comprehensive analysis' of refugee law, and the crux of judicial dialogue, is in Australia, Canada, New Zealand, the UK, and the US.[54] A glance at the index of other major texts on refugee law demonstrates the comparatively greater attention given to common law decisions, and those from the Global North.[55] An emphasis on anglophone, common law, Global North decisions may place a disproportionate emphasis on one strain of State practice and promote a false sense of consistency in decision-making.[56]

For the interpreter, these conclusions demonstrate a need for caution when relying on domestic and regional decisions in the interpretative process. A survey will be necessary to determine whether the high standard of 'agreement of the parties' is met. If it is not, these materials remain relevant to interpretation but should not be adopted uncritically. Certainly, a given judgment may be useful in demonstrating how careful minds have applied the general rule in the Vienna Convention, and persuasive in this sense. However, it should not be mechanically applied as an *ipse dixit* to declare the proper interpretation of a clause.

---

[51] ibid (footnotes omitted).

[52] Goodwin-Gill, 'Search' (n 1) 238–39.

[53] See Foster (n 11) 23.

[54] ibid 22–23. She notes however that '[r]eference to relevant findings or analysis by civil law jurisdictions will occasionally be made ...': at 23.

[55] See eg, Guy S Goodwin-Gill and Jane McAdam, with Emma Dunlop, *The Refugee in International Law* (4th edn, OUP 2021) xxxv–xlix; James C Hathaway and Michelle Foster, *The Law of Refugee Status* (2nd edn, CUP 2014) xvii–lxvi.

[56] On UNHCR's Guidelines, see Cecilia M Bailliet, 'National Case Law as a Generator of International Refugee Law: Rectifying an Imbalance within UNHCR Guidelines on International Protection' (2015) Emory International Law Journal 2059, 2064. On the tendency of international law to privilege certain elements of the 'international', see Anthea Roberts, *Is International Law International?* (OUP 2017) 5.

2.2.2   UNHCR Handbook, Guidelines on International Protection, and Other Interpretative Materials

A second question is the weight that can be given to UNHCR's Handbook, its Guidelines on International Protection, and other materials (such as its Notes on International Protection) in the interpretative process. As Goodwin-Gill notes, UNHCR's status in the interpretative process is somewhat ambiguous. Its duty of 'supervising the application' of the 1951 Convention[57] does not position it as an authoritative interpreter of the Convention's terms, nor is its institutional role equivalent to that of a 'treaty supervisory body'.[58] However, despite its lack of a clear institutional mandate in the field of interpretation:

> UNHCR now has nearly sixty years' experience of working with states in the provision of protection and the promotion of solutions … In addition, states have requested its guidance, accepted the *Handbook* as an authoritative basis of interpretation, and encouraged the promulgation of later Guidelines on protection issues, particularly in the application of the refugee definition.[59]

How, if at all, can such guidance be used in the context of the Vienna Convention rules to interpret the 1951 Convention?

The UNHCR Handbook was first issued in 1979 'at the request of Member States of the Executive Committee of the High Commissioner's program'.[60] It was reissued in 1992, 2011, and 2019, with updates to the annexes on accessions to the 1951 Convention and its 1967 Protocol, but no changes to the substantive text.[61] The origins of the UNHCR Handbook are set out by Goodwin-Gill, who emphasises that Contracting States to the Convention (as members of ExCom) not only instigated the project but also commented on the Handbook's contents in the course of the drafting process.[62] Despite the role of Contracting States in its development and UNHCR's duty under the 1951 Convention, Goodwin-Gill concludes that the Handbook 'does not clearly come within the Vienna Convention's frame of reference'.[63] He leaves open the possibility that the Handbook may be 'evidence of

---

[57] 1951 Convention, article 35. See also UNHCR's role under its Statute of '[p]romoting the conclusion and ratification of international conventions for the protection of refugees, supervising their application and proposing amendments thereto': Statute of the Office of the United Nations High Commissioner for Refugees, annexed to UNGA Res 428(V) (14 Dec 1950), paragraph 8(a).

[58] Goodwin-Gill, 'Search' (n 1) 219. On the role of such bodies in interpretation, see ILC, 'Draft conclusions on subsequent agreements and subsequent practice' (n 11) draft conclusion 13.

[59] Goodwin-Gill, 'Search' (n 1) 219.

[60] UNHCR, *Handbook on Procedures and Criteria for Determining Refugee Status and Guidelines on International Protection under the 1951 Convention and the 1967 Protocol relating to the Status of Refugees* (1979, reissued Feb 2019), HCR/1P/4/ENG/REV.4, 9 ('Foreword').

[61] ibid.

[62] Goodwin-Gill, 'Search' (n 1) 210–12. See also McAdam, 'Interpretation' (n 1) 110–12.

[63] Goodwin-Gill, 'Search' (n 1) 212.

subsequent practice establishing agreement on interpretation' under article 31(3) (b), at least regarding practice before its publication in 1979.[64]

McAdam argues that the UNHCR Handbook, like 'commentaries and explanatory documents', may have 'persuasive value as aids to construing the treaty to which they relate'.[65] It is not clear if McAdam sees the Handbook's persuasive value as having a formal place within the Vienna Convention rules—as, for example, an 'agreement relating to the treaty' under article 31(2)(a), which covers explanatory reports prepared by representatives of Contracting States. Hill seems to distinguish the Handbook from other instruments in his discussion of article 31(2)(a), by using it as an example of an instrument produced after the conclusion of a treaty which is nonetheless 'generally treated as an authoritative commentary on the Refugee Convention 1951 and practice under it, and … often referred to by domestic courts and tribunals'.[66] As Hill implicitly recognises, however, it is difficult to argue that the UNHCR Handbook amounts to 'context' under article 31(2) (a). Ultimately, and despite the influence of ExCom members, the Handbook was drafted by UNHCR rather than 'all the parties' to the 1951 Convention. The fact that it was drafted well after the finalisation of the Convention also speaks against its characterisation as 'context'.

Is the Handbook nonetheless a relevant consideration under article 31(3)(b) of the Vienna Convention rules? Article 31(3)(b) provides that along with context, '[a]ny subsequent practice in the application of the treaty which establishes the agreement of the parties regarding its interpretation' shall be 'taken into account'. Linderfalk argues that:

> 'practice' does not necessarily emanate only from the parties themselves. All appliers of a treaty are potential creators of 'practice', whether it be the state parties themselves, or the non-state organ—possibly an international organisation—with which the application might have been entrusted.[67]

Given that UNHCR has not been directly 'entrusted' with the application of the 1951 Convention, its practice cannot be considered as equivalent to 'State practice' for the purposes of interpretation. However, there are indications that States accept that the Handbook provides 'evidence' of State practice.[68] This position is

---

[64] See ibid.
[65] McAdam, 'Interpretation' (n 1) 110.
[66] Hill (n 9) 246 (footnotes omitted).
[67] Linderfalk (n 7) 166 (footnotes omitted).
[68] See, eg, *R v Secretary of State for the Department (ex parte Adan)* [1999] 3 WLR 1274, 1296 cited in McAdam (n 1) 97 (The Court of Appeal noted: 'While the *Handbook* is not by any means itself a source of law, many signatory States have accepted the guidance which on their behalf the U.N.H.C.R. was asked to provide, and in those circumstances it constitutes, in our judgment, good evidence of what has come to be international practice within article 31(3)(b) of the Vienna Convention.'). This position was noted without comment in the House of Lords in *R v Secretary of State for the Home Department, ex parte Adan* [2001] 2 AC 477, 524 (Lord Hutton). Lord Steyn also noted that '[i]t is not surprising … that

also accepted by the ILC. In its commentary to its draft conclusions on subsequent agreements and subsequent practice in relation to the interpretation of treaties,[69] the ILC states:

> the view that the UNHCR Handbook itself expresses State practice has correctly been rejected [but] … *the UNHCR Handbook nevertheless possesses considerable evidentiary weight as a correct statement of subsequent State practice.*[70]

The acceptance of the Handbook as 'evidence' of State practice is significant. Despite lacking a formal, authoritative role in articulating the meaning of the Convention, UNHCR has effectively positioned itself as a potential source of agreed interpretations that reflect the general position of Contracting States. This is a more robust authority than UNHCR would have if its statements were considered merely on par with State practice. Rather than being viewed as one voice amongst 149, UNHCR is considered capable of synthesising and compiling the practice of multiple parties. This role has a particular value for a multilateral convention with multiple parties, given the difficulties in presenting a unified account of what are likely to be quite disparate practices.

The Handbook is perhaps the most visible UNHCR output that has been taken to synthesise State practice. However, other texts prepared by the organisation that purport to synthesise State practice may have a similar claim to authority.[71] The UNHCR 'Guidelines on International Protection', many of which were developed through UNHCR's Global Consultations on International Protection, are one example.[72] Goodwin-Gill notes that the Guidelines were similarly developed 'by UNHCR on the basis of its experience and in light of jurisprudential developments, and in consultation with states', at the behest of, and with on-going supervision from, ExCom.[73] Certain Guidelines expressly advert to State practice, through for example an introductory note stating that they 'seek to consolidate appropriate

the UNHCR Handbook, although not binding on states, has high persuasive authority, and is much relied on by domestic courts and tribunals': at 520.

[69] See n 32.

[70] 'Draft conclusions on subsequent agreements and subsequent practice' (n 11) Commentary to draft conclusion 5, para 14, fn 161 (emphasis added).

[71] But not, however, all outputs of the organisation. As Goodwin-Gill notes, 'UNHCR possesses no clear, single mechanism through which to express its views, otherwise perhaps than by "official" publication': Goodwin-Gill, 'Search' (n 1) 219. UNHCR materials should therefore be examined on a case-by-case basis to determine whether they do purport to reflect State practice (rather than the views of the organisation) and to assess the strength of their analysis.

[72] For discussion of the Global Consultations process see Erika Feller, 'Preface' in Erika Feller, Volker Türk, and Frances Nicholson (eds), *Refugee Protection in International Law: UNHCR's Global Consultations on International Protection* (CUP 2003), xvii–xix; 'Global Consultations on International Protection, Update 1 August 2002' (UNHCR) <http://www.unhcr.org/3d4928164.html>.

[73] Goodwin-Gill, 'Search' (n 1) 219.

standards and practice ... in light of recent developments in State practice,[74] statements in the main text,[75] or a note that they are the result of 'broad consultation'.[76]
These statements are less significant, however, than the content of the individual
Guidelines.[77] Formally, to determine what weight a particular statement in a
Guideline should have in the interpretative process, it should be examined on a
case-by-case basis to see if it reflects a synthesis of State Practice or an analytic
approach proposed by UNHCR itself.[78] If the former, the statement may provide
evidence of State practice that is relevant to interpretation under article 31(3)(b).
If the latter, the statement will not have a formal role in the interpretative process.

The fact that UNHCR's positions carry weight due to the organisation's long experience and deep knowledge of the law reveals a grey area in treaty interpretation.
It suggests that recognition of certain of UNHCR's pronouncements as 'evidence'
of State practice has less to do with the substance of those positions, and more to
do with the need to articulate some basis for the long-standing practice of both domestic courts and scholars to advert to UNHCR's views, despite the organisation's
lack of any formal standing when it comes to the interpretative process. In Venzke's
view, UNHCR's various outputs, from the Handbook through to its Guidelines and
Guidance Notes, 'portray themselves as clarifications of the law', but are in fact 'interpretations of international law and form part of the practice of interpretation
that shapes the meaning of the relevant provisions'.[79] Venzke has reflected at length
on the organisation's role as an interpreter, finding that it has 'relied on its function
of supervising the implementation of the Convention in order to develop weighty
interpretations of the law and to intervene in seminal cases', investing 'considerable efforts into shifting the interpretation of the Convention in order to meet
the exigencies of new refugee situations'.[80] He views the organisation as having,

---

[74] UNHCR, 'Guidelines on International Protection: "Internal Flight or Relocation Alternative"
within the Context of Article 1A(2) of the 1951 Convention and/or the 1967 Protocol relating to the
Status of Refugees', HCR/GIP/03/04 (23 July 2003).

[75] See UNHCR, 'Guidelines on International Protection: Cessation of Refugee Status under Article
1C(5) and (6) of the 1951 Convention relating to the Status of Refugees (the "Ceased Circumstances"
Clauses)', HCR/GIP/03/03 (10 Feb 2003), paras 5, 21.

[76] See, eg, UNHCR, 'Guidelines on International Protection No. 11: Prima Facie Recognition of
Refugee Status', HCR/GIP/15/11 (24 June 2015); UNHCR, 'Guidelines on International Protection
No. 12, Claims for refugee status related to situations of armed conflict and violence under Article
1A(2) of the 1951 Convention and/or 1967 Protocol relating to the Status of Refugees and the regional
refugee definitions', HCR/GIP/16/12 (2 Dec 2016). This consultation is not necessarily limited to
States, however: see the statement in Guideline No 13 that it has benefitted from 'broad public consult-
ation': UNHCR, 'Guidelines on International Protection No 13: Applicability of Article 1D of the 1951
Convention relating to the Status of Refugees to Palestinian Refugees', HCR/GIP/17/13 (Dec 2017).

[77] For an assessment of the Guidelines and 'discrepancies' in their coverage of national case law, see
Bailliet (n 56).

[78] See for example, the Guidelines on "Membership of a particular social group" within the context
of Article 1A(2) of the 1951 Convention and/or its 1967 Protocol relating to the Status of Refugees,
HCR/GIP/02/02 (7 May 2002), contains a section providing a 'summary of State practice'. As practice is
mixed, with 'two approaches' clear in common law jurisdictions, UNHCR then provides its own analysis of the situation and proposes a 'single standard that incorporates both dominant approaches': at 3.

[79] Venzke (n 3) 116.

[80] Venzke (n 3) 75, and 110.

successfully, 'subtly influenced the contents of the legal commitments that states entered into as parties to the Refugee Convention'.[81] An example is the general recognition of the expansive scope of 'particular social group', even if there are differences of approach on particular groups, and even at times of the foundational test which applies. Through a process of institutional evolution, UNHCR has succeeding in positioning itself in fact, if not in law, as an authoritative interpreter of the Convention.[82]

The widespread treatment of UNHCR's guidance, in varying forms, as persuasive may ultimately be a self-fulfilling prophecy. Acceptance of UNHCR's analysis by domestic courts transforms interpretations that would otherwise fall in the grey zone into clear examples of State practice.[83] However, even in cases where UNHCR's practice stands alone (albeit as the practice of an international organisation, and the creature to some extent of its founding States), it is likely to be relied upon by a range of interpreters, including both scholars and diplomats. This suggests an unusual outcome—could recognition of UNHCR's persuasive, albeit non-binding, authority in the interpretation of refugee issues be itself considered a 'subsequent practice' of Contracting States in the interpretation of the Convention?

2.2.3 ExCom Conclusions

ExCom Conclusions are a second set of documents that may be relevant to the interpretation of the 1951 Convention.[84] ExCom was first established by UN Economic and Social Council (ECOSOC) in 1958.[85] Originally consisting of twenty-four States,[86] ExCom's membership has now grown to 107;[87] 101 members are parties either to the 1951 Convention or its 1967 Protocol, leaving only six members that are not parties to either instrument.[88] Since 1962, ExCom has prepared formal 'Conclusions' based on its annual discussions on international

---

[81] ibid 109.

[82] See, eg, Geoff Gilbert, 'UNHCR and Courts: *Amicus curiae … sed curia amica est?*' (2016) 28 IJRL 623, 633–34, noting ways in which UNHCR's practice parallels that of formal treaty bodies to other Conventions.

[83] See Venzke, noting that UNHCR's intervention as an amicus curiae aims to '[find] recognition for interpretative claims in judicial decisions': Venzke (n 3) 110.

[84] On the history of ExCom, see Jerzy Sztucki, 'The Conclusions on the International Protection of Refugees Adopted by the Executive Committee of the UNHCR Programme' (1989) 1 International Journal of Refugee Law 285; Elihu Lauterpacht and Daniel Bethlehem, 'The Scope and Content of the Principle of *Non-refoulement*: Opinion' in Erika Feller, Volker Türk, and Frances Nicholson (eds), *Refugee Protection in International Law: UNHCR's Global Consultations on International Protection* (CUP 2003) 95–98.

[85] Resolution 672 (XXV), 'Establishment of the Executive Committee of the Programme of the United Nations High Commissioner for Refugees' E/RES/672 (30 Apr 1958).

[86] ibid para 1.

[87] As of 2023. See 'UNHCR Executive Committee of the High Commissioner's Programme Composition for the period October 2022-October 2023' (UNHCR, undated), available via <https://www.unhcr.org/en-au/excom/scaf/5bbc66644/excom-composition-period-october-2022-october-2023.html>.

[88] Namely, Bangladesh, India, Jordan, Lebanon, Pakistan, and Thailand.

protection.[89] In 1975, ExCom established a 'Sub-Committee of the Whole on International Protection' which took charge of the development of 'Conclusions'.[90] From 1975–2022, ExCom agreed on 116 Conclusions on various protection-related matters.[91] Sztucki's 1989 study of ExCom notes that approximately half of the Conclusions prepared at that time consisted of 'provisions which have more or less pronounced or veiled regulatory, normative purport'.[92]

It is clear that ExCom's Conclusions constitute 'soft law', in that they provide guidance to, but impose no binding obligations on, Contracting States to the 1951 Convention. Sztucki, writing in 1989, considered that they fell 'rather low on the relative scale of *de facto* values of non-legal instruments', and were not on par with General Assembly resolutions.[93] Several commentators nonetheless recognise that ExCom Conclusions may bolster the development of customary international law. Lauterpacht and Bethlehem emphasise that ExCom represents States whose 'interests are specially affected' by refugee issues,[94] while Goodwin-Gill and McAdam consider that the conclusions may 'contribute ... to the formulation of *opinio juris*'.[95]

What is less clear, however, is whether ExCom's conclusions fit into the interpretative exercise under the Vienna Convention rules as subsequent practice establishing the agreement of States Parties under article 31(3)(b). Generally, the Conclusions are couched in hortatory language. At least insofar as they encompass statements evincing an intention to be bound under international law, ExCom's broad membership—encompassing 101 of the 149 parties to the Convention or its Protocol—supports the view that they amount to State practice. The presence of non-parties in the make-up of the Commission in no way lessens this role. Given the generally 'soft' nature of ExCom's conclusions, however, many statements in the Conclusions will not reach the standard of 'subsequent practice ... which *establishes the agreement of the parties regarding its interpretation*'. McAdam notes that the real influence of ExCom Conclusions may come through their inclusion in UNHCR amicus curiae briefs and academic commentary, raising the potential

---

[89] Sztucki (n 84) 293.
[90] ibid. Sztucki notes however that the Committee continued to prepare its own, 'General' conclusions, based on the High Commissioner's annual Notes on International Protection: at 294.
[91] See UNHCR, 'Conclusions on International Protection adopted by the Executive Committee of the UNHCR Programme: 1975–2017 (Conclusion No. 1–114)' (Oct 2017); UNHCR, 'Conclusion of the executive committee on international protection and durable solutions in the context of a public health emergency' (October 2021); ExCom, 'Conclusion No. 116 (LXXIII) on mental health and psychosocial support' (2022).
[92] Sztucki (n 84) 300ff.
[93] ibid 308. He proposed that the Conclusions be regularly endorsed by the General Assembly as a means of improving their relative heft: at 312, 316.
[94] Lauterpacht and Bethlehem (n 84) 148, citing the ICJ's judgment in *North Sea Continental Shelf Cases (Federal Republic of Germany/Denmark; Federal Republic of Germany/Netherlands, Judgment* [1969] ICJ Rep 3, 42.
[95] Goodwin-Gill and McAdam (4th edn) (n 55) 256. See also McAdam, 'Interpretation' (n 1) 112; Goodwin-Gill, 'Sources' (n 3) 9 (referring instead to the Conclusions as 'evidence' of *opinio juris*).

that their positions may be transposed, through acceptance by domestic courts, into a clearer example of State practice.[96] These 'soft' materials can also be picked up by regional courts. The Inter-American Court of Human Rights (IACtHR), for example, considers that the corpus of international human rights law includes, in addition to treaty rules and general principles of law, 'a series of general norms or soft law, that serve as guidelines for the interpretation of the former, because they provide greater precision as to the basic contents of the treaties'.[97] In the *Pacheco Tineo Family* case, Bolivia initially argued that interpreting the American Convention on Human Rights (American Convention)[98] by reference to UNHCR materials was beyond the competence of the Court, as it would have the effect of converting 'soft law' into 'hard law'.[99] The Court determined it was appropriate to advert to 'the significant evolution of the principles and regulation of international refugee law, based also on the *directives, criteria and other authorized rulings of agencies such as UNHCR*'.[100] Ultimately, the Court relied on UNHCR materials and ExCom Conclusions at several points in its judgment, including for the elaboration of procedural standards in the case of refugee status determination.[101] While ExCom Conclusions do not, of themselves, constitute 'subsequent practice' due to their generally hortatory nature, they contribute to a well of 'soft' instruments that are practically drawn on by domestic and regional courts in the interpretative process.

3. A Human Rights Approach? Evolutionary and Teleological Interpretations of the 1951 Convention

3.1 An Evolutionary Approach to the 1951 Convention

3.1.1 Article 31(3)(c)—Relevant rules of international law
Article 31(3)(c) provides that along with context, 'any relevant rules of international law applicable in the relations between the parties' shall be 'taken into

---

[96] McAdam, 'Interpretation' (n 1) 113.

[97] Advisory Opinion OC-21/14, *Rights and Guarantees of Children in the Context of Migration and/or in need of International Protection* (IACtHR, 19 Aug 2014), para 60.

[98] American Convention on Human Rights, 1144 UNTS 123 (signed 22 Nov 1969, entered into force 18 July 1978).

[99] *Case of the Pacheco Tineo Family v Plurinational State of Bolivia* (Preliminary Objections, merits, reparations and costs) (IACtHR, 25 Nov 2013), para 34.

[100] ibid para 143 (emphasis added), referring to its obligations under article 29(d) of the American Convention.

[101] See, eg, ibid paras 159 (on RSD) and 172 (on accelerated procedures). Cantor also notes this reliance on UNHCR materials and ExCom Conclusions: see David James Cantor, 'Reframing Relationships: Revisiting the Procedural Standards for Refugee Status Determination in Light of Recent Human Rights Treaty Body Jurisprudence' (2015) 34 Refugee Survey Quarterly 79, 101–03. He notes: '[b]y framing UNHCR guidance as part of "international refugee law", the Court effectively takes UNHCR soft law standards concerning status determination by States and gives them hard form': at 103.

account'. Villiger sees subparagraph (3)(c) as 'envisag[ing] treaty interpretation against the whole background of international law'.[102] He notes that '[t]hese rules need have no particular relationship with the treaty other than assisting in the interpretation of its terms'.[103] 'Relevant rules' encompass 'all the sources of international law, including custom, general principles, and, where applicable, other treaties'.[104] They do not, however, cover 'soft-law' or non-binding instruments.[105] A preliminary question is whether the 'relevant rules' to be examined are those in force at the time of the treaty's adoption or those in force at the moment of interpretation. The answer to this question of 'intertemporal law'[106] is dependent on the terms of the treaty at issue, and whether the text evinces an intention to retain a fixed meaning, or to be interpreted in a dynamic and evolutionary manner.

The ICJ's *Namibia* Advisory Opinion is commonly cited for its evolutionary approach:

> [m]indful as it is of the primary necessity of interpreting an instrument in accordance with the intentions of the parties at the time of its conclusion, the Court is bound to take into account the fact that the concepts embodied in Article 22 of the Covenant – 'the strenuous conditions of the modern world' and 'the well-being and development' of the peoples concerned-were not static, but were by definition evolutionary, as also, therefore, was the concept of the 'sacred trust'. The parties to the Covenant must consequently be deemed to have accepted them as such. That is why ... the Court must take into consideration the changes which have occurred in the supervening half-century, and its interpretation cannot remain unaffected by the subsequent development of law, through the Charter of the United Nations and by way of customary law. Moreover, an international instrument has to be interpreted and applied within the framework of the entire legal system prevailing at the time of the interpretation.[107]

The Court has applied this approach in some subsequent cases when considered appropriate.[108] In other cases, it has adopted the 'contemporary' approach (looking

---

[102] Villiger (n 11) 432 (footnotes omitted).
[103] ibid (footnotes omitted).
[104] See ILC, 'Fragmentation' (n 8) 215, and 233. See also Sinclair (n 7) 119 (footnotes omitted).
[105] See Villiger (n 11) 433 (arguing that the use of the word 'applicable' demonstrates that only *binding* rules are covered in article 31(3)(c)).
[106] See discussion in 'Draft conclusions on subsequent agreements and subsequent practice' (n 11) commentary to draft conclusion 8; ILC, 'Fragmentation' (n 8) 240–44.
[107] *South West Africa* Opinion (n 23) 31.
[108] See discussion in *Dispute regarding Navigational and Related Rights case (Costa Rica v Nicaragua)*, Judgment [2009] ICJ Rep 213, 242–43, cited in Gardiner (n 11) 469 (who also notes that while the Court largely eschews the term 'evolutionary' in later jurisprudence, it implicitly takes this approach when interpreting terms it deems to be 'generic').

only to the rules in force at the time of the treaty's adoption).[109] In the 2009 *Navigational and Related Rights case (Costa Rica v Nicaragua)*,[110] the Court set out indicia of whether an evolutionary approach is warranted:

> where the parties have used generic terms in a treaty, the parties necessarily having been aware that the meaning of the terms was likely to evolve over time, and where the treaty has been entered into for a very long period or is 'of continuing duration', the parties must be presumed, as a general rule, to have intended those terms to have an evolving meaning.[111]

A final issue (particularly relevant in the case of multilateral treaties) is whether all parties to the treaty being interpreted must also be bound by the 'relevant rules' that are taken into account. A textual analysis of article 31(3)(c) supports this view, since a rule that does not bind a Party cannot be said to be 'applicable in the relations between the parties'. However, the ILC makes a counter-argument, based on the need for an 'effective' interpretation of the clause. It challenges the view that article 31(3)(c) is limited to agreements binding all members of a given convention as having 'the ironic effect that the more the membership of a multilateral treaty such as the WTO covered agreements expanded, the more those treaties would be cut off from the rest of international law'.[112] It considers this outcome to be 'contrary to the legislative ethos behind most of multilateral treaty-making and, presumably, with the intent of most treaty-makers'.[113] As a solution, the ILC proposes that reference to another treaty should be allowed so long as 'the *parties in dispute* are also parties to that other treaty', with a certain flexibility in cases where parties can be said to have 'implicitly' accepted or at least tolerated the instrument to be taken into account.[114] This approach seems sensible in practice, but does not assist when a general interpretation is sought in the absence of a particular dispute. In such cases, support may be sought through investigation of the nature of the treaty and its object and purpose. The application of these principles to the 1951 Convention is addressed in Section 3.1.2 of this chapter.

---

[109] See, eg, *Case concerning rights of nationals of the United States of America in Morocco (France v United States of America), Judgment* [1952] ICJ Rep 176, 189 and *Kasikili/Sedudu Island case* (n 13) 1062, each cited as examples of this approach in *Navigational and Related Rights case* (n 108) 242.

[110] *Navigational and Related Rights case* (n 108) 243, discussed in Gardiner (n 11) 469 (footnote omitted).

[111] ibid para 66. See further Gardiner (n 11) 469.

[112] ILC, 'Fragmentation' (n 8) 237, citing Gabrielle Marceau, 'WTO Dispute Settlement and Human Rights' (2002) 13 European Journal of International Law 757, 781.

[113] ILC, 'Fragmentation' (n 8) 238.

[114] ibid 238–39.

3.1.2 Application to the 1951 Convention

It is broadly accepted that the 1951 Convention warrants a dynamic or evolutionary approach that allows attention to be paid to the relevant rules in force at the time that its terms are interpreted.[115] An evolutionary approach is built into the Convention—article 7 provides that a State shall 'accord to refugees the same treatment as is accorded to aliens generally', except where the Convention provides more favourable terms. Article 7 makes express what would otherwise be implied—that the 1951 Convention should be interpreted consistently with changing standards of 'aliens law and international human rights law'.[116] In *R v Secretary of State for the Department (ex parte Adan)*, the UK Court of Appeal (Civil Division) held:

> [i]t is clear that the signatory states intended that the Convention should afford continuing protection for refugees in the changing circumstances of the present and future world. In our view the Convention has to be regarded as a living instrument: just as, by the Strasbourg jurisprudence, the European Convention on Human Rights is so regarded.[117]

Application of the indicia set out by the ICJ in the *Navigational and Related Rights case*, a decade after *Adan* was decided,[118] supports this approach. Although the reach of the 1951 Convention was initially restricted to those who met the refugee definition as a result of 'events occurring before 1 January 1951,[119] it has been extended by means of the 1967 Protocol to cover all refugees who may be in need of protection.[120] First, terms in the Convention are largely framed in a generic manner that suggests their content should evolve over time. A key example is the terms of the refugee definition itself, which affords protection to those outside their country of nationality and unable or unwilling to seek protection of that State 'owing to well-founded fear of being persecuted for reasons of race, religion, nationality, membership of a particular social group or political opinion'.[121] However it is also apparent in more technical terms, which are framed

---

[115] See sources cited in McAdam, 'Interpretation' (n 1) 103–04.

[116] Achilles Skordas, 'Article 7' in Andreas Zimmermann (ed), *The 1951 Convention Relating to the Status of Refugees and its 1967 Protocol: A Commentary* (OUP 2011) 753.

[117] *Adan* [1999] (n 68) 1296, noted without comment by Lord Hutton in the House of Lords in *Adan* [2001] (n 68) 524.

[118] See n 110.

[119] 1951 Convention, article 1A(2). Parties originally had the choice of whether to further restrict their obligations to 'events occurring in Europe before 1 January 1951', by means of a declaration at their time of signature, ratification or accession: see article 1B(1)(a)–(b). If this dateline had been maintained, an evolutionary interpretation may have been more difficult to support.

[120] The 1967 Protocol removed the temporal restriction in the 1951 Convention as well as the option to limit the scope of Contracting States' obligations to 'events occurring in Europe' (save for those States that had already made a declaration to that effect).

[121] See for example the interpretation of 'particular social group' under article 1(A)(2) of the 1951 Convention, which has been extended to apply to homosexuals, women, and conscientious objectors to military service, among others.

in a manner that allows adaptation to changing laws and practices. Examples include the definition of 'in the same circumstances'[122] and the use of the yardsticks of such as treatment 'accorded to aliens',[123] 'the same treatment as a national',[124] and 'most favourable treatment'.[125] Second, the treaty is of 'continuing duration', and is, as the Court of Appeal noted in *Adan*, intended to provide 'continuing protection for refugees in the changing circumstances of the present and future world.'[126]

The 1951 Convention therefore warrants a dynamic or evolutionary interpretation in the application of article 31(3)(c) of the Vienna Convention. It must be 'interpreted in the light of present-day conditions and in accordance with developments in international law'.[127] But what does this mean in practice? To what extent can developments in international law shape the interpretation that is given to particular terms of the Convention?[128] This question is relevant given the significant developments in international human rights law since the Convention's adoption in 1951.[129]

The ILC Report on Fragmentation argues that article 31(3)(c) represents the principle of 'systemic integration', which calls for international obligations to be 'interpreted by reference to their normative environment'.[130] The outcome of this consideration of a treaty in light of relevant rules of international law is very much a matter for the interpreter:

> [t]he point is only—but it is a key point—that the normative environment cannot be ignored and that when interpreting the treaties, the principle of integration should be borne in mind. This points to the need to carry out the interpretation so as to see the rules in view of *some comprehensible and coherent objective*, to prioritize concerns that are more important at the cost of less important objectives. This is all that article 31(3)(c) requires; the integration into the process of legal reasoning—including reasoning by courts and tribunals—of a sense of coherence

---

[122]   1951 Convention, article 4.
[123]   1951 Convention, articles 7, 18, 21, 22(2).
[124]   1951 Convention, article 16. See also, on protection accorded to nationals, articles 14, 22(1), 24.
[125]   1951 Convention, article 15 and 17.
[126]   *Adan* [1999] (n 68) 1296.
[127]   Goodwin-Gill, 'Search' (n 1) 207 (footnotes omitted).
[128]   An analogy can be made to international environmental law. In his separate opinion in the *Gabčíkovo-Nagymaros* case, Judge Weeramantry stated that article 31(3)(c) of the Vienna Convention 'scarcely covers [the inter-temporal] aspect with the degree of clarity requisite to so important a matter', noting that '[e]nvironmental concerns are live and continuing concerns whenever the project under which they arise may have been inaugurated'. He equates environmental rights to human rights, noting that '[t]reaties that affect human rights cannot be applied in such a manner as to constitute a denial of human rights as understood at the time of their application': *Gabčíkovo-Nagymaros Project (Hungary/Slovakia), Judgment* [1997] ICJ Rep 7, 114 (Sep. Op Weeramantry J), the latter quote cited by Lauterpacht and Bethlehem (n 84) 105.
[129]   See further discussion in Chapter 5, Section 1.
[130]   ILC, 'Fragmentation' (n 8) 208ff. See also at 243–44.

and meaningfulness. Success [or] failure here is measured by how the legal world will view the outcome.[131]

How far developments in human rights law can be 'taken into account' in the interpretation of the 1951 Convention, is the subject of the next section. As will be seen, a human rights approach is bolstered by the 1951 Convention's object and purpose.

3.2 A Teleological Approach to Interpretation, and Its Limits

3.2.1 The teleological approach

How developments in international human rights law affect the interpretation of the 1951 Convention has been an animating question for both scholars and courts. Although legal developments are relevant to the interpretation of many treaties, they are particularly significant when examining human rights instruments.[132] This is due to a tendency to adopt a 'teleological' approach in the interpretation of human rights law. The ILC Report on Fragmentation refers to human rights bodies' inclination 'to adopt readings of human rights conventions that look for their *effet utile* to an extent perhaps wider than regular treaties'.[133] A key example of this trend is interpretation of the European Convention on Human Rights (ECHR) by the ECtHR, which Gardiner considers to provide 'the cradle for development of an "evolutive" interpretation in line with the concept of the Convention as a "living instrument"'.[134] Discussing the jurisprudence of the ECtHR,[135] Gardiner recognises the general tendency:

> there are elements of underpinning for this type of evolutive interpretation of the Vienna rules: the principles of good faith, effectiveness, taking into account context, object and purpose, considering general rules of international law and obligations in other instruments, and so forth; but these only provide a limited platform in the case of a treaty whose provisions are vague and are combined with establishment of institutions which, even if not originally designed for evolutive initiatives, have been revamped to give sharper focus to that end. *A possible conclusion is that human rights treaties warrant distinct consideration, not because interpretative rules different from those in the Vienna Convention apply but because the treaty provisions are drawn up in a way which takes the interpreter beyond the*

---

[131] ibid 211 (emphasis added).
[132] Gardiner also points to the emergence of environmental law as a 'particular issue': see (n 11) 333.
[133] ILC, 'Fragmentation' (n 8) 216.
[134] Gardiner (n 11) 471.
[135] Specifically, the case of *Tyrer v United Kingdom,* App no 5856/72 (ECtHR, Court (Chamber), 25 Apr 1978). Gardiner makes these comments after noting that 'the difficulty with the approach in *Tyrer* is that the analysis of the growing consensus is sparse and not based on materials constituting obligations which would fit within article 31(3)(c)': (n 11) 473.

rules. The case law which human rights treaties have generated illustrates particularly well the way in which the Vienna rules lead to interpretation embracing development of doctrines necessary to give meaning to "vague" provisions when accompanied by institutions to this end.[136]

Letsas' interpretation of the ECHR provides a justification for an 'evolutive' approach that is based less on subsequent practice than it is on an attempt to uncover the 'autonomous' truth of certain human rights-orientated provisions of the 1951 Convention.[137] He argues that the ECHR 'enshrines human rights that are legal and liberal: they entail liberal egalitarian principles that impose conditions on the legitimate use of coercion by Member States'.[138] Letsas characterises the ECtHR's more evolutionary jurisprudence as seeking a meaning that is 'towards the truth of the substantive protected right':[139]

> [the case law discussed] suggests that (a) there is an objective substance or value of the protected right; (b) evolution is important only because and so far as it gets this value right; and (c) for the evolution to constitute a standard of correctness for the ECHR, it is not necessary to establish a concrete consensus among the majority of Contracting States. The idea *is more that of a hypothetical consensus: given the principles we now believe underlie the Convention, how would reasonable people agree to apply these principles to common human rights cases?*[140]

The IACtHR has taken a similar approach to the interpretation of the American Convention. In its 2014 Advisory Opinion on the *Rights and Guarantees of Children in the Context of Migration and/or in Need of International Protection,*[141] the Court recalled that it has:

> indicated repeatedly that human rights treaties are living instruments, the interpretation of which must evolve with the times and current living conditions. This evolutive interpretation is consistent with the general rules of interpretation established in Article 29 of the American Convention, as well as those established by the Vienna Convention on the Law of Treaties.[142]

As already discussed, the Court noted in the *Pacheco Tineo Family* case that determining the scope of obligations under the American Convention required

---

[136] Gardiner (n 11) 473–74 (emphasis added).
[137] George Letsas, *A Theory of Interpretation of the European Convention on Human Rights* (OUP 2007).
[138] ibid 17.
[139] ibid 79.
[140] ibid.
[141] Advisory Opinion OC-21/14 (n 97).
[142] ibid para 55 (footnotes omitted).

consideration of 'the significant evolution of the principles and regulation of international refugee law'.[143]

These approaches contain some guidance for interpreters seeking to find the 'one true meaning' of the 1951 Convention.[144] However, the 1951 Convention lacks an authoritative interpreter, in the nature of the ECtHR, or the IACtHR and Inter-American Commission on Human Rights, which limits the weight of interpretations that take a robust 'human rights' approach.

Such authority may be built up incrementally through the practice of domestic courts. However scholars may feel a greater pressure to justify, rigorously, expansive definitions of the Refugee Convention under the accepted principles of interpretation.[145] Justification for such an approach, drawing on the 1951 Convention's object and purpose, is set out in Section 3.2.2 below.

3.2.2. Application to the 1951 Convention

Support for a teleological approach is often found in the 'object and purpose' of a treaty, and is bound up with questions of that treaty's 'effectiveness'.[146] Although the preamble is often turned to as a first step in determining the object and purpose of a treaty, it should be established through an examination of the full text.[147] A treaty may have multiple 'objects and purposes', and it is not necessary to limit attention to the dominant or primary purpose.[148]

The role of 'object and purpose' in the interpretative process will vary depending on the type of the treaty at issue. In some cases, a reference to object and purpose may be confirmatory.[149] In others, a teleological approach will be appropriate if it is established that this is in fact consonant with the intentions of the parties, as expressed in the text of the treaty. Villiger notes that the teleological approach has typically been used in interpretation of 'multilateral "legislative" conventions', including the constitutions of international organisations, and human rights treaties.[150]

---

[143] *Pacheco Tineo Family case* (n 99) para 143.

[144] *Adan* [2001] (n 68) 517 (Lord Steyn). See also Goodwin-Gill, 'Search' (n 1).

[145] For a wry account of the risk posed by academic interpreters paying too little heed to State practice and finding themselves out of step with State interpretations of international obligations (as articulated by government lawyers), see John Dugard, 'The Future of International Law: A Human Rights Perspective—With Some Comments on the Leiden School of International Law' (2007) 20 Leiden Journal of International Law 729, 731–35. See also Sandesh Sivakumaran, 'The Influence of Teachings of Publicists on the Development of International Law' (2017) 66 International and Comparative Law Quarterly 1 (distinguishing between 'State-empowered entities', expert groups, and 'ordinary' publicists respectively in the context of article 38(1)(d) of the ICJ Statute).

[146] Linderfalk notes that '[s]een in its proper context, what the principle of effectiveness is all about is not that appliers shall attempt to interpret a treaty to make it as effective as possible, but that appliers shall attempt to make sure that the treaty is not *ineffective*': Linderfalk (n 7) 219 (footnotes omitted).

[147] See Gardiner (n 11) 213.

[148] Linderfalk (n 7) 211–17.

[149] Though Hill considers that it is not to be taken 'merely as a check': Hill (n 9) 209 (footnotes omitted).

[150] Villiger (n 10) 427–28 (footnotes omitted). See also 'Report of the International Law Commission' (n 15) 218 (commentary on articles 27 and 28).

Differing opinions have been given on the object and purpose of the 1951 Convention, and indeed, whether it is a 'human rights' treaty at all. Goodwin-Gill and McAdam take what can be considered as the orthodox view, arguing that the Convention's object and purpose to be 'extending the protection of the international community to refugees, and assuring to "refugees the widest possible exercise of ... fundamental rights and freedoms"', as set out in its preamble.[151]

Chetail, however, argues that the 1951 Convention 'is not a human rights treaty in the orthodox sense, for both historical and legal reasons'.[152] He characterises the Convention as a 'duty-based' rather than a 'rights-based' treaty, concerned more with 'spelling out [Contracting States'] obligations' than with human rights.[153] However, Chetail argues that the passage of time has re-orientated the 1951 Convention from the primary instrument relating to refugees to a secondary instrument within the broader human rights regime. The Convention 'has thus been reconstructed as a human rights treaty' in an environment where human rights law has displaced refugee law as the central source of protection.[154]

Foster's detailed study of the object and purpose of the Convention also draws attention to alternate views, noting that while:

[t]he leading courts in common law jurisdictions have highlighted the significance of the Preamble for the human-rights based approach to an interpretation of the Refugee Convention ... there is an alternative view that perceives the Refugee Convention's aim as being to resolve a difficult and inconvenient problem of mutual concern to state parties, and thus more clearly concerned with providing assistance to states than with conferring rights on individuals.[155]

After careful analysis, Foster nonetheless concludes that a balanced reading of the preamble and attention to the text of the Convention reveals its 'overriding human rights purpose'.[156] This textual study leads her to conclude that 'the key purpose of the Refugee Convention was not so much to define who constitutes a refugee but to provide for the rights and entitlements that follow from such recognition'.[157]

---

[151] Goodwin-Gill and McAdam (4th edn) (n 55) 6; see also Guy S Goodwin-Gill, 'Article 31 of the 1951 Convention Relating to the Status of Refugees: Non-penalization, Detention, and Protection' in Erika Feller, Volker Türk, and Frances Nicholson (eds), *Refugee Protection in International Law: UNHCR's Global Consultations on International Protection* (CUP 2003) 188–89.

[152] Vincent Chetail, 'Are Refugee Rights Human Rights? An Unorthodox Questioning of the Relations between Refugee Law and Human Rights Law' in Ruth Rubio-Marin (ed), *Human Rights and Immigration* (OUP 2014).

[153] Chetail (n 152) 39. He notes, however, that one 'should not overestimate the difference between rights of individuals and obligations of states, given that the state remains the primary guarantor of human rights': at 40.

[154] ibid 70.

[155] Foster (n 11) 43–44 (footnotes omitted).

[156] ibid 45, see more generally 44–47.

[157] ibid 46.

A midway view of the Convention as a 'compromise of competing interests' was endorsed by Lord Bingham in the *Roma Rights* case.[158]

While the Convention does reflect a carefully negotiated compromise of the Contracting States' interests, it is undeniably directed towards the protection of refugees and the assurance of the 'widest possible exercise of . . . fundamental rights and freedoms'. The preambular reference to the UN Charter and the UDHR[159] affirms the Convention's concern to realise the principle that 'human beings shall enjoy fundamental rights and freedoms without discrimination', while references to the UN's 'profound concern with refugees' and the desire to 'extend the scope of and protection accorded by' previous agreements aimed towards the protection of refugees clarify its specific object and purpose. As Foster notes, the reference in the preamble to a risk that the 'grant of asylum may place unduly heavy burdens on certain countries' is mediated by the clear preambulatory preference for cooperative solutions.[160]

The text of the Convention therefore supports the position that its object and purpose is directed towards enhancing and ensuring refugee protection. Although negotiated between Contracting States and reflecting their obligations, the ultimate beneficiaries of the protection afforded by the Convention are refugees (and, in the case of certain clauses, asylum seekers who have not yet been granted refugee status in the territory of a State Party).[161] This can be characterised as a humanitarian and human rights-directed purpose.

The humanitarian and human rights-directed purpose of the 1951 Convention provides a basis for a more robust application of the 'teleological' approach to interpretation. As Goodwin-Gill notes, 'it is now widely accepted that "human rights" treaties call for a more dynamic approach to interpretation than is offered by the "textual" and "intentions" methods'.[162] However, there are limits to the constructions that a treaty interpreted via a teleological approach can bear. In the UK House of Lords' *Roma Rights* case, Lord Steyn held:

> [i]t is true, of course, that the Refugee Convention is a living instrument and must be interpreted as such. It must also be interpreted in accordance with good faith: article 31 of the Vienna Convention on the Law of Treaties. These are very

---

[158] Those interests being 'the need to ensure humane treatment of the victims of oppression on the one hand and the wish of sovereign states to maintain control over those seeking entry to their territory on the other': *R v Immigration Officer at Prague Airport, ex parte European Roma Rights Centre* [2004] UKHL 55, [15] (Lord Bingham), cited in McAdam, 'Interpretation' (n 1) 92. Note however that Lord Bingham did not expressly state that these 'competing interests' constituted the Convention's 'object and purpose'.

[159] On this point see McAdam, 'Rights Blueprint' (n 5) 272.

[160] Namely that a 'satisfactory solution' cannot be achieved 'without international cooperation': Foster (n 11) 44–45.

[161] See further discussion in Chapter 6, Section 2.2.1.

[162] Goodwin-Gill, 'Search' (n 1) 220.

important principles of interpretation. But they are not capable of filling gaps which were designedly left in the protective scope of the Refugee Convention.[163]

The fact that States are the ultimate masters of the treaties into which they enter should also be borne in mind when adopting a teleological approach. An interpretation consonant with the object and purpose of a treaty and its effectiveness should not be stretched beyond what the text of the treaty—interpreted in good faith and in light of its context and any relevant rules of international law—can sustain. It is one thing to accept that a treaty evinces an intention to be interpreted dynamically, but it is another to marshal that dynamic intention in favour of an interpretation that goes beyond what the text can support.

4. Conclusion

In the absence of an authoritative interpreter, scholars have an important role to play in interpreting the 1951 Convention. This role requires a careful, methodical, and rigorous approach if it is to provide useful guidance on the Convention's scope and content. To Goodwin-Gill, the role of the scholar is 'not to create law but, by distilling the practice and views of States through the prism of objectivity and principle, to show where and how the law can be found'.[164] This chapter has argued that a teleological approach to the interpretation of the 1951 Convention is justified under the general rule of interpretation established in the Vienna Convention. It is incumbent on the interpreter (and, particularly, the scholarly interpreter) to pay careful attention to the limits of an such an approach and the appropriate weight to be afforded to materials prepared by UNHCR and ExCom, as well as to domestic judicial decisions as evidence of State practice.[165] An over-enthusiastic approach to human rights developments since the adoption of the 1951 Convention should not be applied in a manner that denudes the terms of the 1951 Convention of their 'ordinary meaning ... in their context and in the light of its object and purpose'.[166] There is, of course, a role for normative scholarship that argues for a progressive push to the law. But these studies should be clearly distinguished from an analysis of the law as it stands and be clear in their intentions to encourage courts to take a more liberal approach in the hope of transforming ideas into State practice.

---

[163] *Roma Rights* case (n 158) para 43, cited in Gardiner (n 11) 175.

[164] Goodwin-Gill, 'Sources' (n 3) 31.

[165] Consider Lord Hope's comment on the scope of article 1C(5): 'There is a profound gap between what various commentators would like the proviso to mean and what it has actually been taken to mean in practice': *R (Hoxha) v Special Adjudicator* [2005] UKHL 19; [2005] 1 WLR 1063, 1065.

[166] Vienna Convention, article 31(1).

The chapters that follow seek to apply these principles when interpreting article 16 and situating it in its context. First, Chapter 4 provides an account of the origins of article 16 in early treaties and an analysis of debates in the *travaux préparatoires*. Second, Chapter 5 surveys developments in international human rights law since the drafting of the 1951 Convention, assessing whether the provision has been overtaken by broader legal developments. Finally, Chapter 6 provides a principled interpretation of the scope and content of article 16.

4

The Development of Article 16 of the 1951 Convention

1. Introduction

Article 16 of the 1951 Convention did not materialise in a vacuum. It was informed by the content of earlier treaties and shaped over the course of the 1951 Convention's drafting. Section 2 of this chapter gives an overview of clauses guaranteeing aliens access to courts in early commercial treaties, as well as those included in earlier refugee instruments. Section 3 then sets out the historical background to the adoption of the 1951 Convention, before moving to analysis of the *travaux préparatoires* in Sections 4–5. Section 4 covers debates on article 16, while Section 5 takes a wider survey to investigate why the *travaux préparatoires* are silent on refugee status determination (RSD) and what can be gleaned from discussions on related provisions. The purpose of this examination is not to defend a conclusive interpretation of article 16, but rather to situate the provision in its historical context, to illuminate its perceived purpose and scope, and to provide insights into why the *travaux préparatoires* are silent on certain issues.

The survey in Section 2 provides an insight into debates at the time the 1951 Convention was framed and the preoccupations of its drafters. It supports the view that article 16 was framed deliberately to grant refugees broader protections than those generally afforded to aliens under commercial treaties of the time. These broader protections responded to the perceived vulnerabilities of refugees—particularly the risk that they may face indigence and be restricted from accessing the courts for reasons of cost.

Analysis of the *travaux préparatoires* to the 1951 Convention in Parts 4–5 gives further insight on the intended scope and application of the provision. A note of caution is, however, required, as the *travaux préparatoires* suffer from their own limitations. McAdam notes that '[w]hile the *travaux* may help to illuminate the meaning of particular treaty terms ... they are often an incomplete or inaccurate record of treaty negotiations'.[1] Although considering that a

---

[1] Jane McAdam, 'Interpretation of the 1951 Convention' in Andreas Zimmermann (ed), *The 1951 Convention Relating to the Status of Refugees and its 1967 Protocol* (OUP 2011) 101. See also Ian Sinclair, *The Vienna Convention on the Law of Treaties* (2nd edn, Manchester University Press 1984) 142.

Access to Courts for Asylum Seekers and Refugees. Emma Dunlop, Oxford University Press. © Emma Dunlop, 2024.
DOI: 10.1093/oso/9780198885597.003.0004

summary record prepared by an 'independent and skilled secretariat' (which was certainly the case in the drafting of the 1951 Convention) will 'carry more weight',[2] Hill notes that *travaux préparatoires* are 'often ... incomplete and misleading',[3] and that many significant decisions will take place informally and off the record.[4] In a warning to the researcher, he states: '[t]heir investigation is time-consuming, their usefulness often being marginal and very seldom decisive'.[5] Keeping these caveats in mind, the analysis in Parts 4–5 supports several general conclusions on how the drafters understood article 16 to operate. These are, first, that the drafters were concerned to avoid rendering a refugee's access to the courts 'illusory'; second, that the silence of the *travaux préparatoires* on RSD in the context of article 16—and more generally—was due to broad uncertainty as to how RSD would function rather than to a specific conclusion that article 16 had no application to such procedures; and third, that the drafters did not consider article 16 to impose obligations on States in relation to administrative procedures. In addition, the debates contain many scattered references to the views of individual delegates. It is often difficult to extrapolate, from one delegate's view, general agreement on the meaning of the provision. These additional references therefore have lesser weight as 'preparatory work' capable of confirming the meaning of article 16 under article 32 of the Vienna Convention.

2. Access to Courts Clauses in Early Treaties

The inclusion of a provision on access to courts in the draft Convention was not an innovation, and perhaps as a result of this fact, the debates on the clause in the *travaux préparatoires* to the 1951 Convention were brief. Free access to courts provisions were a feature of a number of treaties relating to the treatment of aliens in the early twentieth century (Section 2.1). However, these provisions were generally understood to have a narrower scope than the protections ultimately guaranteed in article 16 of the 1951 Convention. Access to courts clauses were also included in several early instruments relating to refugee rights (Section 2.2). The scope of certain of these clauses was broader than typical 'access to courts' clauses in commercial agreements, and reflected the special vulnerabilities that refugees were perceived to face.

---

[2] Jeremy Hill, *Aust's Modern Treaty Law and Practice* (4th edn, CUP 2023), 256.
[3] ibid 255.
[4] ibid 257. See also Sinclair (n 1) 142.
[5] ibid 258.

2.1 Access to Courts Clauses in Treaties Generally

The general right of foreigners to access domestic courts was well-established prior to the development of a legal status for refugees,[6] and is considered by certain scholars to be a principle of customary international law.[7] It was a feature of certain, but not all, bilateral commercial treaties and multilateral treaties.[8] Wilson notes that between 1824 and 1923, the US concluded over eighty commercial treaties, of which 'approximately half' contained access to courts clauses.[9]

In the early twentieth century, refusal to afford foreigners access to courts was generally recognised to constitute a denial of justice. However, the scope of this concept was contested, with Latin American States in particular arguing for a narrow conception of denial of justice, that was essentially limited to a refusal to grant access to the courts, while traditional imperial powers tended towards a more encompassing set of protections.[10] In the context of these debates, 'access to courts' was understood to have a confined scope. The Guerrero Report supported a narrow conception of 'denial of justice', considering States were simply obliged to grant foreigners 'a legal status, which they can assert through appropriate laws and independent tribunals to which they are allowed access on the same footing as nationals'.[11] Under this view, access to courts did, however, encompass access to any avenues of judicial appeal available to nationals.[12] Fitzmaurice characterised the report's approach as finding that 'nothing short of a refusal or failure on the part of

---

[6] See Edwin M Borchard, *The Diplomatic Protection of Citizens Abroad or the Law of International Claims* (The Banks Law Publishing Co. 1928) 334.

[7] See Borchard, ibid; Jan Paulsson, *Denial of Justice in International Law* (CUP 2005) 1 (footnotes omitted) (considering 'the duty to provide decent justice to foreigners' to be one of customary international law's 'oldest principles'). Wilson also argues that '[t]here appears to be a recognized principle of customary international law giving to aliens rights of access to courts on a reasonable basis', although '[t]he manner in which this principle shall be applied has presented practical questions for legislators and judges, as well as for treaty-makers': Robert R Wilson, 'Access-to-Courts Provisions in United States Commercial Treaties' (1953) 47 American Journal of International Law 20, 47.

[8] Wilson's study notes that in addition to commercial treaties, such clauses also appear in peace treaties, patent and copyright conventions, and consular conventions: Wilson (n 7) 21, 30–32.

[9] ibid 34.

[10] Fitzmaurice characterises this division as between 'creditor' or 'plaintiff' countries and 'debtor' or 'defendant' countries: see GG Fitzmaurice, 'The Meaning of the Term "Denial of Justice"' (1932) 13 British Yearbook of International Law 93, 93–94. See also JW Garner, 'International Responsibility of States for Judgments of Courts and Verdicts of Juries amounting to Denial of Justice' (1929) 10 British Yearbook of International Law 181, 184, displaying an attitude which should be read against Borchard (n 6) 331. On the Latin American argument specifically, see Fitzmaurice, 99–100; Hans W Spiegel, 'Origin and Development of Denial of Justice' (1938) 32 American Journal of International Law 63, 80 (noting that the South American approach is to characterise denial of justice as 'the refusal of access to justice'); Borchard (n 6) 334–35.

[11] 'Annex to Questionnaire No. 4, Report of the Sub-Committee' (Guerrero Report), in League of Nations, Committee of Experts for the Progressive Codification of International Law, 'Report of the Council of the League of Nations on the Questions which appear Ripe for International Regulation (Questionnaires No 1 to 7)', C.196.M.70.1927.V (20 Apr 1927) 92, 98.

[12] ibid 99 ('if the nationals of a State are allowed to appeal from the decision of a court of first instance, the same privilege must be accorded to foreigners when their recognised rights are in dispute').

a court to hear a case or to give judgment therein can constitute a denial of justice'.[13] He considered that this would nullify the protections of 'denial of justice' since '[i]n nearly every country foreigners have access to the courts on the same terms (subject perhaps to the giving of security) as nationals'.[14]

The scope of 'access to courts' was an issue facing the Institut de Droit International in the preparation of its 1927 draft convention on the international responsibility of States for damage caused in their territory to the person or property of foreigners.[15] Article 8 of the draft convention set out a State's responsibility for denial of justice, which included situations in which courts were not equally accessible to foreigners and nationals in a manner not justified by procedural needs.[16] The Rapporteur's first report noted that acceptable distinctions between nationals and foreigners included charging foreigners security for costs, or *cautio judicatum solvi*.[17]

This limited reading of the protection afforded by 'access to courts' clauses was affirmed by later State practice. The propriety of charging security for costs to foreigners was accepted by Austria, Czechoslovakia, and Poland in deliberations in the League of Nations.[18] Poland noted that while it was:

> universally agreed that, subject to reciprocity, a State is under an international obligation to accord foreigners the protection of the courts which must in principle be equal to those accorded to its own nationals ... it cannot be claimed that the rights of a foreign national have been infringed when the latter is required, before bringing an action, to furnish certain guarantees designed to safeguard the interests of the Polish citizens against whom he is bringing proceedings: a case in point is the obligation, laid down in all the laws relating to judicial procedure in the Polish Republic, whereby the plaintiff is required, on the demand of the defendant, to deposit security for the execution of the judgment (*cautio judicatum solvi*), unless otherwise provided in some special international convention.[19]

[13] Fitzmaurice (n 10) 100, with reference to the Guerrero Report.
[14] ibid 101.
[15] Annuaire de l'Institut de Droit International, *Travaux préparatoires de la Session de Lausanne, Septembre 1927, Tome I* (Bruxelles 1927) 455–562.
[16] ibid 559, art 8(2) ('Lorsque en l'absence de raisons justifiées par les besoins de la procédure, les tribunaux ne sont pas également accessibles aux étrangers comme aux nationaux' ('When, in the absence of reasons justified by procedural needs, the courts are not equally accessible to foreigners and nationals'—author's translation)).
[17] ibid 477 (noting that in this case, 'la distinction entre les étrangers et les nationaux s'explique dans ce cas par les exigences de la procédure').
[18] League of Nations, 'Conference for the Codification of International Law: Bases of Discussion for the Conference drawn up by the Preparatory Committee: Volume III. Responsibility of States for Damage caused in their Territory to the Person or Property of Foreigners', C.75.M.69.1929.V et Erratum et Supplément (a) (15 May 1929) 42 (Austria); 45–46 (Poland); 48 (Czechoslovakia).
[19] ibid 45–46.

Czechoslovakia additionally stressed that a guarantee of 'equal judicial protection' to foreigners did not extend to granting legal assistance. It noted that 'the State should not be expected to grant aliens judicial assistance whether reciprocity were granted or not'.[20]

This narrow reading of 'access to courts'—essentially sanctioning certain procedural distinctions between nationals and foreigners—was also accepted in certain court decisions in this period. In 1934, the German Supreme Court in Civil Matters held that article 4 of the German–Latvian Treaty, which guaranteed free access to the courts under the same conditions as residents, could not be read as exempting the appellant from the duty to provide security for costs.[21] According to the International Law Reports' summary of the case, the Court considered clauses that:

> merely provided for free access to courts … did not assure to foreigners exemption from regulations specially laid down by municipal law for aliens. In particular, such clauses did not give foreigners the benefit of poor persons' procedure, nor did they dispense with the requirement of security for costs.[22]

The Swiss Federal Tribunal took a similar view in the 1934 case of *Instant Index Corporation v Tribunal of the Canton of Vaud*.[23] In that case, a treaty clause guaranteeing contracting parties 'free access to the courts and [freedom] to avail themselves of their legal rights in the same way as nationals, either personally or through such attorneys or other agents as they may please to appoint' was found to have a 'precise and limited meaning', which did not exempt a foreigner from the duty to provide security for costs.[24] The International Law Reports noted that the court recalled the purpose of a guarantee of security for costs, namely 'the legal and practical difficulty of enforcing, outside the State where it is given, a judgment giving costs against the plaintiff'.[25]

Finally, the *Ambatielos* case—a contractual dispute under an 1886 treaty resulting in a 1953 judgment in the ICJ and a subsequent Arbitral Award—adds a little complexity to the generally narrow approach taken to 'free access' in commercial treaties.[26]

---

[20] ibid 48.

[21] Case No 125, *L v P (Security for Costs Case)*, Germany, Supreme Court in Civil Matters, 16 Oct 1934, 7 ILR 305.

[22] ibid 306.

[23] Case No 126, *Instant Index Corporation v Tribunal of the Canton of Vaud*, Switzerland, Federal Tribunal, 12 July 1934, 7 ILR 307.

[24] ibid 307–08.

[25] ibid 308. This suggests that a reason for exempting a refugee from the obligation to give security for costs may be that, unlike other aliens, they were not expected to return to their country of origin.

[26] See *Ambatielos Case (Greece v United Kingdom), Merits: Obligation to Arbitrate* [1953] ICJ Rep 10; *The Ambatielos Claim (Greece, United Kingdom of Great Britain and Northern Ireland)*, 6 Mar 1956, Recueil des Sentences Arbitrales, Vol XII, 83–153, available via <http://legal.un.org/riaa/cases/vol_XII/83-153_Ambatielos.pdf> (*Ambatielos Award*).

The dispute arose between Mr Ambatielos, a Greek shipowner, and the UK Ministry of Shipping. Mr Ambatielos' attempts to seek redress for breach of contract had foundered in the UK courts. Greece then brought a claim on the international level, arguing that 'Mr Ambatielos did not enjoy "free access" to the courts, because of the "withholding" by the executive branch of the United Kingdom Government of evidence considered to be vital to his case'.[27] It sought to rely on article XV of the 1886 treaty, which provided for 'free access to the Courts of Justice for the prosecution and defence of their rights, without other conditions, restrictions, or taxes beyond those imposed on native subjects'.[28] Greece argued for a wide reading of the clause (encompassing the 'prosecution of rights by the foreign litigant in the local courts free from restrictions imposed by the executive authorities'[29]), while the UK favoured a narrow interpretation. Greece's attempt to read freedom from executive interference into the term 'free access' suggests an early attempt to mount an argument that free access must entail 'effective' access to the courts.

In its judgment, the ICJ ultimately avoided the question of the appropriate scope of article XV,[30] an unsurprising move since the Court had previously determined that it had 'no jurisdiction to decide on the merits of the Ambatielos claim', but should instead limit itself to the question of whether the UK was required to go to arbitration.[31] However, in a joint dissenting opinion, President McNair and Judges Basdevant, Klaestad and Read did comment directly on the appropriate scope of the provision, noting:

> This Article promises free access to the Courts; it says nothing with regard to the production of evidence.... The free access clause frequently found in treaties, more commonly in the past than at the present, has as its purpose the removal, for its beneficiaries, of the obstructions, which existed in certain countries as the result of old traditions, to the right of foreigners to have recourse to the Courts. Its object is, as it states, to ensure free access to the Courts, not to regulate the different question of the production of evidence.... Free access to the Courts is one thing; the proper administration of justice is another. A distinction is traditionally drawn between the two.[32]

---

[27] As summarised in the judgment: *Ambatielos Case (Merits)* (n 26) 22.

[28] Cited in *Ambatielos Case (Merits)* (n 26) 20.

[29] *Ambatielos Case (Merits)* (n 26) 22. The Court notes that under the Greek view, 'Mr. Ambatielos did not enjoy "free access" to the courts, because of the "withholding" by the executive branch of the United Kingdom Government of evidence considered to be vital to his case.'

[30] ibid.

[31] *Ambatielos Case (Greece v United Kingdom), Preliminary Objection* [1952] ICJ Rep 28, 39, 46; recalled in *Ambatielos Case (Merits)* (n 26) 10, 14.

[32] *Ambatielos Case (Merits)* (n 26) Dissenting Opinion by Sir Arnold McNair, President and Judges Basdevant, Klaestad, and Read, 25, 33.

The weight of this statement—by eminent authorities—is tempered by its presence in a dissenting opinion (particularly in circumstances where the Court had found that it did not have grounds to enter into the merits of the dispute). To further complicate matters, the Arbitral Commission eventually convened to hear the claim favoured a more expansive interpretation.[33] It considered 'free access' under the 1886 treaty to include 'the right to use the Courts fully and to avail themselves of any procedural remedies or guarantees provided by the law of the land *in order that justice may be administered on a footing of equality with nationals of the country*'.[34] The Commission continued:

> [t]he modern concept of 'free access to the Courts' represents a reaction against the practice of obstructing and hindering the appearance of foreigners in Court, a practice which existed in former times and in certain countries, and which constituted an unjust discrimination against foreigners. Hence, the essence of 'free access' is adherence to and effectiveness of the principle of non-discrimination against foreigners who are in need of seeking justice before the courts of the land for the protection and defence of their rights. Thus, when 'free access to the Courts' is covenanted by a State in favour of the subjects or citizens of another State, the covenant is that the foreigner shall enjoy full freedom to appear before the courts for the protection or defence of his rights, whether as plaintiff or defendant; to bring any action provided or authorised by law; to deliver any pleading by way of defence, set off or counterclaim; to engage Counsel; to adduce evidence, whether documentary or oral or of any other kind; to apply for bail; to lodge appeals and, in short, to use the Courts fully and to avail himself of any procedural remedies or guarantees provided by the law of the land in order that justice may be administered on a footing of equality with nationals of the country.[35]

Ultimately, Mr Ambatielos' treatment was not considered to be a breach of this standard, as non-disclosure of documents 'was in conformity with English law and practice'.[36] The Commission's approach treated non-discrimination as a component of 'free access', such that any practices discriminating between foreigners and nationals were suspect.[37]

The Commission's interpretation in *Ambatielos* is an outlier, giving a broader scope to 'free access' clauses in commercial treaties than was usually taken. As a general rule, these clauses were interpreted narrowly, in a manner that recognised

---

[33] *Ambatielos Award* (n 26).
[34] ibid 110 (emphasis added).
[35] ibid 111.
[36] ibid 118.
[37] See also ibid 117: 'The non-disclosure here alleged would constitute a denial of "free access" if it could be shown that the act of non-disclosure does not conform with English law or that that law gives to British subjects, and not to foreigners, a right to discovery, thereby establishing a discrimination between nationals and foreigners. No evidence to that effect has been produced in the present case.'

aliens and nationals may be subject to different procedures when accessing domestic courts.

2.2 Access to Courts Clauses in Early Refugee Instruments

Access to courts clauses were included in a number of early refugee conventions
and arrangements, including the 1928 Arrangement relating to the Legal Status
of Russian and Armenian Refugees ('1928 Arrangement'),[38] the 1933 Convention
relating to the International Status of Refugees ('1933 Convention'),[39] the 1936
Provisional Arrangement concerning the Status of Refugees coming from Germany
('1936 Provisional Arrangement'),[40] and the 1938 Convention Concerning the
Status of Refugees Coming from Germany ('1938 Convention'),[41] which replaced
the 1936 Provisional Arrangement as between mutual parties.[42]

These early arrangements and conventions were limited in scope, both in terms
of the categories of refugees covered and their total number of parties. The refugees who were protected under each instrument were, respectively, 'Russian and
Armenian refugees' (the 1928 Arrangement);[43] 'Russian, Armenian and assimilated refugees' (the 1933 Convention);[44] and refugees 'coming from Germany' (the
1936 Provisional Arrangement and 1938 Convention).[45] The framing of access to
courts clauses differed slightly across these instruments, but generally reflected live
concerns at the time of drafting. Perhaps drawing on the broader debates regarding

---

[38] Arrangement relating to the Legal Status of Russian and Armenian Refugees, signed at Geneva, 30
June 1928, registered 2 May 1929, [1929] LNTSer 101; 89 LNTS 53. Available via <http://www.worldlii.
org/cgi-bin/sinodisp/int/other/treaties/LNTSer/1929/101.html?query=Refugees>.

[39] Convention relating to the International Status of Refugees, No 3663 [1935] LNTSer 91; 159
LNTS 199 (signed 28 Oct 1933, entered into force 13 June 1935) (1933 Convention), art 6. See Atle
Grahl-Madsen, *Commentary on the Refugee Convention 1951, Articles 2-11, 13-37* (Republished by the
Division of International Protection of the United Nations High Commissioner for Refugees 1997)
Article 16, V.

[40] Provisional Arrangement concerning the Status of Refugees coming from Germany, and Annex.
Signed at Geneva, July 4th 1936, No 3952 [1936-1937] LNTSer 77 (1936 Provisional Arrangement). See
Grahl-Madsen (n 39) Article 16, V.

[41] Convention concerning the Status of Refugees coming from Germany, with Annex. Signed at
Geneva, February 10th 1938, No 4461 [1938] LNTSer 61 (1938 Convention), art 8.

[42] See 1938 Convention, art 18.

[43] 1928 Arrangement, preamble.

[44] '[A]s defined by the Arrangements of May 12th, 1926 and June 30th, 1928, subject to such modi-
fications or amplifications as each Contracting Party may introduce in this definition at the moment of
signature or accession': 1933 Convention, art 1.

[45] As defined in article 1 of the 1936 Provisional Arrangement and 1938 Convention respectively.
The 1938 Convention includes in this term '[s]tateless persons not covered by previous Conventions
or Agreements who have left German territory after being established therein and who are proved
not to enjoy, in law or fact, the protection of the German Government'. A Protocol also extended
the 1936 Provisional Arrangement and the 1938 Convention to cover Austrian refugees: League of
Nations, Additional Protocol to the Provisional Arrangement and to the Convention concerning the
Status of Refugees Coming from Germany, 14 Sept 1939, No 4634, League of Nations Treaty Series Vol
CXCVIII, 141.

access to courts clauses in this period, the general right of refugees to access courts was uncontroversial,[46] while the ability of refugees to access legal assistance and to avoid paying security for costs were considered more pressing concerns to address.[47]

The 1928 Arrangement, framed as a series of resolutions, included a recommendation that 'the benefit of legal assistance and if possible exemption from the *cautio judicatum solvi* shall be granted to Russian and Armenian refugees irrespective of reciprocity'.[48] The Arrangement was, however, frustrated by its lack of binding obligations. A Study of Statelessness[49] completed by the Secretary-General in 1949 at the request of the Economic and Social Council (ECOSOC) concluded that the 1928 Arrangement was 'ineffective', and that 'of all the various recommendations contained in the Arrangement ... only one, in a single country, was incorporated in domestic legislation'.[50] The commentary to the draft 1933 Convention considered that a non-binding recommendation was insufficient to guarantee access to courts and that a binding provision was required.[51]

The 1933 Convention was drafted in the throes of the Great Depression, which placed ever greater pressures on refugee populations.[52] The drafting process culminated in a robust instrument that was 'the major model' for the 1951 Convention.[53] The Belgian delegate framed the 1933 Convention's intention as

[46] 'Procés-Verbaux de la Conférence Intergouvernementale pour les Réfugies. Tenue à Genève du 26 au 28 octobre 1933', C.113.M.41.1934 (1 Mar 1934), Annex I, 75 ('[à] l'heure actuelle, il n'existe pas de pays où la compétence des tribunaux en matière de litige entre les réfugiés soit mise en doute où contestée' ('At the present time, there is no country in which the competence of the courts to hear suits between refugees is questioned or challenged'—author's translation)). I am grateful to Guy S. Goodwin-Gill for sharing this document.

[47] ibid ('La situation est bien moins satisfaisante en ce qui concerne l'admission des réfugiés au bénéfice de l'assistance judiciaire et leur exemption de la *caution judicatum solvi*' ('The situation is much less satisfactory as regards the admission of refugees to the benefit of legal assistance and their exemption from *cautio judicatum solvi*'—author's translation)).

[48] 1928 Arrangement, (5). See also Grahl-Madsen (n 39) Article 16, V; Björn Elberling, 'Article 16' in Zimmermann (n 1) 934.

[49] Developments leading to the drafting of this study are discussed further in Section 3.2.

[50] UN Ad Hoc Committee on Refugees and Stateless Persons, 'A Study of Statelessness, United Nations, August 1949, Lake Success - New York' (1 Aug 1949) E/1112; E/1112/Add.1, available via <http://www.refworld.org/docid/3ae68c2d0.html>, 38.

[51] Procés-Verbaux, 1933 Conference (n 46) Annex 1, 75 ('L'article 5 de l'Arrangement du 30 juin 1928 a recommandé que ce bénéfice [de l'assistance judiciaire] et cette exemption [de la caution judicatum solvi] soient accordés aux réfugiés. Mais une recommandation n'a pas été suffisante pour produire l'effet voulu. Une règle conventionnelle est indispensable pour que suite soit donnée aux dispositions adoptées.' ('Article 5 of the Arrangement of 30 June 1928 recommended that this benefit [legal assistance] and exemption (from security for costs] be accorded to refugees. But a recommendation has not been sufficient to produce the desired effect. A conventional rule is essential to give effect to the clauses adopted.'—author's translation)). See further League of Nations, 'Report of the Inter-Governmental Advisory Commission for Refugees on the Work of its Fifth Session and Communication from the International Nansen Office for Refugees', C.266.M.136.1933 (18 May 1933), 4–5.

[52] See Louise W Holborn, *Refugees: A Problem of Our Time: The Work of the United Nations High Commissioner for Refugees, 1951–1972* (The Scarecrow Press, Inc. 1975), vol I , 15 (noting tightening labour regulations for foreigners, reductions in the relief earmarked for refugees, and a rise in incidents of refoulement).

[53] ibid 160.

both to give refugees a juridical status, and to provide them with a form of legal protection.[54] It contained the first binding obligation on Contracting States to provide refugees with 'free and ready access to the courts of law'. Within their countries of domicile or regular residence, the Convention also guaranteed refugees 'the same rights and privileges as nationals' regarding access to the courts. This expressly included, on the same conditions as nationals, legal assistance and exemption from *cautio judicatum solvi*.[55] A reference to the parties' desire to ensure that refugees enjoyed free and ready access to the courts was also included in the Convention's preamble.

The Convention was concluded at an intergovernmental conference held from 26–28 October 1933.[56] The draft text contained a liberal 'access to courts' clause that was diluted over the course of debate. In its original form, the clause guaranteed *all* refugees in a Contracting State's territory the 'same rights and privileges as nationals' in relation to access to the courts, including the benefit of legal assistance on the same conditions as nationals and exemption from *cautio judicatum solvi*.[57] The commentary to the draft convention, which is available only in French, notes the practical need for such protections:

> [l]'intérêt pratique de ces dispositions est d'autant plus grand que nombreux sont les réfugiés qui ne disposent pas des moyens pour demander aux tribunaux la protection de leurs droits.[58]

In the course of discussion, however, several delegates proposed limiting the scope of rights under the draft provision. Bulgaria unsuccessfully argued that courts should be given discretion as to whether to exempt a party from *cautio judicatum solvi*, and eventually entered a reservation to this effect.[59] Poland argued that it was inappropriate to grant refugees national treatment and that the appropriate standard was either the best, or the general, treatment available

---

[54] Procés-Verbaux, 1933 Conference (n 46) 11 (M. Myers) ('Le projet élaboré peut être considéré comme ayant un double objet: celui de donner aux réfugiés un statut juridique proprement dit, et celui de leur assurer en quelque sorte un régime de protection légale').

[55] 1933 Convention, art 6.

[56] The Procés-Verbaux suggest that the text which formed the basis of discussion was drafted by M. le sénateur A. François: Procés-Verbaux, 1933 Conference (n 46) 6.

[57] The original clause read: 'Les réfugiés auront, dans les territoires des parties contractants, libre et facile accès devant les tribunaux; ils jouiront, sous ce rapport, des mêmes droits et privilèges que les nationaux; ils seront, aux mêmes conditions que ceux-ci, admis au bénéfice de l'assistance judiciaire et seront exemptés de la *caution judicatum solvi*' (emphasis added in part): Procés-Verbaux, 1933 Conference (n 46) Annex I, 68.

[58] ibid 6 ('the practical interest of these provisions is enhanced since refugees lack the means to petition the courts for the protection of their rights'– author's translation).

[59] ibid 28 (M. Mikoff, Bulgaria), proposing that the text be amended to include 'Leur exemption de la *caution judicatum solvi* sera soumise chaque fois à l'appréciation des tribunaux' (emphasis added in part); see also Bulgaria's reservation to article 6 of the 1933 Convention, League of Nations Treaty Series Vol CLIX, No 3663, 215.

to foreigners.[60] Austria, Czechoslovakia, and Switzerland (supported by the Intergovernmental Commission) successfully argued for the specific exemption from *cautio judicatum solvi* to be available only to those refugees who were domiciled in the relevant Contracting State,[61] which Austria justified on the basis that a more restrictive scope was consistent with the 1905 Hague Civil Procedure Convention.[62]

The text of the revised draft article is remarkably similar to the final form of article 16 of the Refugee Convention. While 'free and ready access to courts' remained a right of all refugees, the guarantees of the specific rights and principles in the article were restricted to those refugees with domicile or regular residence in the State in question. In a second discussion of the draft article, eight of the fifteen participating States accepted the principle that refugees were guaranteed free and ready access to the courts of all Contracting States.[63] Six States were prepared to accept the second principle regarding the specific rights of refugees.[64] The 1933 Convention was ratified by eight States,[65] of which only Bulgaria made a reservation on access to courts.[66]

Read against the background of commercial 'free access' clauses, the provisions in the refugee instruments demonstrate a concern to respond to the particular vulnerabilities of refugee populations (such as impecuniosity). The 1933 Convention represented the high watermark of 'access to courts' prior to the 1951 Convention. While the 1936 Provisional Arrangement and the 1938 Convention both included an 'access to courts' clause and a corresponding preambular reference, the text of

---

[60] Procés-Verbaux, 1933 Conference (n 46) 28 (M. Kulski, Poland), arguing for the best treatment available to foreigners; and 49–50 (M. Kulski, Poland), arguing for the lower standard of the general treatment available to foreigners.

[61] ibid 28 (M. Matsch, Austria, and M. Künzl-Jizersky, Czechoslovakia), 28–29 (Baron Nolde, Intergovernmental Commission), 29 (M. Kappeler, Switzerland). In the debates Austria and Switzerland indicated their acceptance of draft art 5(2) subject to the reservation that the exemption would only be available in those countries that executed 'décisions relatives au recouvrement de frais': 49. It is also notable that Belgium argued that the exemption should only be available to refugee plaintiffs, and not to defendants, while Baron Nolde (of the Intergovernmental Commission) took the converse view: see 28 29.

[62] ibid 28 (M. Matsch, Austria). See also the note by the Swiss delegate that a clause should be included 'assurant l'exécution des decisions concernant les frais et dépens relative à la procedure civile du 17 juillet 1905': ibid 29 (M. Kappeler, Switzerland ('ensuring the execution of decisions concerning costs and expenses with respect to the civil procedure of 17 July 1905'—author's translation)).

[63] Belgium, Bulgaria, Czechoslovakia, Estonia, France, Poland, Romania, and Switzerland: ibid 49. No record is provided of dissenting or abstaining positions.

[64] Czechoslovakia, Romania, Latvia, Belgium, Egypt, and France: ibid 50.

[65] Bulgaria, Czechoslovakia, Denmark, France, Italy, Norway, and the UK. It was reported that the US, Estonia, Finland, Greece, Iraq, Latvia, Sweden, and Switzerland declined to accede to the Convention on the grounds that 'refugees already enjoy in their respective countries the majority of rights provided for under the Convention, or even more': see League of Nations, Nansen International Office for Refugees (under the Authority of the League of Nations), 'Report of the Governing Body for the Year ending June 30th, 1937 on the Russian, Armenian, Assyrian, Assyro-Chaldean, Saar and Turkish Refugee problems', A.21.1937.XII (20 Aug 1937), 4–5. See also Study of Statelessness (n 50) 78.

[66] League of Nations Treaty Series Vol CLIX, No 3663, 215 (to note that 'exemption from *cautio judicatum solvi* shall be at the discretion of the courts in each individual case').

the clauses included a caveat that weakened the strength of the guarantee. In each text, the enjoyment of the same rights and privileges as nationals was available 'save where otherwise expressly provided by law'.[67] Commenting on these provisions in his Study of Statelessness, the Secretary-General expressed a preference for the 1933 Convention's wording, noting that the caveat in the 1938 Convention 'reduce[d] the practical value of the provisions'.[68] In addition, these instruments suffered low ratification rates that diminished their effectiveness.[69]

3. The Drafting of the 1951 Convention

3.1 The Historical Context

In February 1946, the UN General Assembly adopted resolution 8(I) on the Question of Refugees, recognising that 'the problem of refugees and displaced persons of all categories is one of immediate urgency', and deciding to refer the issue to ECOSOC 'for thorough examination'.[70] ECOSOC moved quickly in response to this request, establishing a Special Committee on Refugees and Displaced Persons,[71] and adopting a draft constitution for the future International Refugee Organization (IRO),[72] which was approved by the General Assembly before the year was out.[73]

The IRO was the peak agency for refugee protection throughout its existence from 1 July 1947 and 28 February 1952. An operational agency, it was the first body to confront the refugee problem 'in all of its phases: identification, registration, and classification; care and assistance; and repatriation or resettlement and reestablishment in countries able to receive those refugees who were under the

---

[67] See also Elberling (n 48) 934, who also discusses other minor textual differences in ft 9. There was little discussion of these clauses in the drafting process of either the 1936 Provisional Arrangement or the 1938 Convention: see League of Nations, 'Inter-Governmental Conference on the Legal Status of Refugees coming from Germany: Provisional minutes, Fourth meeting', Conf. S.R.A./1st Session/ P.V.4 (16 July 1936), 13 and League of Nations, 'Inter-Governmental Conference on the Legal Status of Refugees coming from Germany: Provisional minutes, Sixth meeting', Conf. S.R.A./1st Session/P.V.6 (16 July 1936), 2, both accessed via United Nations Archives at Geneva (digital), Ref Code R5761/50/ 24919/24499 (1936 Provisional Agreement); and League of Nations, 'International Conference for the Adoption of a Convention concerning the Status of Refugees coming from Germany: Provisional Minutes, Fifth meeting', Conf. C.S.R.A/P.V.5 (9 Feb 1938), 5 and 12, accessed via United Nations Archives at Geneva (digital), Ref Code 5793/50/32794/32089 (1938 Convention).

[68] Study of Statelessness (n 50) 48.

[69] See, on the 1936 Provisional Agreement, Volume CLXXI [1936–1937] LNTS 84–85 (Belgium, United Kingdom of Great Britain and Northern Ireland, Denmark, Spain, France, Norway, The Netherlands, Switzerland); and on the 1938 Convention, Study of Statelessness (n 50) 97–98; Holborn (n 52) 16.

[70] UNGA Res 8(I), 'Question of refugees' (12 Feb 1946). Cited in Study of Statelessness (n 50) 30.

[71] See ECOSOC, Resolution 18(III) 'Refugees and displaced persons' (3 Oct 1946), transmitting a draft resolution citing these achievements to the General Assembly.

[72] ibid.

[73] UNGA Res 62(I), 'Refugees and Displaced Persons' (15 Dec 1946).

mandate of the IRO'.[74] The decision to replace the IRO with the (originally non-operational)[75] UNHCR was due in part to the heavy financial burden that the IRO placed on its eighteen members, and their sense that the refugee problem 'should be the responsibility of the entire membership of the UN'.[76] Discussions in the UN turned to the drafting of the UNHCR Statute and a new Convention to better guarantee the rights of refugees.

3.2 The Drafting Process

The genesis of the Refugee Convention was complicated, involving several committees and myriad drafts, proposals, and meetings.[77] In the words of one delegate to the ECOSOC Social Committee, 'the circular movement which brought the same question periodically either to Lake Success or to Geneva reminded him of a merry-go-round'.[78]

In 1947, the Commission on Human Rights adopted a resolution 'express[ing] the wish' that 'early consideration be given by the United Nations to *the legal status of persons who do not enjoy the protection of any Government*, in particular pending the acquisition of nationality as regards their legal and social protection and their documentation'.[79] In 1948, ECOSOC took note of that resolution and requested the Secretary-General to study 'national legislation and international agreements and conventions relevant to statelessness', and to 'submit recommendations to the Council as to the desirability of concluding a further convention on this subject'.[80] The Secretary-General accordingly completed a Study of Statelessness in 1949.[81] The scope of 'statelessness' in the Study differs slightly from contemporary use of the term.[82] The Study distinguished between two types of statelessness—'de jure'

---

[74] Holborn (n 52) 31 (footnotes omitted).

[75] See Holborn (n 52) 88; Guy S Goodwin-Gill, 'Introductory Note', Audiovisual Library of International Law, available via <http://legal.un.org/avl/ha/prsr/prsr.html>.

[76] Holborn (n 52) 37.

[77] Guy S Goodwin-Gill's section on the 1951 Convention and its 1967 Protocol in the on-line Audiovisual Library of International Law sets out the procedural history and key documents from the drafting process: see <http://legal.un.org/avl/ha/prsr/prsr.html>. See also Terje Einarsen, 'Drafting History of the 1951 Convention and the 1967 Protocol' in Zimmermann (n 1) 37–73.

[78] ECOSOC, 11th sess, Social Committee, 156th meeting, E/AC.7/SR.156 (14 Aug 1950), 6 (Mr Rochefort (France)).

[79] ECOSOC, Official Records, Third Year, 6th sess, Supp 1 (New York, 1948), 13–14 available via <https://documents-dds-ny.un.org/doc/UNDOC/GEN/GL9/011/01/pdf/GL901101.pdf?OpenElem ent> (emphasis added).

[80] ECOSOC, Resolution 116(VI)D, Resolutions of 1–2 Mar 1948, available via <https://documents-dds-ny.un.org/doc/RESOLUTION/GEN/NR0/072/51/img/NR007251.pdf?OpenElement>.

[81] Study of Statelessness (n 50).

[82] For an example of the use of the term 'stateless' during the period, see Maître JL Rubenstein, 'The Refugee Problem' (Sept 1936) 15 International Affairs 716, 721, noting that '[a]ll refugees are stateless, whether it be *de jure* (the Russians and a group of Armenians) or *de facto*'. While it is still recognised that refugees with a nationality can be characterised as '*de facto* stateless', on the basis that they are unable or unwilling to avail themselves of the protection of their country of nationality, there is a preference

statelessness (a lack of any nationality), and 'de facto' statelessness (which covered refugees who had fled their country of origin and no longer enjoyed 'the protection and assistance of their national authorities').[83] The Study concluded that ECOSOC should:

> instruct either the Secretary-General in consultation with the Director-General of the IRO and the administrative heads of the other specialized agencies concerned, or an ad ho[c] Committee appointed by the Council, to prepare a draft convention including provisions concerning:
> (a) The following subjects . . .
> 8. The right to appear before the courts as plaintiff or defendant.[84]

The Secretary-General's Study was discussed at the 9th session of ECOSOC, which in resolution 248(IX)B appointed a thirteen-member 'Ad Hoc Committee on Statelessness and Related Problems'[85] to, inter alia:

> (a) Consider the desirability of preparing a revised and consolidated convention relating to the international status of refugees and stateless persons and, if they consider such a course desirable, draft the text of such a convention.[86]

The Ad Hoc Committee had extensive discussions on the draft convention, holding thirty-two meetings during its first session from January–February 1950.[87] It worked on the basis of draft conventions prepared by the UN Secretary-General (in consultation with the IRO)[88] and France[89] respectively. By the conclusion of the session, the Committee had prepared a report setting out, inter alia, a draft

---

not to refer to them as such in order to avoid 'confusion': see UNHCR, 'Expert Meeting: The Concept of Stateless Persons under International Law: Summary Conclusions' (2010), available via <https://www.unhcr.org/4cb2fe326.pdf>, 6.

[83] Study of Statelessness (n 50) 59.
[84] Study of Statelessness (n 50) 60.
[85] The Ad Hoc Committee consisted of representatives of Belgium, Brazil, Canada, China, Denmark, Israel, Poland, Turkey, the USSR, the UK, the US, and Venezuela. The USSR and Poland left the Committee at its first meeting after a USSR draft resolution to 'exclude the representative of the Kuomintang group from membership of the Committee' was rejected, and did not take part in any of its later debates. Several Observers and Consultants of NGOs were also in attendance. See ECOSOC, 'Report of the Ad Hoc Committee on Statelessness and Related Problems', E/1618, E/AC.32/5 (17 Feb 1950) 3-4; ECOSOC, 'Ad Hoc Committee on Statelessness and Related Problems: Summary Record of the First Meeting', E/AC.32/SR.1 (23 Jan 1950) 2–4.
[86] ECOSOC, Resolution 248(IX)B (8 Aug 1949) in ECOSOC, Official Records: Fourth Year, Ninth sess, Suppl No 1, 60.
[87] The Summary Records of these discussions are contained in E/AC.32/SR.1–E/AC.32/SR.32.
[88] ECOSOC, 'Ad Hoc Committee on Statelessness and Related Problems: Status of refugees and stateless persons—Memorandum by the Secretary-General', E/AC.32/2 (3 Jan 1950) Annex.
[89] See 'Report of the Ad Hoc Committee' (n 85) 5; ECOSOC: 'Ad Hoc Committee on Statelessness and Related Problems: France: Proposal for a draft Convention', E/AC.32/L.3 (17 Jan 1950) and its CORR.1 (18 Jan 1950) and CORR.2 (25 Jan 1950) ('French proposed draft').

convention and commentary,[90] which was then circulated to governments for comment.[91]

The Ad Hoc Committee's Report and comments received from governments were discussed by ECOSOC[92] and its Social Committee[93] from late July to early August 1950. ECOSOC then passed Resolution 319(XI)B, which requested the Secretary-General:

(1) To reconvene the Ad Hoc Committee on Refugees and Stateless Persons in order that it may prepare revised drafts of [the agreements set out in the Ad Hoc Committee Report] in the light of comments of Governments and of specialized agencies and the discussions and decisions of this Council at its eleventh session, which shall include the definition of 'refugee' and the Preamble approved by the Council, making such other revisions as appear necessary; and

(2) To submit the drafts, as revised to the General Assembly at its fifth session.[94]

The Ad Hoc Committee (now renamed the Ad Hoc Committee on Refugees and Stateless Persons)[95] accordingly met again from 14–25 August 1950, and pre-pared a revised draft of the Convention.[96] This revised draft was then considered by the Third Committee of the UN General Assembly at its Fifth Session.[97] The UN General Assembly ultimately decided to convene a 'Conference of Plenipotentiaries', so as to 'enabl[e] the governments of States not Members of the United Nations to participate in the final stages of the drafting of the Convention.'[98]

The Conference of Plenipotentiaries was held from 2–25 July 1951 to finalise the Convention.[99] Although it appears that the Secretariat sent eighty invitations to the Conference,[100] only twenty-six delegations took part,[101] leading one delegate to

---

[90]   See 'Report of the Ad Hoc Committee' (n 85) Annexes I and II.

[91]   See Guy S Goodwin-Gill, 'Procedural History', Audiovisual Library of International Law, available via <http://legal.un.org/avl/ha/prsr/prsr.html>.

[92]   ECOSOC, 11th sess, 399th Meeting, E/SR.399 (2 Aug 1950); 406th meeting, E/SR.406 (11 Aug 1950); and 407th meeting, E/SR.407 (11 Aug 1950), as cited in the Procedural History and Documents sections of the Audiovisual Library of International Law <http://legal.un.org/avl/ha/prsr/prsr.html>.

[93]   See Procedural History and Documents sections of the Audiovisual Library of International Law <http://legal.un.org/avl/ha/prsr/prsr.html>.

[94]   ECOSOC, Resolution 319(XI) (Resolutions of 11 and 16 Aug 1950); E/1818 (12 Aug 1950).

[95]   See E/SR.399, 217.

[96]   See ECOSOC, 'Report of the Ad Hoc Committee on Refugees and Stateless Persons: Second Session' E/1850; E/AC.32/8 (25 Aug 1950).

[97]   On 22–27 November, 29–30 November, and 1, 4 and 6 December 1950 (A/C.3/SR.324–30, 332, 334, 337, and 338), as cited in the Procedural History and Documents sections of the Audiovisual Library of International Law.

[98]   UNGA Res 429(V), 'Draft Convention relating to the Status of Refugees' (14 Dec 1950) preamble, para 1.

[99]   The Summary Records of the Conference of Plenipotentiaries are contained in A/CONF.2/SR.1–A/CONF.2/SR.35. I am grateful to Jane McAdam for sharing the *travaux préparatoires*.

[100]   See comments by the representative of France, A/CONF.2/SR.3, 12; A/CONF.2/SR.27, 21.

[101]   The delegations that participated in all or part of the debates were: Australia, Austria, Belgium, Brazil, Canada, Colombia, Denmark, Egypt, Federal Republic of Germany, France, Greece, Iraq, Israel, Italy, Luxembourg, Monaco, Netherlands, Norway, Sweden, Switzerland, and Liechtenstein

comment that it had the 'appearance of being nothing more than a meeting of the Council of Europe, slightly enlarged'.[102] The Convention was opened for signature on 28 July 1951, and entered into force on 22 April 1954 after the sixth State deposited its instrument of ratification.

Participants in these debates were men (and, much less frequently, women)[103] who in some cases had first-hand experience of flight, which informed their discussions in practical ways. Consider for example France's proposal to restrict protection against penalties for illegal entry to a refugee coming 'direct from his country of origin'.[104] In critiquing the proposal, Mr van Heuven Goedhart, the first United Nations High Commissioner for Refugees, used the example of his own flight from the Netherlands:

> in 1944, he had himself left the Netherlands on account of persecution and had hidden in Belgium for five days. As he had run the risk of further persecution in that country, he had been helped by the resistance movement to cross into France. From France he had gone on into Spain, and thence to Gibraltar. Thus, before reaching Gibraltar, he had traversed several countries in each of which the threat of persecution had existed. He considered that it would be very unfortunate if a refugee in similar circumstances was penalized for not having proceeded direct to the country of asylum.[105]

The ultimate wording of article 31 of the Convention contained the more generous formulation of 'refugees ... coming directly from a territory where their life or freedom was threatened'. Participants may also have had experience in negotiating more than one of the critical human rights instruments drafted in this period. Sir Samuel Hoare, for example, appears to have represented the UK in the drafting of both the European Convention on Human Rights and the 1951 Convention.[106]

(represented by the same delegate), Turkey, the UK, the US, Venezuela, Yugoslavia, and the Holy See. Others participated as Observers (Cuba and Iran); Representatives of International Organisations and Specialized Agencies (including the High Commissioner for Refugees and the IRO); and representatives of non-governmental organisations. See the lists of attendees at the beginning of each Summary Record: A/CONF.2/SR.1–A/CONF.2/35.

[102] A/CONF.2/SR.3, 12 (France).
[103] See, eg, the interventions of 'Miss Sender', on behalf of the International Confederation of Free Trade Unions, who asked delegates why sex was not included as a ground of prohibited discrimination under article 3 of the draft convention. No response is recorded in the travaux: A/CONF.2/SR.33, p. 7. For background on Toni Sender's life and work, see Richard Critchfield, 'Toni Sender: Feminist, socialist, internationalist' (1992) 15 History of European Ideas 701; 'Toni Sender, 76, Socialist Leader—Reichstag Foe of Nazis Dies—Aided Labor at U.N.' (New York Times, 27 June 1964) 25. I am grateful to Tristan Harley for bringing these pieces to my attention.
[104] 'France—Amendment to Article 26', A/CONF.2/62 (10 July 1951).
[105] A/CONF.2/SR.14, p 5.
[106] Bates notes comments by a Mr Hoare at the Senior Officials Conference in Ed Bates, *The Evolution of the European Convention on Human Rights: From its Inception to the Creation of a Permanent Court of Human Rights* (OUP 2010) 112, fn 20. Mr Hoare represented the United Kingdom at the Conference

4. The *Travaux Préparatoires*—Article 16

Article 16 underwent few changes over the course of its drafting process, which was described by one commentator as 'rather uneventful'.[107] The article was relatively uncontroversial, and was adopted unanimously on the second reading of the draft convention at the Conference of Plenipotentiaries.[108] While summaries of the debates in the *travaux préparatoires* relating specifically to article 16 have been set out elsewhere,[109] the key points are restated here and supplemented by the author's broader reading of the *travaux préparatoires*. This broader reading gives further guidance on delegates' views of the scope of article 16. It is also helpful in indicating the kinds of actions that the framers anticipated refugees may bring before domestic courts (discussed under article 16(1)), and in interpreting terms that appear in multiple articles (such as 'habitual residence', discussed under article 16(2)). Finally, this general reading assists in understanding the silence of the *travaux préparatoires* on the issue of RSD. This issue is addressed separately in Section 5.1.

4.1 Preliminary Memoranda and Draft Articles

Discussion on including an 'access to courts' provision in the 1951 Convention drew on precedents in earlier instruments relating to the status of refugees. In his 1949 Study of Statelessness, the Secretary-General noted that while '[i]t is universally recognized today that foreigners have the right to appear before the courts as plaintiff or defendant':

> [i]n the case of indigent stateless persons the obligation to furnish the *cautio judicatum solvi* and exclusion from the benefit of legal assistance reduce the right to appear before the courts as plaintiff or defendant to a *nudum jus*.[110]

The 'right to appear before the courts as plaintiff or defendant' was accordingly included in the list of subjects that the Secretary-General considered should be included in the draft convention.[111]

---

of Plenipotentiaries on the Status of Refugees and Stateless Persons: see A/CONF.2/SR.1–A/CONF.2/SR.35.

[107] Elberling, 'Article 16' in Zimmermann (n 1) 934. See also Nehemiah Robinson, *Convention Relating to the Status of Refugee: History, Contents and Interpretation: A Commentary* (Institute of Jewish Affairs, World Jewish Congress 1953) 112 (noting that the Conference 'introduced only verbal changes in the wording of the draft').

[108] A/CONF.2/SR.24, 23. During the Conference of Plenipotentiaries' first discussion on draft article 11, the article was adopted as a whole 19-0 with 1 abstention: A/CONF.2/SR.8, 14.

[109] See, eg, Paul Weis (ed), *The Refugee Convention, 1951* (CUP 1995) 130–34, Elberling (n 48) 934-36.

[110] Study of Statelessness (n 50) 24.

[111] ibid 60.

A preliminary convention for consideration by the Ad Hoc Committee was circulated in a 1950 Memorandum by the UN Secretary-General.[112] The preliminary
convention included a draft article based on article 6 of the 1933 Convention entitled 'The right to sue and be sued'. The key changes in the draft article as compared
to the 1933 Convention were a shortening of the phrase 'free and ready access' from
the earlier article to 'free access',[113] and the addition of extra-territorial guarantees
in a new third sub-provision, which read:

> [i]n the matters referred to in Paragraphs 1 and 2 above, refugees (and stateless
> persons) shall be treated, in the countries of the High Contracting Parties in
> which they do not reside, as national of the country where they have their domi-
> cile or regular residence.[114]

The commentary on paragraphs 1 and 2 of the draft article noted that:

> [a]lthough in principle the right of a refugee to sue and be sued is not challenged,
> in practice there are insurmountable difficulties to the exercise of this right by
> needy refugees: the obligation to furnish *cautio judicatum solvi* and the refusal
> to grant refugees the benefit of legal assistance make the right illusory. In many
> countries, legal assistance is available solely to nationals and only foreigners who
> can invoke a treaty of reciprocity are granted the benefit of such assistance.
>
> Refugees should therefore be exempted, as was done in the Conventions of
> 1933 and 1938, from the obligation to furnish *cautio judicatum solvi* and should
> enjoy the benefit of legal assistance on the same conditions as nationals.[115]

On the new paragraph 3, it noted:

> [r]efugees are to have free access to justice, not only in their country of residence
> but in any other country party to the convention. They would be entitled in this
> respect to benefit under the system applied to nationals of the country of asylum
> in pursuance of the treaties in force.[116]

An alternate draft article prepared by the French delegation,[117] which was entitled 'Right to appear before the courts as plaintiff or defendant', followed largely

---

[112] Secretary-General Memorandum (n 88) Annex. In response to the ECOSOC Resolution No
248(IX)B (n 86), the Memorandum addressed 'the desirability of preparing a revised and consolidated
convention' relating to the status of refugees and stateless persons: at 4.

[113] This is not clear from the Secretary-General's Memorandum, however, which includes the anno-
tation 'same text' in comparing draft article 9(1) to article 6 of the 1933 Convention.

[114] Secretary-General Memorandum (n 88) 29–30, art 9.

[115] ibid 30 (underlined emphasis in original replaced by italics). Also cited in Weis (n 109) 131.

[116] ibid.

[117] French proposed draft (n 89) 4–5, art 7.

similar lines to the draft article in the Secretariat's preliminary convention. The key substantive difference was the use of the phrase 'free and ready access' rather than 'free access' in paragraph 1.[118]

4.2 Discussion of Article 16 During the Drafting Process

4.2.1 Heading to article 16

As noted in Section 4.1, the original draft articles prepared by the Secretary-General and France were entitled 'The right to sue and be sued' and 'Right to appear before the courts as plaintiff or defendant', respectively. However, a new title, 'Access to Courts' was adopted by the Ad Hoc Committee's Working Group during its first session.[119] This title was maintained in the first report of the Ad Hoc Committee, without comment as to why the change was made.[120]

It is not possible to read a great deal into this change, as the headings to article 16 ('Access to Courts'), and to Chapter II as a whole ('Juridical Status') have no interpretative value. This fact results from the Conference of Plenipotentiaries' decision, recorded in its Final Act, that 'the titles of the chapters and of the articles of the Convention are included for practical purposes and do not constitute an element of interpretation.'[121]

4.2.2 Article 16(1)

Article 16(1), as adopted, reads '[a] refugee shall have free access to the courts of law on the territory of all Contracting States.'

4.2.2.1 Free access

In the first session of the Ad Hoc Committee, delegates discussed the Secretariat draft ('free access'), and the French draft ('free and ready access'). The UK representative noted his preference for the Secretariat language, 'since in English the words "free" and "ready" were synonymous in the context if used alone, but in conjunction might mean without payment of court fees'.[122] At the suggestion of the Israeli representative, it was agreed that the French text would read 'free and ready access' ('libre et facile accès'), while the English text would use the term 'free access'.[123] The

---

[118] ibid art 7; see also discussion in E/AC.32/SR.11, 6–7.

[119] See ECOSOC, 'Ad Hoc Committee on Statelessness: Draft Convention Relating to the Status of Refugees: Decision of the Working Group taken on 9 February 1950', E/AC.32/L.32 (9 Feb 1950) 6, art 11 (previously art 9).

[120] See Report of the Ad Hoc Committee (n 85) 16, art 11. See also Elberling (n 48) 935.

[121] Final Act of the United Nations Conference of Plenipotentiaries on the Status of Refugees and Stateless Persons, II. For discussion by the Conference of Plenipotentiaries see A/CONF.2/SR.34, 15; A/CONF.2/SR.35, 37–41.

[122] E/AC.32/SR.11, 7.

[123] ibid.

adoption of the UK representative's proposal shows that the Committee did not expect refugees to be granted access to the courts free of cost.

4.2.2.2 Scope of clause

In discussions, the US representative, Louis Henkin, also commented on the scope of article 16(1) as compared to paragraphs (2) and (3). He noted that 'persons who had recently become refugees and therefore had no habitual residence were not covered by the provisions of paragraphs 2 or 3, but only by those of paragraph 1'.[124]

During the Conference of Plenipotentiaries, the Chairman took the floor in response to a comment by the Egyptian representative to clarify that draft article 11 (now article 16) guaranteed refugees free access to courts 'in the territory of all contracting States', not simply in the state of residence.[125] This point was emphasised in a textual change later made by the Style Committee, amending the phrase 'free access to the courts of law on the territory of *the* Contracting States' to '*all* Contracting States'.[126]

The question whether obligations under article 16 were to extend to those unlawfully present in a host State does not appear to have been the subject of much discussion. However, it is instructive to note the Belgian representative's retort to Australia's comments in the Conference of Plenipotentiaries. In debate on a new draft article proposed by Australia,[127] France had asked whether the Australian government would consider that it had the right to impose on refugees who entered clandestinely 'conditions of stay based on considerations of race, religion or country of origin'.[128] The Australian representative replied that such cases would be 'regarded as an illegal entry' and '[h]e did not presume that the intention was to alter the existing legal arrangements for dealing with such cases'.[129] The Belgian representative said that this reply 'did not appear to him to be satisfactory':

> In the case where a refugee who had entered clandestinely the territory of a contracting state brought a judicial action, would he enjoy the rights and privileges laid down in [draft article 16]?[130]

At the very least, the Belgian representative seems to have accepted that the draft provision applied both to the 'legally' and 'illegally' present refugee.

---

[124] E/AC.32/SR.25, 6.

[125] A/CONF.2/SR.8, 13.

[126] See the Report of the Style Committee: A/CONF.2/102 (24 July 1951) 8, art 16.

[127] The proposed article read: '[n]othing in this Convention shall be deemed to absolve a refugee from observing the conditions under which he was or shall be admitted to, or authorized to stay in, the territory of a Contracting State.': A/CONF.2/25, as amended in comments by Mr Shaw (Australia): A/CONF.2/SR.5, 14.

[128] A/CONF.2/SR.5, 16 (Mr Rochefort, France).

[129] ibid (Mr Shaw, Australia). The French response was that this position 'amounted to a negation of the right to asylum': ibid.

[130] ibid (Mr Herment, Belgium). The numbering of draft article 16 was, at that time, article 11.

4.2.2.3   Types of cases foreseen

Records of the drafting process also indicate the types of matters that the drafters expected refugees to bring before domestic courts. As examples, representatives of the Ad Hoc Committee referred to the prospect of civil actions regarding wills[131] and divorce proceedings.[132] It is also clear that refugees were to be subject to criminal law.[133]

A broader reading of the *travaux préparatoires* also suggests that the drafters expected that refugees would have the ability to claim entitlement to the rights set out in the Convention. The US representative noted early in the meetings of the Ad Hoc Committee that dependence on the 'good will' of States was insufficient, as 'refugees ... *would have no legal rights they could press*' (emphasis added). In his view, it was the Committee's role 'to draft a convention endowing them with such rights.'[134]

The Committee's discussion on labour regulations and social security (in the context of what is now article 24) also supports this view. The Committee decided to use article 6 of the 1949 International Labour Organization (ILO) Migration for Employment Convention as a basis for its discussions on the draft provision. Article 6 guaranteed that lawful immigrants would receive national treatment in several areas, including article 6(1)(d): 'legal proceedings *relating to the matters referred to in this Convention*'.[135] When discussing the draft article, the Belgian representative (who had in fact chaired an ILO commission that drafted the 1949 Convention),[136] proposed the deletion of article 6(1)(d) from the draft on the basis that its 'substance was covered in other parts of the draft convention'.[137]

This proposal, which was adopted by the Committee, is significant. The draft article on access to courts had been discussed only a few days prior by the Committee and would have been fresh in the representatives' minds. That article did not expressly state that refugees were entitled to the same treatment as nationals in relation to legal proceedings *concerning rights in the Refugee Convention*. Nonetheless,

---

[131] See the statement of the Chairman regarding wills in the context of the draft article on Personal Status: 'The reference to wills had been deleted because it would entail conflict with domestic law. The courts of reception countries could be relied upon to deal fairly with refugees in the matter.' E/AC.32/SR.10, 4 (Chairman).

[132] See Study of Statelessness (n 50) 45 ('It should therefore be made possible for him to apply for divorce to the courts of his country of residence'); although the Danish representative noted in the course of the debates that 'the question of the free access of refugees to the courts of law raised a delicate problem in the matter of divorce action.': E/AC.32/SR.11, 7.

[133] See 1951 Convention, art 2 ('Every refugee has duties to the country in which he finds himself, which require in particular that he conform to its laws and regulations'); E/AC.32/SR.19, 10 (Mr Lewin, Agudas Israel World Organisation, noting that if a refugee 'committed criminal acts, he should be punished according to the normal laws of the country').

[134] E/AC.32/SR.2, 9 (Mr Henkin, US).

[135] See ECOSOC, 'Communication from the International Labour Organisation', E/AC.32/L.9, 2, art 6(1)(d) (emphasis added).

[136] See E/AC.32/SR.25, 15, correcting the record in E/AC.32/SR.14, 5.

[137] E/AC.32/SR.14, 12.

the adoption of the Belgian representative's proposal suggests that this was how it was interpreted by the Committee. This is not to suggest that delegates would expect rights on the international level could be directly pursued on the domestic level in all Contracting States. However, the good faith performance of a treaty may require that a State take legislative action to secure the rights guaranteed under the Convention for refugees within its territory.

4.2.2.4 Decision to prohibit reservations to article 16(1)

The right of free access to courts in article 16(1) of the 1951 Convention is one of the few rights to which States cannot enter a reservation.[138] It was emphasised at several points in the drafting process that a liberal policy towards reservations should be adopted, with only 'essential' clauses listed as not subject to reservation.[139] An early draft of the clause by the Committee's Working Group suggested allowing reservations to all provisions except article 1 (the refugee definition) and 23 (travel documents),[140] and several representatives were willing to make the clause even more liberal, allowing reservations to all provisions except article 1.[141] In discussion, however, it was agreed that the Committee would delay drafting the article until governments had had the opportunity to comment,[142] although scant feedback was, in fact, received.[143] The decision to include article 16(1) in the reservations clause was made at the Ad Hoc Committee's second session.[144] During the discussion, Israel initially suggested that draft article 11(3) (now article

---

[138] See 1951 Convention, art 42. States are likewise unable to enter reservations in respect of the definition of refugee (art 1); non-discrimination (art 3), religion (art 4), the prohibition on expulsion or return (art 33), and arts 36–46 of the executory and transitory provisions in Chapter VI.

[139] See, eg, the Study of Statelessness (n 50) which suggested that making a 'fairly liberal provision' for reservations in the Convention was necessary to encourage States to become parties to the instrument: 55; Secretary-General Memorandum (n 88) 55 (noting that the Convention 'embodie[d] a number of provisions which might be considered essential and could not be subject to reservation, since otherwise accession to the Convention would have little or no value ... ').

[140] E/AC.32/L.32 (n 119) 16.

[141] E/AC.32/SR.25, 15 (Turkey); E/AC.32/SR.26, 3 (UK); E/AC.32/L.33 (Denmark–United Kingdom: Proposed Text for Article 36). The UK justified its stance on the basis that the Convention was 'more in the nature of a declaration by States in favour of individuals than a contract between States conferring rights with corresponding obligations', and that therefore, 'reservation should be accepted more freely than in the case of other conventions, especially if it were taken into account that some of the provisions of the existing draft would not be acceptable to all Governments': E/AC.32/SR.26, 3–4. See however the US representative's response (E/AC.32/SR.26, 4).

[142] E/AC.32/SR.26, 5.

[143] Austria noted that it was not in a position to exclude article 1 and 23 from the right to make reservations; the UK proposed allowing reservations to all articles save article 1, and the US simply agreed that the provision should be inserted after comments from governments were received: see 'Refugees and Stateless Persons: Compilation of the Comments of Governments and Specialized Agencies on the Report of the Ad Hoc Committee on Statelessness and Related Problems (Document E/1618) (Memorandum by the Secretary-General)', E/AC.32/L.40, 63.

[144] The Committee discussed article 36 on the basis of a Working Document, X.10. The author was unable to find a copy when researching this chapter. From the discussion, is not clear which sections of the 'access to courts' clause were initially flagged for removal.

16(3)) be listed as not being subject to reservation 'in view of its extraterritorial effects'.[145] While agreeing with Israel, the Chairman queried whether the Committee would 'serve the refugee best by permitting reservations or precluding them and possibly preventing signatures to the Convention'.[146] As a 'compromise' solution, France proposed that reservations to draft article 11(1) (now article 16(1)) be prohibited.[147] The Chairman commented that he '*could scarcely imagine any country wishing to make a reservation in that respect* but the question was, if any did so wish, how best to serve the cause of the refugees'.[148] With the support of the US, the Chairman put the French proposal to the vote, and it was adopted 7–0 with four abstentions.[149] While there were some changes to the provisions listed as not subject to reservation during the Conference of Plenipotentiaries,[150] there was no challenge to the inclusion of the article 16(1).[151] This discussion reflects the drafters' acceptance of the 'essential' nature of article 16(1), but provides little guidance on why the decision was made to allow that reservations be made both to article 16(2) and (3).

4.2.3 Article 16(2)

Article 16(2), as adopted, reads:

> A refugee shall enjoy in the Contracting State in which he has his habitual residence the same treatment as a national in matters pertaining to access to the Courts, including legal assistance and exemption from *cautio judicatum solvi*.

Article 16(2) underwent certain changes over the course of the drafting process, in particular:

- replacing the standard 'domicile or regular residence' with 'habitual residence';
- replacing the phrase 'same rights and privileges as nationals' with 'same treatment as a national';

---

[145] E/AC.32/SR.43, 10. During the discussion, the UK also suggested stating that article 4(1) (on exemption from reciprocity) be listed included as a non-derogable provision, which would remove the need to specifically mention the provisions on access to courts and moveable and immoveable property, however this proposal was not taken up: E/AC.32/SR.43, 9.

[146] ibid.

[147] ibid.

[148] ibid (emphasis added).

[149] ibid.

[150] See Alain Pellet, 'Article 42' in Zimmermann (n 1) 1621. A French proposal to allow reservations to be made to article 35 (draft article 30) was adopted: See A/CONF.2/SR.27, 10–16.

[151] During the Conference, the representative of Yugoslavia proposed insulating nine additional articles from reservations, but withdrew his proposal on the basis of 'the trend of the discussions in the Conference that governments would be forced to enter a great many reservations, and [the fact that] he did not wish his amendment to discourage them from acceding to the Convention.' see A/CONF.2/SR.27, 10; A/CONF.2/31 (namely articles 10, 12, 15, 16, 17, 18, 19, 20, 24).

- replacing the phrase 'in this respect' with the clearer words 'in matters pertaining to access to the Courts';
- deleting a proviso that refugees enjoyed the benefit of legal assistance and exemption from *cautio judicatum solvi* 'on the same conditions as a national'; and
- adding the word 'including', implying that the examples of legal assistance and exemption from *cautio judicatum solvi* are incidents of a broader right of refugees to national treatment on access issues.

However, it is difficult to read too much into these changes. With one exception—the decision to apply the 'habitual residence' standard—all the changes set out here were made by the Conference of Plenipotentiaries' Style Committee, *after* the substantive discussion of the draft articles by the Conference.[152] Although the Style Committee's amended text was approved unanimously by the Conference,[153] there was no further discussion of the rationale for the Style Committee's changes and it can be assumed that they were not intended to alter the draft article substantively. In light of this, discussion focuses on three issues in the *travaux préparatoires*: (1) the scope of 'habitual residence'; (2) the standard of 'national treatment'; and (3) the interpretation of the phrase 'matters pertaining to access to the Courts, including legal assistance and exemption from *cautio judicatum solvi*'.

4.2.3.1 Habitual residence

The term 'habitual residence' was introduced in the course of the drafting process. The Secretariat and French draft articles discussed during the Ad Hoc Committee's first session both used the term 'domicile or regular residence' in paragraphs 2 and 3.[154] During the first session, the UK representative suggested deleting 'domicile or' from the draft article to reflect that refugees were to be given the right to sue and be sued in their country of residence.[155] The Committee agreed to this change.[156] However, the term 'regular residence' was changed to 'habitual residence' in the draft article adopted by the Ad Hoc Committee's Working Group on 9 February 1950.[157] There do not appear to be records of the meetings of the Working Group, so there is no record of why this change was made.[158] The Working Group's new

---

[152] Compare 'Text of Articles adopted by the Conference on 4-5 July 1951', A.CONF.2/L.1 (5 July 1951), 3, art 11, with the Report of the Style Committee (n 126) 8.

[153] A/CONF.2/SR.34, 23.

[154] Secretary-General Memorandum (n 88) 29, art 9; French proposed draft (n 89) 5, art 7.

[155] E/AC.32/SR.11, 7. The UK also proposed changing 'and shall be exempt' to 'and be exempt' in paragraph 2 of the French draft (which was taken as the base text), to emphasise that 'refugees were subject to the same conditions as nationals regarding both the benefit of legal assistance and the exemption from *cautio judicatum solvi*': at 7.

[156] E/AC.32/SR.11, 8.

[157] E/AC.32/L.32 (n 119) 6, art 11 (previously art 9). The Working Group consisted of five members of the Ad Hoc Committee (Belgium, France, Israel, the UK, and the US), and the Chairman (from Canada) ex-officio: See E/AC.32/SR.21, 2.

[158] Based on research conducted for this chapter.

formulation was included in the Ad Hoc Committee's First Report, such that paragraph 2 read:

> In the country in which he has his habitual residence, a refugee shall enjoy in this respect the same rights and privileges as a national. He shall, on the same conditions as a national, enjoy the benefit of legal assistance and be exempt from *cautio judicatum solvi*.[159]

The scope of 'habitual residence' was considered in the drafting discussions, particularly in the context of article 14 of the 1951 Convention (Artistic Rights and Industrial Property). The term provoked debate on what exactly 'habitual residence' entailed.[160] In the Conference of Plenipotentiaries, the Austrian representative drew a distinction between three kinds of attachment: 'fixed abode, habitual residence, and temporary residence'.[161] He noted that a refugee 'had no fixed or ordinary abode, as he had had to abandon it', and that 'the only kind of residence possible for him was habitual or temporary residence, the latter applying where the refugee moved about or took a holiday.'[162] The French representative characterised 'habitual residence' as 'a happy medium' between the narrower term 'domicile' and broader term 'residence'.[163] In discussions of draft article 1(D), the UK representative also reflected that '[i]n the sense in which it had been used in other parts of the Convention, the phrase "habitual residence" implied much less than permanent residence'.[164]

The concept of 'habitual residence' therefore seems to have been considered flexible, and it is not clear from discussions how long a refugee must stay in a country to meet the threshold.[165] Some indications can be pieced together. For example, the Belgian representative counselled against setting up a dichotomy between 'residence' and 'habitual residence' on the basis that 'the former might cover a stay lasting a few days only',[166] which suggests, by implication, that habitual residence must be a stay of more than a few days. The US representative considered that persons who had 'recently become refugees' may not have a place of habitual

---

[159] See E/AC.32/L.32 (n 119) 6, art 11 (previously art 9); 'Report of the Ad Hoc Committee' (n 85) 16, art 11.

[160] See, eg, A/CONF.2/SR.7, 20 (Colombia) (asking '[w]hat length of stay did that concept involve in actual fact?'); A/CONF.2/SR.7, 9 (UK) (noting that 'if the concept of 'habitual residence' were introduced, certain countries might find themselves in difficulties, because the concept had not formerly existed in their legal system and would require interpretation by the courts').

[161] A/CONF.2/SR.8, 5.

[162] ibid.

[163] ibid 7. Compare however comments of the French representative during the second session of the Ad Hoc Committee, noting that the term 'résidence habituelle' implied some considerable length of residence, and that 'résidence regulière' was 'far less restrictive': E/AC.32/SR.42, 12.

[164] A/CONF.2/SR.23, 26. Also cited in Guy S Goodwin-Gill and Jane McAdam, with Emma Dunlop, *The Refugee in International Law* (4th edn, OUP 2021), 598, fn 189.

[165] See, eg, A/CONF.2/SR.7, 20.

[166] ibid 8.

residence.[167] France and the UN High Commissioner for Refugees had different views on the 'habitual residence' of certain refugees who travelled regularly for work, with the High Commissioner suggesting that such refugees may have no habitual residence, and the French representative arguing that '[r]efugees had to have a place of habitual residence; otherwise it would be impossible for them to proceed from one country to another'.[168] This difference of opinion on whether it was possible for a refugee to have no place of habitual residence is also reflected in later commentaries.[169]

4.2.3.2 National treatment

The phrase 'same treatment as a national in matters pertaining to access to the courts' was introduced by the Conference of Plenipotentiaries' Style Committee at the very end of the drafting process.[170] While there is no direct account of why the Style Committee chose this phrase over the original phrase, 'enjoy in this respect the same rights and privileges as a national',[171] an earlier Note prepared by the representatives of Israel and the UK suggests that the change may have been adopted to enhance consistency within the Convention.[172]

4.2.3.3 Matters pertaining to access to the Courts

The *travaux préparatoires* show that certain States were hesitant to guarantee eligible refugees the right to exemption from *cautio judicatum solvi*. When governments were asked to comment on the Ad Hoc Committee's First Report,[173] Austria was the only State to comment specifically on draft article 11 (now article 16). Austria proposed that the *guarantees* of public assistance and exemption from security for costs in paragraph 2 be downgraded to *recommendations*.[174] As a justification, Austria noted that 'refugees change their residence more frequently than other persons, even if they have their habitual residence on the national territory or in a foreign State which grants reciprocity in this respect'.[175] Austria's proposal was not adopted. In the Conference of Plenipotentiaries, Egypt also raised concerns about this provision, noting that it could not 'vote for the paragraph which provided that the refugee should be exempt from *cautio judicatum solvi*', since in Egypt this exemption 'was granted subject to reciprocity'.[176] However, the Belgian

---

[167]   See E/AC.32/SR.25, 6.
[168]   A/CONF.2/SR.8, 7.
[169]   See Chapter 2, Section 2.1.5.
[170]   Compare the text of the article adopted by the Conference: A/CONF.2/L.1 (5 July 1951), 3; the initial text of articles adopted by the Style Committee: A/CONF.2/AC.1/R.2 (18 July 1951), 4; and the Report of the Style Committee (n 126) 8, art 16 (formerly art 11). See also Section 4.2.3.
[171]   Based on research conducted for this chapter.
[172]   See the discussion of the different formulations for 'national treatment' in the Israel/UK Note on Article 3(B): A/CONF.2/84 (17 July 1951), 3.
[173]   By a note of 10 March 1950: see E/AC.32/L.40, 1.
[174]   ibid 42.
[175]   ibid.
[176]   A/CONF.2/SR.8, 13.

representative recalled that 'the practice of demanding *cautio judicatum solvi* was dying out, and that in Belgium, for instance, it was no longer required, except in commercial litigation'. He also drew attention to the fact that this exemption was 'one of the first few clauses in all bilateral treaties'.[177]

As noted in Section 4.2.3, the word 'including' was only introduced into the clause by the Style Committee. However, the summary records show that at least one delegate understood two rights listed (the benefit of legal assistance and exemption from *cautio judicatum solvi*) to be examples of a broader class of rights guaranteed to refugees under article 16. In response to Egypt's request that draft article 11 be voted on in two parts, with 'a separate vote being taken on the phrase 'be exempt from *cautio judicatum solvi*', the Belgian representative observed:

> the exemption from *cautio judicatum solvi* was already provided for under the first sentence of paragraph 2, which provided that a refugee should enjoy in that respect the same rights and privileges as a national.[178]

Although the Conference nonetheless proceeded to vote on paragraph 2 in two parts,[179] the Belgian representative's point, which was not disputed, seems best to reflect the plain meaning of the draft clause.

A final issue in the *travaux préparatoires* concerned the conditions that a refugee must meet to avail himself or herself of national treatment. The draft article debated in the Conference of Plenipotentiaries stated that a refugee 'shall, *on the same conditions as a national*', enjoy legal assistance and exemption from *cautio judicatum solvi*.[180] The fact that the deletion of the reference to 'conditions' occurred in the Style Committee suggests that the change was not intended to alter the substantive meaning of the clause. An Israel–UK Note on draft article 3(B)(b) also supports this view.[181] It therefore appears that the Conference intended that rights would be granted under article 16(2) on the same conditions as applied to nationals.

There is one notable caveat to this conclusion. The Israeli and UK representatives considered that 'the special circumstances' of refugees should be recognised when deciding whether refugees met conditions that would generally be applied to nationals. The draft article that was the subject of the Israel–UK Note (which

---

[177] ibid.
[178] ibid.
[179] This procedure seems somewhat problematic. In essence, the Committee voted on the two specific examples listed in art 16(2) (the 'benefit of legal assistance' and exemption 'from *cautio judicatum solvi* on the same conditions as a national'), without voting on the broader umbrella principle in paragraph 2 that a refugee enjoys 'the same rights and privileges and a national'. Nonetheless, after this piecemeal voting the paragraph as a whole was adopted by the Conference, reflecting their general agreement: See A/CONF.2/SR.8, 13–14.
[180] A/CONF.2/1, available via <https://www.refworld.org/docid/3ae68ce944.html>, 9, art 11.
[181] The Note proposed deleting the reference to 'conditions' in draft article 11(2) (now article 16(2)), on the basis that the draft convention necessarily implied that national treatment 'is given under the same conditions as to nationals': see A/CONF.2/84, 4.

was eventually omitted from the Convention) read: '[i]n those cases in which the refugee enjoys the 'same treatment accorded to nationals' the refugee must satisfy the conditions required of a national for the enjoyment of the right in question'.[182] In debates on the draft provision, Israel considered that draft article 3(B)(b) was 'too rigid', and that 'the special circumstances of refugees must be recognized'.[183] The UK agreed, noting that Israel had 'rightly pointed out ... that a refugee may not be able to satisfy the "conditions required", precisely because he was a refugee and not a national'.[184] The UK representative felt that 'it would be very difficult to redraft [draft article 3(B)(b)] so as to exclude those conditions which a refugee was incapable of fulfilling'. The Israel–UK proposal to delete article 3(B)(b), on the basis that it was 'meaningless',[185] was adopted by the Conference.[186] This debate reflects acceptance—at the very least by Israel and the UK—that when implementing 'national treatment' standards, States should be alive to the particular circumstances of refugees. To give effect to these standards, some flexibility was therefore warranted.

4.2.4 Article 16(3)

Article 16(3), as adopted, reads:

> A refugee shall be accorded in the matters referred to in paragraph 2 in countries other than that in which he has his habitual residence the treatment granted to a national of the country of his habitual residence.

The original drafts of article 16(3) discussed in the Ad Hoc Committee did not differ greatly from the final article adopted by the Conference of Plenipotentiaries. In the first session of the Ad Hoc Committee, a reference to 'domicile or regular residence' was replaced with 'habitual residence' (as was the case for paragraph 2). A link to paragraph 1 was also deleted.[187] Although there is no discussion of this edit in the *travaux préparatoires*, it seems a sensible recognition of the fact that the right guaranteed by article 16(1) is applicable in all Contracting States. Surprisingly, there was no discussion at all of paragraph 3 of the draft article in the Ad Hoc Committee's first report, despite the fact that it was an innovation as compared to previous instruments.[188]

---

[182] A/CONF.2/1 (n 180), 6, art 3(B).
[183] A/CONF.2/SR.5, 19 (the comment 'too rigid' was made specifically on draft art 3(B)(a), but Israel notes that 'the same argument applied to sub-paragraph (b)').
[184] A/CONF.2/SR.6, 4.
[185] A/CONF.2/84, 4.
[186] A/CONF.2/SR.26, 10.
[187] Compare the draft articles in Secretary-General Memorandum (n 88) 30, art 9 and French proposed draft (n 89) 5, art 7 with the draft article in the Report of the Ad Hoc Committee (n 85).
[188] 'Report of the Ad Hoc Committee' (n 85) 48.

Between the Ad Hoc Committee's first report and the Conference of Plenipotentiaries' final decision, only minor textual changes were made to article 16(3). In the Conference of Plenipotentiaries, the representative for Yugoslavia tabled an amendment to include the words 'and if he is considered by such countries as being a refugee under the terms of this Convention' after 'habitual residence' in paragraph 3.[189] The proposed amendment was intended to ensure that 'persons who were not refugees should not be treated as such' (the representative seemed to have in mind particularly Nazis and other war criminals who had settled in Argentina).[190] However, after discussion Yugoslavia agreed to withdraw the amendment on the basis that it referred to a more general question.[191] As can be seen from this brief summary, the *travaux préparatoires* do not provide a great deal of insight into the drafters' views on the scope of article 16(3).

5. The *Travaux Préparatoires*—Other Guidance

This section surveys broader discussion in the *travaux préparatoires* that sheds light on the drafters' intentions when drafting article 16.

5.1 Refugee Status Determination—The Silence of the *Travaux Préparatoires*

The silence in the *travaux préparatoires* on whether article 16 covers issues related to RSD has been noted by commentators.[192] Clues as to why there was no comment on this point are found in more general discussions in the *travaux préparatoires*. In early debates in the Ad Hoc Committee, France called for a liberal approach to the Convention, which would grant 'a minimum of rights ... in the receiving countries, to all categories of refugees present and future'.[193] However, to the Belgian representative, 'the problem was to define the rights of persons who had already been granted asylum'.[194] The US representative endorsed a similar view during discussion of a draft article on admission, which was omitted from the draft

---

[189] See A/CONF.2/31, 1.
[190] A/CONF.2/SR.8, 11. For the text of the proposed amendment see A/CONF.2/31, 1.
[191] A/CONF.2/SR.8, 12.
[192] See, eg, Dana Baldinger, *Vertical Judicial Dialogues in Asylum Cases: Standards on Judicial Scrutiny and Evidence in International and European Asylum Law* (Brill Nijhoff 2015) 25; Jean-Yves Carlier, *Droit d'asile et des réfugiés: de la protection aux droits* (Vol 332), Collected Courses of the Hague Academy of International Law (Brill Nijhoff 2008) 320.
[193] E/AC.32/SR.3, 13.
[194] E/AC.32/SR.4, 6.

Convention.[195] He noted that 'the question of admission, while vital for the individuals concerned, was not the main question to be settled by the Committee':

> [a]dmission into a country of refugees from camps or from initial reception countries constituted a political problem which the States concerned would have to solve. The convention must deal with the rights of refugees *who had already been admitted into a country, without seeking to establish who should admit them and in what circumstances.*[196]

An additional element that may have influenced the drafters was a level of uncertainty as to the role that the UN High Commissioner for Refugees would eventually play in RSD procedures. At the time of the Ad Hoc Committee and Conference's discussions, the IRO, which preceded UNHCR, was slated for termination.[197] The Statute of the Office of the High Commissioner for Refugees was only adopted in December 1950, after the discussions of the Ad Hoc Committee and six months before the Conference of Plenipotentiaries.

The IRO had been involved in RSD, developing what the Secretary-General referred to as 'somewhat elaborate machinery to determine whether applicants for assistance [came] within the constitutional definitions of refugees'.[198] This system included 'a trained body of eligibility experts and a semi-judicial tribunal of appeals'.[199] However, many States opted instead to conduct their own status determination.[200] There appears to have been a lack of clarity on exactly what role the new High Commissioner would play in status determination at the time the debates took place, although France considered it 'inconceivable that the High Commissioner, with the small staff at his disposal, could undertake individual screening of refugees'.[201]

---

[195]   See Secretary-General Memorandum (n 88) art 3, 22; French proposed draft (n 89) art 2, 3; E/AC.32/SR.7, 2–13.

[196]   E/AC.32/SR.7, 8 (emphasis added).

[197]   See ECOSOC, Resolution 248(IX)A (6 Aug 1949), which notes in its preamble that 'the question of the protection of refugees who are the concern of the IRO is an urgent one owing to the fact that IRO expects to terminate its services about 30 June 1950'. The IRO was eventually dissolved in 1952 by Resolution No 108 of the General Council of the IRO: see United Nations Treaty Collection, <https://treaties.un.org/pages/ViewDetails.aspx?src=TREATY&mtdsg_no=V-1&chapter=5&clang=_en>.

[198]   See UNGA, 'Refugees and Stateless Persons: Report of the Secretary-General' (26 Oct 1949), A/C.3/527, available via <http://www.refworld.org/docid/3ae68bf00.html#_edn15> para 12. The report notes that '[i]n actual practice, the IRO requires the completion by applicants of a written form which is reviewed, normally with personal interview, by an Eligibility Officer assigned to the area in which the applicant appears. An applicant rejected as not falling within the mandate of the Organization must be notified by the Eligibility Officer of his right to appeal to a semi-judicial Review Board. This Review Board with headquarters in Geneva and panels which travel on circuit throughout the principal areas in which refugees are located, was established by the IRO in accordance with Annex I of the Constitution.': ibid n 15.

[199]   Holborn (n 52) 77.

[200]   See comment by France in the ECOSOC Social Committee: E/AC.7/SR.166 (22 Aug 1950) 8.

[201]   ibid.

The tendency to focus on the rights to be granted to refugees already within a jurisdiction, coupled with uncertainty as to the way that RSD would be carried out in the future, may therefore have influenced the content of the debates. There is no discussion of how, or whether, article 16 would apply in the case of RSD, despite its potential significance. As the representative for Belgium pointed out in the Conference of Plenipotentiaries, 'the authorities of the country of reception would be at the same time both judge and party in every appeal submitted by a refugee and in every request concerning the exercise of a right by a refugee'.[202]

5.2 Comparing the Use of 'Courts' and 'Due Process of Law'

Article 32(2) sets out specific legal safeguards afforded to refugees in the case of expulsion. Following from the guarantee in article 32(1) that a Contracting State 'shall not expel a refugee lawfully in their territory save on grounds of national security and public order', the provision provides that:

> [t]he expulsion of such a refugee shall be *only in pursuance of a decision reached in accordance with due process of law*. Except where compelling reasons of national security otherwise require, the refugee shall be allowed to *submit evidence to clear himself, and to appeal to and be represented for the purpose* before competent authority or a person or persons specially designated by the competent authority.[203]

This provision is relevant to an understanding of States' obligations to provide refugees with access to courts for two reasons. First, discussion on the term 'due process of law' supports the view that the drafters considered the reference to 'courts' in article 16 had a narrower scope. Second, article 32(2) sets out specific guarantees that must be afforded to refugees who face an expulsion procedure which may supplement the protections guaranteed in article 16.

5.2.1 'Due Process of Law': Scope and Significance
Article 32(2) provides that a refugee may only be expelled following a decision 'reached in accordance with due process of law'. The *travaux préparatoires* regarding article 32 show that the drafters expressly chose the phrase 'due process of law' so as to cover both administrative and judicial decision-making.

The phrase was included in the draft on the suggestion of the Chairman of the Conference, speaking in his capacity as representative of Canada[204] and replaced the initial text 'in pursuance of the decision of a judicial authority'.[205] The

---

[202] A/CONF.2/SR.27, 11.
[203] 1951 Convention, art 32(2) (emphasis added).
[204] E/AC.32/SR.20, 7 (Mr Chance, Chairman (speaking as representative of Canada)).
[205] E/C.2/242, art 24(2). Compare E/AC.32/L.22, art 24(2).

amendment was a compromise after an earlier Canadian proposal (to replace 'decision of a judicial authority' with 'the decision of a judicial or administrative authority')[206] had been criticised by the US. The US representative thought the initial amendment would 'deprive the refugee of the safeguards which every individual was entitled to expect from the judicial authority', leaving the refugee 'to the discretion of police measures'.[207] However, he was prepared to accept the term 'due process of law', noting that '[t]he essential thing was that it should not be possible to expel refugees other than in accordance with a regular procedure provided by the law, whether administrative or judicial'.[208]

The context of these discussions supports the view that the drafters considered 'due process of law' to cover both administrative and judicial procedures.[209] The debates highlighted significant variations between States' expulsion regimes, some of which were wholly administrative, while others included judicial review elements.

In Belgium, expulsion was 'a royal prerogative', and the law 'did not specify in what cases it might take place'.[210] In France, the expulsion of aliens was an administrative procedure, carried out 'through an Appeals Board under the authority of the Minister of the Interior'.[211] However, the French representative noted that this procedure was 'in no way discretionary, since aliens had the right of resort, if necessary, to courts of appeal on administrative matters just as had French nationals'.[212]

Canada similarly had an administrative regime in place for expulsion orders.[213] Under the Canadian procedure, an alien could appear or be represented by counsel before a three-member board of inquiry, which would then send its findings to the Federal Authorities in Ottawa, and 'if an order of deportation was found necessary it was issued under the authority of the Minister'.[214] At the Conference of

---

[206]   E/AC.32/SR.20, 6 (Mr Chance, Chairman (speaking as representative of Canada)).

[207]   ibid 6 (Mr Henkin, US).

[208]   ibid 12 (Mr Henkin, US).

[209]   See, eg, the Chairman (speaking as the representative for Canada) at E/AC.32/SR.20, 16, noting that '[h]e saw no objection to the adoption of paragraph 2, as in his country all expulsions were ordered only in pursuance of a decision reached by due process of law'. He had already clarified that in Canada expulsion orders 'were issued by the administrative and not by the judicial authority': E.AC.32/SR.20, 6. Austria's written comment suggests an even broader view: 'it is assumed that "due process of law" covers not only the procedure before the courts, but also before the administrative authorities and the police': E/AC.32/L.40, 55. This view was countered in the debates however, where the Chairman noted that the term ' "final" decision' was used 'in order to avoid the possibility of a person being expelled on the decision of a mere policeman for example': see E/AC.32/SR.20, 18 (Mr Chance, Chairman).

[210]   E/AC.32/SR.40, 20 (Mr Herment, Belgium).

[211]   ibid 18 (Mr Juvigny, France).

[212]   ibid 18. However, a contradictory statement was given by Mr Ordonneau, also representative for France, in an earlier session. Mr Ordonneau noted that expulsion was 'a matter for the executive authorities', and 'such measures could only be taken by the prefects or the Ministry of the Interior': E/AC.32/SR.20, 7. Mr Ordonneau further noted that '[i]n France an expulsion order was issued by the Prefect, and no administrative authority could usurp his right. His order was therefore final. It was always possible to appeal to the Council of State which could countermand the order, but that took time and, in any case, an appeal did not stay execution': see E/AC.32/SR.20, 18. On the specificities of the French procedure, see A/CONF.2/SR.14, 22 (Mr Rochefort, France).

[213]   See E/AC.32/SR.20, 6 (Mr Chance, Chairman (speaking as representative of Canada)).

[214]   A/CONF.2/SR.14, 23 (Mr Chance, Canada).

Plenipotentiaries, the Canadian representative noted that '[n]o appeal could be made against [the Minister's] decision, for obvious reasons'.[215] However, in the Ad Hoc Committee the same representative noted that courts could rule on the legality of an expulsion order as part of a habeas corpus application, and remit the matter back to the administrative authority for a new decision if necessary.[216] Italian expulsion decisions were also made by the Minister under domestic law, and there were different views put to the committee as to whether appeals were allowed.[217]

In the UK, 'no alien lawfully resident [could] be deported save under an Order made personally by the Secretary of State'.[218] While safeguards were built into this administrative procedure, namely a right to 'make representations' to the Secretary of State, and the possibility of bringing a habeas corpus action,[219] an alien had no right 'to appear or to be represented before the Secretary of State personally',[220] and there was 'no appeal tribunal' in place.[221] During the Conference of Plenipotentiaries, the UK representative noted its presumption that the right to appeal referred to in the draft article did not require it to establish an appeal tribunal.[222] The UK challenged the reference to a right to 'representation' in the draft article several times over the course of debates in the Ad Hoc Committee as inconsistent with its own procedure,[223] noting that '[e]very method of making representations was open [to an applicant] under English law except that chosen in the draft Convention'.[224] The amendment to the draft article to enable that representations be made to 'a person or persons specially designated by the competent authority' was proposed by the UK and adopted by the Conference to allow for this procedural peculiarity.[225]

Use of the term 'due process of law' was motivated by the need to encompass these quite different systems.[226] As Paul Weis (representing the IRO) pointed out

---

[215] ibid. Interestingly, Mr Chance added that 'the Canadian government did not believe that the provisions of [the draft article] would call for any alteration of the procedure.': ibid 24.

[216] E/AC.32/SR.20, 6 (Mr Chance, Chairman (speaking as representative of Canada): '[w]hen a writ of *habeas corpus* had been obtained, the judge dealing with the case decided whether the expulsion order had been legal or not; in the event of his declaring it illegal, it was necessary for expulsion proceedings to be initiated anew before the administrative authority').

[217] Compare the statement by Mr Theodoli, Italy, in A/CONF.2/SR.15, 13 (that 'in Italy, the law authorizing the Minister to execute an expulsion order made no provision for appeals') with the statement by Mr des Drago, also representing Italy, on the previous day: A/CONF.2/SR.14, 23 ('in Italy refugees under order of expulsion could appeal against the order to the competent authority').

[218] E/AC.32/L.40, 56 (UK comments).

[219] ibid.

[220] ibid.

[221] A/CONF.2/SR.14, 25 (Mr Hoare, UK).

[222] ibid.

[223] See, eg, comments by Sir Leslie Brass, UK: E/AC.32/SR.22, 23; E/AC.32/SR.25, 10; E/AC.32/SR.40, 13; E/AC.32/SR.40, 29.

[224] E/AC.32/SR.40, 29 (Sir Leslie Brass, UK).

[225] See A/CONF.2/60 (proposed UK amendment to article 27); A/CONF.2/SR.15, 16.

[226] See, eg, the comment of Mr Hoare, UK, noting that '[t]he first sentence of [paragraph 2 of the draft article] had been very carefully drafted in order to cover the different systems of expulsion, which might be broadly classified in two groups, judicial and administrative.': A/CONF.2/SR.14, 24.

in the Ad Hoc Committee, 'due process of law' is sufficiently broad as to encompass either regime.[227]

This survey supports the view that article 32(2) was expressly and carefully drafted to cover both administrative and legal proceedings. As such, it can usefully be compared with article 16 of the 1951 Convention, which refers only to 'access to courts'. The drafters' decision to use a more specific term in article 16 suggests that they did not intend the clause to impose obligations on Contracting States in relation to administrative procedures.

6. Conclusion

The *travaux préparatoires* shed some light on drafters' perceptions of the scope and content of article 16 of the 1951 Convention. The historical survey of access to courts provisions in early treaties in Section 2, coupled with analysis of the *travaux préparatoires* in Sections 4–5, support some general conclusions on the drafters' intentions regarding the scope and content of the provision. First, it is clear that article 16 was deliberately framed to grant refugees broader protections than those generally afforded to aliens under commercial treaties of the time. The risk of indigence was understood as a particular concern that, if unremedied, could render refugees' access to courts 'illusory'. Second, it appears that the silence of the *travaux préparatoires* on RSD in the context of article 16 was driven more by a general uncertainty as to how RSD would be carried out than a specific view that article 16 had no application. Third, reading article 16 in light of debates on article 32(2) supports the view that the drafters did not intend article 16 to impose obligations on States in relation to administrative procedures.

In addition to these general conclusions, there are also indications of the views of particular delegates, which fall short of a conclusive view of the drafters' general intentions overall. Analysis of the debates shows that at least one delegate considered that refugees should be able to claim their rights under the Convention in domestic courts; that article 16 applied to both 'legally' and 'illegally' present refugees; that article 16(2) had a broader application than the two protections it expressly includes; and that, when comparing the treatment of a refugee to that of a national, the special circumstances of a refugee should be taken into account. The scattered nature of these references, and the difficulty of discerning the extent to which they were generally accepted by other delegates, weakens their status as material capable of 'confirming the meaning' of the provision under article 32 of the Vienna Convention.

---

[227] E/AC.32/SR.40, 15 (noting 'the term "due process of law", used in paragraph 1 of article 27, was applied to processes, usually juridical but also administrative, attended by certain safeguards').

5

Access to Courts and Related Rights under International Law

1. Introduction

This chapter now turns to relevant developments in international law since 1951. The approach that courts and human rights bodies have taken to provisions that protect access to courts rights and fair trial protections under other treaties is relevant to the task of interpreting article 16. But it also raises a more fundamental question—have developments in international law, and international human rights law in particular, left article 16 with any work to do at all?

Although the Universal Declaration of Human Rights, which includes rights to an effective remedy and to a fair hearing, was adopted before the 1951 Convention was drafted,[1] it was not supported by any binding legal instrument. The subsequent decades have seen the adoption and entry into force of several treaties of universal application incorporating fair trial guarantees, including the International Covenant on Civil and Political Rights (ICCPR),[2] the International Convention on the Elimination of All Forms of Racial Discrimination (ICERD),[3] the Convention on the Elimination of All Forms of Discrimination against Women (CEDAW),[4] the Convention on the Rights of the Child (CRC),[5] and the Convention on the Rights of Persons with Disabilities (CRPD),[6] amongst others.[7] Similar rights are included in regional human rights instruments adopted in this period, in some cases together with institutions in which claims under those instruments can be heard.[8]

---

[1] UNGA res 217 A(III) (adopted 10 Dec 1948) (UDHR), arts 8, 10.
[2] 999 UNTS 171 (adopted 16 Dec 1966, entered into force 23 Mar 1976) art 14.
[3] 660 UNTS 195 (adopted 7 Mar 1966, entered into force 4 Jan 1969) art 5(a).
[4] 1249 UNTS 13 (adopted 18 Dec 1979, entered into force 3 Sept 1981) art 15(2).
[5] 1577 UNTS 3 (adopted 20 Nov 1989, entered into force 2 Sept 1990) art 12(2).
[6] 2515 UNTS 3 (adopted 13 Dec 2006, entered into force 3 May 2008) art 13.
[7] See also generally Ian Brownlie and Guy S Goodwin-Gill (eds), *Brownlie's Documents on Human Rights* (6th edn, OUP 2010).
[8] See the African Charter on Human and People's Rights, 1520 UNTS 217 (adopted 27 June 1981, entered into force 21 Oct 1986) (Banjul Charter), art 7; American Convention on Human Rights, 1144 UNTS 123 (signed 22 Nov 1969, entered into force 18 July 1978) (American Convention), art 8; Arab Charter on Human Rights (22 May 2004, entered into force 15 Mar 2008) arts 12–13; Charter of Fundamental Rights of the European Union (2012/C 326/02) OJ C 326/391 (26 Oct 2012) (CFR), art 47; and, predating the 1951 Convention, the European Convention for the Protection of Human Rights and Fundamental Freedoms (originally adopted 1950, see now the text as amended by Protocols Nos. 11 and 14) (ECHR), art 6.

Access to Courts for Asylum Seekers and Refugees. Emma Dunlop, Oxford University Press. © Emma Dunlop, 2024.
DOI: 10.1093/oso/9780198885597.003.0005

As article 7(1) of the 1951 Convention makes clear, '[e]xcept where this Convention contains more favourable provisions, a Contracting State shall accord to refugees the same treatment as is accorded to aliens generally'.[9] If the protection afforded to individuals under international human rights law has reached a point which surpasses the protections afforded by article 16, that law, rather than the 1951 Convention, will be the primary source of rights.

Some scholars have expressly stated that article 16 has been subsumed by these developments. Schultz and Einarsen, for example, consider that article 16 is 'not as comprehensive as the human rights guarantee to the right to a fair hearing'.[10] Chetail takes a similar approach to article 16,[11] arguing more generally that international human rights law has displaced the 1951 Convention from the core of refugee protection to its margins.[12] Any analysis of State obligations in article 16 must therefore contend with whether those obligations have been subsumed by States' more general obligations under international human rights law.

To answer this question, the chapter undertakes a broad survey of access to courts provisions, both express and implied, in international human rights law, together with procedural or substantive rights broadly related to such access.[13] This analysis extends to procedural guarantees that relate to administrative proceedings under non- or quasi-judicial 'tribunals'. It begins with an analysis of relevant rights and obligations under 'universal' international conventions, specialised instruments, and regional treaties (Section 2). It then turns to a brief discussion of customary international law (Section 3) and general principles of law (Section 4), before concluding by examining an indicative selection of soft law instruments (Section 5). The scope of this exercise necessarily limits discussion of specific 'fair

---

[9] 1951 Convention, art 7(1). This provision 'enables the co-evolution of the refugee regime with aliens law and international human rights law': Achilles Skordas, 'Article 7' in Andreas Zimmermann (ed), *The 1951 Convention Relating to the Status of Refugees and its 1967 Protocol* (OUP 2011) 753.

[10] Jessica Schultz and Terje Einarsen, 'The Right to Refugee Status and the Internal Protection Alternative: What Does the Law Say?' in Bruce Burson and David James Cantor (eds), *Human Rights and the Refugee Definition: Comparative Legal Practice and Theory* (Brill Nijhoff 2016) 309.

[11] 'Article 16(1) of the Refugee Convention provides free access to domestic courts but says nothing about judicial proceedings and due process guarantees. While equal access to courts is inherent in the right to a fair trial, human rights law enriches and upgrades refugee law by granting a significant set of due process guarantees': Vincent Chetail, 'Moving towards an integrated approach of refugee law and human rights law' in Cathryn Costello, Michelle Foster and Jane McAdam (eds), *The Oxford Handbook of International Refugee Law* (OUP 2021) 218 (footnotes omitted).

[12] ibid 207. See also Vincent Chetail, 'Are Refugee Rights Human Rights? An Unorthodox Questioning of the Relations between Refugee Law and Human Rights Law' in Ruth Rubio-Marin (ed), *Human Rights and Immigration* (OUP 2014) 70.

[13] This analysis does not extend to discussion of international humanitarian law (IHL), though certain due process rights in this field are considered to have the force of customary international law. See the ICRC IHL database, rule 100 ('No one may be convicted or sentenced, except pursuant to a fair trial affording all essential judicial guarantees') and related practice. The summary to rule 100 notes: 'State practice establishes this rule as a norm of customary international law applicable in both international and non-international armed conflicts.': ICRC, 'IHL Database', 'Rule 100. Fair Trial Guarantees' available via <https://ihl-databases.icrc.org/customary-ihl/eng/docindex/v1_rul_rule100>; also ICRC, 'IHL Database', 'Practice Relating to Rule 100. Fair Trial Guarantees', available via <https://ihl-databases.icrc.org/customary-ihl/eng/docindex/v2_rul_rule100>.

trial' protections, such as those guaranteed in the criminal process. The chapter instead focuses on specific procedural rights most relevant to asylum seekers and refugees, including any protections that are applicable to the refugee status determination (RSD) process, both at the first instance and appeal stages. It aims to provide a comprehensive overview of current law on access to courts clauses and related protections, drawing on recent jurisprudence and guidance from human rights bodies. In this endeavour, the chapter builds on academic work in this area— particularly Cantor's study of procedural guarantees for asylum seekers across human rights instruments,[14] treaty commentaries,[15] and work focused more generally on access to justice and access to courts.[16]

The chapter concludes that international human rights instruments provide asylum seekers and refugees with an uneven patchwork of protection. While asylum seekers and refugees are generally entitled to benefit from 'fair trial' guarantees under international human rights law, judicial review of negative RSD decisions has been expressly excluded from the scope of two key treaty regimes— the universal ICCPR and the regional but broad-reaching ECHR, which has forty-six States parties. More robust protections can be found in other regional regimes and in specialised treaties designed to protect specific classes of people (for example minors or those living with a disability). Asylum seekers and refugees who fall within the scope of these instruments will therefore be entitled to more robust rights, though even here, some gaps remain. The gaps in protection identified are unlikely to be filled by customary international law or general principles of law. Recognition of rights as custom requires meeting a high bar, while general principles may ultimately prove a fragile basis on which to rely for protection.

2. International Human Rights Treaties

This section provides a survey of relevant rights under universal, specialised, and regional treaties. It covers the ICCPR (Section 2.1); the CRC and the CRPD, as specialised international human rights treaties providing rights to children and those living with a disability respectively (Section 2.2); and the ECHR, EU law, the Inter-American human rights system, the Banjul Charter, and the Arab Charter

---

[14] David James Cantor, 'Reframing Relationships: Revisiting the Procedural Standards for Refugee Status Determination in Light of Recent Human Rights Treaty Body Jurisprudence' (2015) 34 Refugee Survey Quarterly 79. Cantor compares international human rights law favourably with international refugee law, finding that that latter offers a 'relatively fragile legal basis for the elaboration of procedural standards': at 85.

[15] The exception, at the time of writing, is the Arab Charter on Human Rights.

[16] See eg Francesco Francioni (ed), *Access to Justice as a Human Right* (OUP 2007) and Nihal Jayawickrama, *The Judicial Application of Human Rights Law* (CUP 2002) ch 16.

on Human Rights, as regional human rights instruments (Section 2.3). It reaches three conclusions.

First, fair trial and due process protections exist across a range of international human rights treaties, although their phrasing, and how they have been interpreted, differs. The survey affirms Cantor's finding that an asylum seeker seeking review of a rejected protection claim would fall outside the scope of article 6 of the ECHR and article 14 of the ICCPR, but remain protected under the American Convention on Human Rights (American Convention) and the African Charter on Human and People's Rights (Banjul Charter).[17]

Second, the survey highlights trends in how human rights treaties are interpreted by judicial and non-judicial bodies. A concern to ensure the *effective* protection of rights, which may require States to make positive accommodations for individual claimants, is evident across several treaty regimes.

Finally, as a result of their age and institutional trappings, some treaties have been the subject of deeper, and more authoritative, interpretation than others. The ECHR and the American Convention have each been extensively analysed by their respective judicial interpreters. In contrast, the Arab Charter of Human Rights has received relatively little scrutiny. Other treaties are unconnected to a court, and, as a result, interpreting their terms relies largely on non-judicial bodies. While States remain the ultimate arbiters of the meaning of a treaty's text, non-binding interpretations by treaty bodies do 'play a significant role'.[18] This chapter does not ignore the rich interpretative work of the various commissions, but emphasises the need to examine their findings closely. Greater value should be afforded to documents that have been drafted with the input of States parties, at least as evidence of possible directions for progressive development of the law. Communications drafted by independent committees of experts should be assessed not as authoritative interpretations of treaty terms, but with an eye to their logic and persuasiveness.[19] This is not to deny Byrnes' point that 'States themselves accept that general comments and views have a certain level of authority and persuasiveness', and may 'invoke their output';[20] it is simply to note that States are able to make use of soft instruments in a way that the scholar may not, by virtue of their ultimate status as law-makers in the international community.

---

[17] See particularly Cantor, 'Reframing Relationships' (n 14) 94–96 (Banjul Charter); 99–104 (American Convention); 104–105. Cantor notes that ECtHR and HRC procedural guarantees can however be drawn from jurisprudence on risks of harm upon expulsion or arbitrariness in that context: at 104 and fn 191. He also discusses due process protections that the Inter-American Commission on Human Rights draws from the American Declaration of the Rights and Duties of Man: at 97–99.

[18] Andrew Byrnes, 'Kirby Lecture in International Law 2014: The Meaning of International Law: Government Monopoly, Expert Precinct, or the People's Law?' (2014) 32 Australian Year Book of International Law 11, 17.

[19] See ibid 23.

[20] ibid.

2.1 International Covenant on Civil and Political Rights (ICCPR)

2.1.1 Article 14 ICCPR

A right of access to courts is not expressly included in core international human rights treaties. However, the Human Rights Committee (HRC) has recognised that access to courts is an inherent element of article 14(1) of the ICCPR, which guarantees equality before courts and tribunals, as well as the right to 'a fair and public hearing by a competent, independent and impartial tribunal established by law' in the determination of a criminal charges, or of an individual's 'rights and obligations in a suit at law'.[21] Article 14 is complemented by article 16 ICCPR on the right to 'recognition everywhere as a person before the law'.

In its General Comment No. 32, the HRC notes that '[a]ccess to administration of justice must effectively be guaranteed in all such cases to ensure that no individual is deprived, in procedural terms, of his/her right to claim justice'.[22] This implied right is limited to first instance decisions and does not encompass the right to an appeal.[23] While there is no legal obligation to provide free legal assistance in non-criminal proceedings,[24] the HRC notes that it may be required 'in some cases', for example, where necessary to meet the requirements of article 14(1) and the right to an effective remedy.[25] Charging fees that would 'de facto prevent ... access to justice' may also be inconsistent with article 14(1).[26] These examples show the HRC's concern for 'effective' access, which is alive to practical matters that hinder parties' access to the courts.[27] Translation is not mentioned in the context of the implied right of access to courts, but the Committee does note that a free interpreter may be required 'in exceptional cases' to ensure equality of arms.[28] While article 14 is not included in the list of non-derogable rights enumerated in article 4(2), the HRC considers that deviation from 'fundamental principles of fair trial' would violate a *jus cogens* norm and cannot be justified under the Convention.[29] In

---

[21] HRC, 'General Comment No. 32: Article 14 Right to Equality before courts and tribunals and to a fair trial', CCPR/C/GC/32 (23 Aug 2007), para 9; see also paras 10–12; 17–18 (HRC, General Comment No. 32). As discussed in Section 2.3.1.1, the ECtHR has also recognised an implied right of access to courts under article 6 of the ECHR.

[22] ibid para 9.

[23] ibid para 12. An appeal is however guaranteed for those convicted of a crime: see ICCPR, art 14(5) and ibid paras 45–51.

[24] For rights in criminal proceedings, see ICCPR, art 14(d) (which states that an individual is entitled to 'have legal assistance assigned to him, in any case where the interests of justice so require'); HRC, General Comment No. 32 (n 21) para 38.

[25] ibid para 10.

[26] ibid para 11.

[27] The Committee also notes that the systematic frustration of an individual's attempts to access 'the competent courts or tribunals' may be inconsistent with the right of equality before the courts and tribunals in article 14(1): ibid para 9 (footnotes omitted).

[28] ibid para 13. See also, in the criminal context, ICCPR art 14(3)(f); HRC, General Comment No. 32 (n 21) para 40.

[29] HRC, 'General Comment No. 29: State of Emergency (Article 4)', CCPR/C/21/Rev.1/Add.11 (32 August 2001) para 11. Clooney and Webb identify 13 component rights to the right to a fair trial, based

addition, the HRC considers that fair trial guarantees 'may never be made subject to measures of derogation that would circumvent the protection of nonderogable rights'.[30]

The HRC considers that the right of access to courts inherent in article 14 extends to all individuals within a State's territory, regardless of 'nationality' or 'status', and expressly cites asylum seekers and refugees.[31] The ICCPR therefore offers broad protection of access to the courts to refugees and asylum seekers across a range of civil and criminal matters. Rights under article 14 are, however, limited to those cases which are either criminal or fall within the parameters of a 'suit at law'. The HRC does not consider that 'suit of law' covers the judicial review of negative asylum decisions, although this conclusion seems out of step with its broader jurisprudence on the scope of 'suit of law',[32] which has been characterised as lacking 'clear guidance'.[33]

In the 1986 decision of *YL v Canada*, the HRC noted that the concept of a 'suit of law' was:

> based on the nature of the right in question rather than on the status of one of the parties (governmental, parastatal or autonomous statutory entities), or else on the particular forum in which individual legal systems may provide that the right in question is to be adjudicated upon.[34]

This interpretation has been applied across a range of decisions and is accepted in General Comment No. 32.[35] As outlined there, and in Joseph and Castan's survey of the jurisprudence,[36] 'suit at law' is considered to cover judicial proceedings relating to private law matters, as well as 'equivalent notions in the area of administrative law'. These include, amongst others, 'the determination of social security benefits',[37] and 'procedures regarding the use of public land or the taking of private property'.[38] It may, 'in addition', 'cover other procedures which ... must be assessed

---

on article 14 ICCPR: see Amal Clooney and Philippa Webb, *The Right to a Fair Trial in International Law* (OUP 2020) 7–8.

[30] HRC, General Comment No. 32 (n 21) para 6.
[31] ibid para 9. See also ICCPR, art 2(1).
[32] A conclusion also reached by Hathaway: James C Hathaway, *The Rights of Refugees under International Law* (2nd edn, CUP 2021) 804.
[33] Sarah Joseph and Melissa Castan, *The International Covenant on Civil and Political Rights: Cases, Materials and Commentary* (3rd edn, OUP 2013) 439.
[34] *YL v Canada*, Comm no 112/1981 (8 Apr 1986), para 9.2.
[35] See HRC, General Comment No. 32 (n 21) para 16.
[36] ibid; Joseph and Castan (n 33) 434–39.
[37] HRC, General Comment No. 32 (n 21) para 16, citing *Garcia Pons v Spain*, Comm no 454/1991, CCPR/C/55/D/454/1991 (8 Nov 1995) para 9.3. See also Joseph and Castan (n 33) 437.
[38] HRC, General Comment No. 32 (n 21) para 16, citing, in relation to the use of public land, *Äärelä and Näkkäläjärvi v Finland*, Comm no 779/1997, CCPR/C/73/D/779/1997 (24 Oct 2001) paras 7.2–7.4. See also, on this communication, Joseph and Castan (n 33) 445–47.

on a case by case basis in the light of the nature of the right in question.[39] By analogy, it might be assumed that the judicial review of an administrative decision to deny refugee status would engage the protections under article 14(1) (if such review is available under a State Party's municipal legal system).[40] In a line of cases, however, the HRC has characterised the review of a negative RSD decision claims as 'deportation' decisions that are entitled only to the benefit of the 'expulsion' protections set out in article 13.[41]

Zundel v Canada, the first of these cases, concerned an application submitted by a Holocaust denier who had claimed asylum in Canada and was ultimately deported on national security grounds.[42] The HRC found that:

> proceedings relating to an alien's expulsion, the guarantees of which are governed by article 13 of the Covenant, do not also fall within the ambit of a determination of 'rights and obligations in a suit at law', within the meaning of [article 14(1)].[43]

In reaching this conclusion, it recalled its general position that the concept of a suit at law is 'based on the nature of the right in question.'[44] It characterised the right that the author sought to vindicate as a right 'to continue residing in the State party's territory.'[45]

Since *Zundel*, the HRC has pinpointed the nature of the 'rights' sought to be vindicated by asylum seekers with greater specificity, and in a manner which suggests that the essence of the right is less focused on 'expulsion' than on recognition as refugees and the rights that status entails.[46] Despite this, it has maintained its rigid view that such cases are entitled only to the expulsion guarantees in article 13 of the ICCPR. In *PK v Canada,* the HRC considered a complaint by a Pakistani woman whose application for asylum was denied by the Immigration and Refugee Board on credibility grounds.[47] Leave to appeal to the Federal Court was also denied.[48] The HRC characterised the proceedings as relating to 'the author's right to receive protection in the State party's territory.'[49] However, without analysing the nature of

---

[39] HRC, General Comment No. 32 (n 21) para 16.
[40] Consider for example the proposed test for whether public law rights are engaged by article 14(1) in Joseph and Castan (n 33) 439 (footnotes omitted).
[41] This move is discussed in Cantor, 'Reframing Relationships' (n 14) 87–89 and in Hathaway, *Rights* (2nd edn) (n 32) 801–805, who identifies cases that suggest a different view prior to the HRC's General Comment No. 32.
[42] *Zundel v Canada*, Comm no 1341/2005, CCPR/C/89/D/1341/2005 (20 Mar 2007), paras 2.7–2.14. See also Hathaway, *Rights* (2nd edn) (n 32) 803.
[43] *Zundel v Canada* (n 42) para 6.8.
[44] ibid.
[45] ibid.
[46] These decisions are noted in Cantor, 'Reframing Relationships' (n 14) 87, n 59 and in Hathaway, *Rights* (2nd edn) (n 32) 804.
[47] *PK v Canada*, Comm no 1234/2003 (decided 20 Mar 2007) para 2.2. This decision was adopted on the same date as *Zundel v Canada*.
[48] ibid para 2.3. See also Joseph and Castan (n 33) 420.
[49] ibid para 7.5.

this right, it immediately recalled the exclusion of 'proceedings relating to an alien's expulsion' from 'suit at law' under article 14(1), and concluded that 'the deportation proceedings of the author' were beyond the scope of article 14(1).[50] A similar move was made in *Chadzjian v Netherlands*, where the Committee considered the right in question to be 'the author's right to receive protection for herself and her children in the State party's territory.'[51] Following *PK v Canada*, the HRC then reaffirmed that 'proceedings relating to aliens' expulsion, the guarantees in regard to which are governed by article 13 of the Covenant, do not fall within the ambit of a determination of rights and obligations in a suit at law"', and duly found the article 14 claim to be inadmissible.[52] In *X v Denmark*, the HRC did not even identify a right at issue, simply reiterating that proceedings relating to the expulsion of aliens are not covered by article 14(1).[53]

As has been recognised elsewhere,[54] the HRC's reasoning in these cases is problematic. The 'right to receive protection' as a refugee is, in essence, the right to an internationally recognised protected status. This status, in turn, obliges States to guarantee a host of other rights, depending on the refugee's level of connection to the State, including rights of association,[55] the right to the most favourable treatment accorded to foreign national in relation to wage-earning employment,[56] and the right of national treatment with respect to social security.[57] As already noted, the HRC has recognised a 'right to social security' as engaging article 14(1).[58] Decisions on citizenship applications are also considered to constitute a 'suit at law', with the Committee noting that 'whenever ... a judicial body is entrusted with the review of an administrative decision on such an application, it must respect the guarantees of a fair hearing [in article 14(1)]'.[59] In contrast, article 13 is applicable to 'all procedures aimed at the obligatory departure of an alien, whether described in national law as expulsion or otherwise'.[60] The finding that the right to protection can be subsumed into a simple question of expulsion[61] is a reductive approach

---

[50] ibid.
[51] *Arusjak Chadzjian v Netherlands*, Comm no 1494/2006, CCPR/C/93/D/1494/2006 (22 July 2008), para 8.4.
[52] ibid. See, to similar effect, *Kaur v Canada*, Comm no 1455/2006, CCPR/C/94/D/1455/2006 (30 Oct 2008) para 7.5.
[53] *X v Denmark*, Comm no 2007/2010, CCPR/C/110/D/2007/2010 (26 Mar 2014), para 8.5.
[54] See Hathaway, *Rights* (2nd edn) (n 32) 804–805; Violeta Moreno-Lax, *Accessing Asylum in Europe: Extraterritorial Border Controls and Refugee Rights under EU Law* (OUP 2017) 404, considering the HRC's position to be 'unsustainable'.
[55] 1951 Convention, art 15 (available to refugees 'lawfully staying').
[56] ibid art 17 (available to refugees 'lawfully staying').
[57] ibid art 24 (available to refugees 'lawfully staying').
[58] See n 37.
[59] *Gonzales v Guyana*, Comm no 1246/2004, CCPR/C/98/D/1246/2004 (25 Mar 2010) para 13.4 (footnotes omitted).
[60] HRC, General Comment No. 15, 'The Position of Aliens Under the Covenant' HRI/GEN/1/Rev.1 at 18 (1986) para 9.
[61] A point highlighted by Cantor in 'Reframing Relationships' (n 14) 89.

which fails to recognise true nature of RSD and the full gamut of rights which are contingent on the grant of that status.[62]

2.1.2 Article 13 ICCPR

It could be argued that critique of the interpretation of article 14 ICCPR is merely academic, since asylum seekers will in any event benefit from the protection provided by article 13. Article 13 provides that a lawfully present alien may only be expelled from a State party 'in pursuance of a decision reached in accordance with law', and is also entitled, absent 'compelling reasons of national security':

> to submit the reasons against his expulsion and to have his case reviewed by, and be represented for the purpose before, the competent authority or a person or persons especially designated by the competent authority.

The HRC's General Comments[63] and jurisprudence show that the protection afforded by article 13 is less robust than that in article 14,[64] although there may be some movement towards recognition of a stronger right to legal assistance under the former article.

Article 13 is essentially a procedural guarantee that States will carry out expulsion decisions in line with their domestic law.[65] Critically, its protections are only available to an alien who is 'lawfully' present in a State party, which has been interpreted by the HRC as requiring an examination of domestic law.[66] A State that denied an asylum seeker the benefit of article 13 on the basis that he or she was illegally present could, perhaps, find itself in breach of the prohibition on illegal penalties in article 31 of the 1951 Convention,[67] although this may be a complicated argument to mount in the individual case. Its application therefore raises immediate problems for asylum seekers who enter a State's territory irregularly. Article 13 is not included in the list of non-derogable rights enumerated in article 4(2).

As a procedural guarantee, article 13 requires that an individual decision be taken in each case, precluding mass expulsions.[68] In addition, General Comment

---

[62] On this point see also Hathaway, *Rights* (n 32) 805.

[63] HRC, General Comment No. 15 (n 60); HRC, General Comment No. 32 (n 21).

[64] See also Joseph and Castan (n 33) 420 (noting that Article 14 provides 'far more comprehensive' rights).

[65] HRC, General Comment No. 15 (n 60) para 10 (observing that article 13 'regulates only the procedure and not the substantive grounds for expulsion'), though see Joseph and Castan (n 33) 418, 429. See also *Anudo Ochieng Anudo v Tanzania* (African Court on Human and Peoples' Rights, Judgment, 22 Mar 2018) para 101 (considering that article 13 has the objective of 'protect[ing] a foreigner from any form of arbitrary expulsion by providing him with legal guarantees').

[66] HRC, General Comment No. 15 (n 60) para 9. See also *Maroufidou v Sweden*, Comm no 58/1979 (1984), paras 9.3–10.1; Joseph and Castan (n 33) 422. General Comment No. 15 notes, however, that if 'the legality of an alien's entry or stay is in dispute, any decision on this point leading to his expulsion or deportation ought to be taken in accordance with article 13': at para 15.

[67] See discussion of art 31 in Chapter 6, Section 2.2.1.

[68] HRC, General Comment No. 15 (n 60) para 10; see also Joseph and Castan (n 33) 419.

No. 15 notes that '[a]n alien must be given full facilities for pursuing his remedy against expulsion so that this right will in all the circumstances of his case be an effective one'.[69] Joseph and Castan consider that any review must have suspensive effect, since reviews conducted *in absentia* would not meet this standard.[70]

The implied right of access to courts or tribunals does not apply under article 13 of the ICCPR.[71] However, certain guarantees in article 14(1) will apply if a State arranges its affairs such that expulsion and deportation hearings are conducted before judicial bodies, including 'the guarantee of equality of all persons before the courts ... and the principles of impartiality, fairness and equality of arms'.[72]

A series of cases against Denmark shed some light on the parameters of article 13 in the asylum context. Under Denmark's RSD system, asylum decisions are made at first instance by the Danish Immigration Service and can be appealed to the Refugee Appeal Board, characterised as an 'independent and quasi-judicial body'.[73] The decision of the Board is final and cannot be appealed on its merits in domestic courts.[74] Under the Danish Constitution an asylum seeker may, however, seek judicial review on points of law.[75] The Committee has consistently found challenges to this system under article 13 to be inadmissible.[76] In *MM v Denmark*, the Committee recalled that article 13 'offers asylum seekers some of the protection afforded under article 14 of the Covenant, but not the right of appeal to judicial bodies'.[77] In that case, the author also claimed a violation of article 26 of the ICCPR (equality before the law and non-discrimination), noting that in Denmark, 'decisions of a great number of administrative boards, which have the same composition as the Refugee Appeals Board, can be appealed before the ordinary courts'.[78]

---

[69] HRC, General Comment No. 15 (n 60) para 10.

[70] Joseph and Castan (n 33) 423.

[71] HRC, General Comment No. 32 (n 21) para 17. See also *MN v Denmark*, Comm no 2458/2014, CCPR/C/133/D/2458/2014 (28 January 2022), para 8.4; *Omo-Amenaghawon v Denmark*, Comm no 2288/2013, CCPR/C/114/D/2288/2013 (23 July 2015), para 6.4.

[72] ibid para 62.

[73] See, eg, Denmark's observations set out in *Omo-Amenaghawon v Denmark* (n 71) para 4.7, also noting that the Board is 'considered a court within the meaning of article 39 of the [2005 Procedures Directive]'. The author in *Omo-Amenaghawon* challenged this system primarily on article 14 grounds; the Committee declared this claim inadmissible: see para 6.4. In *M.S. aka M.H.A.D v Denmark*, Comm no 2601/2015, CCPR/C/120/D/2601/2015 (27 July 2017), Denmark noted that the Board became the responsibility of the Ministry of Immigration, Integration and Housing in June 2015, but that the independence of its Members was nonetheless assured under s 53(1) of the Aliens Act: at para 6.5.

[74] For a summary of the system, see ibid paras 4.6–4.8. Denmark's observations elsewhere note that 'the Board's assessment of evidence is not subject to review': *MS aka MHAD v Denmark* (n 73) para 6.4.

[75] ibid para 4.7.

[76] See, eg, *SZ v Denmark*, Comm no 2625/2015, CCPR/C/120/D/2625/2015 (28 July 2016) para 7.12; *HA v Denmark*, Comm no 2328/2014, CCPR/C/123/D/2328/2014 (9 July 2018) para 8.5; *SAH v Denmark*, Comm no 2419/2014, CCPR/C/121/D/2419/2014 (8 Nov 2017) para 10.5.

[77] *MM v Denmark*, Comm no 2345/2014, CCPR/C/125/D/2345/2014 (14 Mar 2019) para 7.5 and citations therein. See also *SF v Denmark*, Comm no 2494/2014, CCPR/C/125/D/2494/2014 (14 Mar 2019) para 7.4.

[78] *MM v Denmark* (n 77) para 3.4. See also para 5.4 and the State Party's response, in para 4.20–4.21. The author initially claimed that his rights under article 14 and article 26 (non-discrimination) had been violated, but later amended his claim to rely on article 13 in place of article 14: ibid para 3.6. See also *SF*

In finding the claim to be insufficiently substantiated,[79] the HRC implicitly rejected the author's suggested comparison between asylum seekers and nationals (in accordance with the argument that asylum claims, unlike most other administrative claims, could not be reviewed by the courts). The Committee instead recalled Denmark's statement that the author 'had been treated no differently than any other person applying for asylum'. This suggests that the Committee considers the appropriate comparator for the purposes of non-discrimination as 'discrimination as between asylum seekers', rather than 'discrimination as between asylum seekers and other members of society'. This aligns with the statement in General Comment No. 15 that discrimination 'between different categories of aliens' is prohibited when applying article 13.[80]

Nowak interprets article 13 as providing separate rights to a 'hearing' (which need not be in person) and an 'appeal' (which need not be before judicial authority).[81] This position gains some support from General Comment No. 15, which refers to 'appeal against expulsion and the entitlement to review by a competent authority' under article 13.[82] However, Joseph and Castan note that it is 'not ... clear whether this appeal/review relates to consideration of the alien's arguments against expulsion, or whether the words refer to a *subsequent* review after an initial decision has taken those arguments into account'.[83] In *MP v Denmark*, the author argued that article 13 guaranteed a 'two stage expulsion procedure, with one stage relating to the expulsion itself and the other to the review of the order'.[84] In that case, the author's initial asylum application had, in fact, been examined and rejected by the Danish Immigration Service and the Refugee Appeal Board. The author challenged the Board's subsequent refusals to reopen her case after she admitted to having lied in her initial application under pressure from her husband.[85] The Committee did not clearly state whether a two-stage procedure is required under article 13.[86] It remains to be seen whether the HRC would find a single-stage procedure to be inconsistent with article 13.[87] Its 2015

---

v Denmark (n 77) paras 5.4, 7.4, in which the author argued that under s 63 of the Danish Constitution, 'all administrative decisions, including Board decisions, can be appealed before the courts'; and *SZ v Denmark* (n 76) para 3.5.

[79] *MM v Denmark* (n 77) para 7.6. See also *SF v Denmark* (n 77) para 7.4; *SZ v Denmark* (n 76) para 7.11.

[80] HRC, General Comment No. 15 (n 60) para 10.

[81] Manfred Nowak, *U.N. Covenant on Civil and Political Rights: CCPR Commentary* (NP Engel 1993) 228–31, and communications cited therein.

[82] HRC, General Comment No. 15 (n 60) para 10.

[83] Joseph and Castan (n 33) 423–24.

[84] *MP v Denmark*, Comm no 2643/2015, CCPR/C/121/D/2802/2016 (9 Nov 2017) para 5.4.

[85] See ibid paras 2.9–2.11 and 5.3–5.5 (author); and 4.4–4.5, 6.4–6.9 (State party observations).

[86] ibid para 7.4.

[87] See, eg, the situation of excluded fast-track applicants under Part 7AA of the Australian Migration Act 1958, who are denied access to merits review. Judicial review remains available.

Concluding Observations on Canada suggest that a system that lacked any appeal on the merits, but allowed judicial review, could be deemed inconsistent with article 13.[88]

Article 13 does entitle an alien to 'representation' before a competent authority when submitting reasons against expulsion (except in cases in which 'compelling reasons of national security' can be invoked).[89] Nowak's view was that this was not an entitlement to '*legal* counsel', although legal representation could be arranged at an individual's own cost.[90] There is, however, some evidence that stronger protection is afforded in the context of asylum applications. The Committee has recommended access to 'fair and efficient refugee status determination procedures'.[91] In its 2019 Concluding Observations on Estonia, the HRC raised concerns about limited access to free legal counselling or assistance when asylum decisions were made at the border and called on Estonia to provide free legal aid in '*suitable cases*'.[92] Commenting on South Africa, it used a different formulation, calling on the State to 'facilitate access to documentation and fair procedures for asylum seekers, including translation services and, *where the interests of justice so require*, access to legal representation'.[93] The HRC's 2022 Concluding Observations on Ukraine call for free legal aid and translation services to be provided 'at the border'.[94] Concluding observations on Greece and Israel are more definitive, finding that asylum seekers should have access to counsel and an interpreter 'from the outset of the [RSD] procedure' (in the case of Greece) and access to free legal aid 'throughout asylum procedures' (in the case of Israel).[95] And in its observations on Mexico in December 2019, the Committee recommended that the State Party

---

[88] See HRC, 'Concluding observations on the sixth periodic report of Canada', CCPR/C/CAN/CO/6 (13 Aug 2015) para 12 (noting concern that individuals who are nationals of Designated Countries of Origin cannot appeal a rejected refugee claim before the Refugee Appeal Division and are limited to judicial review).

[89] For elaboration and critique, see Joseph and Castan (n 33) 424–28.

[90] Nowak (n 81) 231.

[91] HRC, 'Concluding observations on the sixth periodic report of Hungary', CCPR/C/HUN/CO/6 (9 May 2018) para 48; HRC, 'Concluding observations on the sixth periodic report of Australia', CCPR/C/AUS/CO/6 (1 Dec 2017) para 34.

[92] See HRC, 'Concluding observations on the fourth periodic report of Estonia', CCPR/C/EST/CO/4 (18 Apr 2019) paras 27–28 (emphasis added). The HRC notes that its concerns relate to arts 2, 6, 7, and 13: ibid. Compare however the phrasing in the Concluding Observations on South Africa, referring to access to legal representation 'where the interests of justice so require': HRC, 'Concluding observations on the initial report of South Africa', CCPR/C/ZAF/CO/1 (27 Apr 2016) paras 34–35.

[93] HRC, 'South Africa' (n 92) para 35. The HRC notes that its concerns relate to arts 6, 7, and 13: para 34. See also HRC, 'Concluding observations on the fourth periodic report of Bulgaria' CCPR/C/BGR/CO/4 (15 November 2018) para 30(d) (recommending that 'asylum seekers and migrants have access to qualified legal aid when the interests of justice so require').

[94] HRC, 'Concluding observations on the eighth periodic report of Ukraine', CCPR/C/UKR/CO/8 (9 February 2022), para 38(b).

[95] HRC, 'Concluding observations on the second periodic report of Greece', CCPR/C/GRC/CO/2 (3 Dec 2015) para 30 (the HRC notes that its concerns relate to arts 6–7 and 13: para 29); HRC, 'Concluding observations on the fifth periodic report of Israel', CCPR/C/ISR/CO/5 (5 May 2022), para 41 (likewise referring to concerns under both arts 6–7 and 13: para 40).

should '[e]nsure that asylum seekers have access to legal aid and the right to initiate appeal proceedings'.[96]

It is not clear in these observations whether the HRC considers any obligation to provide legal aid to derive from article 13 or from the *non-refoulement* obligations inherent in articles 6 and 7 of the ICCPR.[97] In earlier observations, the Committee based its recommendations solely on article 13, noting for example in its 2009 Concluding Observations on Switzerland that '[t]he State party should review its legislation in order to grant free legal assistance to asylum-seekers during all asylum procedures, whether ordinary or extraordinary'.[98] The weight of these statements is weakened first by the HRC's practice of presenting the recommendations in its observations in non-obligatory terms ('The State Party should . . . '), and the quite significant inconsistencies in formulation across reports. They nonetheless suggest that there may be some movement towards strengthening the right of representation under article 13, at least in those cases in which it is required for the applicant to effectively fulfil his or her rights under that article. This development would imbue certain cases under article 13 with more robust rights than are afforded to civil cases under article 14. The Committee recalls in its General Comment No. 32 that civil cases lack the guarantees of legal assistance available in criminal cases under ICCPR article 14(3)(b), but 'encourages' States 'to provide free legal aid in other cases, for individuals who do not have sufficient means to pay for it'.[99]

To some commentators, the right to an effective remedy under article 2(3) provides substitute protection to a failed asylum seeker.[100] Applied in combination with articles 6 and 7 of the ICCPR, this clause bolsters the protection available to asylum seekers by preventing their deportation or expulsion to a State where they are at risk of death, torture, or cruel, inhuman or degrading treatment, or punishment.[101] Cantor notes that the HRC 'clearly views any expulsion that may expose an alien to Article 7 (or Article 6) ICCPR harm in the destination country as requiring

---

[96] HRC, 'Concluding observations on the sixth periodic report of Mexico', CCPR/C/MEX/CO/6 (4 Dec 2019), para 33(e).

[97] In HRC, *AB and PD v Poland*, Comm no 3017/2017, CCPR/C/135/D/3017/2017 (3 February 2023), the Committee referred to failure to provide access to legal assistance in the context of a violation of article 7 in conjunction with article 2(3), but not in the context of a violation of article 13.

[98] HRC, 'Concluding observations of the Human Rights Committee', CCPR/C/CHE/CO/3 (3 Nov 2009) para 18, cited in Joseph and Castan (n 33) 424.

[99] HRC, General Comment No. 32 (n 21) para 10.

[100] See Cantor (n 14) 89; Vincent Chetail, 'The Transnational Movement of Persons under General International Law—Mapping the Customary Law Foundations of International Migration Law' in Vincent Chetail and Céline Bauloz (eds), *Research Handbook on International Law and Migration* (Edward Elgar 2014) 57–58; Moreno-Lax (n 54) 404–405.

[101] Joseph and Castan (n 33) 421 (referring to article 7 only); Cantor, 'Reframing Relationships' (n 14) 87. Cantor also infers certain 'procedural parameters' from the Committee's jurisprudence and Concluding Observations, noting that its views also suggest that article 2(3) ICCPR may oblige States to guarantee asylum seekers the right to 'appeal first-instance decisions to an independent body': at 87–88.

proper evaluation by the expelling State'.[102] The Denmark Communications show some examples of this approach.[103] The protection against deportation offered by the implicit *non-refoulement* obligations in these articles is, however, a thin protection. It guarantees asylum seekers none of the substantive rights to which they would be entitled under the 1951 Convention if their claim to refugee status were accepted. This remedy must therefore be seen as a partial solution which does not guarantee an asylum seeker who has a valid claim to refugee status the full civil status to which he or she is entitled.[104]

2.2 Specialised International Human Rights Treaties

Treaties that protect specific groups in society reaffirm certain guarantees set out in the ICCPR, such as the right to equality before courts and tribunals.[105] The CRC and the CRPD, discussed in Parts 2.2.1 and 2.2.2, supplement these guarantees with additional protections.[106] These treaties therefore bolster the rights of asylum seekers who are children or who live with a disability.

2.2.1 Convention on the Rights of the Child

The CRC provides specific guarantees to children—and asylum seeker and refugee children in particular—that supplement rights set out in the 1951 Refugee Convention and in other international human rights treaties. This is significant given that UNHCR estimates in its 2021 Global Trends report that children constitute around 41 per cent of those forcibly displaced.[107]

Article 22(1) requires States to take 'appropriate measures' to ensure that a child asylum seeker or refugee receives 'appropriate protection and humanitarian assistance in the enjoyment of applicable rights' under the CRC and any other international human rights treaties. Pobjoy argues that this provision:

> extends beyond simply guaranteeing beneficiaries of article 22(1) enjoyment of 'applicable rights' on a non-discriminatory basis, but imposes a further requirement on states to take into account any additional protection and humanitarian assistance that a refugee child or child seeking refugee protection may, on account

---

[102] Cantor, 87 (footnotes omitted). Though he considers it as yet unclear whether the HRC's RSD standards derive from article 13 or from the combined effect the right to an effective remedy in article 2(3) and the *non-refoulement* protections implicit in articles 6–7: at 89.

[103] See, eg, *KH v Denmark*, Comm no 2423/2014, CCPR/C/123/D/2423/2014 (16 July 2018) para 9; *MS aka MHAD v Denmark* (n 73) para 9.3; *Omo-Amenaghawon v Denmark* (n 71) para 8.

[104] A point made by Cantor: 'Reframing Relationships' (n 14) 104–105.

[105] CEDAW, art 15(2); ICERD, art 5(a); CRPD, art 12.

[106] Children are also protected of course by article 14(1) ICCPR.

[107] UNHCR, *Global Trends: Forced Displacement in 2021* (UNHCR 2022) 3.

of their distinct vulnerabilities and development needs, require in order to *effectively enjoy those rights.*[108]

A key provision relevant to judicial and administrative proceedings is article 12(2), which guarantees a child 'the opportunity to be heard in any judicial and administrative proceedings affecting the child, either directly, or through a representative or an appropriate body, in a manner consistent with the procedural rules of national law'.[109] In line with the CRC's inclusive approach to the rights of asylum seekers, the Committee on the Rights of the Child has affirmed that article 12 is applicable to asylum seekers and refugees,[110] including in administrative proceedings that relate to 'asylum requests from unaccompanied children'.[111] It notes:

[c]hildren who come to a country following their parents in search of work or as refugees are in a particularly vulnerable situation. For this reason it is urgent to fully implement their right to express their views on all aspects of the immigration and asylum proceedings.... In the case of an asylum claim, the child must additionally have the opportunity to present her or his reasons leading to the asylum claim.[112]

The benefit of article 12 applies to a child 'who is capable of forming his or her own views'.[113] The Committee on the Rights of the Child considers that this 'imposes no age limit' and discourages States from doing so in law or practice. States should presume that a child has such capacity; a child is not required to prove it.[114] In *YB and NS v Belgium*, the Committee found a violation of article 12 in relation to a decision regarding a five-year old child, noting that the child was, at that age, 'perfectly capable of forming views of her own'.[115]

Article 12 covers the right to be heard in both administrative and judicial proceedings.[116] It does not guarantee a child a judicial or administrative 'hearing',

---

[108] Jason M Pobjoy, 'Article 22. Refugee Children' in John Tobin (ed), *The UN Convention on the Rights of the Child: A Commentary* (OUP 2019) 824 (emphasis added).

[109] CRC, article 12(2). See further Laura Lundy, John Tobin, and Aisling Parkes, 'Article 12: The Right to Respect for the Views of the Child' in John Tobin (ed), *The UN Convention on the Rights of the Child: A Commentary* (OUP 2019) 419–32.

[110] Committee on the Rights of the Child, 'General Comment No. 12 (2009): The right of the child to be heard', CRC/C/GC/12 (20 July 2009) para 32.

[111] ibid para 67. The provision has also been applied more generally to guarantee a child the right to be heard in relation to residency permit proceedings: see *YB and NS v Belgium*, Comm no 12/2017, CRC/C/79/D/12/2017 (27 Sept 2018), para 8.8. See also UNHCR, 'Guidelines on International Protection: Child Asylum Claims under Articles 1A(2) and 1(F) of the 1951 Convention and/or the 1967 Protocol relating to the Status of Refugees', HCR/GIP/09/08 (22 Dec 2009) para 8 (UNHCR, 'Guidelines on Child Asylum Claims').

[112] 'General Comment No. 12' (n 110) para 123.

[113] CRC, art 12(1).

[114] ibid paras 20–21.

[115] *YB and NS v Belgium* (n 111) para 8.8.

[116] See 'General Comment No. 12' (n 110) paras 50–67; Jason M Pobjoy, *The Child in International Refugee Law* (OUP 2017) 59.

but rather the right to *be* heard in the course of any administrative or judicial procedures afoot. In criminal matters, it applies to 'all stages of the process, starting from the moment of contact'.[117] The right to be heard is engaged both in those proceedings commenced by a child, and those in which a child is a third party but nonetheless affected by the outcome.[118] There is no suggestion in article 12 or the Committee's General Comment that a child's intervention need be expressed orally, nor in the presence of the decision maker. To the contrary, article 12(2) makes it clear that a child may be heard 'through a representative or an appropriate body', while General Comment No. 12 notes that the preferred format is not to have a child express his or her views in open court but in a context which is 'enabling and encouraging'.[119] The child may also express his or her views, for example, to a teacher, social worker, or caregiver involved in the matter at issue, an institutional decision-maker, or a specialist.[120] 'Due weight' must, however, be given to the child's views, in accordance with his or her 'age and maturity'.[121]

In its General Comment on article 12 and its Communications, the Committee sets out several practical guarantees necessary to make the right in article 12(2) effective. These requirements include, first, that a State provide due process in the initial assessment of whether a young person is in fact a 'child' for the purposes of the CRC; second, that a State take measures to facilitate a child's expression of views; and third, that remedies are provided if a child's right to be heard is not upheld. Finally, specific rights are available to children depending on the nature of the proceedings (for example, detained children or those accused of a crime). These guarantees are discussed in turn.

First, the Committee has consistently stated that since determining the age of a young person is critical to engaging his or her rights under the CRC, it is 'imperative that there be due process to determine a person's age, as well as the opportunity to challenge the outcome through an appeals process'.[122] Unaccompanied young persons who claim to be minors are entitled to be provided with a representative

[117] See Committee on the Rights of the Child, 'General Comment No. 24 (2019) on children's rights in the child justice system' CRC/C/GC/24 (18 Sept 2019) para 45.

[118] 'General Comment No. 12' (n 110) para 33.

[119] ibid para 42. See also para 23 (on the need to ensure that the environment in which the child expresses his or her views is one in which the child feels 'respected and secure'). See further Lundy, Tobin and Parkes (n 109) 424–27; 'General Comment No. 24' (n 117) para 67.

[120] ibid. See also para 110.

[121] CRC, art 12(1). Lundy, Tobin and Parkes therefore consider that 'children's views are not necessarily determinative in matters affecting them': (n 109) 403.

[122] Committee on the Rights of the Child, *RYS v Spain*, Comm no 76/2019, CRC/C/86/D/76/2019 (4 Feb 2021); see also *RK v Spain*, Comm no 27/2017, CRC/C/82/D/27/2017 (18 Sept 2019) para 9.3; *MT v Spain*, Comm no 17/2017, CRC/C/82/D/17/2017 (18 Sept 2019) para 13.3; Committee on the Rights of the Child, *AL v Spain*, Comm no 16/2017, CRC/C/81/D/16/2017 (31 May 2019), para 12.3; Committee on the Rights of the Child, *JAB v Spain*, Comm no 22/2017, CRC/C/81/D/22/2017 (31 May 2019), para 13.3; *NBF v Spain*, Comm no 11/2017, CRC/C/79/D/11/2017 (27 Sept 2018) para 12.3.

during the age assessment process, as 'an essential guarantee of respect for their best interests and their right to be heard'.[123] A failure to provide such representation constitutes a breach of articles 3 and 12 of the CRC, and delayed provision of representation could result in 'substantial injustice'.[124]

Second, the requirement that States 'assure' that a child who meets the conditions of article 12 can express his or her views requires that States 'undertake *appropriate* measures to fully implement this right for all children'.[125] General Comment No. 12 sets out a series of requirements for the 'effective, ethical and meaningful' implementation of article 12. These cover the need for certain pre-requisites to the exercise of the right, for example the provision of information on a child's right to be heard; the facilitation of participation by 'marginalized children' and those 'experiencing difficulties in making their views heard'; and the adaptation of 'environments and working methods' to a child's capacity.[126] These requirements must be tailored to the specific needs of individual children, taking into account language, disability, age, and other factors. The proceedings themselves are required to be 'accessible and child-appropriate'.[127]

In asylum cases, children are to receive information on their entitlements in their own language, and to the appointment of a guardian or advisor without charge.[128] A 2017 Joint General Comment of the Committee suggests that additional rights may be applicable in the context of international migration, referring, for example, to children's rights to legal assistance at all stages of proceedings, 'free legal aid', and appeal to 'a higher court or independent authority, with suspensive effect'.[129] However, the language of the Joint Comment here and elsewhere appears to conflate legal obligations derived from treaties,[130] or from the principle of effectiveness, with indications of 'best practice', in a manner which is not altogether helpful.[131] UNHCR's 2009 Guidelines on Child Asylum Claims take a

---

[123] *RYS v Spain* (n 122) para 8.9; see also *RK v Spain* (n 122) para 9.8; *MT v Spain* (n 122) para 13.5; *AL v Spain* (n 122) para 12.8; *JAB v Spain* (n 122) para 13.7; *NBF v Spain* (n 122) para 12.8.

[124] See, eg, *RYS v Spain* (n 122) para 8.9; *RK v Spain* (n 122) para 9.8; *MT v Spain* (n 122) para 13.5.

[125] 'General Comment No. 12' (n 110) para 19 (emphasis added).

[126] ibid paras 133–34; para 21.

[127] ibid para 34.

[128] ibid para 124. See also paras 34, 40–47, 80, 133–34 (on general measures to ensure that a child can be heard effectively); Committee on the Rights of the Child, 'General Comment No. 6: Treatment of Unaccompanied and Separated Children outside their Country of Origin', CRC/GC/2005/6 (1 Sept 2005) para 25; UNHCR, 'Guidelines on Child Asylum Claims' (n 111) para 69.

[129] See 'Joint General Comment No. 4 (2017) of the Committee on the Protection of the Rights of All Migrant Workers and Members of Their Families and No. 23 (2017) of the Committee on the Rights of the Child on State Obligations regarding the Human Rights of Children in the context of International Migration in Countries of Origin, Transit, Destination and Return', CMW/C/GC/4-CRC/C/GC/23 (16 Nov 2017) ('Joint General Comment No. 4') para 17(f) and (h).

[130] The Joint General Comment is concerned with legal obligations set out in two treaties, the CRC and the International Convention on the Protection of the Rights of All Migrant Workers and Members of their Families (adopted 18 Dec 1990, entered into force 1 July 2003) 2220 UNTS 3.

[131] See 'Joint General Comment No. 4' (n 129) para 14–19 (noting, for example, that children '*should* be guaranteed *the right* to ... [b]e heard') (emphasis added).

more restrictive view, stating that children '*who are the principal applicants* in an asylum procedure' are entitled to legal representation, and making no comment on whether legal aid must be provided.[132] As these Guidelines are non-binding, they should not be viewed as a definitive statement of the rights to which children are entitled under other treaties.

Third, children are entitled to be informed whether their views were taken into account by decision-makers and to a remedy in the event that their article 12 rights are breached. The Committee notes that in both administrative and judicial proceedings, a child 'must have access to appeals and complaints procedures which provide remedies for rights violations'.[133]

Finally, specific rights exist for children who are liable to be detained or who are accused of a crime. Article 37(b) provides that the arrest, detention, or imprisonment of a child 'shall be in conformity with the law and shall be used only as a measure of last resort and for the shortest appropriate period of time'. A right of access to a court to review an administrative decision or to appeal a judicial decision is also implied.[134] The Committee on the Rights of the Child has affirmed that '[e]very child, at all times, has a fundamental right to liberty and freedom from immigration detention'.[135] Such detention can never be a 'measure of last resort' under article 37(b), as it is inherently inconsistent with the best interests of the child.[136] This provision provides substantive protection to asylum seeker children, provided that it is transposed into domestic law and access to courts is guaranteed. In the criminal justice context, the CRC also sets out tailored guarantees.[137] These rights are not comprehensive and are supplemented by those available under other international instruments to which a State is party.[138] In particular, the child is entitled to 'legal or other appropriate assistance in the preparation and presentation of his or her defence'.[139] Unlike the ICCPR, this provision does not state that such assistance will be assigned 'where the interests of justice so require', leading Tobin and Read to argue that the CRC imports an 'unqualified obligation' to provide access.[140] The CRC does not specify that this representation be free of charge (in contrast, for example, to the right to interpretation),[141] and the Committee on

---

[132] UNHCR, 'Guidelines on Child Asylum Claims' (n 111) para 69 (emphasis added).

[133] ibid para 47.

[134] 'General Comment No. 24' (n 117) para 91.

[135] See 'Joint General Comment No. 4' (n 129) para 5.

[136] See ibid para 10 (citing an inconsistency also with the right to development).

[137] See CRC, art 41; 'General Comment No. 24' (n 117).

[138] See CRC, art 41; John Tobin with Cate Read, 'Article 40. The Rights of the Child in the Juvenile Justice System' in Tobin (ed) (n 108) 1617–21; 1630 (on the right to a fair hearing).

[139] CRC, art 40(2)(b)(ii). The Committee considers that states 'should' ensure that this assistance is available from the outset of proceedings until all appeals are exhausted: see 'General Comment No. 24' (n 117) para 49.

[140] Tobin with Read (n 138) 1629.

[141] Compare CRC, art 40(2)(b)(ii) and (vi).

the Rights of the Child has implied that there is no general obligation to provide free assistance.[142] The principle of effectiveness would, however, support the existence of an obligation to provide free representation in a case in which a child was unaccompanied and/or indigent.[143] A child is also entitled under the CRC to an appeal in the event that he or she is found to have infringed penal law.[144] The Committee considers that access to justice considerations call for a 'broader interpretation' of the clause, 'allowing reviews or appeals on any procedural or substantive misdirection'.[145]

In sum, the CRC supplements the ICCPR by guaranteeing a child the right to be heard in any matter affecting him or her, regardless of whether he or she is a party to the proceedings. It does not extend, however, to a guarantee of a right to an administrative or judicial hearing itself. Second, it guarantees certain substantive protections in the case of detained children and children accused of a crime. The effective implementation of these rights may require that States parties guarantee the provision of information, legal assistance, translation or certain adaptations to general procedure. Where necessary to ensure the effective exercise of the right in question, these adaptations constitute obligations on States parties rather than mere guidance.

2.2.2 Convention on the Rights of Persons with Disabilities
The CRPD, which entered into force in 2008, is the first international human rights treaty to provide expressly for a right to 'access to justice'.[146] Article 13 obliges States parties to ensure:

> effective access to justice for persons with disabilities on an equal basis with others, including through the provision of procedural and age-appropriate accommodations, in order to facilitate their effective role as direct and indirect participants, including as witnesses, in all legal proceedings, including at investigative and other preliminary stages.[147]

---

[142] See Committee on the Rights of the Child, 'General Comment No. 10 (2007) Children's rights in juvenile justice', CRC/C/GC/10 (25 Apr 2007) para 49 ('It is left to the discretion of States parties to determine how this assistance is provided but it *should* be free of charge': emphasis added); 'General Comment No. 24' (n 117) para 51 ('The Committee *recommends* that States provide effective legal representative, free of charge, for all children who are facing criminal charges': emphasis added).

[143] See also Tobin with Read (n 138) 1629.

[144] CRC, art 40(2)(b)(v).

[145] 'General Comment No. 24' (n 117) para 62.

[146] As noted in Eilionóir Flynn, 'Article 13 [Access to Justice]' in Valentina Della Fina, Rachele Cera, and Giuseppe Palmisano (eds), *The United Nations Convention on the Rights of Persons with Disabilities: A Commentary* (Springer 2017) 282; and in Eilionóir Flynn, 'Article 13 Access to Justice' in Ilias Bantekas, Michael Ashley Stein, and Dimitris Anastasiou (eds), *The UN Convention on the Rights of Persons with Disabilities: A Commentary* (OUP 2018) 383.

[147] CRPD, art 13(1).

As discussed in Chapter 4, 'access to courts' has its roots in the general need to ensure that foreigners can access domestic courts, and has traditionally been treated as having a confined, legalistic, scope. In contrast, the notion of 'access to justice' is broader and more amorphous.[148] A United Nations Development Programme (UNDP) Practice Note on access to justice states that the term entails 'much more than improving an individual's access to courts, or guaranteeing legal representation' and 'must be defined in terms of ensuring that legal and judicial outcomes are just and equitable'.[149] Article 13 appears to limit its scope to judicial proceedings through the inclusion of the phrase 'in all legal proceedings'. However, the Committee on the Rights of Persons with Disabilities treats this obligation as also extending to administrative proceedings.[150] For example, in its 2019 report on Greece, the Committee recommended that Greece ensure:

> effective access to legal services and legal aid, cost-free assistive technologies and quality translation and interpretation in sign language, Braille and other alternative formats, provided free of charge at all stages of civil, criminal *and administrative proceedings*.[151]

The reference to 'effective' access to justice in article 13 makes express what would otherwise be implied; namely, that steps must be taken to ensure that the right is practically available.[152] A 2017 report on article 13 CRPD considers that persons

---

[148] See, eg, OECD/Open Society Foundations, 'Legal Needs Surveys and Access to Justice' (OECD Publishing, Paris 2019) 24; Committee on the Elimination of Discrimination against Women, 'General recommendation No. 33 on women's access to justice', CEDAW/C/GC/33 (3 Aug 2015), para 1. 'Access to justice' is also enshrined in Sustainable Development Goal 16, but the initial agreed indicators to measure the goal related only to the criminal justice sphere and did not cover access for settlement of civil disputes: See UNGA Res 70/1, 'Transforming our world: the 2030 Agenda for Sustainable Development' (25 Sept 2015); Margaret L Satterthwaite and Sukti Dhital, 'Measuring Access to Justice: Transformation and Technicality in SDG 16.3' (Jan 2019) 10 Global Policy 96. A new global indicator addressing civil justice has since been approved—'*Proportion of the population who have experienced a dispute in the past two years and who accessed a formal or informal dispute resolution mechanism, by type of mechanism*': see 'People-centred measurement of access to civil justice: the new global SDG indicator 16.3.3' (OECD, undated) <https://www.oecd.org/governance/global-roundtables-acc ess-to-justice/people-centredmeasurementofaccesstociviljusticethenewglobalsdgindicator1633. htm>; 'Targets and Indicators', (United Nations, Department of Economic and Social Affairs, undated) <https://sdgs.un.org/goals/goal16>, target 16.3.3.

[149] UNDP, 'Access to Justice: Practice Note' (9 Mar 2004) 6.

[150] As noted by Flynn in Bantekas, Stein, and Anastasiou (n 146) 398, citing in particular CRPD Committee, 'Concluding Observations on the initial report of New Zealand', CRPD/C/NZL/CO/1 (31 Oct 2014) para 24.

[151] CRPD Cttee, 'Concluding observations on the initial report of Greece', CRPD/C/GRC/CO/1 (29 Oct 2019) para 20 (emphasis added).

[152] Flynn suggests that 'effective' means that this right could be interpreted 'mutatis mutandis with the right to an effective remedy', requiring, in Roht-Arriaza's words, a remedy that is 'both individualized and adjudicatory': Flynn in Bantekas, Stein, and Anastasiou (n 146), citing Naomi Roht-Arriaza, 'State Responsibility to Investigate and Prosecute Grave Human Rights Violations in International Law' (1990) 78 California Law Review 449, 475. However, given the general applicability of the principle of effectiveness, there is no need to tie the term too strictly to the right to an effective remedy.

with disabilities are most commonly denied access to justice 'as a result of lack of accessibility of and access to information, procedural accommodations, the right to claim justice and stand trial, respect for the presumption of innocence and legal aid'.[153]

Flynn notes that while the CRPD drafters 'were under a mandate not to create any new rights,'[154] this provision also includes some innovations, most notably the requirement that access be provided through 'the provision of *procedural and age-appropriate accommodations*'.[155] This phrasing differs from that of 'reasonable accommodation', a core concept in the CRPD that is defined in article 2. The Office of the UN High Commissioner for Human Rights notes that the omission of 'reasonable' was intentional:

> 'procedural accommodations' … are not limited by the concept of 'disproportionate or undue burden' [as in the definition of reasonable accommodation]. This differentiation is fundamental, because the right of access to justice acts as the guarantor for the effective enjoyment and exercise of all rights.[156]

The Committee's Concluding Observations on article 13 provide examples of the scope and content of such accommodations, as well as several recommendations that relate to accessibility.[157] A State party's obligations to ensure accessibility, which are unconditional, are set out in article 9 of the CRPD.[158] In General Comment No. 2, the Committee notes that the concept of accessibility is an 'ex ante' obligation 'related to groups', while 'reasonable accommodation' refers to measures taken in relation to an individual request. Therefore, while accessibility measures are 'broad and standardized', reasonable accommodation may be called for in the case of rarer conditions.[159] The distinction between obligations of accommodation and accessibility is arguably less crucial in the context of article 13, since the provision creates an unconditional obligation to provide accommodation that is

---

[153] UNGA, 'Right to access to justice under article 13 of the Convention on the Rights of Persons with Disabilities: Report of the Office of the United Nations High Commissioner for Human Rights', A/HRC/37/25 (27 December 2017) para 19.

[154] Flynn in Bantekas, Stein, and Anastasiou (n 146) 383.

[155] CRPD, art 13(1) (emphasis added); ibid 390.

[156] Human Rights Council, 'Equality and non-discrimination under article 5 of the Convention on the Rights of Persons with Disabilities: Report of the Office of the United Nations High Commissioner for Human Rights' A/HRC/34/26 (9 Dec 2016) para 35. UNGA, 'Right to access to justice under article 13 of the Convention on the Rights of Persons with Disabilities' (n 153) para 25.

[157] This was noted in 2017 by Flynn in Della Fina, Cera, and Palmisano (eds) (n 146) 290. The examples discussed here are drawn from more recent reports which confirm many of the trends that she identifies.

[158] See also UNGA, 'Right to access to justice under article 13 of the Convention on the Rights of Persons with Disabilities' (n 153) para 15 (noting that access to justice is a cross-cutting right and that article 13 should be read in conjunction with article 9).

[159] CRPD Cttee, 'General Comment No. 2 (2014): Article 9: Accessibility', CRPD/C/GC/2 (22 May 2014) para 25.

not subject to a 'reasonableness' test. Alternatively, references to accessibility in the context of article 13 could be read as an extension of the duty of 'effective access' under that provision. In the context of the CRPD, any such implied obligations are bolstered by article 12(3), which obliges States parties to 'take appropriate measures to provide access by persons with disabilities to the support they may require in exercising their legal capacity'. Rights of access to justice guaranteed to detained persons with disabilities are also elaborated in non-binding guidelines adopted by the Committee in 2015.[160]

In Committee reports, examples of recommendations under article 13 that relate to accommodation or accessibility include ensuring accessibility of facilities,[161] accessibility of legal services and legal information (through, for example translation in sign language or braille),[162] free interpretation and translation during proceedings (into, for example, sign language or braille),[163] and access to legal aid.[164] The Committee has also addressed intersectionality concerns, pointing to the need for gender-sensitive accommodations.[165]

Legal assistance is clearly a key concern of the Committee, which noted in its first General Comment that under article 13, States parties 'must also ensure that persons with disabilities have access to legal representation on an equal basis with others'.[166] The 2017 report on article 13 CRPD noted that '[t]he right to legal counsel is a fair trial right and includes the right to free legal aid', but goes on to recommend that States parties 'increase their efforts to guarantee legal aid for persons with

---

[160] CRPD Cttee, 'Guidelines on article 14 of the Convention on the Rights of Persons with Disabilities: The right to liberty and security of persons with disabilities' (adopted 14th sess, Sept 2015), XIV.

[161] See CRPD Cttee, 'Concluding observations on the initial report of Estonia', CRPD/C/EST/CO/1 (5 May 2021) para 26(d) (recommending the adoption of an 'action plan to ensure physical access to all justice facilities, including through accessible transportation'); CRPD Cttee, 'Concluding observations on the combined second and third periodic reports of Ecuador', CRPD/C/ECU/CO/2-3 (21 Oct 2019) para 28 (recommending that Ecuador 'take due account of accessibility considerations with respect to the physical environment, information and communications in all facilities having to do with the administration of justice'); CRPD Cttee, 'Greece' (n 151) para 20; CRPD Cttee, 'Concluding observations on the initial report of India', CRPD/C/IND/CO/1 (29 Oct 2019) para 29; CRPD Cttee, 'Concluding observations on the initial report of Kuwait', CRPD/C/KWT/CO/1 (18 Oct 2019), para 27 (recommending that Kuwait ensure the accessibility of both '*police* and judicial premises': emphasis added).

[162] CRPD Cttee, 'Estonia' (n 161) para 26(d); CRPD Cttee, 'Greece' (n 151) para 20; CRPD Cttee, 'Concluding observations on the initial report of Iraq', CRPD/C/IRQ/CO/1 (23 Oct 2019) para 26.

[163] CRPD Cttee, 'Greece' (n 151) para 20; 'Concluding observations on the initial report of Myanmar' CRPD/C/MMR/CO/1 (22 Oct 2019) para 26.

[164] CRPD Cttee, 'Estonia' (n 161) para 26(c); CRPD Cttee, 'Greece' (n 151) para 20; CRPD Cttee, 'India' (n 161) para 29; CRPD Cttee, 'Kuwait' (n 161) para 27(b); 'Concluding observations on the initial report of Albania', CRPD/C/ALB/CO/1 (14 Oct 2019) para 26. See also Flynn in Bantekas, Stein, and Anastasiou (n 146) 391.

[165] See CRPD Cttee, 'India' (n 161) para 29; CRPD Cttee, 'Iraq' (n 162) para 26; CRPD Cttee, 'Myanmar' (n 163) para 26. For earlier examples, see Flynn in Bantekas, Stein, and Anastasiou (n 146) 394.

[166] CRPD Cttee, 'General Comment No. 1 (2014): Article 12: Equal recognition before the law', CRPD/C/GC/1 (19 May 2014) para 38.

disabilities'.[167] In reports, it is unclear whether free legal aid is required. In its 2019 report on Iraq, for example, the Committee recommended the provision of 'free or affordable legal aid for persons with disabilities in all areas of the State party', and that Iraq 'ensure the necessary budgetary allocations'.[168] This aligns with the Committee's observations on Albania, which recommended that 'persons with disabilities, particularly those still living in institutions, have access to free legal aid'.[169] However, its report on Turkey simply recommends that human and financial resources are ensured to 'provide persons with disabilities with legal aid, which is accessible *and affordable*',[170] while the report on Greece makes no mention of cost, referring only to the need to 'ensure effective access to legal services and legal aid'.[171] These inconsistencies suggest that the Committee has not yet committed itself to the position that free legal aid is required for all individuals who have a disability, although in many cases, it may be a necessary accommodation to ensure 'access to justice'. Additional guidance is provided in the International Principles and Guidelines on Access to Justice for Persons with Disabilities, adopted in 2020.[172] Principle 6 states that '[p]ersons with disabilities have the right to free or affordable legal assistance'.[173] It calls for free legal assistance to be provided to those who cannot afford it in a range of cases, including loss of life or liberty, forfeiture of parental rights, loss of housing, and other cases in which a person with disabilities may face a disadvantage in 'communicating, understanding or being understood in the process'.[174]

The 2018 communication of *Al Adam v Saudi Arabia* provides guidance on the scope of article 13—and, ultimately, the practical challenges of enforcing human rights through international treaty bodies. The case concerned a Saudi Arabian citizen who was detained by security forces at a checkpoint and subsequently tortured. As a result of the torture and inadequate medical care, the author's slight hearing impairment from childhood worsened to the point that he lost all hearing in one ear. The

---

[167] UNGA, 'Right to access to justice under article 13 of the Convention on the Rights of Persons with Disabilities' (n 153) paras 40-41.

[168] CRPD Cttee, 'Iraq' (n 162) para 26.

[169] 'Albania' (n 164) para 26. See also CRPD Cttee, 'India' (n 161) para 29; CRPD Cttee, Concluding observations on the combined second and third periodic reports of Hungary', CRPD/C/HUN/CO/2-3 (20 May 2022), para 27 (recommending that free and effective legal representation be available to those who have restricted legal capacity and those placed in residential and psychiatric facilities).

[170] CRPD Cttee, 'Concluding observations on the initial report of Turkey', CRPD/C/TUR/CO/1(1 Oct 2019) para 28 (emphasis added). See similarly CRPD Cttee, Concluding observations on the combined second and third periodic reports of Mexico, CRPD/C/MEX/CO/2-3 (20 April 2022), para 38.

[171] CRPD Cttee, 'Greece' (n 151) para 20. See also CRPD Cttee, 'Estonia' (n 161) para 26(c).

[172] 'International Principles and Guidelines on Access to Justice for Persons with Disabilities' (Aug 2020), available via <https://www.ohchr.org/Documents/Issues/Disability/SR_Disability/GoodPracti ces/Access-to-Justice-EN.pdf>. Drafting of the Principles was spearheaded by the Special Rapporteur on the rights of persons with disabilities and involved wide consultations: see 'International Principles and Guidelines on access to justice for persons with disabilities' (Office of the High Commissioner for Human Rights, undated) <https://www.ohchr.org/EN/Issues/Disability/SRDisabilities/Pages/GoodPracticesEffectiveAcces sJusticePersonsDisabilities.aspx>.

[173] ibid Principle 6.

[174] ibid Guideline 6.2 to Principle 6.

author claimed that he had been forced to make a confession, and that, on the basis of that confession, he was sentenced to death. Commenting on the judicial process, the Committee noted that article 13 'entails the respect of all components of the right to fair trial, including the right to be represented and not to be submitted to any direct or indirect physical or undue psychological pressure from the investigating authorities, with a view to obtaining a confession of guilt'.[175] The Committee also considered the intersection of rights and obligations of equality and non-discrimination with article 13 of the CRPD, finding that Saudi Arabia was required 'to take all procedural accommodation that is necessary to enable [the applicant's] effective participation in the process, taking into account his hearing impairment'.[176] The lack of such measures constituted a breach of article 13 of the CRPD, and the Committee recommended that his conviction be reviewed.[177] Despite the Committee's findings, Al Adam was executed by Saudi Arabia on 23 April 2019.[178]

2.3 Regional Human Rights Treaties

Regional treaties are also a source of rights for those individuals falling within their jurisdiction. Relevant rights established under the ECHR, EU law, the Inter-American human rights system, the Banjul Charter, and the Arab Charter on Human Rights are set out in Parts 2.3.1–2.3.5. As will be seen, interpretation of the ECHR echoes that of the ICCPR in excluding the judicial review of RSD decisions from the scope of its article 6 on the right to a fair trial. Beyond this exclusion, article 6 ECHR has been given a robust interpretation through reliance on the principle of effectiveness. The asylum regime established under EU law considers the 1951 Convention to be the 'cornerstone' of refugee protection,[179] and in some cases mandates greater obligations than those that bind Contracting States under the 1951 Convention. Robust rights for asylum seekers are enshrined in the Inter-American human rights system and under the Banjul Charter, while the Arab Charter is limited to general fair trial guarantees. The jurisdictional scope of each of these treaties is narrower than that of the 1951 Convention.

---

[175] CRPD Cttee, *Al Adam v Saudi Arabia*, Comm no 38/2016, CRPD/C/20/D/38/2016 (20 Sept 2018) para 11.4 (footnotes omitted).
[176] ibid para 11.5. The Committee relied in particular on the intersection of articles 4 and 13 CRPD.
[177] See ibid (finding a breach of article 13 'read alone and in conjunction with article 4'); and ibid para 12(a)(ii).
[178] See Human Rights Council, Working Group on Arbitrary Detention, 'Opinion No. 26/2019 concerning Abdelkarim Mohamed Al Hawaj and Mounir Abdullah Ahmad Aal Adam (Saudi Arabia)' (2 May 2019).
[179] See Directive 2011/95/EU of the European Parliament and of the Council of 13 December 2011 on standards for the qualification of third-country nationals or stateless persons as beneficiaries of international protection, for a uniform status for refugees or for persons eligible for subsidiary protection, and for the content of the protection granted (recast), OJ L 337/9 (recast Qualification Directive) recital 4.

2.3.1 European Convention on Human Rights

2.3.1.1 Exclusion of asylum proceedings from article 6 ECHR

Article 6 of the ECHR states that '[i]n the determination of his civil rights and obligations or of any criminal charge against him, everyone is entitled to a fair and
public hearing within a reasonable time by an independent and impartial tribunal
established by law'. The European Court of Human Rights' interpretation of the
scope of this clause the echoes that taken by the HRC in relation to article 14 of the
ICCPR.[180] The ECtHR considers article 6 to contain an 'inherent' right of access
to courts which is subject to certain limitations.[181] This protected right of access
to courts is intended to be 'practical and effective' rather than 'theoretical or illusory'.[182] Guaranteeing effective access may require States to take certain procedural
steps (or remove certain procedural bars). For example, although article 6 is silent
on the issue of legal aid in civil proceedings,[183] the Court has found that it may be
breached by a refusal to grant aid in circumstances where it is necessary to ensure
effective access to the courts.[184]

This implied right therefore provides relatively robust protection to all individuals within a Member State's jurisdiction across a range of actionable claims
under domestic law.[185] However, like the HRC, the Court determined in *Maaouia
v France* that 'decisions regarding the entry, stay and deportation of aliens do not
concern the determination of an applicant's civil rights or obligations or of a criminal charge against him, within the meaning of [article 6(1)] of the Convention'.[186]

---

[180] See discussion in Section 2.1.1 and in Cantor, 'Reframing Relationships' (n 14) 91–94.

[181] *Golder v United Kingdom,* App no 4451/70 (ECtHR, Court (Plenary), 21 Feb 1975), paras 36–38;
Zubac v Croatia, App no 40160/12 (Grand Chamber, 5 apr 2018), para 76. See also ECtHR, 'Guide on
Article 6 of the European Convention on Human Rights: Right to a fair trial (civil limb)' (Council of
Europe/European Court of Human Rights, updated to 31 August 2022) paras 105–151.

[182] See, eg, *Zubac v Croatia* (n 181) para 77; *Airey v Ireland,* App no 6289/73 (ECtHR, Chamber, 9
Oct 1979) para 24 (noting that while this is generally true of the rights protected by the Convention, it
is 'particularly so of the right of access to the courts in view of the prominent place held in a democratic
society by the right to a fair trial', a principle echoed in *Zubac*).

[183] In criminal proceedings, article 6(3)(c) guarantees free legal assistance where a defendant is unable to pay and 'the interests of justice so require'.

[184] See *Airey v Ireland* (n 182) discussed further in Chapter 6, Section 2.2.4. While the Court found
it 'most improbable that a person in Mrs. Airey's position … can effectively present his or her own case',
it stressed that there was no general requirement of legal aid in civil cases. See paras 24, 26. See also
Gnahoré v France, App no 40031/98 (3rd Section, 19 Sept 2000) para 38 (reiterating that article 6(1)
'only compels the State to provide for the assistance of a lawyer when such assistance proves indispensable for an effective access to court either because legal representation is rendered compulsory or by
reason of the complexity of the procedure or of the case'); *Del Sol v France,* App no 46900/99 (ECtHR,
3rd Section, 26 Feb 2002) paras 20–21; 24–27 (on factors relevant to whether a refusal of legal aid
'infringe[s] the very essence of [an applicant's] right of access to a court'). For these and other cases on
the implied right of access to a court under article 6, see Christoph Grabenwarter, *European Convention
on Human Rights—Commentary* (C.H. Beck, Hart, Nomos 2014) 127–33; ECtHR, 'Guide on Article 6'
(n 181) paras 113–133 (on the requirement that the right of access to a court be 'practical and effective'
generally) and 157–164 (on principles regarding legal aid).

[185] On this point, see *Z and others v United Kingdom,* App no 29392/95 (Grand Chamber, 10 May
2001), para 92, cited in ECtHR, 'Guide on Article 6' (n 181) para 107.

[186] *Maaouia v France,* App no 39652/98 (ECtHR, Grand Chamber, Judgment, 5 Oct 2000), para 40.

The applicant in *Maaouia v France* was not an asylum seeker, but a Tunisian national issued with a deportation order after his imprisonment for armed robbery and assault.[187] However, in *Katani v Germany*,[188] the Court extended its finding in *Maaouia* to the review of failed RSD decisions, noting '[l]a Cour rappelle que les garanties de l'article 6 de la Convention *ne sont pas applicables aux procédures en matière d'asile politique*'.[189] As a result, an asylum seeker is not entitled to the benefit of article 6(1) in the context of asylum claims.[190]

The Court has also found that proceedings considered to be 'closely connected' to asylum proceedings are excluded from the protection of article 6. In *Panjeheighalehei v Denmark*, the applicant had sought damages in relation to the Danish Refugee Board's earlier failure to grant him asylum, following which he was deported and tortured.[191] Despite the fact that the applicant was a recognised refugee at the time of the application, and the Court's acknowledgment that his claim was 'formulated as an ordinary tort action',[192] it ultimately considered that the compensation claim 'amounted, in reality ... to a challenge to the merits of the decisions of the Refugee Board' and found article 6(1) to be inapplicable.[193] In *MN and others v Belgium*, the Grand Chamber took the same approach to a complaint that the applicants were unable pursue execution of a Belgian court judgment effectively requiring Belgium to issue them with humanitarian visas.[194] Finding article 6(1) of the ECHR to be inapplicable, the Court noted that 'the underlying proceedings do not become "civil" merely because their execution is sought before the courts and they give rise to a judicial decision'.[195] These two decisions demonstrate the far-reaching consequences for asylum seekers and refugees of the ECtHR's position on the scope of article 6.

---

[187] See ibid paras 9–13.

[188] *Katani et autres contre l'Allemagne*, App no 67679/01 (ECtHR, 4th Section, Décision sur la Recevabilité, 31 May 2001).

[189] ibid, 'En droit', para 4 ('The Court recalls that the guarantees of article 6 of the Convention are not applicable to procedures regarding political asylum'—author's translation). For the allegations of the claimants, see also ibid, 'Griefs', para 4 (alleging that they had not benefited from a fair process as required under art 6(1) before the 'juridictions administratives' (administrative courts); and complaining of the refusal to grant them legal aid, amongst other issues).

[190] The question of why the ECtHR might take a more restrictive interpretative approach where the rights of asylum seekers and other migrants are concerned is the subject of some reflection elsewhere: see Marie-Bénédicte Dembour, *When Humans Become Migrants: Study of the European Court of Human Rights with an Inter-American Counterpoint* (OUP 2015) 9, 36, 42, 61, 247–48, 433 (noting that protection of citizens, not aliens, was the impetus for the development of the ECtHR, and suggesting that '[t]he propensity of "the beauty to fall back to sleep" in Article 3 return cases' may 'have been triggered by the general tide against asylum seekers which engulfed Europe in the mid-1980s and the fear that an opening of the "flood gates" would see Europe "invaded" by migrants': at 248). See also Jaya Ramji-Nogales, 'Undocumented Migrants and the Failures of Universal Individualism' (2014) 47 Vanderbilt Journal of Transnational Law 699, 750 (on institutional legitimacy in the eyes of States).

[191] *Panjeheighalehei v Denmark*, App no 11230/07 (ECtHR, 5th Section, Admissibility Decision, 13 Oct 2009). I am grateful to Grabenwarter (n 184) 105, n 42, for directing me to this reference.

[192] *Panjeheighalehei v Denmark* (n 191) 11.

[193] ibid.

[194] *MN and others v Belgium*, App no 3599/18 (ECtHr, Grand Chamber, 5 Mar 2020) para 140.

[195] ibid paras 139–140.

One basis for the ECtHR's finding that article 6 is not engaged in 'decisions regarding the entry, stay and deportation of aliens' appears to be that the two categories of 'criminal' and 'civil' claims do not cover the full field of possible legal actions brought or defended by an individual.[196] This characterisation of deportation and/or asylum procedures was criticised in a dissenting judgment in *Maaouia*, which argued that 'the term "civil" should be interpreted as covering all other legal rights which are not of a criminal nature' and that 'the object and purpose of Article 6 was to ensure, through judicial guarantees, a fair administration of justice to any person in the assertion or determination of his legal rights or obligations.[197] In the Grand Chamber's later decision in *Hirsi*, Judge Pinto de Albuquerque expressed support for the dissentients in a Concurring Opinion:

> I also have serious doubts about the proposition that, on account of the alleged discretionary and public-order element of the decisions taken in these procedures [expulsion and asylum claims], they are not to be seen as determining the civil rights of the person concerned. I have two major reasons: firstly, these decisions will necessarily have major repercussions on the alien's private and professional and social life. Secondly, these decisions are not discretionary at all and do have to comply with international obligations, such as those resulting from the prohibition of *refoulement*.[198]

The ECtHR's position on the scope of article 6 does not mean that asylum seekers lack any protection under the ECHR in relation to their asylum applications.[199] However, the inquiry shifts from the asylum application itself to any associated breach of ECHR-guaranteed rights.[200] These rights centre on expulsion, not asylum. First, the prohibition on torture or inhuman or degrading treatment or punishment in article 3 of the ECHR prevents the removal of individuals who face a real risk of such harm.[201] Article 3 guarantees protection

---

[196] See *Maaouia v France* (n 186) Dissenting opinion of Judge Loucaides joined by Judge Traja, 18–19 (noting that '[i]t was assumed that by the use of that word the drafters of the Article intended to confine the rights and obligations in question only to those falling within the domain of private law. I do not agree with this approach'). The Court's judgment focused on the fact that article 1 of Protocol No. 7 contains procedural guarantees related to expulsion as evincing an intention on the part of States not to include deportation proceedings within the scope of article 6(1): see paras 36–37.

[197] Ibid, Dissenting opinion of Judge Loucaides joined by Judge Traja, 19–20.

[198] *Hirsi Jamaa and Others v Italy,* App no 27765/09 (Grand Chamber, 23 Feb 2012), Concurring opinion of Judge Pinto de Albuquerque, 74, fn 1. For academic support, see also Geoffrey Care, *Migrants and the Courts: A Century of Trial and Error?* (Routledge Ashgate 2013) 272.

[199] See, eg, *Hirsi v Italy* (n 198) Concurring opinion of Judge Pinto de Albuquerque, 74, n 2.

[200] This point is made by Cantor (n 14) 91. See also Jean-François Durieux, 'Salah Sheekh is a Refugee: New Insights into Primary and Subsidiary Forms of Protection', Refugee Studies Centre, Working Paper Series No 49 (Oct 2008) 8.

[201] See *Soering v United Kingdom*, App no 14038/88 (EctHR, Court (Plenary), 7 July 1989), para 111; see also Guy S Goodwin-Gill and Jane McAdam, with Emma Dunlop, *The Refugee in International Law* (4th edn, OUP 2021) Ch 7.

both against removal to the country where the real risk of harm is feared, and removal to a third country which lacks an adequate asylum procedure (with the consequent risk of so-called chain *refoulement*).[202] Second, article 4 of Protocol No. 4 to the ECHR precludes the collective expulsion of aliens. Finally, article 1 of Protocol No. 7 regulates the expulsion of 'lawfully resident' aliens.[203] The reference to 'lawfully' is directed to the domestic law of the host State.[204] In *SC c Roumanie*, the ECtHR considered whether being an asylum applicant was sufficient to engage article 1. The court noted that while asylum applicants had the right to remain in a State's territory until the conclusion of asylum procedures under certain national and European laws, this right did not automatically confer the status of 'resident' or regularise that residence so as to engage the provision.[205] Accordingly, the ability of this article to protect asylum seekers may be limited.[206]

---

[202] See *MK and others v Poland*, App nos 40503/17, 42902/17 and 43643/17 (EctHR, 1st Section, 23 July 2020) paras 173, 179, 185; citing also at para 173 to *Ilias and Ahmed v Hungary*, App no 47287/15 (ECtHR, Grand Chamber, 21 Nov 2019) para 134.

[203] A 'lawfully resident' alien may only be expelled in accordance with a lawful decision and has the right to 'submit reasons against his expulsion'; 'have his case reviewed'; and be represented for that purpose. However, these rights of review will not have suspensive effect 'when … expulsion is necessary in the interests of public order or … grounded on reasons of national security': Protocol No. 7 to the Convention for the Protection of Human Rights and Fundamental Freedoms, ETS No 117 (adopted 22 Nov 1984, entered into force 1 Nov 1988), art 1(1)–(2). See also Council of Europe, 'Explanatory Report to the Protocol No. 7 to the Convention for the Protection of Human Rights and Fundamental Freedoms' (Strasbourg, 22 November 1984), paras 12–14, noting in particular that the form of review is determined by domestic law; that it need not be a two-stage procedure; and that, if domestic law does provide for an appeal of a review decision, article 1 does not require that it have suspensive effect (para 13.2). The Explanatory Report also notes that review may be on the papers (para 14).

[204] See 'Explanatory Report to the Protocol No. 7' (n 203) para 9; *SC c Roumanie*, Req No. 9356/11 (ECtHR, 3rd Section, 10 February 2015) para 81.

[205] *SC c Roumanie* (n 204) paras 83–85 (« Elle observe également que, en vertu des différentes dispositions légales applicables—nationales et européennes –, les demandeurs d'asile dont les procédures étaient en cours avaient le droit de rester sur le territoire du pays jusqu'à la finalisation desdites procédures … ce droit ne confère pas automatiquement auxdites personnes le statut de « résident » d'un certain pays et ne « régularise » pas leur séjour »). See similarly *NM c Roumanie*, Req No 75325/11 (ECtHR, 3rd Section, 10 February 2015) paras 104–105. The French text of Protocol No. 7 uses the expression « un étranger résidant régulièrement » for 'an alien lawfully resident'. The decisions in *SC c Roumanie* and *NM c Roumanie* seem inconsistent with the court's earlier finding in *Ahmed c Roumanie*, Req No 34621/03 (ECtHR, 3rd Section, 13 July 2010) para 46, that article 13 of Government ordinance 102/2000 (framed in similar terms to article 17 of Government ordinance 122/2006, which was at issue in the later cases) gave the applicant a right of residence that satisfied the 'lawful residence' requirement in article 1 of Protocol No. 7.

For other examples of cases in which an applicant was found not to be lawfully resident for the purposes of article 1 of the Protocol, see *ST c France*, Req no. 20649/92 (European Commission of Human Rights, 8 February 1993) (applicant lacked a residence permit because his application for asylum had been definitively rejected) and *Voulfovitch and others v Sweden*, App no 19373/92 (European Commission of Human Rights, 13 January 1993) (applicants outstayed a one-day transit visa to await a decision on their applications for asylum and residence permits). See further 'Guide to Article 1 of Protocol No. 7 to the European Convention on Human Rights: Procedural safeguards relating to expulsion of aliens' (Council of Europe, updated 31 August 2022).

[206] See also Cantor, noting that a claim of asylum is unlikely to satisfy 'lawful residence' by the Court 'absent applicable national law to that effect': (n 14) 91.

Coupled with the right to an effective remedy in article 13 of the ECHR, these primary rights generate additional procedural protections for individuals at risk of removal, both in first-instance decision-making and on appeal.[207]

The procedural guarantees engaged by articles 3 and 13 of the ECHR were set out in the case *MK and others v Poland*.[208] There, the Court reaffirmed that where an individual alleges a risk of torture or ill-treatment in breach of article 3, an effective remedy requires an independent assessment by 'a national authority', a prompt response, and automatic suspensive effect preventing removal.[209] The authority need not be judicial, although if it is administrative, 'its powers and the guarantees that it affords are relevant in determining whether the remedy before it is effective'.[210] There is no requirement to set up a second level of appeal.[211] The remedy must be both formally and practically available.[212] An effective remedy under article 13 need not have suspensive effect when the prohibition on collective expulsion article 4 of Protocol No. 4 is engaged, unless the applicant also claim a real risk of ill-treatment contrary to article 3 or a violation of his or her right to life.[213]

In *MK*, these protections were found to apply to individuals alleging a risk of ill-treatment who presented at a border checkpoint—with the result that Poland was required to *grant* entry while an appeal against the *refusal* of entry was on foot.[214] In *Hirsi*, the Court applied these protections to a group of applicants who were intercepted by an Italian vessel on the high seas and returned to Libya without access to an asylum procedure.[215] In finding a violation of the right to an effective remedy, the Court drew attention to the fact that 'no provision was made for such procedures' on the military ships onto which the applicants were transferred, and

---

[207] A point made by Cantor: ibid.

[208] *MK and others v Poland* (n 202).

[209] ibid paras 143, 179; see also *MSS v Belgium and Greece*, App no. 30696/09 (ECtHR, Grand Chamber, 21 Jan 2011) para 293, cited in Cantor (n 14) 91. See also Goodwin-Gill and McAdam (4th edn) (n 201) 380.

[210] *MK and others v Poland* (n 202) para 142.

[211] *AM v The Netherlands*, App no 29094/09 (ECtHR, 3rd Section, 5 July 2016) para 70.

[212] *MSS v Belgium and Greece* (n 209) para 290.

[213] *Khlaifia and others v Italy*, App no 16483/12 (ECtHR, Grand Chamber, 15 Dec 2016) paras 276–277; 281. Compare the Court's earlier approach in *Hirsi* (n 198) para 199; citing also *Čonka v Belgium,* App no 51564/99 (ECtHR, 3rd Section, 5 Feb 2002) para 79 ff. On this case law see Diego Boza Martínez, 'Procedural Rights Protecting Immigrants Right to a Fair Trial (Article 6) and Right to an Effective Remedy (Article 13)' in David Moya and Georgios Milios (eds), *Aliens before the European Court of Human Rights: Ensuring Minimum Standards of Human Rights Protection* (Koninklijke Brill 2021) 37–39.

[214] ibid para 179. In this case, the applicants' efforts to claim asylum at the Polish border were repeatedly stymied by the Polish authorities. While an appeal against the refusal of entry decision was available, it did not have suspensive effect. The Court found this in itself sufficient to deny the appeal the character of an effective remedy (at para 147). The Court unanimously found a violation of article 13 in conjunction with article 3 of the ECHR and article 4 of Protocol No. 4 to the Convention. For discussion of previous case law, see Cantor (n 16) 91–93.

[215] *Hirsi* (n 198) paras 185; 197–200; 201–207. The Court unanimously found a violation of article 13 in conjunction with article 3 and article 4 of Protocol No. 4 respectively.

that '[t]here were neither interpreters nor legal advisers among the personnel on board'.[216] The Court also reiterated its views on the importance of access to information for an accessible asylum process.[217] A limit was reached in *ND and NT v Spain*. In that case, the Court declined to find a violation of article 13 in combination with article 4, Protocol No. 4 on the basis that, rather than using available legal procedures, the applicants had 'placed themselves in an unlawful situation by deliberately attempting to enter Spain by crossing the Melilla border protection structures ... as part of a large group and at an unauthorised location'.[218]

The Court has also found a violation of article 13 in combination with article 3 where rigid procedural requirements preclude an effective remedy. In *Jabari*, a breach was found in the government's (non-appealable) refusal to consider the applicant's asylum request on the basis that it was out of time.[219] Excessively short timeframes for filing an application or appealing a removal decision are also suspect, unless adequate safeguards are in place.[220]

It may be accepted that, as Cantor argues, these procedural standards are 'hardly inferior', to those from which asylum seekers are excluded under article 6(1).[221] However, as he recognises, the standards are 'ultimately created by subsuming the process of refugee status determination under the concept of expulsion to harm'.[222] The test for harm under article 3 (that '[n]o one shall be subjected to torture or to inhuman or degrading treatment or punishment') is not contiguous with the test for persecution under article 1A(2) of the 1951 Convention (which refers to 'being persecuted for reasons of race, religion, nationality, membership of a particular social group or political opinion').[223] As the Court itself stresses, its concern is with the risk of *refoulement*, not with the rights accompanying a grant of refugee status.[224] This leads to the situation identified by Durieux, in which:

---

[216] *Hirsi* (n 198) para 202.

[217] ibid para 204; citing *MSS v Belgium and Greece* (n 209) para 304.

[218] *ND and NT v Spain*, App nos 8675/15 and 8697/15 (ECtHR, Grand Chamber, 13 Feb 2020) paras 242–244.

[219] *Jabari v Turkey*, App no 40035/98 (4th Section, 11 July 2000) paras 48–50. The existence of a non-suspensive right to challenge the legality of the deportation decision via judicial review was insufficient to cure the breach.

[220] See ECtHR, 'Guide on Article 13 of the European Convention on Human Rights: Right to an effective remedy' (updated 31 Aug 2022) para 124, citing *IM c France*, Req no 9152/09 (Former 5th Section, 2 Feb 2012) paras 136–60; *RD c France*, Req no 34648/14 (ECtHR, Fifth Section, 16 June 2016) paras 55-64; and *EH c France*, Req no 39126/18 (ECtHR, 5th Section, 22 July 2021) paras 174–207.

[221] Cantor (n 14) 93.

[222] ibid 91, 94.

[223] Although article 33 of the 1951 Refugee Convention refers to a prohibition of return to 'the frontiers of territories where ... *life or freedom* would be threatened on account of ... race, religion, nationality, membership of a particular social group or political opinion' (emphasis added), this is considered a rule 'clearly designed to benefit the refugee': Goodwin-Gill and McAdam (4th edn) (n 201) 244. It is engaged even in the absence of formal recognition of refugee status: see further Chapter 6, Section 2.2.1.

[224] See *MK and others v Poland* (n 202) para 169, citing *MSS v Belgium and Greece* (n 209) para 286. See also Cantor (n 14) 93–94, citing *MSS*; and Durieux (n 200) 13 (calling for exposure of 'the impropriety of addressing what are essentially refugee definition matters in the ECHR forum').

'asylum' cases continue to be heard in Strasbourg—and to be adjudicated on ECHR grounds in domestic jurisdictions—in *de facto* appeals against denials of Convention refugee claims, but without reference, let alone deference, to Convention refugee criteria.[225]

Protection against *refoulement* in breach of the ECHR does not necessarily result in recognition as a refugee, as Durieux emphasises. An asylum seeker whose claim is rejected, but is nonetheless protected against return, may be granted subsidiary protection, but precluded from accessing the full suite of rights that accompany refugee status.[226] Again, as is the case under the ICCPR, this is a partial solution which stops short of guaranteeing to an asylum seeker all rights to which they may be entitled under the 1951 Convention.

2.3.1.2 Exclusion of asylum seekers from protection against detention

The Court's jurisprudence on the detention of asylum seekers shows a high level of deference to States, at the expense of individual protection. Article 5(1)(f) of the ECHR provides that:

> No one shall be deprived of his liberty *save in the following cases* and in accordance with a procedure prescribed by law: … (f) the lawful arrest or detention of a person to prevent his effecting an unauthorised entry into the country or of a person against whom action is being taken with a view to deportation or extradition. [Emphasis added.]

In *Saadi v United Kingdom*,[227] the ECtHR considered whether the general guarantee against deprivation of liberty in article 5 protected an asylum seeker subject to detention. The applicant, an Iraqi Kurd, had claimed asylum upon his arrival at Heathrow Airport. As there was no room in the reception centre used to detain asylum seekers, the applicant was given 'temporary admission' to stay at a hotel and advised to return to the airport the following morning. He did so, and was again granted temporary admission, on the condition that he return to the airport for two consecutive days. Upon his return on the second day, he was detained and transferred to the reception centre, where he remained for one week.[228] When initially detained, the applicant was given a standard form titled 'Reasons

---

[225] Durieux (n 200) 8.
[226] This may be the result either of being granted a lesser suite of rights under a complementary protection regime, or being relegated to 'legal limbo' as an unremovable person without a fixed status: see Goodwin-Gill and McAdam (n 201) 398. On the more general risk of 'legal limbo' in the gap between *non-refoulement* and the grant of asylum, see Goodwin-Gill and McAdam (4th edn) (n 201) 415.
[227] *Saadi v United Kingdom*, App no 13229/03 (ECtHR, Grand Chamber, 29 Jan 2008).
[228] See facts in ibid paras 10–12.

for Detention and Bail Rights', which the Court noted 'indicated that detention was used only where there was no reasonable alternative'.[229] The applicant was ultimately granted refugee status on appeal and challenged the legality of his detention under article 5 of the ECHR.

In its judgment, the Court reaffirmed that 'States enjoy an "undeniable sovereign right to control aliens' entry into and residence in their territory"',[230] and that 'a necessary adjunct to this right [is] that States are permitted to detain would-be immigrants who have applied for permission to enter, *whether by way of asylum or not*'.[231] The Court accordingly determined that the detention of asylum seekers, like that of other migrants, was 'capable of being compatible with [article 5(1)]'.[232] The Court nonetheless set certain limits on such detention, namely that it must not be arbitrary. It held:

> such detention must be carried out in good faith; it must be closely connected to the purpose of preventing unauthorised entry of the person to the country; the place and conditions of detention should be appropriate, bearing in mind that 'the measure is applicable not to those who have committed criminal offences but to aliens who, often fearing for their lives, have fled from their own country' ... and the length of the detention should not exceed that reasonably required for the purpose pursued.[233]

In the applicant's case, the Court was prepared to accept that the detention was carried out in good faith, and that the purpose of 'quickly and efficiently' enabling the authorities to determine the applicant's asylum claim was sufficiently connected to the purpose of preventing unauthorised entry.[234] The fact that legal assistance was available to the applicant was considered an important aspect of the assessment of the 'place and conditions' of detention.[235] In a clear recognition of the political elements of the issue, the Court concluded that '*given the difficult administrative problems with which the United Kingdom was confronted during the period in question, with increasingly high numbers of asylum-seekers* ... it was not incompatible with Article 5 § 1 (f) of the Convention to detain the applicant for seven days in suitable conditions to enable his claim to asylum to be processed speedily'.[236] Accordingly, no violation of article 5 was found. The Court's reasoning

[229] ibid para 13.
[230] ibid para 64.
[231] ibid (emphasis added).
[232] ibid para 64.
[233] ibid para 74. See also *Abou Amer v Romania*, App no 14521/03 (Third Section, 24 May 2011) para 37.
[234] *Saadi* (n 227) para 77.
[235] ibid para 78.
[236] ibid para 80 (emphasis added).

was challenged in a joint partly dissenting opinion by six judges,[237] who noted that they 'fail[ed] to see what value or higher interest can justify the notion that these fundamental guarantees of individual liberty in a State governed by the rule of law cannot or should not apply to the detention of asylum-seekers'.[238] Departing from the characterisation of the purpose of the detention in the judgment, the partly dissenting opinion noted that the applicant's detention furthered 'a purely bureaucratic and administrative goal, unrelated to any need to prevent his unauthorised entry into the country'.[239]

The dissenting judges' arguments have not gained traction, and later case law confirms the Court's willingness to countenance the detention of asylum seekers, so long as certain basic conditions are met.[240] Where asylum seekers are held in transit zones on land borders, the Court has declined to find a deprivation of liberty that engages article 5 at all. In *Ilias and Ahmed v Hungary*,[241] the Grand Chamber considered the detention of two Bangladeshi asylum seekers for over three weeks in the Röszke transit zone on the border of Hungary and Serbia. The applicants' complaints under articles 5(1) and 5(4)[242] were found to be inadmissible by the Court. The Court did not consider the circumstances constituted a *de facto* deprivation of liberty, and placed weight on the applicants' ability to return to Serbia, a country in which they did not face 'a direct threat [to] their life or health'.[243]

The rights set out in articles 5 and 6 of the ECHR are universal and will provide protection to asylum seekers and refugees in a host of legal matters that may arise while they are under the jurisdiction of a State Party. However, by carving out the asylum procedure, and many cases of detention, from these provisions, the ECtHR limits an asylum seeker's capacity to claim any rights to which he or she may be entitled as a result of refugee status. The Court's position reflects a certain deference both to States' inherent powers of immigration control and to political exigencies. The result, however, is to accept that asylum seekers are entitled to lesser rights than would be granted to other individuals. By situating asylum seekers and their claims as exceptional under international human rights law, the Court risks entrenching a two-tiered system of rights.

---

[237] See ibid, 'Joint Partly Dissenting Opinion of Judges Rozakis, Tulkens, Kovler, Hajiyev, Spielmann and Hirvelä'.

[238] ibid, 'Joint Partly Dissenting Opinion', 35.

[239] ibid, 'Joint Partly Dissenting Opinion', 34.

[240] There are of course limits: see *ZA and Others v Russia*, App nos 61411/15, 61420/15, 61427/15, and 3028/16 (ECtHR, Grand Chamber, 21 Nov 2019), finding the applicants' extended confinement to an airport boarding area in 'appalling material conditions' (para 195) without a strictly defined statutory basis for detention or access to access to information on asylum procedures amounted to violation of Article 3 and 5(1) ECHR: paras 197 and 171, also paras 40–42, 164–165, 191–195.

[241] *Ilias and Ahmed v Hungary* (n 202).

[242] Which provides that '[e]veryone who is deprived of his liberty by arrest or detention shall be entitled to take proceedings by which the lawfulness of his detention shall be decided speedily by a court and his release ordered if the detention is not lawful.'

[243] *Ilias and Ahmed v Hungary* (n 202) para 246.

2.3.2 EU law

EU Member States are subject to the Common European Asylum System (CEAS), a regime based on the 'full and inclusive application' of the 1951 Convention.[244] The CEAS consists of three Directives that set out minimum standards for the treatment of asylum seekers and refugees, a Regulation establishing which European State is responsible for determining an asylum claim,[245] a supporting Regulation on the comparison of fingerprints,[246] and a support agency. The three Directives are the recast Procedures Directive, on decision-making on refugee and subsidiary protection status; the recast Qualification Directive, setting out the grounds on which protection shall be granted and the rights accorded; and the recast Reception Conditions Directive, on the standards for the reception of applicants, including detention standards.[247] Although the CEAS is to be implemented 'in accordance' with the 1951 Convention,[248] UNHCR and academic commentators have queried whether certain of the Directives' provisions are, in fact, consistent with it.[249]

These Directives guarantee a range of procedural and substantive rights to applicants seeking protection from an EU Member State. These include rights both during the application process as well as those contingent on the grant of refugee

---

[244] See, eg, recast Qualification Directive (n 179) recital 3; Directive 2013/32/EU of the European Parliament and of the Council of 26 June 2013 on common procedures for granting and withdrawing international protection (recast), OJ L 180/60 (recast Procedures Directive), recital 3. Note however that some States have opted out of certain Directives—Denmark is not bound by either the original or recast Qualification Directive: recast Qualification Directive (n 179) recital 51; Council Directive 2004/83/EC of 29 April 2004 on minimum standards for the qualification and status of third country nationals or stateless persons as refugees or as persons who otherwise need international protection and the content of the protection granted, OJ L 304/12, recital 40.

[245] Namely, Regulation (EU) No 604/2013 of the European Parliament and of the Council of 26 June 2013 establishing the criteria and mechanisms for determining the Member State responsible for examining an application for international protection lodged in one of the Member States by a third-country national or a stateless person (recast), OJ L 180/31 (Dublin Regulation).

[246] Regulation (EU) No 603/2013 of the European Parliament and of the Council of 26 June 2013 on the establishment of 'Eurodac' for the comparison of fingerprints for the effective application of Regulation (EU) No 604/2013 establishing the criteria and mechanisms for determining the Member State responsible for examining an application for international protection lodged in one of the Member States by a third-country national or a stateless person and on requests for the comparison with Eurodac data by Member States' law enforcement authorities and Europol for law enforcement purposes, and amending Regulation (EU) No 1077/2011 establishing a European Agency for the operational management of large-scale IT systems in the area of freedom, security, and justice (recast), OJ L 180/1.

[247] Recast Procedures Directive (n 244); recast Qualification Directive (n 179); Directive 2013/33/EU of the European Parliament and of the Council of 26 June 2013 laying down standards for the reception of applicants for international protection (recast), OJ L 180/96 (recast Reception Directive).

[248] See Consolidated version of the Treaty on the Functioning of the European Union, 2016/C 202/01 (TFEU), art 78(1)–(2).

[249] See, eg, UNHCR, 'UNHCR comments on the European Commission's proposal for a Directive of the European Parliament and of the Council on minimum standards for the qualification and status of third country nationals or stateless persons as beneficiaries of international protection and the content of the protection granted (COM(2009)551, 21 October 2009)' (UNHCR, July 2010), 13–14 (with respect to articles 12 and 14); Goodwin-Gill and McAdam (4th edn) (n 201) 66 (on the Qualification Directive's limitation to third-country nationals); Cathryn Costello, *The Human Rights of Migrants and Refugees in European Law* (OUP 2016) 201–203.

or subsidiary protection status. If an application is refused and all avenues of appeal are exhausted, an applicant will nonetheless have an avenue 'to appeal against or seek review of decisions related to return' under the Returns Directive, which is not addressed in detail here.[250] The Temporary Protection Directive, also not addressed in detail here, establishes minimum standards in the case of mass influx and was first activated in the wake of Russia's invasion of Ukraine in 2022.[251] The rights set out here, whether procedural or substantive, should also be interpreted in light of the effective remedy and fair trial guarantees set out in article 47 the Charter of Fundamental Rights of the European Union (CFR). These are addressed at the end of the section.

2.3.2.1 Recast Procedures Directive

Procedural guarantees to which asylum seekers are entitled while having their status determined are set out in the recast Procedures Directive.[252] These protections apply to all applications for international protection (ie, applications either for refugee status or subsidiary protection) made within a Member State's territory, including in border zones, transit areas, and territorial waters.[253]

The Directive is premised on the principles of efficiency and fairness.[254] Member States are required to designate a 'determining authority'—a 'quasi-judicial or administrative body'—tasked with determining international protection claims in the first instance.[255] These bodies must be appropriately resourced and staffed.[256]

In its preamble, the Directive affirms the importance of ensuring an accurate decision at first instance in RSD processes.[257] To this end, the Directive requires that applicants be provided, upon request, with 'legal and procedural information free of charge, including, at least, information on the procedure in light of the applicant's particular circumstances'.[258] Member States may task NGOs with

---

[250] Directive 2008/115/EC of the European Parliament and of the Council of 16 December 2008 on common standards and procedures in Member States for returning illegally staying third-country nationals, OJ L 348/98, art 13 (Returns Directive).

[251] Council Directive 2001/55/EC of 20 July 2001 on minimum standards for giving temporary protection in the event of a mass influx of displaced persons and on measures promoting a balance of efforts between Member States in receiving such persons and bearing the consequences thereof, OJ L 212/12, art 1 (Temporary Protection Directive); and Council Implementing Decision (EU) 2022/382 of 4 March 2022 establishing the existence of a mass influx of displaced persons from Ukraine within the meaning of Article 5 of Directive 2001/55/EC, and having the effect of introducing temporary protection, OJ L 71/1. Article 3(1) of the Temporary Protection Directive provides that temporary protection 'shall not prejudge recognition of refugee status' under the 1951 Convention. See also, on access to the asylum procedure, arts 17–19.

[252] See n 244.

[253] Recast Procedures Directive (n 244) art 3. Article 3 notes that the Directive also applies to the withdrawal of international protection.

[254] See ibid recital 18 and art 31(2) ('Member States shall ensure that the examination procedure is concluded as soon as possible, without prejudice to an adequate and complete examination').

[255] See ibid arts 2(f); 4.

[256] See ibid art 4.

[257] ibid recital 22.

[258] ibid art 19. See also recital 22.

providing this information.[259] Certain limitations on its provision are set out in article 21(4).[260] A higher threshold applies where third-country nationals are detained or present at external border crossing points or in transit zones. In these cases, a State is obliged to provide information on the possibility of applying for international protection '[w]here there are indications [that the person] may wish to make an application',[261] and to 'make arrangements for translation to the extent necessary to facilitate access to the asylum procedure'.[262] Individuals and organisations giving advice to applicants are to have 'effective access' to applicants in border and transit areas.[263] Applicants who require 'special procedural guarantees' (due for example to their 'age, gender, sexual orientation, gender identity, disability, serious illness, mental disorders or as a consequence of torture, rape or other serious forms of psychological, physical or sexual violence') must receive 'adequate support' throughout the asylum procedure.[264]

The Directive also sets out States' obligations on the provision of free legal assistance and representation. There is no requirement to provide free legal assistance in first instance procedures, but if a State chooses to do so, it is relieved of its duty to provide free legal and procedural information.[265] At the appeals stage, however, States must grant free legal assistance and representation to applicants who request it.[266] This assistance shall, at a minimum, include 'the preparation of the required procedural documents and participation in the hearing before a court or tribunal of first instance on behalf of the applicant'.[267] The right to free legal assistance is subject to both conditions and safeguards. Conditions are set out in article 21. Member States may limit free assistance to those lacking resources; regulate who provides such assistance; and limit assistance for first instance appeals only.[268] In addition, article 20(3) states that legal assistance need not be provided if an appeal is considered by a court, tribunal, or other competent authority to have no prospects of success.[269] As safeguards, the Directive provides that an applicant must be provided with an effective remedy to challenge a decision not

[259] ibid art 21, noting that it may also be provided by 'professionals from government authorities or from specialised services of the State'.

[260] Member States may, eg, 'impose monetary and/or time limits on the provision of legal and procedural information free of charge … provided that such limits do not arbitrarily restrict access to the provision of legal and procedural information': ibid art 21(4)(a).

[261] ibid art 8(1).

[262] ibid.

[263] See ibid art 8(2) (also setting out permissible limits on access) and art 12(1)(c). For information that must be provided to all applicants on the procedure, see art 12(1)(a). For information on the outcome of the decision, see art 12(1)(e)–(f).

[264] ibid, recital 29 and art 24(3). See also art 2(d).

[265] ibid art 20(2), referring to procedures set out in Chapter III and the duties to provide information in art 19.

[266] ibid art 20(1). See also recital 23. Applicants are expressly entitled to consult with legal advisers at their own cost at any time: see art 22; recital 23.

[267] ibid art 20(1), referring to the appeals procedures set out in Chapter V.

[268] ibid art 21(2).

[269] ibid art 20(3).

to grant free legal assistance, and that legal assistance shall not be 'arbitrarily restricted' or 'the applicant's effective access to justice' hindered.[270] Legal advisers and counsellors are guaranteed access to detention facilities and transit zones for the purpose of consulting with the applicant.[271] The European Commission's proposal for a Regulation establishing a common international protection procedure, which would replace the recast Procedures Directive if adopted, extends the obligation to provide free legal assistance and representation on request to both first instance and appeals decisions.[272] UNHCR has welcomed this aspect of the proposal, noting that '[e]specially in complex European asylum procedures, the right to legal assistance and representation is an essential safeguard'.[273]

The recast Procedures Directive allows for the use of accelerated procedures in circumstances 'where an application is likely to be unfounded',[274] including if an applicant is considered to have come from a safe country of origin, so long as basic principles and guarantees are met.[275] Accelerated procedures are expressly condoned in transit zones or border areas.[276] However, they may not be applied to applicants in need of special procedural guarantees who could not be adequately supported in a fast-track process.[277]

The Directive also sets out guarantees for applicants at the point at which the first instance decision is made, and on appeal. At the first instance, an applicant who is not assisted by a lawyer or other counsellor must be informed of the outcome of the decision 'in a language that they understand or are reasonably supposed to understand'.[278] Decisions on international protection must be in writing, and if the application is unsuccessful, written information on how to challenge the decision must also be provided.[279]

Applicants are guaranteed an effective remedy 'before a court or tribunal' to challenge a decision that their application for protection is inadmissible or unfounded.[280] This guarantee extends to decisions taken at the border or in transit

---

[270] ibid.

[271] ibid art 23(2), citing also the obligations in the recast Reception Directive (n 247) arts 10(4) and 18(2)(b)–(c).

[272] See European Commission, 'Proposal for a Regulation of the European Parliament and of the Council establishing a common procedure for international protection in the Union and repealing Directive 2013/32/EU', COM(2016) 467 final (13 July 2016), art 15(1). This proposal was amended in 2020: see Amended proposal for a Regulation of the European Parliament and of the Council establishing a common procedure for international protection in the Union and repealing Directive 2013/32/EU, COM(2020) 611 final (23 September 2020).

[273] UNHCR, 'UNHCR Comments on the European Commission Proposal for an Asylum Procedures Regulation—COM(2016)467' (Apr 2019), 15.

[274] See recast Procedures Directive (n 244) recitals 20–21; art 31(8).

[275] ibid art 31(8)(b); Chapter II. See also recitals 40 and 42.

[276] See ibid art 31(8); art 43. See also recital 38.

[277] See ibid art 24(3); recital 30.

[278] ibid art 12(1)(f).

[279] ibid art 11. The latter requirement is waived where the applicant already has access to that information.

[280] See ibid arts 46(1) and 33(2). In border zones, see arts 46(1)(a)(iii) and 43(1). Decisions not to conduct an examination, or a full examination, on the basis that the applicant is coming from a safe

zones under accelerated procedures.[281] Member States are required to provide 'a full and *ex nunc* examination of both facts and law ... at least in appeals procedures before a court or tribunal of first instance'.[282] The Court of Justice of the European Union (CJEU) has held that this obligation is intended to confer on the court or tribunal 'the power to give a binding ruling',[283] and that the court or tribunal's assessment must consider evidence that the determining authority 'took into account', 'could have taken into account', or 'any new evidence which has come to light after the adoption of the decision under appeal'.[284] Applicants are entitled to comment on any new evidence that could adversely affect their claim.[285] However, a court or tribunal is entitled to dismiss a manifestly unfounded application without an oral hearing so long as certain conditions are met.[286]

An applicant is to be provided with 'reasonable time limits and other necessary rules ... to exercise his or her right to an effective remedy', and it is expressly stipulated that the time limits 'shall not render such exercise impossible or excessively difficult'.[287] In most cases, applicants are to be granted the right to remain in the Member State until the expiration of the period in which they are entitled to appeal, or, if they choose to appeal, until the outcome is decided.[288] Special conditions apply before an applicant in a border zone can be removed.[289]

2.3.2.2 Recast Reception Directive

Guarantees in the case of detention are set out in the recast Reception Directive.[290] An applicant for international protection cannot be placed in detention 'for the sole reason that he or she is an applicant' and can only be detained for one of the listed grounds in article 8(3).[291] Special guarantees are afforded to vulnerable

---

third country; refusals to reopen an examination; and decisions to withdraw protection are also open to challenge: see art 46(1)(a)(iv); 46(1)(b)–(c); art 39; arts 27–28; art 45. Applicants granted subsidiary status but denied refugee status may also challenge the latter decision, so long as a grant of refugee status would offer distinct rights and benefits: art 46(2).

[281]   ibid arts 46(1)(a)(iii); 43(1); 31(8).

[282]   ibid art 46(3).

[283]   Case C-556/17, *Alekszij Torubarov v Bevándorlási és Menekültügyi Hivatal* (CJEU, Grand Chamber, 29 July 2019), para 65.

[284]   Case C-585/16, *Serin Alheto v Zamestnik-predsedatel na Darzhavna agentsia za bezhantsite* (CJEU, Grand Chamber, 8 Nov 2016), paras 113 and 111.

[285]   ibid para 114. This is considered a requirement of article 47 of the CFR, discussed in Section 2.3.2.4 of this chapter.

[286]   Case C-348/16, *Moussa Sacko v Commissione Territoriale per il riconoscimento della protezione internazionale di Milano* (CJEU, Second Chamber, 26 July 2017), paras 46–49, also cited in Hathaway, *Rights* (2nd edn) (n 32) 805, fn 2841.

[287]   Recast Procedures Directive (n 244) art 46(4).

[288]   ibid art 46(5)–(6). See also Case C-808/18, *Commission v Hungary (Accueil des demandeurs de protection internationale)* (CJEU, Grand Chamber, 17 Dec 2020), paras 314–315, finding Hungary in breach of art 46(5) because the right to remain was subject to conditions that breached EU law.

[289]   ibid art 46(7).

[290]   See Recast Reception Directive (n 247) recitals 15, 21; art 9.

[291]   ibid art 8(1); art 8(3).

applicants, including minors.[292] Detention must be 'for as short a period as possible',[293] and 'speedy' judicial review is guaranteed in all cases of detention ordered by administrative authorities.[294] Applicants are entitled to 'free legal assistance and representation' for the purposes of this judicial review application, although they are entitled to limit its provision only to those in need and to regulate the providers of such assistance.[295] Financial and time limits on the provision of legal assistance may also be instituted, so long as they 'do not arbitrarily restrict access to legal assistance and representation'.[296] States may also provide that applicants will not receive more favourable treatment than nationals in regards to 'fees and other costs' related to legal assistance.[297] Communication with legal advisors 'in conditions that respect privacy' is guaranteed for detained applicants.[298] States must also inform applicants of the reason for their detention; domestic legal procedures for challenging their detention; and 'the possibility to request free legal assistance and representation'.[299]

The Reception Directive also contains some more general protections relating to appeals. Article 26 provides a right to appeal to 'decisions relating to the granting, withdrawal or reduction of benefits' under the Directive, or decisions related to residence and freedom of movement under of article 7.[300] It guarantees an appeal to a judicial authority, both on facts and law, '[a]t least in the last instance'.[301] Member States are obliged to ensure, in appeals before a judicial authority, 'free legal assistance and representation is made available on request in so far as such aid is necessary to ensure effective access to justice'.[302] Again, certain limits on the provision of legal assistance are condoned.[303] Notably, Member States may elect not to provide free legal assistance and representation 'if the appeal or review is considered by a competent authority to have no tangible prospect of success'.[304] In the specific case of appeals against rejected applications for international protection, the Directive provides that access to the labour market

---

[292] See ibid Ch IV (arts 21–25).

[293] ibid arts 8(3); 9(1)

[294] ibid art 9(3). Similarly, the Returns Directive, art 15(2), guarantees either a speedy judicial review of administrative detention or the right to bring proceedings.

[295] Recast Reception Directive (n 247) art 9(6)–(7).

[296] ibid art 9(8)(a).

[297] ibid art 9(8)(b).

[298] ibid 10(4), also setting out permissible limitations on access where 'objectively necessary for the security, public order or administrative management of the detention facility, provided that access is not thereby severely restricted or rendered impossible'. For guarantees of access to legal advisors in reception housing, see art 18(2)(b)–(c).

[299] ibid art 9(4). See also, on information on legal assistance generally, art 5.

[300] ibid art 26(1).

[301] ibid.

[302] Recast Reception Directive (n 247) art 26(2).

[303] ibid art 26(3)–(4).

[304] ibid art 26(3). The article continues—'In such a case, Member States shall ensure that legal assistance and representation is not arbitrarily restricted and that the applicant's effective access to justice is not hindered.'

cannot be withdrawn while an appeal under 'regular procedure' with suspensive effect is ongoing.[305]

2.3.2.3 Recast Qualification Directive

The recast Qualification Directive sets out the rights to be granted to a recognised refugee or a person granted subsidiary protection. Only certain rights are listed, and the list does not include article 16 of the 1951 Convention. However, the Directive notes that the rights granted therein are 'without prejudice to the rights laid down in the Geneva Convention'.[306] Article 16 is only expressly referred to in one situation—that of the rights owed to a person whose refugee status is revoked or denied because he or she is regarded, on reasonable grounds, as a 'danger to the security of the Member State' or, 'having been convicted by a final judgment of a particularly serious crime', as a danger to the community.[307] Despite being denied the full set of rights in Chapter VII of the Directive,[308] a person in this situation is entitled to a small range 1951 Convention rights, including article 16, 'in so far as [he or she is] present in the Member State'.[309] This is significant in that it makes article 16 'actionable' in such situations within the EU context, by operation of article 47 of the CFR. The operation of article 47 of the CFR, and its effect on the rights established in these three Directives, is now discussed.

2.3.2.4 Article 47 of the Charter of Fundamental Rights (CFR)—the right to an effective remedy and to a fair trial

The rights set out in the three Directives discussed may be substantive (such as the rights established in article 10 of the recast Reception Directive on the conditions of detention), or procedural (such as article 26 of the Reception Directive, on appeals, or article 46 of the recast Procedures Directive, a right to an effective remedy). All these rights, whether procedural or substantive, are bolstered by the right to an effective remedy and a fair trial in the CFR.

Article 47 of the CFR establishes a right to an effective remedy before an independent and impartial tribunal for all individuals 'whose rights and freedoms guaranteed by the law of the Union are violated'. It also guarantees individuals a 'fair and public hearing', and the possibility of 'being advised, defended, and represented'. States are obliged to provide legal aid to those who 'lack sufficient resources in so far as such aid is necessary to ensure effective access to justice'.[310]

---

[305] ibid art 15.

[306] Recast Qualification Directive (n 179) art 20(1).

[307] ibid art 14(4)–(5). The language used in article 14(4) is 'revoke, end, or refuse to renew'. Article 14(5) extends the application of article 14(4) to situations where a decision has not yet been taken.

[308] See Joined Cases C-391/16, C-77/17 and C-78/17, *M v Ministerstvo vnitra (C-391/16) and X (C-77/17), X (C-78/17) v Commissaire général aux réfugiés et aux apatrides* (CJEU, Grand Chamber, 14 May 2019), para 99.

[309] Recast Qualification Directive (n 179) art 14(6); see also ibid; *ND and NT* (n 218) para 183.

[310] Charter of Fundamental Rights of the European Union, (2012/C 326/02) OJ C 326/391 (26 Oct 2012) (CFR), art 47.

The right to a fair trial in article 47 of the CFR corresponds to the right to a fair trial in article 6(1) of the ECHR, but, unlike article 6(1), it is not limited to civil rights and obligations or criminal charges.[311] As a result, decisions regarding the entry, stay, or deportation of aliens, which are excluded from the scope of article 6(1) of the ECHR, are covered by the guarantees of article 47 of the CFR to the extent that they are regulated by EU law.[312] The preamble to the recast Procedures Directive states that '[i]t reflects a basic principle of Union law that the decisions taken on an application for international protection … are subject to an effective remedy before a court or tribunal.'[313]

In order to ensure effective judicial protection, article 47 of the CFR guarantees 'the rights of the defence, the principle of equality of arms, the right of access to a court or tribunal and the right to be advised, defended and represented.'[314] The capacity of article 47 to bolster procedural rights under individual Directives is illustrated by the 2020 CJEU Grand Chamber decision of *FMS, FNZ, SA and SA Junior*.[315] The case concerned two Afghan and two Iranian asylum seekers who had entered Hungary via Serbia. Their applications were rejected as inadmissible[316] and Hungary's attempts to deport them to Serbia were thwarted by Serbia's refusal to accept them.[317] The Hungarian authorities then amended the deportation documents to change the country of deportation from Serbia to Afghanistan and Iran, respectively, and ordered their removal.[318] This decision was taken administratively and, under Hungarian legislation, was not subject to judicial review.[319] The four applicants brought actions before the referring court arguing, inter alia, that the removal orders 'constitute[d] return decisions which must be amenable to judicial action.'[320] The referring court stayed the proceedings and referred several questions to the CJEU, including whether, in light of article 47 of the CFR, a third-country national's right to appeal 'decisions related to return' required a national

---

[311] See 'Explanations relating to the Charter of Fundamental Rights', 2007/C 303/02 (14 Dec 2007), 303/30, noting that 'in all respects other than their scope, the guarantees afforded by the ECHR apply in a similar way to the [European] Union'. See also Case C-619/10, *Trade Agency Ltd v Seramico Investments Ltd* (CJEU, First Chamber, 6 Sept 2012), para 52; Case C-279/09, *DEB Deutsche Energiehandels- und Beratungsgesellschaft mbH v Bundesrepublik Deutschland* (CJEU, Second Chamber, 22 Dec 2010), para 32.

[312] See, eg, Case C-662/17, *EG v Republika Slovenija* (CJEU, Seventh Chamber, 18 Oct 2018), paras 46–48.

[313] Recast Procedures Directive (n 244) recital 50.

[314] *EG v Republika Slovenija* (n 312) para 48. See also para 49, referring to the 'fundamental right to effective judicial protection enshrined in Article 47 of the Charter'.

[315] Joined Cases C-924/19 PPU and C-925/19 PPU, *FMS, FNZ (C-924/19 PPU) SA, SA junior (C-925/19 PPU) v Országos Idegenrendészeti Főigazgatóság Dél-alföldi Regionális Igazgatóság, Országos Idegenrendészeti Főigazgatóság* (CJEU, Grand Chamber, 14 May 2020).

[316] The applications were considered to be inadmissible under art 51(2)(f) of Hungary's Law on the right of asylum, on the basis that the four had entered Hungary via Serbia. The Grand Chamber found this provision to be inconsistent with EU law: ibid paras 51, 84, 151, 165, 177, 184.

[317] ibid paras 55, 88.

[318] ibid paras 57, 90.

[319] ibid paras 58, 77.

[320] ibid para 59.

court to review a decision upon application if the domestic law failed to provide for an effective remedy.[321] The particular Directive considered against article 47 of the CFR here was the Returns Directive, but the CJEU's reasoning nonetheless has implications for the procedural rights discussed.

Article 13(1) of the Returns Directive provides that a third-country national is entitled to an 'effective remedy to appeal against or seek review of decisions related to return ... before a competent judicial or administrative authority or a competent body composed of members who are impartial and who enjoy safeguards of independence'. In its judgment, the CJEU considered that while States are entitled to vest administrative authorities with the power to review returns decisions under article 13(1) of the Directive, a State's obligations under article 47 of the CFR must also be considered. It held that article 47 'requires Members States to guarantee, at a certain stage of the proceedings, the possibility for the third-country national concerned to bring any dispute relating to a return decision adopted by an administrative authority before a court'.[322] Ultimately, the CJEU found that article 13 of the Directive, read in light of article 47 of the CFR:

> must be interpreted as precluding legislation of a Member State under which the amendment by an administrative authority of the country of destination stated in an earlier return decision can be contested by the third-country national concerned only by means of an action brought before an administrative authority, *without a subsequent judicial review of the decision of that authority being guaranteed.*[323]

Although it was open to a State to allow 'authorities other than judicial authorities' to assess return decisions, the CJEU held that doing so did not exempt States from their responsibility to uphold article 47 of the CFR.[324] Accordingly, 'the decision of an authority that does not itself satisfy the conditions' set down in article 47 must be reviewable before a judicial body with 'jurisdiction to consider all the relevant issues'.[325] Having found an attempt to oust judicial review to be inadmissible, the CJEU went one step further, recalling the primacy of EU law and compelling the referring court to declare that it had such jurisdiction in such cases, and to 'disapply, if necessary, any national provision prohibiting it from proceeding in that way'.[326] A similar finding was made in relation to any domestic laws that purported

---

[321] ibid para 79.
[322] Unless the challenge is brought by the public prosecutor's office: ibid para 129. The word 'court' is a gloss, as the CFR in fact refers to a 'tribunal'.
[323] ibid Operative Part, para 1 (emphasis added).
[324] ibid para 128.
[325] ibid (footnotes omitted).
[326] ibid para 146 (footnotes omitted).

to oust a court's jurisdiction to review the legality of an applicant or third-country national's detention.[327]

2.3.2.5 Conclusions on EU law

The CEAS regime is one of the most robust, and justiciable, of the world's legal protection regimes. It might be asked whether the broader scope of the CFR has the effect of 'curing' the exclusion of decisions on the entry, stay, or deportation of aliens from the protections in article 6(1) of the ECHR. However, the fact remains that the number of States parties to the ECHR vastly outnumbers the EU Member States. Forty-six Member States are parties to the ECHR,[328] whereas only the twenty-seven EU Member States are bound by the CFR. As a result, many individuals who lack protection under article 6(1) of the ECHR are likewise left unprotected by the CEAS regime.

Finally, acknowledgment that the CEAS is a robust legislative regime is not to suggest that all asylum seekers will be empowered to access the remedies available in the event of a breach of their rights. Implementation is a general challenge, particularly when those whose rights are at stake lack familiarity with a legal system, do not speak the language, or are detained in a border zone or airport facility.[329] It is also well recognised that the quality of procedural guarantees offered, reception standards provided, and protection granted, differ greatly across the EU Member States.[330] Those inconsistences were laid bare in the well-known *MSS* judgment of the ECtHR Grand Chamber.[331] The Court accepted that in practice, asylum seekers in Greece faced a flawed status determination process characterised by 'shortcomings in access to the asylum procedure and in the examination of applications . . . insufficient information for asylum seekers about the procedures to be followed . . . a shortage of interpreters . . . [and] a lack of legal aid effectively depriving the asylum-seekers of legal counsel', amongst other deficiencies.[332] The 'extremely low' rate of successful applications, as compared to other EU Member States, tended, in the

---

[327] In line with the requirements of the Reception Directive (n 247) arts 9(3) and 9(5) and the Returns Directive, art 15(2)–(3): see ibid paras 261, 272, 290–291.

[328] As Members of the Council of Europe. See 'Chart of signatures and ratifications of Treaty 005' (Council of Europe, status as of 11 April 2023) <https://www.coe.int/en/web/conventions/full-list/-/conventions/treaty/005/signatures?p_auth=Lv2PfBpi/>.

[329] See, eg, discussion of difficulties that lawyers are faced with in Hungary in Júlia Iván, 'Where do State Responsibilities Begin and End: Border Exclusions and State Responsibility' in Maria O'Sullivan and Dallal Stevens (eds), *States, the Law and Access to Refugee Protection: Fortresses and Fairness* (Hart Publishing 2017) 63–64.

[330] See, eg, European Commission, 'Proposal for a Regulation of the European Parliament and of the Council on standards for the qualification of third-country nationals or stateless persons as beneficiaries of international protection, for a uniform status for refugees or for persons eligible for subsidiary protection and for the content of the protection granted and amending Council Directive 2003/109/EC of 25 November 2003 concerning the status of third-country nationals who are long-term residents', COM(2016) 466 final (13 July 2016), 2.

[331] *MSS v Belgium and Greece* (n 209).

[332] ibid para 301.

Court's view, 'to strengthen the applicant's argument concerning his loss of faith in the asylum procedure'.[333] Detention conditions were so appalling as to constitute a breach by Greece of its obligations under article 3 of the ECHR not to subject any person to 'degrading treatment'.[334] Belgium, by returning the applicant to Greece for assessment of his protection claim, had itself breached its article 3 obligations.[335] In reaching this last finding, the Court recalled that:

> the existence of domestic laws and accession to international treaties guaranteeing respect for fundamental rights in principle are not in themselves sufficient to ensure adequate protection against the risk of ill-treatment where, as in the present case, reliable sources have reported practices resorted to or tolerated by the authorities which are manifestly contrary to the principles of the Convention.[336]

Reality can often fall short of the legislative ideal—a fact that only reinforces the importance of ensuring that rights are effectively justiciable.

2.3.3 The Inter-American human rights system

The Inter-American human rights system enshrines strong due process protections for those falling within its jurisdiction. These protections are derived from the American Declaration of the Rights and Duties of Man (ADHR, or 'Declaration')[337] and the American Convention on Human Rights (American Convention),[338] as interpreted by the Inter-American Commission on Human Rights (IACmHR, or 'Commission') and the Inter-American Court of Human Rights (IACtHR) respectively. The scope, and legal effect, of these two instruments differs. The Declaration applies to a larger number of States than the American Convention, but its legal status is somewhat murkier. The American Convention—a treaty—has only twenty-three States parties,[339] of which twenty recognise the jurisdiction of the

---

[333] ibid para 313.

[334] ibid paras 231–234. See also para 230, where the Court refers to findings by organisations who visited the centre that detainees 'had no access to the water fountain outside and were obliged to drink water from the toilets'; that 145 detainees were held in a 110 sqm space; that some cells had only one bed for 14 to 17 people; that there was 'insufficient room for all the detainees to lie down and sleep at the same time'; and that the cells were 'unbearably hot'. Police also admitted that detainees had to urinate in plastic bottles due to restrictions on accessing toilets. It is little surprise that the Court considered these conditions 'unacceptable': para 233.

[335] ibid paras 360, 368.

[336] ibid para 353, citing *Saadi v Italy*, App no 37201/06 (ECtHR, Grand Chamber, 28 Feb 2008), para 147.

[337] American Declaration of the Rights and Duties of Man (adopted by the Ninth International Conference of American States, 1948), in Brownlie and Goodwin-Gill (n 7) 949 (ADHR).

[338] American Convention on Human Rights, 1144 UNTS 123 (adopted 22 Nov 1969, entered into force 18 July 1978) (AHCR).

[339] See 'Inter-American Human Rights System' (Inter-American Court of Human Rights, undated) <https://www.corteidh.or.cr/que_es_la_corte.cfm?lang=es> (accessed 11 April 2023). Trinidad and Tobago and Venezuela have each denounced the Convention in accordance with its article 78, in 1998 and 2012 respectively.

IACtHR.[340] The Declaration—which was not drafted as a binding instrument—is relevant to all thirty-five members of the Organization of American States (OAS).

Despite its non-binding origins, the IACtHR and Commission's practice gives the Declaration 'a certain normative effect'.[341] The IACtHR considers itself competent to interpret the ADHR,[342] elliptically stating that the fact that the Declaration 'is not a treaty does not ... lead to the conclusion that it does not have legal effect'.[343] Cerna describes this conclusion as a 'set of triple negatives' that 'does little to define [the Declaration's] normative status'.[344] Nonetheless, in its advisory jurisdiction, the IACtHR applies the Declaration to States—such as the US and Canada—that are OAS Members but not parties to the American Convention.[345] For its part, the Commission, a body of experts serving in their personal capacity, is empowered to monitor the observance of ADHR rights by non-parties to the American Convention under its Statute.[346] It is also empowered to interpret the American Convention, but as Cantor notes, its work on asylum issues has largely involved OAS States that are not parties to the American Convention.[347] As a result, its reporting and decision-making on asylum focuses on protections under the ADHR.

[340] ibid.

[341] Brownlie and Goodwin-Gill (n 7) 949.

[342] Under article 64 of the American Convention (which empowers the Court to interpret the Convention or 'other treaties').

[343] Advisory Opinion OC-10/89, *Interpretation of the American Declaration of the Rights and Duties of Man within the Framework of Article 64 of the American Convention on Human Rights* (IACtHR, 14 July 1989), para 47. Essentially, the Court concluded that that it was agreed the Declaration 'contains and defines the fundamental human rights referred to in the [OAS] Charter', and that the Court was authorised to interpret the Declaration when necessary to a process of interpreting the Charter or Convention: see paras 43–44.

[344] Christina M Cerna, 'Reflections on the Normative Status of the American Declaration of the Rights and Duties of Man' (2009) University of Pennsylvania Journal of International Law 1211, 1230.

[345] See, eg, Advisory Opinion OC-21/14, *Rights and Guarantees of Children in the Context of Migration and/or in need of International Protection* (IACtHR, 19 Aug 2014), para 32 (noting that 'everything indicated in this Advisory Opinion also has *legal* relevance for all the OAS Member States that have adopted the American Declaration, irrespective of whether they have ratified the American Convention' (emphasis added, citing Advisory Opinion OC-18/03, *Juridical Condition and Rights of Undocumented Migrants* (IACtHR, 17 Sept 2003), para 60). The Court considers its contentious jurisdiction to be based on the American Convention, not the ADHR: *Case of Maidanik et al v Uruguay* (IACtHR, Merits and Reparations, 15 November 2021) para 18, citing Advisory Opinion OC-10/89, *Interpretation of the American Declaration of the Rights and Duties of Man within the Framework of Article 64 of the American Convention on Human Rights* (IACtHR, 14 July 1989), para 46 and *Case of Argüelles et al v Argentina* (IACtHR, Preliminary Objections, Merits, Reparations and Costs, 20 November 2014), paras 32–38. For other applications of the ADHR, see Cerna (n 344).

[346] See Statute of the Inter-American Commission on Human Rights (approved in Resolution No 447 adopted by the OAS General Assembly, Oct 1979), available via <http://www.oas.org/en/iachr/mandate/basics/statuteiachr.asp>, arts 1(2)(b); 18; 20. The role of the Commission is enshrined in article 106 of the Charter of the Organization of American States, 119 UNTS 3 (signed 30 Apr 1948, entered into force 13 Dec 1951), but it also has functions specific to American Convention Member States under the Convention and its Statute. See further David James Cantor and Stefania Barichello, 'Protection of Asylum Seekers under the Inter-American Human Rights System' in Ademola Abass and Francesca Ippolito (eds), *Regional Approaches to the Protection of Asylum Seekers: An International Legal Perspective* (Ashgate 2014).

[347] Cantor (n 14) 97.

This section gives a brief summary of key provisions in the ADHR and its interpretation by the Commission, before focusing on two recent cases handed down by the IACtHR. As will be seen, the IACtHR has confirmed that 'judicial guarantees' under the American Convention apply to RSD procedures and has elaborated a robust set of procedural rights to protect asylum seekers during that process.

2.3.3.1 American Declaration of the Rights and Duties of Man

The ADHR[348] pre-dates the American Convention and was 'an important source of inspiration' for it.[349] Article XVIII of the ADHR provides that '[e]very person may resort to the courts to ensure respect for his legal rights', and also enshrines the concept of amparo in relation to 'acts of authority' that 'violate any fundamental constitutional rights'.[350] Habeas corpus protections are guaranteed under article XXV, while article XXVI contains additional due process rights. Article XXVII establishes the right 'to seek and receive' asylum.

In 2014, Cantor and Barichello documented a strong set of procedural protections for asylum seekers that the Commission has derived from article XXVII of the Declaration and broader human rights protections under the Inter-American system.[351] At that time, the IACtHR was yet to respond to a petition from an asylum seeker. The intervening years have seen the IACtHR engage directly with these protections in the context of asylum applications and expulsions and confirm the existence of substantive procedural guarantees in the context of asylum applications.[352]

2.3.3.2 American Convention on Human Rights

Article 8 of the American Convention establishes the 'right to a hearing ... by a competent, independent, and impartial tribunal' covering both criminal proceedings and 'the determination of [an individual's] rights and obligations of a civil, labor, fiscal, or any other nature'.[353] On its face, the 'civil' rights and obligations limb of article 8 covers a broader class of decisions than the equivalent limb of article 6 ECHR. Its broad scope has been confirmed by the IACtHR's jurisprudence. The Court considers that due process rights, 'expressed, above all, by the "judicial guarantees" ... in Article 8' encompass:[354]

---

[348] ADHR (n 337).

[349] Cantor and Barichello (n 346) 267, 270.

[350] Article XVIII provides: 'There should likewise be available to him a simple, brief procedure whereby the courts will protect him from acts of authority that, to his prejudice, violate any fundamental constitutional rights.'

[351] See Cantor and Barichello (n 346) 267, 276–280; 283–287.

[352] On these developments see also Cantor, 'Reframing Relationships' (n 14) 99–104.

[353] American Convention (n 8) art 8.

[354] While noting that many other provisions, including article 25, 'also contain regulations that correspond, substantially, to the procedural and substantive components of due process': see Advisory Opinion OC-21/14 (n 345) para 110.

the procedural requirements that should be observed to ensure that people are able to defend their rights adequately *vis-à-vis* any act of the State, adopted by any public authority, whether administrative, legislative or judicial, that may affect them.[355]

The IACtHR has held that article 8 may require a decision-making body—whether administrative or judicial—to ensure that certain procedural protections are built into the initial stage of decision-making. The nature of the decision-making body is less significant than the nature of the power exercised when determining if the protections of article 8 are engaged.[356] In *Baruch Ivcher Bronstein v Peru,* the IACtHR noted that the application of article 8 was 'not strictly limited to judicial remedies', and that it was also engaged where 'a public rather than a judicial authority issues resolutions that affect the determination of [rights within the scope of article 8(1)]'.[357] It concluded that the Migration and Naturalization Directorate, an administrative body, was bound by article 8 when issuing a resolution annulling the applicant's Peruvian nationality title.[358] The IACtHR has since confirmed that minimum guarantees under articles 8 and 25 of the American Convention are also engaged in administrative decisions on whether to grant asylum.[359]

Article 8(2) of the American Convention sets out minimum guarantees in the context of criminal proceedings, which include a right to be assisted by a translator or interpreter if required; a right to be assisted by counsel, 'paid or not as the domestic law provides'; and the right of judicial appeal.[360] In another expansive move, the IACtHR has held that the guarantees set out in article 8(2) also apply in non-criminal matters 'to the extent that [the right to due process is represented by those guarantees] is applicable to the respective procedure'.[361]

Article 25 enshrines a 'Right to Judicial Protection'. Article 25(1) guarantees to all persons 'the right to simple and prompt recourse, or any other effective recourse,

---

[355] ibid para 109 (footnotes omitted).

[356] Kosař and Lixinski consider that 'once a special body is given the authority to decide on fundamental rights enshrined in the American Convention, it is treated as a "tribunal" and must meet all the procedural guarantees required for ordinary courts.': David Kosař and Lucas Lixinski, 'Domestic Judicial Design by International Human Rights Courts' (2015) 109 American Journal of International Law 713, 723.

[357] *Baruch Ivcher Bronstein v Peru* (IACtHR, 6 Feb 2001), available via: <https://www.refworld.org/cases,IACtHR,44e496434.html>, paras 102, 105 (footnotes omitted).

[358] ibid paras 101–110.

[359] See *Case of the Pacheco Tineo Family v Plurinational State of Bolivia* (IACtHR, Preliminary Objections, Merits, Reparations and Costs, 25 Nov 2013) para 155.

[360] American Convention (n 8) art 8(2)(e); art 8(2)(h). See also the guarantees in art 8(3)–(5) (non-validity of coercive confessions; double jeopardy; general principle of public proceedings, subject to limitations where necessary to protect the interests of justice).

[361] See, eg, *Baruch Ivcher Bronstein v Peru* (n 357) para 103, cited in Amaya Úbeda de Torres, 'The right to due process', in Laurence Burgorgue-Larsen and Amaya Úbeda de Torres, *The Inter-American Court of Human Rights—Case Law and Commentary* (Rosalind Greenstein tr, OUP 2011) 657.

to a competent court or tribunal for protection against acts that violate his fundamental rights recognized by the constitution or laws of the States concerned', or
rights under the American Convention itself. The IACtHR notes that this provision reflects 'the procedural institution known as "amparo"', a 'simple and prompt
remedy designed for the protection of all the rights recognized by the constitutions
and laws of the States Parties and by the Convention'.[362]

This right is expressly guaranteed in the event that the violation was carried out
by a person acting in the course of their official duties.[363] As Burgorgue-Larsen
points out, article 25(1) provides broader protection than that offered under article
13 of the ECHR, which does not afford an effective remedy against breaches of domestic law.[364]

Under article 25(2), States parties undertake to 'ensure that any person claiming
such remedy shall have his rights determined by the competent authority provided
for by the legal system'; 'develop the possibilities of judicial remedy'; and 'ensure
that the competent authorities shall enforce such remedies'.[365]

The State has two key obligations under article 25, being to:

(i) enact into law and ensure the due application of effective remedies before the
competent authorities that protect all persons under its jurisdiction against acts
that violate their fundamental rights or that lead to the determination of their
rights and obligations and (ii) guarantee the means to enforce the decisions and
judgments of those competent authorities in order to effectively protect the declared and recognized rights.[366] [Footnotes omitted.]

The Court considers articles 8, 25 and 1 to be 'interrelated to the extent that "... effective judicial remedies ... must be substantiated in accordance with the rules of
due process of law, ... in keeping with the general obligation of ... States to guarantee the free and full exercise of the rights recognized by the Convention to all
persons subject to their jurisdiction (Art. 1(1))" '.[367]

---

[362] OC-8/87, *Habeas Corpus in Emergency Situations (Arts. 27(2), 25(1) and 7(6) American
Convention on Human Rights)* (IACtHR, 30 Jan 1987), para 32. For discussion of the various forms that
the amparo takes across different States parties, see Laurence Burgorgue-Larsen, 'The right to an effective remedy', in Burgorgue-Larsen and Úbeda de Torres (n 361) 681–83.

[363] American Convention (n 8) art 25(1).

[364] Burgorgue-Larsen (n 362) 681.

[365] American Convention (n 8) art 25(2).

[366] *Case of the National Federation of Maritime and Port Workers (Femapor) v Peru* (IACtHR,
Preliminary Objections, Merits and Reparations, 1 February 2022), para 77 (citations omitted).

[367] *Case of the Former Employees of the Judiciary v Guatemala* (IACtHR, Preliminary Objections,
Merits and Reparations, 17 November 2021), para 77, referring to *Case of Velásquez Rodríguez v
Honduras* (IACtHR, Preliminary Objections, 26 June 1987), para 91, and *Case of Bedoya Lima et al v
Colombia* (IACtHR, Merits, Reparations and Costs, 26 August 2021), para 125.

Remedies 'cannot be considered effective if they are "illusory" '.[368] The effectiveness of a remedy is not assessed with an eye to whether it grants a 'favourable result' to the plaintiff.[369]

In the *Miskito Divers* case, the Court noted that a State's obligation to ensure the existence of 'judicial or extrajudicial mechanisms that provide an effective remedy' for rights violations entailed an obligation to 'eliminate existing legal and administrative barriers that limit access to justice, and adopt those aimed at achieving its effectiveness'.[370] It continued: '[t]he Court emphasizes the need for States to address cultural, social, physical or financial barriers that prevent access to judicial or extrajudicial mechanisms for persons belonging to groups in situations of vulnerability'.[371] The Court has recognised asylum seekers and refugees as a vulnerable group.[372]

The judicial guarantees enshrined in articles 8 and 25 apply to all those present within a State Party's jurisdiction, whether legally or illegally.[373] More generally, the IACtHR has held that '[d]ue process of law … must be ensured to all persons, irrespective of their migratory status'.[374] The Court's emphasis on effectiveness bolsters the protection of those, like asylum seekers and refugees, who may face practical hurdles in accessing the legal system. It considers that justice, a notion 'closely related' to due process, must be effective—'reflected in … access to justice that is not merely formal, but that recognizes and resolves the factors of real inequality'.[375] Asylum seekers and refugees are therefore entitled to general protection under the American Convention 'judicial guarantees', which may require positive action to offset any 'real disadvantages' faced.[376]

In addition, article 7(6) guarantees 'recourse to a competent court' to anyone deprived of liberty (habeas corpus). The IACtHR has found that the legal remedies contained in articles 25(1) and 7(6) may not be suspended, on the basis that

---

[368] *Case of González et al v Venezuela* (IACtHR, Merits and Reparations, 20 September 2021), para 159 (footnotes omitted).

[369] *Case of Pavez Pavez v Chile* (IACtHR, Merits, Reparations and Costs, 4 February 2022), para 155 (footnotes omitted).

[370] *Case of the Miskito Divers (Lemoth Morris et al) v Honduras* (IACtHR, Judgment, 31 August 2021), para 50.

[371] ibid (citations omitted).

[372] *Case of Julien Grisonas Family v Argentina* (IACtHR, Preliminary Objections, Merits, Reparations and Costs, 23 September 2021), para 144.

[373] See American Convention (n 8) art 1(1); *Pacheco Tineo Family case* (n 359), finding Bolivia to have breached, inter alia, articles 8 and 25 in relation to the illegally present Pacheco Tineo family.

[374] Advisory Opinion OC-18/03 (n 345) para 121.

[375] Advisory Opinion OC-21/14 (n 345) para 109.

[376] See Advisory Opinion OC-16/99, *The Right to Information on Consular Assistance in the Framework of the Guarantees of the Due Process of Law* (IACtHR, 1 Oct 1999), para 119, cited in Advisory Opinion OC-18/03 (n 345) para 121; Advisory Opinion OC-21/14 (n 345) para 71 (on factors to determine whether additional positive measures are needed in the case of child migrants); Úbeda de Torres (n 361) 665–66 (on equality in the context of specific guarantees).

they are 'judicial guarantees essential for the protection of the rights and freedoms whose suspension Article 27(2) prohibits'.[377]

In addition to these rights, the IACtHR has now confirmed that asylum seekers are entitled to a specific set of procedural rights in the context of RSD. Article 22(7) of the American Convention guarantees 'the right to seek and be granted asylum ... in accordance with the legislation of the state and international conventions, in the event that [a person] is being pursued for political offenses or related common crimes'. The IACtHR has relied on the references to State legislation and international conventions to support an interpretation that allows for an 'inter-relationship between the scope and content of [relevant American Convention rights] and international refugee law'.[378] Accordingly, the reference to 'asylum' in article 22(7) is not restricted to the traditional Latin American concept of diplomatic asylum,[379] but encompasses refugee status under the 1951 Convention and the expanded definition of refugee under the Cartagena Declaration.[380] This broad reading enables asylum seekers who meet the definition of refugee under international and regional instruments to benefit from asylum-specific rights articulated by the Court under the American Convention.

In the *Pacheco Tineo Family* case, the Court for the first time elaborated American Convention rights relevant to the RSD process.[381] Reading the right to seek and be granted asylum under the American Convention in conjunction with articles 8 and 25, the IACtHR concluded that a series of due process protections apply.[382] These protections in many ways mirror the 'soft law' due process protections set out in ExCom Conclusion No 8 and subsequent UNHCR reports, sources that the Court expressly cites in its judgment.[383] They cover both the initial asylum decision and rights of appeal. In particular, the IACtHR found that States parties are required to guarantee to an applicant: (i) 'the necessary facilities, including the services of a competent interpreter, as well as, if appropriate, access to legal assistance and representation, in order to submit their request to the authorities',

---

[377] *Habeas Corpus case* (n 362) para 44. See also para 42. On the derogability of fair trial and due process rights in the inter-American system generally, see also Inter-American Commission on Human Rights, 'Report on Terrorism and Human Rights', OEA/Ser.L/V/II.116, Doc. 5 rev. 1 corr. (11 October 2002), available via <http://www.cidh.org/terrorism/eng/toc.htm>, para 127 (non-derogable protections in relation to detention) and paras 244–253 (on fair trial and due process). The Commission concludes that 'that the basic components of the right to a fair trial cannot be justifiably suspended', though it recognizes that 'there may be some limited aspects of the right to due process and to a fair trial from which derogation might in the most exceptional circumstances be permissible': at paras 247, 249. See also, in the same report, IV, Recommendations, para 10.

[378] *Pacheco Tineo Family case* (n 359) para 142.

[379] Advisory Opinion OC-21/14 (n 345) para 74.

[380] ibid paras 74–79. See also Cartagena Declaration on Refugees, adopted by the Colloquium on the International Protection of Refugees in Central America, Mexico and Panama, Colombia (22 Nov 1984) conclusion 3.

[381] *Pacheco Tineo Family case* (n 359).

[382] See ibid paras 154–160.

[383] See ibid footnotes to para 159. This aspect of the decision has also been noted by Cantor: see Cantor, 'Reframing Relationships' (n 14) 101–102.

as well as 'the necessary guidance concerning the procedure to be followed, in words and in a way that he can understand and, if appropriate ... the opportunity to contact a UNHCR representative';[384] (ii) that the request 'be examined, objectively, within the framework of the relevant procedure, by a competent and clearly identified authority' and that it 'requires a personal interview';[385] (iii) that decisions are reasoned;[386] and (iv) that in the case of rejection, an applicant is provided with information on how to file an appeal, and granted 'a reasonable period' for doing so.[387] Although the IACtHR did not clarify whether an administrative appeal would suffice, in a subsequent Advisory Opinion it reaffirmed that all people subject to immigration proceedings have 'the right to submit the case to review before the competent *judicial* authority'.[388] The appeal must have suspensive effect unless the application is shown to be 'manifestly unfounded'.[389] The Court also recalled that judicial safeguards exist to remedy other breaches of an applicant's rights, and that:

> regardless of a possible review ... certain judicial actions or remedies may exist, for example, amparo or habeas corpus, that are rapid, adequate and effective to question the possible violation of the rights [to seek and be granted asylum, and of non-refoulement, under the American Convention], or in the Constitution and laws of each State.[390]

While accelerated proceedings may be established to 'decide requests that are "manifestly unfounded or abusive"',[391] they, too, require certain guarantees in light of the 'serious consequences for the applicant [of] an erroneous decision'.[392] Applicants are therefore entitled to a hearing and 'the possibility of a review ... before expulsion'.[393]

Minimum guarantees also apply more generally to decisions that may result in the expulsion or deportation of an alien. In such cases, the Court interprets relevant rights under the American Convention in light of the 'vulnerability' of undocumented migrants, and the 'special needs for protection' that they require.[394]

---

[384] *Pacheco Tineo Family case* (n 359) para 159(a) (footnotes omitted)
[385] ibid para 159(b) (footnotes omitted).
[386] ibid para 159(c) ('duly and expressly founded').
[387] ibid para 159 (e).
[388] Advisory Opinion OC-21/14 (n 345) para 140 (emphasis added). The Court cites, inter alia, the *Pacheco Tineo Family case* (n 359) para 133, which likewise does not specific if the competent authority to which an appeal is directed must be judicial.
[389] *Pacheco Tineo Family case* (n 359) para 159(f). The Court also notes that States parties are required to protect applicants' personal information: para 159(d).
[390] ibid para 160.
[391] ibid para 172 (footnotes omitted).
[392] ibid.
[393] ibid.
[394] See ibid paras 128–129; citing also Advisory Opinion OC-18/03 (n 345) para 117.

It considers that such proceedings must be accompanied by the following guarantees: (i) to be informed of any charges against him or her, and of the reasons for expulsion; (ii) to be provided with information on how to defend himself or herself or how to present reasons as to why her or she should not be deported; (iii) to be informed of '[t]he possibility of requesting and receiving legal assistance, even by free public services if applicable', 'if necessary, translation and interpretation', and consular assistance 'if required'; (iv) the right to review of a negative decision 'before the competent authority', and 'to appear or to be represented before the competent authorities for this purpose'; and (v) that deportation may only follow 'a reasoned decision in keeping with the law, which has been duly notified'.[395] A migrant who raises a fear of danger upon return is entitled, 'at the very least' to an interview before the competent authorities which are required to make a 'prior or preliminary assessment ... respecting ... the minimum guarantees'.[396]

The IACtHR has also clarified that minimum guarantees with 'substantially the same' content as article 8(2) of the American Convention apply to decisions on 'fundamental rights', which include decisions affecting personal liberty, expulsion, or deportation.[397] Immigration policies based on 'obligatory detention' are considered by their nature to be arbitrary.[398] In the context of *non-refoulement*, the Court has held that asylum seekers 'cannot be turned back at the border or expelled without an adequate and individualized analysis of their application'.[399]

In the *Pacheco Tineo Family* case, the IACtHR also considered the specific guarantees owed to children, who are entitled to 'more rigorous' protection under articles 8 and 25 by virtue of their special rights under article 19 of the American Convention.[400] It held that, in line with the CRC principles already discussed,[401] a child seeking asylum 'must enjoy specific procedural and probative guarantees to ensure that fair decisions are taken when deciding their requests for refugee status'.[402]

The specific guarantees to be accorded to children were afforded more extensive analysis in the 2014 Advisory Opinion on the *Rights and Guarantees of Children in the Context of Migration and/or in Need of International Protection*.[403] The Opinion responded to a request for clarification of the human rights of children in light of significant migration to Northern American States and Europe.[404] The IACtHR considered the scope of States' obligations by reference to both the

---

[395] *Pacheco Tineo Family case* (n 359) para 133.
[396] ibid para 135.
[397] ibid para 132.
[398] ibid para 131.
[399] ibid para 153 (footnotes omitted).
[400] ibid para 220.
[401] See Section 2.2.1.
[402] *Pacheco Tineo Family case* (n 359) para 224.
[403] Advisory Opinion OC-21/14 (n 345).
[404] By Argentina, Brazil, Paraguay and Uruguay: see ibid paras 2–3.

American Convention and the ADHR.[405] In the course of its Opinion, the Court reinforced its findings on the due process guarantees owed to asylum seekers and provided further precision on the obligations owed to children in relation to migration decisions, asylum applications, and detention decisions and conditions. It concluded that:

> [i]n order to ensure access to justice under equal conditions, to guarantee effective due process, and to ensure that the best interest of the child is a paramount consideration in all the decisions adopted, States must guarantee that the administrative or judicial proceedings in which a decision is taken on the rights of migrant children are adapted to their needs and are accessible to them.[406]

The Court established a series of procedural protections derived from due process guarantees under the American Convention and ADHR that apply in the case of administrative or judicial decision-making.[407] These include, in particular, 'the right of the child to be heard and to participate in the different stages of the proceedings';[408] 'the right to be assisted without charge by a translator or interpreter', in order to avoid a situation in which the child's participation becomes 'illusory';[409] the right to free legal representation, which should be 'specialized' in terms of rights and the age of the migrant 'in order to guarantee true access to justice';[410] the right to a reasoned decision that has assessed the child's best interests;[411] and the right 'to appeal the decision before a higher court with suspensive effect'.[412] Judicial review was noted generally as 'a basic requirement to ensure adequate control and examination of administrative decisions that affect fundamental rights'.[413]

The IACtHR addressed the due process guarantees that apply to asylum applications separately.[414] From the right to seek and receive asylum in article 22(7) of the

---

[405] The Court also considered obligations under the Inter-American Convention to Prevent and Punish Torture (adopted 9 Dec 1985, entered into force 28 Feb 1987), OAS Treaty Series No 67. The Court's findings on this treaty fall outside the scope of discussion here.

[406] Advisory Opinion OC-21/14 (n 345) para 4; see also paras 108–115.

[407] ibid para 116. See also para 5 of the unanimous Opinion (where the guarantees are described as being in accordance with international human rights law).

[408] ibid paras 116, 122–123.

[409] ibid paras 116, 124–125.

[410] See ibid paras 116, 130.

[411] See ibid paras 116, 137–138.

[412] See ibid paras 116, 140–142.

[413] ibid para 140, citing *Case of Vélez Loor v Panama* (IACtHR, Preliminary Objections, Merits, Reparations and Costs, 23 Nov 2010) para 126 (commenting in the course of discussion of habeas corpus protections under art 7(6) of the American Convention). This conclusion can also be deduced from the Court's discussion of article 8(2) of the American Convention. It notes that in immigration proceedings, the State 'cannot issue administrative orders or adopt judicial decisions without respecting specific basic guarantees, the content of which is *substantially the same* as those established in [article 8(2)]: ibid para 112 (emphasis added). It can therefore be inferred that asylum seekers are entitled to a right of judicial appeal from administrative decisions under article 8(2), amongst other guarantees.

[414] Advisory Opinion OC-21/14 (n 345) paras 243–262.

American Convention and article XXVII of the ADHR, it derived the 'overriding requirement that States must design and implement fair and efficient proceedings to determine whether the applicant meets the criteria to exercise this right and to request refugee status'.[415] While the Court acknowledged that States retain discretion as to the nature of the proceedings and which authorities are deemed competent, it reaffirmed that due process guarantees apply.[416] It noted that child applicants are entitled, 'in addition to the general guarantees provided by article 8 and 25 of the American Convention', to specific guarantees 'to ensure their access to these proceedings and that just decisions are taken'.[417] Guarantees in relation to the asylum interview, for example, were drawn from UNHCR and ExCom materials.[418] Children identified as potential asylum seekers must also be given guidance on how to apply, and receive, 'if appropriate', free legal assistance in order to submit an application and 'during its processing'.[419] In essence, the Court concluded that 'States must adapt the proceedings on asylum or on the determination of refugee status, in order to provide children with a *real access* to these proceedings, allowing their specific situation to be considered'.[420]

In cases of detention, the IACtHR recalled the habeas corpus guarantees under article XXV of the ADHR and article 7 of the American Convention are bolstered by child-specific rights under the American Convention and the CRC.[421] In the Court's view, detained migrant children are in a situation of 'extreme vulnerability', and 'the presence of conditions of real inequality makes it compulsory to adopt compensatory measures that help reduce or eliminate the obstacles and deficiencies that impede or reduce the effective defense of their interests'.[422] This requires, amongst other measures, that detained children be provided with 'prompt and free access to a legal representative who can give them legal assistance'.[423] The IACtHR's findings here pre-date a 2017 Joint General Comment of the Committee on the Protection of the Rights of All Migrant Workers and Members of Their Families and the Committee on the Rights of the Child, which states that '[e]very child, at all times, has a fundamental right to liberty and freedom from immigration detention.'[424] It remains to be seen whether the Court will incorporate the Committee's position into future jurisprudence, as part of its evolutive interpretive approach.[425]

---

[415] ibid para 244.
[416] ibid para 245.
[417] ibid para 246.
[418] See ibid paras 248, 254.
[419] ibid paras 250–251 (footnotes omitted).
[420] ibid para 261 (emphasis added). This obligation includes, inter alia, 'not impeding entry to the country: ibid. On non-rejection at the border, see also para 81.
[421] ibid paras 188–190, 204.
[422] ibid para 190 (footnotes omitted).
[423] ibid para 204. See also para 206, on habeas applications.
[424] 'Joint General Comment No. 4' (n 129), para 5 (footnotes omitted).
[425] See, eg, Advisory Opinion OC-21/14 (n 345) para 55 (on the evolutive approach); and paras 57–59 (on the Court's consideration of other treaties on the rights of the child as well as 'resolutions, rulings, and declarations that have been adopted on an international level': at para 58).

This brief survey demonstrates that the Inter-American human rights system guarantees a much more substantive set of procedural rights than are available to asylum seekers seeking status determination under the ECHR or the ICCPR. Its evolutive approach to interpreting the American Convention and ADHR has given the IACtHR space to draw not merely on other international instruments, but also on the 'soft' interpretative apparatus of UNHCR materials, ExCom resolutions, and General Comments in elaborating on State obligations with regards to asylum seekers. As a result, asylum seekers and refugees who fall within the jurisdiction of the American Convention are entitled to a particularly robust set of protections in relation to access to courts generally, legal assistance and review in the course of the asylum process, and rights to challenge detention status and breaches of rights to which they may be entitled in the course of the asylum application process.

2.3.4 Banjul Charter

The Banjul Charter[426] binds fifty-four States in Africa.[427] The rights under the Charter are supported by a supervisory system comprising the African Commission on Human and Peoples' Rights (the ACmHPR), and the African Court on Human and Peoples' Rights (the ACtHPR).

The ACmHPR, a body of experts serving in their personal capacity, is established under the Banjul Charter.[428] It is mandated, amongst other duties,[429] to receive communications regarding alleged rights breaches from States and other authors.[430] It is required when undertaking its functions to 'draw inspiration from international law on human and peoples' rights',[431] and to take into consideration, 'as subsidiary measures to determine the principles of law, other general or special international conventions'.[432] The ACmHPR considers that the Charter must be interpreted 'in light of international norms and consistently with the approach of other regional and international human rights bodies'.[433]

The ACtHPR was established under a 1998 Protocol to the Charter and handed down its first judgment in 2009.[434] It has a complementary mandate to the

---

[426] See (n 8).

[427] See 'List of countries which have signed, ratified/acceded to the African Charter on Human and Peoples' Rights' (African Union, 15 June 2017) <https://au.int/sites/default/files/treaties/36390-sl-african_charter_on_human_and_peoples_rights_2.pdf>.

[428] Banjul Charter (n 8) arts 30–31.

[429] See Banjul Charter (n 8) art 45.

[430] ibid arts 48–49, 55–57. See also 'Rules of Procedure of the African Commission on Human and Peoples' Rights' (adopted by the Commission during its 27th Extra-ordinary session on 19 Feb–4 Mar 2020), Pt 3, Ch III.

[431] Banjul Charter (n 8) art 60.

[432] ibid art 61 ('laying down rules expressly recognized by member states of the Organization of African Unity, African practices consistent with international norms on human and people's rights, customs generally accepted as law, general principles of law recognized by African states as well as legal precedents and doctrine').

[433] Comm no 313/05, *Kenneth Good v Republic of Botswana* (ACmHPR, 12–26 May 2010), para 112.

[434] See Protocol to the African Charter on Human and Peoples' Rights on the Establishment of an African Court on Human and Peoples' Rights (adopted 10 June 1998, entered into force 25 Jan 2004).

ACmHPR, with jurisdiction over 'all cases and disputes submitted to it concerning the interpretation and application of the Charter ... and any other relevant Human Rights instrument ratified by the States concerned'.[435] It is also empowered to give Advisory Opinions.[436] Individuals and NGOs are not entitled to submit cases to the ACtHPR as a matter of course, but leave may be granted if the State concerned has deposited a declaration allowing such a case to be brought.[437] Only eight such declarations were in effect at the time of writing;[438] four others have been withdrawn to prevent further cases being brought by individuals and NGOs.[439] This may hamper the ACtHPR's ability to respond to individual complaints, but it maintains its general jurisdiction to consider cases submitted by the ACmHPR, amongst others.[440] In 2008, a Protocol on the Statute of the African Court of Justice and Human Rights was adopted, with the intention of merging the ACtHPR with the Court of Justice of the African Union. The Protocol is yet to enter into force.[441]

The key access to justice rights under the Banjul Charter are set out in article 7.[442] The Charter also includes an express right to 'seek and obtain asylum', and specific guarantees related to the expulsion of non-nationals who are legally in the territory of a State Party.[443] However, Cantor notes that the ACmHPR has generally

---

34 States are parties to the Protocol: see 'List of countries which have signed, ratified/acceded to the Protocol to the African Charter on Human and Peoples' Rights on the establishment of an African Court on Human and Peoples' Rights' (African Union, 14 February 2023) <https://au.int/sites/defa ult/files/treaties/36393-sl-PROTOCOL_TO_THE_AFRICAN_CHARTER_ON_HUMAN_AND_ PEOPLESRIGHTS_ON_THE_ESTABLISHMENT_OF_AN_AFRICAN_COURT_ON_HUMAN_A ND_PEOPLES_RIGHTS_0.pdf>.

[435] Protocol (n 434) arts 2–3. Naldi and d'Orsi therefore consider that the Court's jurisdiction extends to the 1951 Convention: see Gino J Naldi and Cristiano d'Orsi, 'The Role of the African Human Rights System with Reference to Asylum Seekers' in Abass and Ippolito (n 346) 45, 49–50.

[436] Protocol (n 434) art 4.

[437] ibid art 5(1) (setting out entities that are entitled to access the Court as of right) and art 5(3); art 34(6).

[438] Guinea Bissau, Niger, Burkina Faso, The Gambia, Ghana, Malawi, Mali, and Tunisia: see 'The Republic of Guinea Bissau becomes the eighth country to deposit a declaration under article 34(6) of the Protocol establishing the Court' (ACtHPR, Press Release, 3 Nov 2021) <https://www.african-court. org/wpafc/the-republic-of-guinea-bissau-becomes-the-eighth-country-to-deposit-a-declaration- under-article-346-of-the-protocol-establishing-the-court/>; (n 434).

[439] Namely Rwanda, Tanzania, Côte d'Ivoire and Benin: see 'African Human Rights System' (International Justice Resource Center (IJRC), undated) <https://ijrcenter.org/regional/african/ #African_Court_on_Human_and_Peoples8217_Rights>.

[440] Protocol (n 434) art 5(1).

[441] Protocol on the Statute of the African Court of Justice and Human Rights (adopted 1 July 2008). Only eight States have ratified the Protocol: see 'List of countries which have signed, ratified/acceded to the Protocol on the Statute of the African Court of Justice and Human Rights' (African Union, 18 June 2020)   <https://au.int/sites/default/files/treaties/36396-sl-PROTOCOL%20ON%20THE%20STAT UTE%20OF%20AFRICAN%20COURT%20OF%20JUSTICE%20AND%20HUMAN%20 RIGHTS.pdf>. Article 9 of the Protocol provides that it will enter into force 30 days after the deposit of the 15th instrument of ratification. Article 7 provides that the 1998 Protocol will remain in force for 'a transition period'.

[442] On article 7, see also Rachel Murray, *The African Charter on Human and Peoples' Rights: A Commentary* (OUP 2019) 205–52.

[443] Banjul Charter, arts 12(2) and 12(4).

analysed 'decisions involving the entry, stay and expulsion of aliens' by reference to general rights in article 7 rather than these specific guarantees.[444] He considers that by placing these protections under the ambit of 'fair trial' rights, the ACmHPR avoids cabining them in a 'separate regime attracting an arguably lesser set of expulsion-related guarantees'.[445] As will be seen, the Court has taken a similar approach in its jurisprudence.

2.3.4.1 The right to be heard generally

Article 7(1) of the Banjul Charter establishes the right of any individual 'to have his cause heard'. This encompasses the right to an appeal 'to competent national organs' in relation to acts that violate 'fundamental rights as recognized and guaranteed by conventions, laws, regulations and customs in force'; the presumption of innocence, the right to a defence, and the right to trial within a reasonable time by an impartial court.[446] The ACtHPR has confirmed that article 7 is not limited to criminal matters but rather 'encompasses the right of every individual to access the relevant judicial bodies competent to have their causes heard and be granted adequate relief'.[447] The ACmHPR considers that this right extends to all people within a State Party's 'territory and jurisdiction',[448] and requires 'unfettered access to a tribunal of competent jurisdiction to hear [an individual's] case'.[449]

The ACmHPR has found breaches of article 7(1) in cases where it was deemed factually impossible for victims to access the courts, for example where non-nationals alleged to be present illegally are detained and then expelled from the country in quick succession.[450] Breaches of article 7(1) have been found in relation to the arrest and deportation of foreign legally employed mine-workers,[451] and certain West-Africans,[452] from Angola; and in the expulsion of allegedly illegally-present West Africans from Zambia.[453] In another case, the ACmHPR found a breach of article 7(1) on the basis that Burundian refugees expelled from Rwanda were 'not allowed to defend themselves before a competent court', but

---

[444] Cantor, 'Reframing Relationships' (n 14) 95.

[445] ibid 96.

[446] Banjul Charter, art 7(1).

[447] *Jebra Kambole v Tanzania* (ACtHPR, Judgment, 15 July 2020) para 98, citing Comm no 245/02, *Zimbabwe Human Rights NGO Forum v Zimbabwe* (2006) AHRLR 128, para 213.

[448] *Good v Botswana* (n 433) para 163.

[449] ibid para 169.

[450] See, eg, Comm no 71/92, *Rencontre Africaine pour la Defense des Droits de l'Homme (RADDHO)/Zambia* (ACmHPR, Oct 1996), paras 14 (on admissibility) and 30 (on article 7); and, citing that decision, Comm no 159/96, *Union Inter Africaine des Droits de l'Homme, Federation Internationale des Ligues des Droits de l'Homme, Rencontre Africaine des Droits de l'Homme, Organisation Nationale des Droits de l'Homme au Sénégal and Association Malienne des Droits de l'Homme v Angola* (ACmHPR, 11 Nov 1997) paras 12 (admissibility) and 19 (article 7).

[451] Comm no 292/2004, *Institute for Human Rights and Development in Africa v Republic of Angola* (ACmHPR, 7–22 May 2008), para 60.

[452] Comm no 159/96 (n 450) paras 12 (admissibility) and 19 (article 7).

[453] Comm no 71/92 (n 450) paras 14 (on admissibility) and 30 (on article 7).

the nature of the prohibition on defence (whether legislative or otherwise) was not expressly stated.[454] These cases also demonstrate the ACmHPR's general trend of requiring 'judicial oversight over executive decisions particularly on issues of deportation'.[455] It considers that deportation without a hearing 'is contrary to the spirit and letter of the Charter and international law'.[456] The ACtHPR took a similar approach in a 2018 case involving an applicant who had had his citizenship revoked and was deported to Kenya because his citizenship documents were issued on the basis of falsified material. Kenya subsequently expelled him to Tanzania, and the applicant found himself living precariously in a 'no man's land' in the border zone.[457] The Court found a breach of article 7 due to both the legal and practical hurdles involved in accessing a court. In the first place, it noted that under Tanzanian law, a declaration that a person was an 'illegal immigrant' was 'final', presumably barring the applicant from appealing the decision.[458] However, the ACtHPR noted that even if Tanzanian law had been silent on the issue, the applicant was prevented from accessing a court by his arrest and expulsion. The Court considered it would be 'very difficult' to seek judicial review from the 'no man's land' in which he resided.[459] Tanzania was subsequently ordered to pay the applicant reparations.[460]

The ACmHPR's decision in *Kenneth Good v Botswana* addressed a situation in which a court was accessible, but legislation precluded its ability to provide an effective review.[461] Good, a Professor of Political Studies at the University of Botswana, was declared an 'undesirable inhabitant of or visitor to Botswana' by the Botswanan President.[462] No reasons were given for the declaration, which came after Good co-authored an article entitled 'Presidential Succession in Botswana: No Model for Africa'.[463] Good, who had lived in Botswana for fifteen years, was deported, leaving behind a seventeen-year-old daughter who had no other relatives in Botswana.[464] He pursued a constitutional challenge in the Botswana High Court prior to his deportation, and, following it, an appeal to the Court of Appeal, the highest authority in Botswana.[465] In both cases, the ouster provisions in the

---

[454] Comm nos 27/89, 46/91, 49/91, 99/93, *Organisation Mondiale contre la Torture and Association Internationale des Juristes Democrates) [sic] Commission International des Juristes (C.I.J), Union Interafricaine des Droits de l'Homme v Rwanda* (ACmHPR, 21–31 Oct 1996) paras 1, 34.

[455] See *Good v Botswana* (n 433), para 178.

[456] Comm no 159/96 (n 450) para 20.

[457] *Anudo v Tanzania* (n 65) paras 4; 69–71, 117, 121.

[458] ibid para 113.

[459] ibid para 114.

[460] *Anudo Ochieng Anudo v Tanzania* (ACtPHR, Judgment (Reparations), 2 December 2021, para 102.

[461] *Good v Botswana* (n 433).

[462] Exercising a discretionary power vested in him under s 7(f) of the Botswana Immigration Act.

[463] *Good v Botswana* (n 433) paras 1–4; 122.

[464] She was unable to accompany him due to 'the critical stage of her studies'. See ibid paras 6, 127, 213.

[465] ibid paras 5–8.

Immigration Act were deemed to have prevented the court from reviewing the President's decision.[466] The ACmHPR considered that:

> while the victim was able to access judicial organs to have his cause heard, the ouster of the jurisdiction of the organs made that access illusory as the organs have been prevented by law from entertaining the victim's grievance.[467]

The ACmHPR found that the ouster clauses had the effect both of violating the right to an appeal in article 7(1) and of 'threaten[ing]' judicial independence, guaranteed under article 26.[468]

Much of the ACtHPR's jurisprudence on article 7 has developed in the context of criminal cases. In several such cases, the Court has read a right to free legal aid into article 7(1)(c), which provides that the right to have one's cause heard encompasses 'the right to defense, including the right to be defended by counsel of his choice'.[469] It justifies this implication by reading the right to defence under the Charter 'in light of ... Article 14(3)(d) [ICCPR]', which addresses rights in relation to criminal charges.[470] In determining whether legal aid should be provided, the Court considers the nature of the charges and the potential sentence faced.[471] It notes that the interests of justice will 'inevitably require that free legal assistance be extended to an accused person where he/she is indigent and is charged with a serious offence which carries a severe penalty'.[472] It is not clear whether the ACtHPR would be willing to imply a right of free legal aid in civil cases and/or administrative appeals if it were deemed necessary in the interests of justice. The reliance on article 14(3)(d), a criminal provision, suggests that this implication is limited to criminal cases. However, in *Mugesera v Rwanda*, the Court noted that free legal assistance was 'an inherent right of the right to a fair trial, *in particular* the right to defence guaranteed in Article 7(1)(c)', suggesting that it may be open to treating legal aid in criminal cases as a single example of a broader class of cases in which legal aid is necessary.[473] In support of this view, the ACmHPR's Principles and Guidelines on

---

[466] The relevant sections of the Immigration Act were ss 11(6) ('[n]o appeal shall lie ... against any notice that the person is a prohibited immigrant by reason of any declaration by the President under Section 7(f) and no court shall question the adequacy of the grounds for any such declaration') and 34(a) ('[n]o person shall have the right to be heard before or after a decision is made by the President in relation to that person under this Act ... '): see ibid, para 166 (setting out the provisions); and paras 179–180.

[467] ibid para 179.

[468] ibid para 180.

[469] See, amongst others, *Léon Mugesera v Rwanda* (ACtHPR, Judgment, 27 Nov 2020) para 52; citing *Alex Thomas v Tanzania* (ACtHPR, Judgment, 20 Nov 2015) para 114; *Matter of James Wanjara and 4 others v Tanzania* (ACtHPR, Judgment, 25 Sept 2020) para 66.

[470] *Thomas v Tanzania* (n 469) para 88. See also *Mohamed Abubakari v Tanzania* (ACtHPR, Judgment, 3 June 2016), paras 138–139.

[471] See *Thomas v Tanzania* (n 469) para 115; *Abubakari v Tanzania* (n 470) para 139.

[472] *Wanjara v Tanzania* (n 469) para 69.

[473] *Mugesera v Rwanda* (n 469) para 52.

the Right to a Fair Trial and Legal Assistance in Africa provide for the right of legal assistance 'in any case where the interest of justice so require', be it civil or criminal.[474] A right to an interpreter has also been implied into article 7(1)(c) in criminal cases.[475] Again, it remains to be seen if the Court will extend this right to apply in civil cases, as provided for in the ACmHPR's Guidelines.[476]

In line with the ECtHR and the IACtHR, the Court considers that article 7 implies a right to a reasoned judgment.[477] This statement was made in the course of a case related to employment termination and therefore clearly extends to both criminal and civil matters. This implied right supports an applicant's right to an appeal.[478] A State is required to 'take necessary actions' to facilitate the right of appeal, including by providing a prospective appellant with copies of the relevant judgments or decisions.[479] Only one level of judicial appeal is guaranteed by article 7,[480] although the ACtHPR has held that a mechanism to review the findings of appellate courts is required in cases where 'there are cogent reasons to believe that the findings ... are no longer valid'.[481]

Equality and equal protection before the law are guaranteed under article 3 of the Banjul Charter. The ACmHPR has noted that the right to equal protection 'relates to the right of all persons to have the same access to the law and courts', and is 'akin to the right to due process of law'.[482] In a 2008 decision, the ACmHPR considered whether the obligation to equal protection had been breached in relation to the deportation of fourteen Gambians from Angola.[483] Although it was prepared to declare the matter admissible on the basis that 'mass expulsions ... deny victims the opportunity to establish the legality of these actions in the courts',[484] it declined to find a breach of article 3(2). The ACmHPR noted that it found no evidence that the victims 'were treated differently from the other nationals arrested and detained under the same conditions'.[485] This statement is a little ambiguous—it is not clear whether by the words 'the other', the ACmHPR intends to compare the victims to other *foreign* nationals, 'tens of thousands' of whom were expelled in the same

---

[474] 'Principles and Guidelines on the Right to a Fair Trial and Legal Assistance in Africa' (2003) available via <https://www.achpr.org/legalinstruments/detail?id=38>, H.a.

[475] *Armand Guehi v Tanzania, Republic of Côte d'Ivoire Intervening* (ACtHPR, Judgment, 7 Dec 2018), considering article 7(1)(c) in light of ICCPR art 14(3)(a) and (f).

[476] 'Principles and Guidelines' (n 474) A.2(g).

[477] *Fidèle Mulidahabi v Rwanda*, App no 004/2017 (ACtHPR, Judgment, 26 June 2020) paras 63–64 (drawing on 'Principles and Guidelines' (n 474) A(2)(i)).

[478] See the court's discussion of Commission findings in para 64, and references therein.

[479] See *Mgosi Mwita Makungu v Tanzania* (ACtHPR, Judgment, 7 Dec 2018) paras 57, 65. Although this was a criminal case, the Court makes no indication that the principle is limited to criminal proceedings.

[480] *Yahaya Zumo Makame and others v Tanzania*, App no 023/2016 (ACtHPR, Judgment, 25 June 2021) paras 74–75.

[481] *Kambole v Tanzania* (n 447) para 96.

[482] *Institute for Human Rights and Development in Africa v Angola* (n 451) para 45.

[483] ibid.

[484] ibid para 40, referring to *RADDHO/Zambia* (n 450).

[485] *Institute for Human Rights and Development in Africa v Angola* (n 451) para 47.

year,[486] or to *Angolan* nationals, who may be detained and arrested in the same conditions, but presumably would not be subject to deportation. If the former, the ACmHPR could be critiqued for choosing a comparator that is, by its nature, discriminatory. If the latter, it accepts that non-nationals should be compared to foreign nationals when determining if equal protection has been breached. Where access to courts is denied generally by a State, therefore, article 3(2) is unlikely to offer redress, and article 7(1) may offer stronger protection.[487]

2.3.4.2 Rights specific to asylum seekers

Asylum-specific obligations are contained in both the Banjul Charter and in other regional instruments.[488] Relevantly for current purposes, article 12(3) of the Banjul Charter establishes a right to 'seek and obtain asylum in other countries in accordance with the law of those countries and international conventions'.[489] Article 12(4) requires that any decision to expel a non-national who has been lawfully admitted must be taken in accordance with the law. Mass expulsion is prohibited under article 12(5).

At the time of writing, the Court had not yet considered the application of article 7 or 12 in the context of an RSD appeal. There is, however, some discussion of these issues within ACmHPR decisions. In one decision in which no breach of article 7 was ultimately found, the ACmHPR appeared to conclude that article 7(1) has more stringent requirements for an appeal from a negative RSD decision than those laid out in ExCom guidance.[490] While ExCom

---

[486] ibid para 67.

[487] In *Institute for Human Rights and Development in Africa v Angola*, a breach of article 7(1)(a) was nonetheless found: ibid para 60. Additional rights are afforded to women and children in relation to access to justice under specialised instruments. See African Charter on the Rights and Welfare of the Child, OAU Doc. CAB/LEG/24.9/49 (1990) (adopted July 1990, entered into force 29 Nov 1999), art 17 (on rights in the context of criminal proceedings); Protocol to the African Charter on Human and Peoples' Rights on the Rights of Women in Africa (adopted 11 July 2003, entered into force 25 Nov 2005), art VIII(a) (providing that States parties take 'all appropriate measures to ensure … effective access by women to judicial and legal services'). Child-specific protections are also established by the Commission in its 'Principles and Guidelines' (n 474) O.

[488] Space does not allow full discussion of these rights, which include an obligation to determine whether an applicant is a refugee, under the OAU Convention governing the specific aspects of refugee problems in Africa, 1001 UNTS 45 (adopted 10 Sept 1969, entered into force 20 June 1974) art 1(6); and to bring perpetrators of violence and rape against asylum seeking women to justice, under the Protocol to the African Charter on Human and Peoples' Rights on the Rights of Women in Africa (n 487) art XI(3).

[489] For critique of the reference to domestic law in this clause, see Ademola Abass and Dominique Mystris, 'The African Union Legal Framework for Protecting Asylum Seekers' in Abass and Ippolito (n 346) 27–28, noting that '[many African States do not have national laws that meet the requirements set out in international let alone regional instruments': at 27. However, a recent study finds that 'at least 46 of 54 States in Africa now possess dedicated national refugee laws', which in some cases go beyond international obligations: see David James Cantor and Farai Chikwanha, 'Reconsidering African Refugee Law' (2019) 31 International Journal of Refugee Law 182, 241. The authors note, however, that 'the quality of such laws remains somewhat mixed': at 242 (footnote omitted).

[490] Comm no 235/2000, *Dr Curtis Francis Doebbler v Sudan* (ACmHPR, 11–25 Nov 2009) para 165. As Cantor notes, the ACmHPR appears to be referring to ExCom Conclusion No 8 here, despite

considers that an appeal may be heard either by an administrative or judicial body,[491] the ACmHPR emphasises 'the need to adopt judicial remedies in the event of the failure of ... administrative mechanisms', such as the RSD mechanism in place.[492]

In the context of admissibility findings, the ACmHPR has shown a general openness to arguments on the practical difficulty that refugees face in accessing courts. In one decision, on crimes committed against Sierra Leonean refugees in Guinea, it accepted that 'the impractical number of potential plaintiffs makes it difficult for domestic courts to provide an effective avenue of recourse'.[493] It reflected that domestic courts 'would be severely overburdened if even a slight majority of victims chose to pursue legal redress in Guinea'.[494] The complaints made no claim of a violation under article 7 in that case, although breaches were found under article 12(5) and other articles.[495] In *Doebbler v Sudan,* the ACmHPR considered the forced repatriation of 14,000 Ethiopian refugees from Sudan. In considering whether local remedies had been exhausted, it concluded that 'it was not reasonable to expect refugees to seize the Sudanese Courts of their complaints, given their extreme vulnerability and state of deprivation, their fear of being deported and their lack of adequate means to seek legal representation'.[496] The perceived difficulty in obtaining a judicial remedy was no doubt enhanced by the fact that an 'Information Notice' posted on the door of the UNHCR compound stated that the loss of the Ethiopians' refugee status after 1 March 2000 would be accompanied by the cessation of rights, including 'legal status in respect of resolving individual cases and the right to appear before the courts etc'.[497]

The ACmHPR's general concern with effective access to courts is also demonstrated in its Fair Trial Principles and Guidelines, which enjoin States to:

> ensure that access to judicial services is not impeded including by the distance
> to the location of judicial institutions, the lack of information about the judicial

referring to Decision no 69. However, it is questionable whether the ACmHPR in fact 'finds that Article 7(1) ACHPR requires administrative authorities determine asylum claims to meet the procedural standards set out in [that conclusion]', as Cantor suggests. The ACmHPR's paraphrasing appears to merely to 'take note' of paragraph (e)(vi) of that Conclusion, which, as Cantor recognises, gives more flexibility to States than article 7(1) of the Charter allows. See Cantor, 'Reframing Relationships' (n 14) 95–96.

[491] ExCom, 'Determination of Refugee Status', Conclusion No 8 (XXVIII) (12 Oct 1977) <http://www.unhcr.org/excom/exconc/3ae68c6e4/determination-refugee-status.html> (ExCom Conclusion No 8), para (e)(vi). See further Chapter 2, Section 2.2.

[492] Comm no 235/2000 (n 490) para 165.

[493] Comm no 249/2002, *African Institute for Human Rights and Development (On Behalf of Sierra Leonean Refugees in Guinea) v Guinea* (ACmHPR, 23 Nov–7 Dec 2004) para 34.

[494] ibid (concluding that exhaustion of domestic remedies was 'impractical').

[495] ibid operative provisions.

[496] Comm no 235/2000 (n 490) para 116.

[497] See ibid para 6.

system, the imposition of unaffordable or excessive court fees and the lack of assistance to understand the procedures and to complete formalities.[498]

However, in a concerning development, the ACmHPR has taken a very restrictive view of the procedural safeguards that are engaged during immigration detention. In *George Iyanyori Kajikabi v Egypt*, the Commission considered whether the detention of the applicants, without access to lawyers or to a court, breached the prohibition on arbitrary arrest or detention under article 6 of the Banjul Charter.[499] Relying on a recommendation in ExCom Conclusion No 44, 'Detention of Refugees and Asylum-Seekers',[500] the Commission found that it did not. It instead considered that:

> in the case of detention of asylum-seekers and refugees, international standards do not require access to a lawyer or a court for purposes of review, only that they be granted access to UNHCR, which was in fact done in the present case. [The] Commission thus finds that being granted access to UNHCR is sufficient and that they did not in addition have to be provided with legal counsel, since the UNHCR could have sufficiently supported them in any administrative review processes.[501]

In reaching this conclusion, the ACmHPR did not consider the habeas corpus obligation in article 9(4) of the ICCPR, which guarantees judicial review to a detained asylum seeker.[502] Nor did it consider whether effective access to courts requires that a detained person be granted direct access to a lawyer.[503] It remains to be seen whether the Commission will take a similarly restrictive view of asylum seeker rights when eventually called on to examine access to the courts in the context of negative RSD decisions.

---

[498] 'Principles and Guidelines' (n 474) K.d.

[499] Comm no 344/07, *George Iyanyori Kajikabi v Egypt* (ACmHPR, 13 July–7 Aug 2020).

[500] ExCom, 'Detention of Refugees and Asylum-Seekers', Conclusion No 44 (XXXVII) (1986), para (g) ('Recommended that refugees and asylum-seekers who are detained be provided with the opportunity to contact the Office of the United Nations High Commissioner for Refugees or, in the absence of such office, available national refugee assistance agencies'). See further Chapter 2, Section 2.2.

[501] Comm no 344/07 (n 499) para 217.

[502] See HRC, 'General Comment No. 35: Article 9 (Liberty and security of person)' CCPR/C/GC/35 (16 Dec 2014) paras 3, 40. In 2010, the Working Group on Arbitrary Detention recalled cases in which States had denied the right of habeas corpus, noting 'a weakened habeas corpus institution has led to a weaker challenge to the practice of arbitrary detention' and that 'administrative detention and a weak or non-existent habeas corpus facility appear to be correlated.' See Human Rights Council, 'Report of the Working Group on Arbitrary Detention', A/HRC/13/30 (18 January 2010), paras 79–80. See also UNGA, 'Report of the Special Rapporteur on the promotion and protection of human rights and fundamental freedoms while countering terrorism' A/63/223 (6 August 2008), para 13. Both these reports are cited in the United Nations Counter-Terrorism Implementation Task Force, Working Group on protecting human rights while countering terrorism, 'Basic Human Rights Reference Guide: Right to a Fair Trial and Due Process in the Context of Countering Terrorism' (United Nations, October 2014), para 25.

[503] See, eg, HRC, 'General Comment No. 35' (n 502) para 46 ('[t]o facilitate effective review, detainees should be afforded prompt and regular access to counsel').

2.3.5 Arab Charter on Human Rights

Article 13 of the Arab Charter on Human Rights, which is non-derogable,[504] enshrines the right to a fair trial 'that affords adequate guarantees before a competent, independent and impartial court that has been constituted by law to hear any criminal charge against him or to decide on his rights or his obligations.'[505] Article 12 establishes a right, available to all within a States parties jurisdiction, to 'seek a legal remedy before courts of all levels.'[506] Equality before the law, equality before the courts, and non-discrimination are also guaranteed,[507] although the Convention has been subject to criticism for its approach to the rights of women and non-citizens, amongst other issues.[508] Several rights are limited to citizens,[509] though not the fair trial guarantees or habeas corpus rights.[510] States parties also commit to providing legal aid to those 'without the requisite financial resources … to enable them to defend their rights.'[511] Article 23 establishes a right to an effective remedy for violations of the Charter.

The Arab Human Rights Committee is responsible for considering reports issued by States parties on their implementation of the Charter and providing comments and recommendations.[512] The Open Society Initiative reports that, according to the Committee's Rules of Procedure, it is also competent to interpret the Charter.[513] In 2014, the Ministerial Council of the League of Arab States approved a Statute for an Arab Court of Human Rights.[514] The Court is not yet operational, and only Saudi Arabia has ratified the Statute.[515] Under the Statute, the Court has

---

[504] See Arab Charter on Human Rights (n 8) art 4(2).

[505] See ibid, art 13 in Brownlie and Goodwin-Gill (n 7) 1120. See also rights afforded in the context of arrest, detention and criminal trial under arts 14–20.

[506] ibid art 12.

[507] ibid arts 11–12.

[508] See commentary in Brownlie and Goodwin-Gill (n 7) 1120, citing comments by Louise Arbour, UN High Commissioner for Human Rights in 'Arab rights charter deviates from international standards, says UN official' (UN News, Press release, 30 Jan 2008); Mervat Rishmawi, 'Arab Charter on Human Rights (2004)', Max Planck Encyclopaedia of Public International Law (June 2008) paras 30–43.

[509] Rishmawi notes that in some cases, these limitations are inconsistent with other human rights treaties: Rishmawi, 'Arab Charter' (n 508) paras 30–34.

[510] For the latter see Arab Charter on Human Rights (n 8) art 14(6) ('Anyone who is deprived of his liberty by arrest or detention shall be entitled to petition a competent court in order that it may decide without delay on the lawfulness of his arrest or detention and order his release if the arrest or detention is unlawful').

[511] ibid art 13(1). See also, in the context of a criminal trial, art 16(4).

[512] ibid arts 45, 48.

[513] Mervat Rishmawi, 'The League of Arab States: Human Rights Standards and Mechanisms: Towards Further Civil Society Engagement: A Manual for Practitioners' (Open Society Foundations/Cairo Institute for Human Rights Studies, undated) 41, available via: <https://www.cihrs.org/wp-content/uploads/2015/12/league-arab-states-manual-en-20151125.pdf>.

[514] See International Commission of Jurists, 'The Arab Court of Human Rights: A Flawed Statute for an Ineffective Court' (2015), available via <https://www.icj.org/wp-content/uploads/2015/04/MENA-Arab-Court-of-Human-Rights-Publications-Report-2015-ENG.pdf>, 9–10.

[515] See Ahmed Almutawa, 'The Arab Court of Human Rights and the Enforcement of the Arab Charter on Human Rights' (2021) 21 Human Rights Law Review 506, 511 and fn 38; 'Arab League Secretary General Welcomes Saudi Arabia's Ratification on the Statute of Arab Court for Human Rights (Saudi Press Agency, 24 June 2016) <https://www.spa.gov.sa/viewfullstory.php?lang=en&newsid=1513644>,

jurisdiction over 'all suits and conflicts resulting from the implementation and in-terpretation' of the Charter.[516] However, individuals lack the right to petition the Court directly.[517] This deficiency has been strongly criticised by the International Commission of Jurists, amongst others.[518]

3. Customary International Law

The survey of treaties in Section 2 demonstrates an uneven patchwork of pro-tection across universal and regional instruments. While this diversity indicates the wealth of material from which evidence of custom can be drawn, it can also exacerbate the challenge of determining whether a specific human rights obliga-tion has attained the status of customary international law. Such an obligation will be binding on all States (excepting persistent objectors), whether or not they are bound by an equivalent right under a universal or regional treaty. The scope of this book prevents a full survey of whether the obligations identified in Section 2 have reached the status of custom. Instead, the purpose of this section is to highlight the challenges involved in that analysis and conclusions in recent scholarship.

International custom, 'as evidence of a general practice accepted as law', is one of the core sources of international law under the ICJ Statute.[519] The dual require-ments of general State practice and *opinio juris*—a sense that that practice is driven by binding obligation—are well established. But how widespread that practice must be, and how best to prove a sense of legal obligation, have long raised diffi-culties.[520] The ILC recently finalised its work on a series of draft conclusions on the formation of customary international law, which, while not resolving all chal-lenges, at least confirm the ground rules within which issues can be debated.[521]

---

cited in 'Middle East and North Africa' (IJRC, undated) <https://ijrcenter.org/regional/middle-east-and-north-africa/>.

[516] See 'English Version of the Statute of the Arab Court of Human Rights' (tr. Mohammed Amin Al-Midani, non-official translation) (Arab Center for International Humanitarian Law and Human Rights Education (ACIHL), undated) <https://acihl.org/texts.htm?article_id=44>, art 16.

[517] See ibid art 19. Access is limited to 'a State Party whose citizen claims to be a victim of a human rights violation', or, with the acceptance of the State concerned, 'one or more NGOs that are accredited and working in the field of human rights' in that State.

[518] See International Commission of Jurists (n 514) 5–6; 26–28; Joe Stork, 'New Arab Human Rights Court is doomed from the Start' (HRW, 26 Nov 2014), available via: <https://www.hrw.org/news/2014/11/26/new-arab-human-rights-court-doomed-start> (with note that it was published in 'International Business Times'). But see also Almutawa (n 515) 531, arguing that 'an imperfect Court is better than no Court at all.'

[519] Per art 38(1)(b).

[520] A bibliography of writings on custom is included as an Addendum to ILC, 'Fourth report on iden-tification of customary international law by Michael Wood, Special Rapporteur', A/CN.4/695/Add.1 (68th sess, 2016). This gives some sense of the wealth of literature and particular issues of debate.

[521] See ILC, 'Draft conclusions on identification of customary international law', in *Report of the International Law Commission*, A/73/10 (70th sess, 2018). The draft conclusions address the identifica-tion of custom, and do not 'systematically' address its formation over time: Commentary to Conclusion

First, identifying a rule of customary international law requires 'systematic and rigorous analysis', with regard to 'the overall context, the nature of the rule, and the particular circumstances in which the evidence in question is to be found'.[522] The two elements of general practice and *opinio juris* are to be ascertained separately.[523] To constitute general practice, State practice must be 'sufficiently widespread and representative, as well as consistent'.[524] '[U]niversal participation', or consistency, is not required.[525] However, inconsistent conduct should 'generally have been treated as [a breach] of that rule, not as indications of the recognition of a new rule'.[526] Accordingly, the existence of breaches of fair trial obligations (as have been found in several of the judgments surveyed here) would not prevent a finding on the customary nature of an obligation absent evidence that the State challenges the binding nature of the obligation itself. While States are the primary source of practice, international organisations may also contribute '[i]n certain cases'.[527]

To prove the requisite *opinio juris*, the relevant practice must be 'undertaken with a sense of legal right or obligation'.[528] It might be thought that a binding treaty obligation in the same terms as the potential rule of customary international law was therefore strong evidence of *opinio juris*.[529] However, the commentary takes the view that:

[s]eeking to comply with a treaty obligation as a treaty obligation ... is not acceptance as law for the purpose of identifying customary international law: practice undertaken with such intention does not, by itself, lead to an inference as to the existence of a rule of customary international law.[530]

1, para 5. The General Assembly has welcomed the conclusion of the ILC's work and encouraged its 'widest possible dissemination': UNGA Res 73/203, 'Identification of customary international law' (20 Dec 2018), paras 1, 4.

[522] See, respectively, 'Draft conclusions on identification of customary international law' (n 521) commentary to draft conclusion 3, para 1 and draft conclusion 3, para 1. For analysis of how nature and context affects the application of the test for identifying customary international law, see Katie A Johnston, 'The Nature and Context of Rules and the Identification of Customary International Law' (2021) 32(4) EJIL 1167. On the Special Rapporteur's engagement with human rights (or lack thereof), see William A Schabas, *The Customary International Law of Human Rights* (OUP 2021) 38; 41.

[523] ibid draft conclusion 3, para 2.

[524] ibid draft conclusion 8.

[525] ibid commentary to draft conclusion 8, paras 3, 7. Although practice should be 'virtually or substantially uniform': at para 7.

[526] *Military and Paramilitary Activities in and against Nicaragua (Nicaragua v United States of America)*, Merits, Judgment [1986] ICJ Rep 14, 98, cited in ibid commentary to draft conclusion 8, para 8.

[527] 'Draft conclusions on identification of customary international law' (n 521) draft conclusion 4, paras 1–2.

[528] ibid draft conclusion 9(1).

[529] In support of this position see, eg, James Crawford, *Brownlie's Principles of Public International Law* (9th edn, OUP 2019) 25; Chetail, 'Transnational movement' (n 100) 20.

[530] 'Draft conclusions on identification of customary international law' (n 521) commentary to draft conclusion 9, para 4 (footnotes omitted).

This position seems unsatisfactory when assessing multiple treaties that cover similar subject matter as evidence. In the case of fair trial guarantees, the patchwork of regional instruments arguably supports the identification of legal obligations that are larger than those treaties' constituent parts (or parties). Scouring for individual examples of States applying those rules to non-parties appears less convincing as evidence of *opinio juris*[531] than the broad agreement of a large majority of the world's states as to the existence of an obligation, even if treaty-based.[532] While the ILC considers that 'near universal' membership of a single treaty can be 'particularly indicative' of whether a rule reflects customary international law,[533] no comment is made on the relevance of broad membership where multiple treaties are involved. The draft conclusions include the (not particularly helpful) guidance that where multiple treaties contain the same rule, it 'may, but does not necessarily, indicate that the treaty rule reflects a rule of customary international law'.[534]

It has long been recognised that proving a human rights principle has reached the status of customary law poses a particular challenge. Writing in 2015, Thirlway noted that it appeared 'to be still a perfectly tenable view that there is in fact no general international customary law of human rights'.[535] As Simma and Alston note, 'an element of [State] interaction—in a broad sense—is intrinsic to, and essential to, the kind of State practice leading to the formation of customary international law'.[536] However human rights treaties involve vertical, not horizonal, relationships.[537] This ill-fit has encouraged some commentators to argue for a flexible approach to the identification of custom where a human rights obligation is concerned. In Simma and Alston's words:

> [g]iven the fundamental importance of the human rights component of a just
> world order, the temptation to adapt or re-interpret the concept of customary law

---

[531] On this point, see ibid.

[532] This issue recalls the Baxter Paradox, namely that 'as the number of parties to a treaty increases, it becomes more difficult to demonstrate what is the state of customary international law dehors the treaty': RR Baxter, *Treaties and Custom (Vol 129): Collected Courses of the Hague Academy of International Law* (Brill Nijhoff 1970) 64. See also discussion in Hugh Thirlway, 'Professor Baxter's Legacy: Still Paradoxical?' (2017) 6(3) ESIL Reflections, available via <https://esil-sedi.eu/wp-content/uploads/2017/03/ESIL-Reflection-Thirlway_0.pdf>, and James Richard Crawford, *Chance, Order, Change: The Course of International Law (Vol 365): Collected Courses of the Hague Academy of International Law* (Brill Nijhoff 2013) 90–112. Crawford considers and rejects the possibility that a presumption of *opinio juris* can be implied from widespread ratification of a treaty: at 109. He ultimately concludes that the Baxter Paradox is 'not so much an insoluble paradox as a valid reflection on the distinct attributes of treaties and custom': at 110.

[533] 'Draft conclusions on identification of customary international law' (n 521) commentary to draft article 11, para 3. This position does not seem entirely consistent with the Special Rapporteur's earlier comments on treaty obligations, cited at n 530.

[534] ibid draft conclusion 11(2). See also commentary to draft article 11, para 8.

[535] Hugh Thirlway, 'Human Rights in Customary Law: An Attempt to Define Some of the Issues' (2015) 28 Leiden Journal of International Law 495 at 497.

[536] Bruno Simma and Philip Alston, 'The Sources of Human Rights Law: Custom, Jus Cogens, and General Principles' (1988–1989) 12 Australian Year Book of International Law 82, 99.

[537] See also Thirlway, 'Human Rights' (n 535) at 498.

in such a way as to ensure that it provides the 'right' answers is strong, and at least to some, irresistible.[538]

Wouters and Rygaert provide an example of this imperative at work. They argue for a 'modern positivism', combining 'customary law with broadly drawn general principles of law':

> the more important the common interests of states or humanity are, the greater the weight that may be attached to opinio juris as opposed to state practice. If the stakes are high, inconsistent state practice may be glossed over, and a high premium may be put on states' statements and declarations ... [539]

Simma and Alston take a more cautious approach. They argue that the list of human rights that reach the threshold of custom 'will inevitably be rather brief and will certainly constitute an unsatisfactory or inadequate basis on which to achieve many of the goals appropriately sought by the strongest proponents of international human rights law'.[540]

Faced with these debates, the ILC Special Rapporteur rejected adopting a formally different approach to the elaboration of custom in the human rights field.[541] He nonetheless recognised the potential for a 'difference in application' of the general rules of custom formation, by accepting for example that 'one particular form of [State] practice would be given "a major role"'.[542] This approach seems appropriate, in that it avoids diluting the rigorous standards of custom or importing normative considerations into a positivist exercise.[543] As Meron notes, '[t]he credibility of international human rights ... requires that attempts to extend their universality utilize irreproachable methods'.[544]

There has been a recent surge of interest on the question of whether access to courts and fair trial rights have reached the status of customary international law.

---

[538] Simma and Alston (n 536) 83. Simma and Alston express 'serious misgivings' about this approach: ibid.

[539] Jan Wouters and Cedric Ryngaert, 'Impact on the Process of Formation of Customary International Law' in Menno T Kamminga and Martin Scheinin (eds), *The Impact of Human Rights Law on General International Law* (OUP 2009) 112.

[540] Simma and Alston (n 536) 100.

[541] ILC, 'Second report on identification of customary international law by Michael Wood, Special Rapporteur', A/CN.4/672 (66th sess, 2014), para 28.

[542] ibid, citing *Jurisdictional Immunities of the State (Germany v Italy: Greece intervening), Judgment*, ICJ Rep 2012, Separate Opinion of Judge Keith, 162, para 4.

[543] See also Ludovica Chiusssi, 'Remarks on the ILC Work on the Identification of Customary Law and Human Rights: Curbing "Droit de l'Hommisme"?' (2018) 27 Italian Yearbook of International Law 163, 164, 169–72, arguing that the draft conclusions 'allow adequate flexibility to accommodate the "speciality" of human rights, while avoiding exceptions to be taken to the extreme': at 164.

[544] Theodor Meron, *Human Rights and Humanitarian Norms as Customary Law* (OUP 1989) 81. See also Chiussi (n 543) 173 ('Special care should be taken to avoid depriving human rights of the authority of general international law').

In a 2021 study, Schabas argues that the 'inherent' right of access to courts 'for the exercise of rights and obligations' has reached customary status,[545] though the precise parameters of that right are not set out. Clooney and Webb argue that there is 'strong evidence' that both the right to a fair trial and 'most of the 13 component rights set out in Article 14 ICCPR' constitute customary international law.[546] Francioni proposes recognition of a liberal right of 'access to justice', characterised as either 'the possibility for the individual to bring a claim before a court and have the court adjudicate it' or the right also to 'have his or her case heard and adjudicated in accordance with substantive standards of fairness and justice'.[547] Francioni concludes that States have an obligation under general international law not to deny justice to aliens before domestic courts,[548] which encompasses civil and judicial remedies, as well as 'the right to seek effective criminal prosecution' if one is the victim of crime.[549] He argues that that the right of access to justice has 'an inclusive scope', noting in particular courts' findings that it may be breached by denying access because a litigant lacks legal personality; restricting access to legal counsel to prepare a criminal defence; or rendering access contingent on an administrative decision.[550]

This scholarship demonstrates a less restrictive approach than that taken in the 1987 Restatement (Third) on the Foreign Relations Law of the United States. No due process rights are included in its list of laws that have reached the level of custom, although the list is not closed.[551] The Restatement does, however, recognise ancillary rights in the case of arbitrary detention. It notes that the customary international law prohibition on 'prolonged arbitrary detention' may be breached

---

[545] Schabas (n 522) 275–76 (concluding that '[c]ustomary law recognises a right of access to the courts for the exercise of rights and obligations'). See also, on the right of foreigners to access courts as custom, M Borchard, *The Diplomatic Protection of Citizens Abroad or the Law of International Claims* (The Banks Law Publishing Co. 1928) 334; Jan Paulsson, *Denial of Justice in International Law* (CUP 2005) 1 (footnotes omitted); Robert R Wilson, 'Access-to-Courts Provisions in United States Commercial Treaties' (1953) 47 American Journal of International Law 20, 47.

[546] Clooney and Webb (n 29) 13; 13–25. Clooney and Webb's study focuses on criminal proceedings, while recognising that 'the boundary between the right to a fair trial in civil and criminal proceedings is not a bright line': at 26. See also Schabas' conclusions on fair trial rights: Schabas (n 522) 287. On interpretation, see also Julia Sherman, 'The Right to an Interpreter under Customary International Law' (2017) Columbia Human Rights Law Review 257, 257 fn 1; 287 (arguing for the customary status of a right to interpretation and translation of 'essential written documents' in criminal proceedings).

[547] See Francesco Francioni, 'The Rights of Access to Justice under Customary International Law' in Francioni (ed) (n 16) 1. He also notes other meanings of the term, that of 'justice' as encompassing 'those remedies offered by competent public authorities, which are not courts of law but can nevertheless perform a dispute settlement function': at 4.

[548] See discussion at ibid 10–15.

[549] ibid 14.

[550] ibid 33–35. However, he also draws attention to 'countervailing objectives' that delimit the scope of the right, including procedural conditions such as time limits (which may nonetheless be subject to a reasonableness test): ibid 38–39.

[551] American Law Institute, *Restatement of the Law Third: The Foreign Relations Law of the United States* (Vol 2, 1987) § 702. The *Restatement (Fourth)* does not cover this issue. Meron considers the Restatement to be 'too cautious' in its approach to due process rights: (n 544) 95.

if the person detained for a prolonged period is not 'given early opportunity to … consult counsel; or is not brought to trial within a reasonable time'.[552] A consistent pattern of arbitrary detention, as a matter of State policy, may violate customary international law even if the detention is not prolonged.[553]

The Inter-American Commission on Human Rights considers it to be 'beyond question' that the right to due process and to a fair trial, as protected under the ADHR, have attained customary international law status.[554] A concurring opinion to the ECtHR Grand Chamber judgment in *Al-Dulimi* considered 'the right of access to a court in criminal proceedings has acquired … the status of a norm of *jus cogens*',[555] though this was rejected in the judgment itself.[556] The concurring opinion considered that the right encompassed 'access to an independent, impartial and regularly constituted court, before which the accused is presumed innocent, is not compelled to testify against himself or herself or to confess and may be heard, contest incriminating evidence and present exonerating evidence, after being informed of the nature and cause of the accusation'.[557] Meron would add to this account the following protections:

> to be tried in his or her presence and to defend himself or herself in person or through legal assistance of his or her own choosing … [and] the right to have one's conviction and sentence reviewed by a higher tribunal according to law.[558]

In the migration context, Chetail argues that customary international law includes 'the right to challenge the lawfulness of detention before a court', which entails four procedural guarantees:

> the review must be prompt; it must be exercised by an independent and impartial judicial body; the procedure must respect the minimum standards of due process (including the equality of arms and the adversarial principle); the judicial review must be effective and include the possibility of ordering release.[559]

---

[552] ibid § 702, Comment, 164.

[553] See ibid, § 702 (g); Comment, 167. Similarly, a consistent denial of fair trial in criminal cases will reach the status of customary international law as a 'gross violation' of human rights: ibid. However, the Reporters' notes state that it 'would be difficult to claim a gross violation of a right whose definition and application are disputed': ibid, 174.

[554] *Mario Alfredo Lares Reyes et al (United States)*, Inter-American Commission on Human Rights, Petition 12.379, Report N° 19/02 (Inadmissibility) (27 February 2002), para 23.

[555] *Al-Dulimi and Montana Management Inc., v Switzerland*, App no 5809/08 (ECtHR, Grand Chamber, Judgment, 21 June 2016), Concurring opinion of Judge Pinto de Albuquerque, joined by Judges Hajiyev, Pejchal, and Dedov, para 28.

[556] *Al-Dulimi and Montana Management Inc., v Switzerland*, App no 5809/08 (ECtHR, Grand Chamber, Judgment, 21 June 2016), para 136.

[557] ibid, Concurring opinion of Judge Pinto de Albuquerque, joined by Judges Hajiyev, Pejchal, and Dedov, para 29.

[558] Meron (n 544) 96–97.

[559] Chetail, 'Transnational movement' (n 100) 52.

Chetail does not consider that the right to judicial review against expulsion decisions has customary status.[560] The ILC draft articles on the expulsion of aliens refer more broadly to the right 'to be heard by a competent authority'.[561] In his sixth report, the Special Rapporteur noted that he considered this broader right to constitute customary international law.[562]

Customary international law is an important source of law for refugee protection, since it binds States that are not signatories to the 1951 Convention or international human rights treaties.[563] While recent scholarship suggests that there is appetite to recognise a broader set of human rights as customary international law than was previously the case, establishing that a right has reached the level of custom—and ascertaining its precise scope and content if so—remains a challenging undertaking. This is particularly the case given the approach taken by the ILC in its recent draft conclusions.[564]

4. General Principles of Law

The ICJ Statute refers to 'general principles of law recognized by civilized nations' (article 38(1)(c)).[565] Meron, writing in 1989, predicted that general principles would 'increasingly become one of the principal methods for the maturation of [human rights] standards into the mainstream of international law'.[566] Goodwin-Gill considers this category to be a particularly useful source of rights for asylum seekers if they are not entitled to protection under article 16 of the 1951 Convention.[567] Goodwin-Gill is correct to note that general principles are an important repository of due process rights.[568] However, the category of 'general principles' suffers from continuing conceptual difficulties which undermine its

---

[560] Though he concludes that 'treaty law largely offers similar guarantees under general human rights instruments': ibid 56–58.

[561] ILC, 'Draft articles on the expulsion of aliens', in *Report of the International Law Commission*, A/69/10 (66th sess, 2014), draft article 26(1)(c).

[562] ILC, 'Sixth report on the expulsion of aliens', by Mr Maurice Kamto, Special Rapporteur, A/CN.4/625 and Add 1–2 (62nd sess, 2010), para 451.

[563] Guy S Goodwin-Gill, 'The Office of the United Nations High Commissioner for Refugees and the Sources of International Refugee Law' (2020) 69 International and Comparative Law Quarterly 1, 26.

[564] Though see the contrary argument put by Schabas (n 522) 39.

[565] The reference to 'civilized nations' has unsurprisingly fallen out of favour over the years; in an on-going ILC project on general principles of law, the Special Rapporteur proposes recasting this category as 'the general principles of law recognized by States': ILC, 'First report on general principles of law by Marcelo Vázquez-Bermúdez, Special Rapporteur', A/CN.4/732 (71st sess, 2019) ('First report'), para 258. See also ILC, 'Second report on general principles of law by Marcelo Vázquez-Bermúdez, Special Rapporteur', A/CN.4/741 (72nd sess, 2020) ('Second report'), para 2(d); ILC, 'Third report on general principles of law by Marcelo Vázquez-Bermúdez, Special Rapporteur', A/CN.4/753 (73rd sess, 2022) ('Third report'), para 4.

[566] Meron (n 544) 88 (considering that the catalyst would be the increasing adoption of human rights into national laws, 'especially in provisions for the administration of justice and due process').

[567] Goodwin-Gill, 'Sources' (n 563) 28.

[568] See ibid 28–29.

usefulness as a source of rights. In addition, the high level of abstraction at which principles are recognised can make it difficult to know precisely what protection is afforded in the individual case.

The key conceptual difficulty with 'general principles' as a category is its apparent importation of natural law considerations into international law. The word 'recognized' in article 38(1)(c) of the ICJ Statute appears on its face to require a lower standard of acceptance than that required by custom. In a dissent in the *South West Africa* cases, Judge Tanaka argued that the reference to recognition demonstrated that 'some natural law elements' were inherent in this source of law:[569]

> [article 38(1)(c)] extends the concept of the source of international law beyond the limit of legal positivism according to which, the States being bound only by their own will, international law is nothing but the law of the consent and auto-limitation of the State. But this viewpoint, we believe, was clearly overruled ... by the fact that this provision does not require the consent of States as a condition of the recognition of the general principles. States which do not recognize this principle or even deny its validity are nevertheless subject to its rule.[570]

As a consequence, Judge Tanaka considered that recognition could be 'of a very elastic nature'—certainly, recognition by '*all* civilized nations' was not required.[571] Goodwin-Gill has previously argued that '[i]t is no longer necessary to appeal to natural law in order to support the proposition that basic human rights are established within the realm of positive international law'.[572] This may be the case insofar as custom and treaty law are concerned (certainly, the adoption of the ICCPR has enshrined rights in positive law, and a thin tranche of rights have reached the level of custom). But a natural law flavour to general principles has lingered. In a separate opinion to the 2010 *Pulp Mills* judgment, Judge Cançado Trindade characterised general principles as 'fundamental principles of law which identify themselves with the very foundation of the legal system ... guiding it, protecting it *against the incongruities of the practice of States*'.[573] In Judge Cançado Trindade's view, general principles 'do not depend on the "will", nor on the "agreement", nor on the consent, of the subjects of law ... [a]bove the will of subjects of law, stands their conscience,

---

[569] *South West Africa Cases (Ethiopia v South Africa; Liberia v South Africa), Second Phase, Judgment* [1966] ICJ Rep 6, Dissenting Opinion of Judge Tanaka, 298ff. On the value of this judgment, despite its dissenting nature, see Guy S Goodwin-Gill, *International Law and the Movement of Persons between States* (Clarendon Press OUP 1978) 77.

[570] *South West Africa Cases* (n 569) Dissenting Opinion of Judge Tanaka, 298ff.

[571] ibid 299.

[572] See Goodwin-Gill, *Movement of Persons* (n 569) 71 (footnotes omitted).

[573] *Case concerning Pulp Mills on the River Uruguay (Argentina v Uruguay), Judgment* [2010] ICJ Rep 14, Separate Opinion of Judge Cançado Trindade, 207 (emphasis added). It should be noted that Judge Cançado Trindade expressly recognises that the conception of general principles laid out in the separate opinion is at odds with the Court's majority: at 137.

as the ultimate material source of all law'.[574] Natural law provides an uneasy foundation for the importation of obligations into a legal system—for who is to be the arbiter of those fundamental values that so bind States? Too liberal an approach to the identification of general principles could sideline customary international law, offering a backdoor for the inclusion of rights that perhaps are insufficiently supported by State practice, but are, nonetheless arguably 'recognized' for the purposes of article 38(1)(c).[575]

Overt references to natural law have not found universal favour. Simma and Alston attempt to distance themselves from a natural law approach, arguing that general principles can be rooted 'in a consensualist conception of international law'.[576] The topic of general principles of law is currently under discussion in the ILC, and the Special Rapporteur charged with the topic (Marcelo Vázquez-Bermúdez) has largely sidestepped natural law debates. Like Simma and Alston, he seems to consider, at least in relation to general principles drawn from domestic law, that 'convincing evidence of acceptance and recognition' is necessary.[577] While Simma and Alston find that acceptance in the legal expression of 'moral and humanitarian considerations',[578] the Special Rapporteur calls for evidence that a principle derived from domestic law is 'common to the principal legal systems of the world', and capable of transposition to the international level.[579]

However, the Special Rapporteur also recognises a second source of general principles, which has proved more contentious than the first. Like Judge Cançado Trindade,[580] he argues that general principles are not limited to those drawn from domestic law. They also encompass principles 'formed within the international legal system'.[581] This is a position that the ICJ itself has implicitly taken, in for example its recognition of *uti possidetis* as a general principle.[582] The process of identifying these principles naturally differs from identifying those drawn from national law. The Special Rapporteur proposes that the category of principles formed within the international system may include a principle 'widely recognized

---

[574] ibid.

[575] On this point, see comments in the ILC debates on general principles of law, cited in Section 4.

[576] Simma and Alston (n 536) 105.

[577] See n 576.

[578] ibid.

[579] See ILC, 'Second report' (n 565) Annex, draft conclusion 4, as well as discussion at paras 17, 19–74; and in ILC, 'First report' (n 565) paras 223–230. Transposability requires that a principle is both 'compatible with fundamental principles of international law', and that 'conditions exist for its adequate application in the international system': ILC, 'Second report' (n 565) Annex, draft conclusion 5, and discussion at paras 75–106.

[580] ibid 146.

[581] See ILC, 'First report' (n 565) Annex, draft conclusion 3; and discussion at para 156ff.

[582] See obiter discussion in *Case concerning the Frontier Dispute (Burkina Faso/Mali), Judgment* [1986] ICJ Rep 554 at 565. See also discussion and cases cited in Giorgio Gaja, 'General Principles of Law' in Max Planck Encyclopedia of International Law [MPIL] (updated Apr 2020), <https://opil-oup law-com.wwwproxy1.library.unsw.edu.au/view/10.1093/law:epil/9780199231690/law-9780199231 690-e1410?print=pdf>, paras 17–20; 33.

in treaties and other international instruments'; one which 'underlies general rules of conventional or customary law'; or one which is 'inherent in the basic features and fundamental requirements of the international legal system'.[583] The identification of 'inherent' or 'underlying' principles offers more space for the importation of value-driven assessments than a consensualist process of identification of general principles drawn from national law.[584]

While the existence of the first category of legal principles (those deriving from national legal systems) was widely accepted in ILC and Sixth Committee debates, this second category provoked serious debate.[585] One concern was that rules lacking the requisite State practice and *opinio juris* to amount to custom could nonetheless be smuggled into the international legal system in the guise of 'general principles'.[586] In the ILC, Sir Michael Wood, the Special Rapporteur for work on custom, cautioned against 'send[ing] the message that, if an applicable rule of customary international law could not be identified, then a general principle of law might nonetheless be invoked because the criteria for its identification were less stringent.'[587] Sir Michael argued against the inclusion of this second category, noting that it 'was perhaps where the confusion between general principles of law and customary international law was most apparent'.[588] These concerns were echoed by other delegates.[589] In the Sixth Committee, some States questioned whether a general principle could derive from the international level, without entering into the detail of the ILC members' critiques.[590]

This discussion shows that there are ongoing debates on the scope of 'general principles' as a source of law. While generally accepted as a means of filling gaps

---

[583] ILC, 'Second report' (n 565) Annex, draft conclusion 7.

[584] Although space also exists in the test proposed for 'general principles' derived from national legal systems—an assessment of whether a principle is 'common to the principle legal systems of the world' will undoubtedly involve some smoothing of inconsistent practice within each legal system. By choosing to focus on legal systems, rather than States, the Special Rapporteur leaves open the possibility of a State being bound to a general principle that has no basis in its own domestic law.

[585] See ILC, 'Second report' (n 565) paras 16 and 114–115 respectively. The Special Rapporteur's inclusion of a note containing pincites to critical views expressed by certain ILC members was of great assistance in the discussion that follows. See also ILC, 'Third Report' (n 565) paras 4; 18–19; 24. The Special Rapporteur notes at para 19 of the Third Report that 'views expressed regarding the second category [in the second debate] were similar to those expressed during the first debate on the topic'.

[586] See, eg, comments by Mr Rajput, in ILC, 'Provisional summary record of the 3490th meeting', A/CN.4/SR.3490 (71st sess, 25 July 2019), 17.

[587] ibid 5. See also, at 7: 'If, arguendo, one were to accept the existence of a second category of general principles of law, doubts would arise regarding the forms of recognition of such category … The propositions in the literature referred to in the report seemed to make it all too easy for a general principle of law to be invoked and could potentially transform the general principles of law into "custom lite".'

[588] ibid 8–9.

[589] See ibid 20 (Mr Rajput); ILC, 'Provisional summary record of the 3493rd meeting', A/CN.4/SR.3493 (71st sess, 29 July 2019), 16 (Mr Šturma), with Mr Park and also raising concerns about the possible confusion of custom and general principles: ILC, 'Provisional summary record of the 3489th meeting', A/CN.4/SR.3489 (71st sess, 24 July 2019), 17.

[590] See Statements referred to in ILC, 'Second report' (n 565) para 115, fn 181 (the statements of the US and Iran, available via the 'PaperSmart portal', could not be accessed).

in the international legal system and avoiding *non liquet*,[591] a lingering natural law element (despite efforts to recast general principles as positive law[592]) may mean that they ultimately prove a more fragile basis on which to ground concrete rights protections. Additionally, rights of access to courts and more specific fair trial guarantees seem to sit oddly between the two categories of legal principles proposed by the Special Rapporteur. Although they are clearly rooted in national law, they are often enshrined in international treaties. A process of 'transposition' to the international level does not seem to be required,[593] since these rights govern the vertical relationship between each State and those within its jurisdiction. The question of how best to characterise general principles of law that will be applied primarily on the domestic level may call for more attention. Ultimately, the answer might be that some flexibility is required when identifying whether a right of this nature, recognised on both national and international bases, has reached the status of a general principle.

This discussion has focused on the form and identification of general principles. But what of their actual substance? This is a question that falls outside the scope of the Special Rapporteur's enquiry.[594] As Goodwin-Gill notes, the right of access to courts and certain fair trial guarantees have be recognised by international and regional courts as general principles.[595] He cites, in particular, the ECtHR's reference to access to courts in *Golder*[596] and the ICJ's discussion of the principle of the equality of the parties in its International Fund for Agricultural Development (IFAD) Advisory Opinion.[597] While this case law does bolster individual protections, principles are stated at a high level of generality and will not afford protection in every case.

In *Golder*, access to courts was recognised as a general principle of law, with the Grand Chamber stating that '[t]he principle whereby a civil claim must be capable of being submitted to a judge ranks as one of the universally "recognised" fundamental principles of law'.[598] Denial of justice, addressed in Chapter 4, was

---

[591] See ILC, 'First report' (n 565) para 25; Goodwin-Gill, 'Sources' (n 563) 28; ILC, 'Third Report' (n 565) paras 39–73.

[592] Compare de Andrade, who notes that 'it seems now widely accepted that [general principles of law] must be ascertained through a positivist methodology': Mariana de Andrade, 'The Two-Step Methodology for the Identification of General Principles of Law' (2022) 71 International and Comparative Law Quarterly 983 at 986.

[593] Since this process is designed to ensure that rights based in national law are capable of exercise on the international level: See ILC 'Second report' (n 565), paras 73–74, and on transposition more generally, para 85.

[594] See ILC, 'First report' (n 565) para 41. Although examples are cited in the Special Rapporteur's two reports to date, they are provided 'for illustration only', 'in line with the practice of the Commission': ibid.

[595] Goodwin-Gill, 'Sources' (n 563) 28–29 and cases cited therein.

[596] *Golder v United Kingdom* (n 181).

[597] *Judgment No 2867 of the Administrative Tribunal of the International Labour Organization upon a Complaint Filed against the International Fund for Agricultural Development*, Advisory Opinion [2012] ICJ Rep 10 (*IFAD Advisory Opinion*)

[598] *Golder v United Kingdom* (n 181) para 35. Golder is discussed in ILC, 'Third Report' (n 565) para 126. See also *Al-Dulimi* (n 555) para 136, noting that 'despite their importance', these guarantees are not *jus cogens* norms.

also recognised as a general principle.[599] However, as discussed in Section 2.3.1.1, the ECtHR does not consider this general principle to be engaged in the review of negative RSD decisions, or of asylum seekers' rights that it deems to be closely connected to those decisions.

The ICJ has commented on the evolving nature of 'equality of arms' as a general principle through its mandate to provide judicial review of certain administrative tribunal decisions.[600] In 1956, the Court first considered the question in an Advisory Opinion. The case concerned the ICJ's jurisdiction to review cases of the International Labour Organisation Administrative Tribunal (ILOAT), which was tasked to settle workplace disputes in international organisations. Under the ILOAT Statute, UNESCO's Executive Board was entitled to seek a binding review of the Tribunal's judgments, while staff members were not. The Court considered that while '[a]ccording to generally accepted practice, legal remedies against a judgment are equally open to either party', the failure to afford staff members the possibility to appeal was not 'an inequality before the Court' but an inequality 'antecedent to [its] examination' that did not prevent the court from exercising its powers of review.[601] The court did not here use the term 'general principles', referring only to 'generally accepted practice'. However, it did note that '[t]he principle of equality of the parties follows from the requirements of good administration of justice', suggesting that 'general principles' was the source of law in the majority's mind.[602]

In the 2012 *IFAD Advisory Opinion*, a challenge to an ILOAT judgment brought by the Executive Board of IFAD, the Court reconsidered the implications of unequal rights of review. Although it did not refer expressly to article 38(1)(c) of its Statute,[603] the Court reiterated that the principle of equality derives from 'requirements of good administration of justice',[604] and applied it as a principle of general international law.[605] Relying on changes between the HRC's General Comments on article 14 ICCPR between 1984 and 2007, the Court found that 'the principle of equality of access to courts and tribunals' had developed to a point at which 'if procedural rights are accorded they must be provided

---

[599]   ibid. See also other references on denial of justice in ILC, 'First report' (n 565) para 84.

[600]   Along with *res judicata*: see *Case Concerning Pulp Mills on the River Uruguay (Argentina v Uruguay), Judgment* [2010] ICJ Rep 14, Separate Opinion of Judge Cançado Trindade, 145, and case references therein. Judge Cançado Trindade also characterises *nullem crimen sine lege* and the presumption of innocence as general principles (referring to their application in international criminal law rather than domestic law): ibid 213 and fn 189.

[601]   *Judgments of the Administrative Tribunal of the ILO upon complaints made against the UNESCO, Advisory Opinion* [1956] ICJ Rep 77, 85 (*UNESCO Advisory Opinion*), cited in *IFAD Advisory Opinion* (n 597) 26.

[602]   ibid 86, cited in *IFAD Advisory Opinion* (n 597) 29.

[603]   *IFAD Advisory Opinion* (n 597) 25; see also 27.

[604]   ibid 29.

[605]   While the Court refers to the ICCPR, it is applying the principles therein to proceedings between international organisations and individuals, not States parties.

to all the parties unless distinctions can be justified on objective and reasonable grounds'.[606] With respect to the ILOAT, the Court considered that 'questions may now properly be asked whether the system ... meets the present-day principle of equality of access to courts and tribunals'.[607] In a Separate Opinion, Judge Greenwood argued that '[t]he Court should not be asked to participate in a procedure whose inequality is at odds with contemporary concepts of due process and the integrity of the judicial function'.[608] Although prepared to answer the Opinion on the grounds that the Court should not withdraw from a longstanding procedure 'without warning', Judge Greenwood considered that 'the inequality of access that exists at present cannot be allowed to persist into the future'.[609] He also made express what the Court had in its Opinion implied—namely, that the system was in 'urgent' need of reform.[610] In an attempt to alleviate the inequities of the system (exacerbated by the fact that the Court considers its own Statute to preclude it from hearing the individuals concerned in person),[611] the Court provided an avenue for the official in question's views to be transmitted to the Court—through IFAD itself—and denied IFAD's request for an oral hearing.[612] To remedy an inequality of arms that it was not within the Court's power to erase entirely,[613] therefore, the Court chose to limit the due process rights to which the more privileged party would otherwise be entitled. This approach was also taken in earlier Advisory Opinions—and excoriated by Judge Córdova in a 1956 dissenting opinion as an 'abnormal procedure' which 'only makes more flagrant the existence of such inequality between the parties'.[614] To Judge Cançado Trindade, the decision to proceed without oral hearings 'has been and is ... most unsatisfactory: rather than a solution, it is a capitulation in the face of a persisting problem'.[615] In a 1973 Advisory Opinion, the Court commented on general principles of law in the context of this situation, finding them to 'require that, even in advisory proceedings, the interested parties should each

---

[606] *IFAD Advisory Opinion* (n 597) 27. The Court attributes this position to the HRC in its General Comment No. 32, but its affirmation of the position is shown by its application of it to the ILOAT case. See also 29, at which the Court notes that equality of the parties now requires 'access on an equal basis to available appellate or similar remedies under an exception can be justified on objective and reasonable grounds'.

[607] ibid 29. See also the Declaration of Judge Greenwood, noting that the procedure 'falls well short of modern standards on equality of the parties': at 94; and the detailed critique in Judge Cançado Trindade's Separate Opinion: at 61–69.

[608] Declaration of Judge Greenwood, *IFAD Advisory Opinion* (n 597) 95.

[609] ibid.

[610] ibid. Compare *IFAD Advisory Opinion* (n 597) 28 ('While the Court is not in a position to reform this system ... ').

[611] See *IFAD Advisory Opinion* (n 597) 30.

[612] ibid. The same set of procedures was adopted by the Court in its 1956 Advisory Opinion, amongst others: see, eg, *UNESCO Advisory Opinion* (n 601) 86.

[613] See *IFAD Advisory Opinion* (n 597) 29.

[614] Dissenting Opinion of Judge Córdova to the *UNESCO Advisory Opinion* (n 601) 166, cited in Judge Cançado Trindade's Separate Opinion to the *IFAD Advisory Opinion* (n 597) 65–66.

[615] Judge Cançado Trindade, Separate Opinion to the *IFAD Advisory Opinion* (n 597) 70.

have an opportunity, and on a basis of equality, to submit all the elements relevant to the questions which have been referred to the review tribunal'—but *not* to require an oral hearing.[616]

The long-standing inequities of the ILOAT system have enabled the Court to expound at length on the substantive requirements of the principle of 'equality of the parties', and the evolving nature of that principle over time. Less guidance is provided on the scope and content of other 'general principles' that the ICJ has recognised, such as 'the right to an independent and impartial tribunal established by law; the right to have the case heard and determined within a reasonable time; [and] the right to a reasonable opportunity to present the case to the tribunal and to comment upon the opponent's case'.[617]

Attempts to ground more specific and concrete rights as 'general principles' are not always successful. The ILC Special Rapporteur has highlighted the International Criminal Court's (ICC) refusal to consider as general principles of law (i) a ban on former prosecutors joining 'the defense immediately after leaving the prosecution'; and (ii) the right to a 'review of decisions of hierarchically subordinate courts disallowing or not permitting an appeal'.[618] The ICJ's refusal to recognise a general right to an oral hearing in review proceedings is another example.[619] The ICJ has also taken a quite restrictive approach to 'the right to a reasoned decision'. While recognizing this as a general principle, it notes that there is no obligation for 'every particular plea ... to be discussed and reasons given for upholding or rejecting each one'. All that is required is that 'a judgment shall be supported by a stated process of reasoning'.[620]

This brief survey highlights individual rights relevant to access to courts or due process that have been recognised as general principles. The nature of dispute resolution is such that courts have not been called on to pronounce on the status of all rights discussed. Questions of application remain, and limits will be set in the concrete case. A concern with avoiding general principles becoming a repository for rights that do not reach the standard of 'custom' may limit a court's willingness to derive concrete protections from the general principles recognised.

---

[616] *Application for Review of Judgment No. 158 of the United Nations Administrative Tribunal, Advisory Opinion* [1973] ICJ Rep 166, 181. The Court specifies that there is no general principle of all requiring 'that in review proceedings the interest parties should necessarily have an opportunity to submit oral statements of their case to the review tribunal'.

[617] Recognised by the Court in ibid 209.

[618] See ILC, 'Second report' (n 565) para 68 citing, respectively, *Situation in Darfur, Sudan, in the Case of the Prosecutor v Abdallah Banda Abakaer Nourain and Saleh Mohammed Jerbo Jamus (Judgment on the appeal of the Prosecutor against the decision of Trial Chamber IV of 30 June 2011)*, No ICC-02/05-03/09 OA (11 Nov 2011), para 33; and *Situation in the Democratic Republic of the Congo, No. ICC-01/04, Judgment on the Prosecutor's Application for Extraordinary Review of Pre-Trial Chamber I's 31 March 2006 Decision Denying Leave to Appeal*, No ICC-01/04 (13 July 2006), para 32.

[619] *Application for Review of Judgment No. 158* (n 616) 181.

[620] See ibid 209–11.

5. Soft Law

Finally, there is also a wealth of soft law guidance on access to the courts and procedural guarantees in relation to RSD, expulsion, and detention. Four indicative examples are: ExCom guidance on status determination; the International
Commission of Jurists' Principles on the role of judges and lawyers in relation to
refugees and migrants;[621] the International Law Commission's draft articles on expulsion of aliens;[622] and UN guidance on legal aid.[623] These sets of principles are
discussed to give a more holistic account of progressive development in this area
of the law. As discussed in Chapter 3, caution is needed when relying on soft law
materials as an interpretative aid. Soft law has no weight in assessments of whether
particular rights have reached the level of custom, but can indicate directions
which courts may take in future if they choose to adopt these soft materials in their
judgments in the process of developing 'hard' law.

ExCom's guidance on RSD has been well covered in the academic literature
and needs only a brief discussion here. As noted in Chapter 2, ExCom Conclusion
No 8 sets out so-called 'basic requirements' for these procedures, which are non-
binding.[624] These include that applicants should receive guidance on the procedure;[625] be given 'necessary facilities', including interpretation, in order to submit
their cases;[626] and, in the case of rejection, 'be given a reasonable time to appeal for
a formal reconsideration of the decision, either to the same or to a different authority, whether administrative or judicial, according to the prevailing [system]'.[627]
It also calls on States to permit an applicant to remain in the host country while
the first instance decision and any appeal is pending, unless the application is considered 'clearly abusive'.[628] A subsequent ExCom Conclusion noted that 'clearly
abusive' or 'manifestly unfounded' applications could be dealt with expeditiously,
so long as 'appropriate' safeguards were in place, including 'a complete personal
interview by a fully qualified official', and the right to have the negative decision
reviewed.[629] This review could be 'more simplified' than that afforded to other rejected asylum seekers.[630] ExCom has also recommended that RSD procedures be

---

[621] International Commission of Jurists, 'Principles on the Role of Judges and Lawyers in Relation to
Refugees and Migrants' (May 2017) available via <https://www.icj.org/wp-content/uploads/2017/07/
Universal-Refugees-Migrants-Principles-Publications-Report-Thematic-Report-2017-ENG.pdf>.

[622] See ILC, 'Analytical Guide on the Work of the International Law Commission: Expulsion of
Aliens', available via <https://legal.un.org/ilc/guide/9_12.shtml>.

[623] 'United Nations Principles and Guidelines on Access to Legal Aid in Criminal Justice Systems',
annexed to UNGA Res 67/187 (20 Dec 2012).

[624] ExCom Conclusion No 8 (n 491) para (e).

[625] ibid para (e)(ii).

[626] ibid para (e)(iv).

[627] ibid para (e)(vi).

[628] ibid para (e)(vii).

[629] ExCom, *The Problem of Manifestly Unfounded or Abusive Applications for Refugee Status or
Asylum*, No 30 (XXXIV) (20 Oct 1983), paras (d)–(e).

[630] ibid para (e)(iii).

accessible to asylum seekers with disabilities and designed in a manner that enables them to 'fully and fairly represent their claims with the necessary support'.[631]

The International Commission of Jurists' Principles also cover RSD safeguards,
along with judicial review of detention and general rights of access to courts. These
safeguards are in some respects more robust than those proposed by ExCom. Like
ExCom, the International Commission of Jurists calls for a 'fair and effective' RSD
process, which includes the right to 'individual examination'.[632] However, while
ExCom would be satisfied by a review to an administrative or a judicial authority,
the Commission calls for merits review by 'a separate, competent and independent
judicial authority'.[633] A judge is to review the case on its merits whenever so requested, so long as that request is not 'manifestly unfounded'.[634] Like ExCom, it
considers that appeals should have suspensive effect.[635]

Procedural safeguards are to be afforded both at first-instance and review.[636] These
include ensuring that access is 'effective' (the example given is that indigent applicants
should not be charged fees); time limits are reasonable; information on processes is
provided; legal advice is available; an in-person hearing is granted which may be attended by a lawyer; and that interpretation and translation is available where necessary and free where the applicant is unable to pay.[637] Adaptions should be made to
account for any 'vulnerabilities', for example in the case of children, those living with
a disability, or victims of torture and sexual and gender-based violence.[638] Decisions
should be reasoned and information provided on appeal rights.[639] States are considered to have a 'positive obligation' to inform applicants of their right to legal advice, which should be free if a person is not in a position to pay.[640] More generally,
the Commission avers that '[r]efugees and migrants' are entitled to 'the right to an
effective remedy and reparation for violations of human rights, which includes access
to the courts', and, if an alleged victim of crime, the right to 'equal access to justice'.[641]
In cases of detention, 'prompt' and 'automatic' judicial review is required.[642]

A third example is the ILC's draft articles on the expulsion of aliens, adopted
in 2014.[643] The draft articles do not focus on asylum seekers specifically and are

[631] ExCom, 'Conclusion on refugees with disabilities and other persons with disabilities protected
and assisted by UNHCR', Conclusion No 110 (LXI) (12 Oct 2010), (j).
[632] International Commission of Jurists (n 621) Principle 3.
[633] ibid Principles 3, 6.
[634] ibid Principle 6.
[635] ibid Commentary to Principle 6.
[636] ibid Commentary to Principle 5.
[637] ibid.
[638] ibid.
[639] ibid.
[640] ibid Principle 7.
[641] ibid Principle 10.
[642] ibid Principle 8.
[643] 'Draft articles on the expulsion of aliens' (n 561). The General Assembly has now taken note of the
draft articles after initial hesitation: see UNGA Res 69/119, 'Expulsion of aliens' (10 Dec 2014), para 3;
UNGA Res 72/117, 'Expulsion of aliens' (7 Dec 2017), paras 2–3.

generally applicable to aliens subject to expulsion. They set out a series of rights that are to apply during expulsion proceedings. Aliens are entitled to be expelled 'only in pursuance of a decision reached in accordance with law',[644] which is to be reasoned.[645] Specific procedural rights are set out, including the right to notice of the expulsion decision, considered a pre-requisite for the exercise of all other procedural rights;[646] the right to challenge the expulsion decision, except where compelling reasons of national security otherwise require'[647] (a caveat derived from ICCPR article 13, which in practice will in many cases be tempered by State's human rights obligations not to return a person to harm); the right to be heard (which may be satisfied by written proceedings);[648] the right to access 'effective remedies', which may be administrative or judicial;[649] the right to representation before the competent authority;[650] and the right to the free assistance of an interpreter where necessary.[651] This final guarantee is considered 'an essential element of the right to be heard'.[652] Finally, 'due regard' is to be given to the vulnerabilities of children and people living with a disability, amongst others.[653] No right to legal aid is included, whether conditionally or otherwise—which one scholar considers a 'conspicuous' absence.[654] The commentary concludes that the right to be represented before the competent authority during expulsion proceedings, based on article 13 ICCPR, 'does not necessarily encompass the right to be represented by a lawyer', or 'an obligation on the expelling State to pay the cost of representation'.[655] The right to legal aid was included in the Special Rapporteur's earlier drafts.[656]

Although these rights are to apply to aliens irrespective of whether they are legally present,[657] an exception is made in the case of illegally present aliens 'who have been unlawfully present in [a State's] territory for a brief duration'.[658] These aliens may be expelled without the benefit of any of the procedural guarantees

---

[644] 'Draft articles on the expulsion of aliens' (n 561) draft article 4.

[645] ibid draft article 5(1). The Commentary notes that the duty to give grounds is 'well-established in international law': Commentary to draft article 5, para 2.

[646] ibid draft article 26(1)(a); Commentary to draft article 26, para 2.

[647] ibid draft article 26(1)(b); Commentary to draft article 26, para 3.

[648] ibid draft article 26(1)(c); Commentary to draft article 26, para 4. The commentary argues that State practice does not support the position that the right to be heard need be in person.

[649] ibid draft article 26(1)(d); Commentary to draft article 26, para 5.

[650] ibid draft article 26(1)(c), Commentary to draft article 26, para 6 notes however, that this 'does not necessarily encompass the right to be represented by a lawyer during expulsion proceedings', and does not require a State to pay the costs of representation.

[651] ibid draft article 26(f).

[652] ibid Commentary to draft article 26, para 7.

[653] ibid draft article 15; Commentary to draft article 15, para 3.

[654] Won Kidane, 'Missed Opportunities in the International Law Commission's Draft Articles on the Expulsion of Aliens' (2017) 30 Harvard Human Rights Journal 77, 85 ('What is conspicuously missing is the right to legal aid or appointed counsel ... ').

[655] 'Draft articles on the expulsion of aliens' (n 561), Commentary to draft article 26, para 6.

[656] As noted by Kidane (n 654) 85–86, referring to draft article C1(1)(g) in 'Sixth report on the expulsion of aliens' (n 562) para 402.

[657] 'Draft articles on the expulsion of aliens' (n 561) Commentary to draft article 26, para 1.

[658] ibid draft article 26(4).

discussed here, if domestic legislation so provides.[659] The commentary frames the denial of procedural guarantees to those unlawfully present for a brief period as in line with State practice, and the extension for procedural rights to those unlawfully present for a 'specified minimum period' as 'an exercise in ... progressive development'.[660] Although the commentary does not fix a specific period, it notes that in some countries 'this period ... must not exceed six months'.[661] This position is concerning given that key international treaty regimes take the view that the rights of asylum seekers who receive a negative status determination decision at first instance can be characterised merely as rights against expulsion.

Draft article 27 provides that aliens 'lawfully present' have the right to an appeal (which need not be judicial) with suspensive effect 'when there is a real risk of serious irreversible harm'.[662] No such right is afforded to unlawfully present aliens generally.[663] Even this limited right to suspensive effect was considered by the Commission to be an exercise in progressive development of the law, unsupported by State practice.[664] Nonetheless, the Commission argued for its inclusion on the basis that a failure to afford suspensive effect to an appeal could render it ineffective.[665] Detention of an alien subject to expulsion is to be 'reviewed at regular intervals', although the draft articles do not expressly provide that such review must be undertaken by a judicial authority.[666] These general provisions are considered to be 'without prejudice to the rules of international law relating to refugees, as well as to any more favourable rules or practice on refugee protection', including the 1951 Convention's provisions on expulsion and *non-refoulement*.[667] In all, the draft articles on expulsion of aliens show high deference to State interests[668] and a more

---

[659] See ibid and Commentary to draft article 26, para 11.

[660] ibid.

[661] ibid.

[662] ibid draft article 27.

[663] See Commentary to draft article 27, para 4. Of course, however, an alien may possess additional rights under a specialised regime (as a refugee, eg): see draft articles 3 and 6. The precise scope of a refugee's rights under the 1951 Convention is addressed in Chapter 6, Section 2.2.1.

[664] In fact, the draft article was highly controversial, with some States rejecting it 'outright': see ILC, 'Ninth Report on the expulsion of aliens submitted by Mr Maurice Kamto, Special Rapporteur', A/CN.4/670 (66th sess, 2014), para 62, cited in Sean D Murphy, 'The Expulsion of Aliens (Revisited) and Other Topics: The Sixty-Sixth Session of the International Law Commission' (2015) 109 American Journal of International Law 125, 128. In the Sixth Committee, the United Kingdom noted its continued belief that 'the expulsion of aliens was not an area suitable for a convention ... it did not agree with those draft articles which claimed to represent the progressive development of international law': UNGA, 69th sess, Sixth Committee, 'Summary record of the 19th meeting', A/C.6/69/SR.19 (17 November 2014), para 165 (Mr MacLeod), referred to in Mathias Forteau, 'A New "Baxter Paradox"? Does the Work of the ILC on Matters Already Governed by Multilateral Treaties Necessarily Constitute a Dead End? Some Observations on the ILC Draft Articles on the Expulsion of Aliens', available via <https://harvardhrj.com/wp-content/uploads/sites/14/2016/06/Forteau.pdf>.

[665] ibid Commentary to draft article 27, paras 1–2.

[666] ibid draft article 19(3)(a). In contrast, the draft articles note that a decision to extend the length of detention can only be carried out by a court or by 'another competent authority' subject to judicial review: article 19(2)(b).

[667] ibid draft article 6.

[668] On this point, see also Kidane, who notes 'it appears that ... both the Draft Articles and the Commentaries settled on the lowest common denominator in pursuit of consensus': (n 654) 78–79.

restrictive approach to rights than that taken either by ExCom or the International Commission of Jurists.

Finally, the UN General Assembly has adopted principles and guidelines on legal aid in criminal proceedings which provide specific protections for refugees and asylum seekers.[669] While these principles are not relevant to RSD proceedings, they provide useful guidance on progressive measures to ensure that asylum seekers and refugees are guaranteed general access to courts. The document, intended as a 'useful framework to guide Member States',[670] provides that '[s]pecial measures should be taken to ensure meaningful access to legal aid' for those with special needs, including asylum seekers and refugees.[671] Guideline 11 provides that the needs of such groups should be taken into account when designing legal aid schemes.[672]

Three points can be drawn from these examples. First, there is a trend towards ensuring that rights can be 'effectively' exercised, through for example waiving fees, providing interpretation, making accommodations to those with disabilities, or designing legal aid schemes with an eye to the needs of vulnerable groups. Second, the first three examples all grapple with the tension in RSD proceedings between, on the one hand, offering meaningful procedural safeguards, and on the other, granting States a measure of liberty to circumvent those safeguards when deemed appropriate. Third, the balance drawn between these two competing impulses leads to inconsistencies in the level of rights afforded to the asylum seeker.

6. Conclusion

This survey of human rights law demonstrates that asylum seekers and refugees are entitled to many rights as individuals under human rights law. However, the HRC and ECtHR have concluded that core rights under the ICCPR and ECHR are not engaged by RSD decision-making, leading to gaps in protection. This chapter has argued that these gaps are not sufficiently filled by the operation of effective remedy clauses, since they focus on the avoidance of *non-refoulement* rather than on the positive recognition of a refugee's legal status. Asylum seekers may be spared expulsion, but denied the legal status to which they are entitled under the 1951 Convention. This shift in focus affects an asylum seeker's ultimate ability to access rights that are contingent upon the grant of refugee status.

Asylum seekers are entitled to robust rights under certain regional regimes, including EU law, the Banjul Charter and the Inter-American human rights system.

---

[669] See UNGA Res 67/187, 'United Nations Principles and Guidelines on Access to Legal Aid in Criminal Justice Systems' (20 Dec 2012), Annex.

[670] ibid para 2.

[671] ibid, Annex, Principle 10, para 32.

[672] ibid, Annex, Guideline 11, para 57.

There are also heightened protections for vulnerable groups, particularly child asylum seekers and asylum seekers with a disability. While it is beyond the scope of the book to analyse whether the right of access to courts and related rights have met the status of customary international law, the high threshold required suggests that only a limited tranche of rights will be recognised. A lower threshold is needed for these rights to be recognised as 'general principles', and certain procedural rights have been recognised on this basis. It can, however, be challenging to identify the concrete rights that flow from the general principle, and courts may be wary to take too robust an approach given the risks of forming a category of 'custom-lite'. As a whole, these findings suggest that gaps remain in the protection afforded to asylum seekers and refugees in respect to access to courts under international human rights law. These gaps suggest that there remains a role for article 16 of the 1951 Convention, a provision which binds 149 Contracting States and grants express rights regarding access to courts to refugees. Furthermore, when interpreting article 16, lessons can be drawn from the interpretative approaches adopted in relation to the rights surveyed in this chapter. This final task—of interpretation—is addressed in Chapter 6.

6

Interpreting Article 16

1. Introduction

The preceding chapters have set the groundwork for the central question of this book—namely, the scope of State obligations under article 16. In this chapter, the various threads are drawn together to develop a reasoned interpretation of the provision. The chapter makes eight key conclusions on the scope of article 16 in the course of a clause-by-clause analysis. These conclusions correspond to the eight issues set out in Chapter 2.

Article 16(1) is interpreted in Section 2.2. Four conclusions are made. First, the term 'refugee' in article 16(1) encompasses asylum seekers. This brings article 16 within a small group of Convention provisions that have previously been recognised as extending to asylum seekers, despite the use of the term 'refugee'.[1] Second, the term 'courts' does not extend to administrative agencies. Article 16 accordingly has no application to administrative refugee status determination (RSD) proceedings. It is also concluded that the provision does not guarantee an inherent right of judicial review of negative administrative RSD decisions.[2] Third, the provision's broad geographic scope is confirmed, guaranteeing free access to the courts of law in any Contracting State, provided that the requisite jurisdictional link exists.[3] Fourth, States must ensure that the right of access to courts in article 16(1) is *effective*.[4] In reaching this finding, the analysis draws on developments in international human rights law.

Article 16(2) is interpreted in Section 2.3, leading to three additional conclusions. First, the standard of 'habitual residence' set out in article 16(2) should be interpreted autonomously, through a flexible, fact-based approach.[5] Under this approach, an asylum seeker may, with the passage of time, attain the standard of 'habitual residence' even where his or her residency status is precarious or inconsistent with domestic law. An asylum seeker meeting this threshold would therefore be entitled to 'the same treatment as a national in matters pertaining to access to the Courts' under article 16(2). Second, 'matters pertaining to access to the Courts' is an open category that is not limited to the specific examples

---

[1] See Section 2.2.1. The same conclusion is made in relation to article 16(2)–(3): see 2.3.1, and 2.4.1.
[2] See Section 2.2.2.
[3] See Section 2.2.3.
[4] See Section 2.2.4.
[5] See Section 2.3.2 and, in relation to article 16(3), Section 2.4.1.

Access to Courts for Asylum Seekers and Refugees. Emma Dunlop, Oxford University Press. © Emma Dunlop, 2024.
DOI: 10.1093/oso/9780198885597.003.0006

expressly noted in article 16(2) (legal assistance and the exemption from security for costs).[6] It is proposed that two classes of 'matters' fall within the scope of the provision: (i) practical matters, such as the availability of translation or legal aid; and (ii) procedural matters that pertain to access to the courts. Third, the appropriate comparator for determining whether an asylum seeker or refugee has been provided with the 'same treatment' as a national is Spijkerboer's standard of 'substantively equal' procedural treatment. This standard calls for a fact-based approach comparing the impugned measure with the specific legal system in which it is located.[7]

Article 16(3) is interpreted in Section 2.4. In Section 2.5, the subject-matter jurisdiction question is addressed.[8] This section makes the final conclusion—namely, that article 16 does not require a Contracting State to establish jurisdiction to hear a dispute where no such jurisdiction otherwise exists. However, while a State is not under a general obligation to guarantee judicial review of negative RSD decisions, a discriminatory bar on appeals may breach the article 16(2)–(3) obligation to guarantee the 'same treatment as a national' to habitually resident asylum seekers. If review of administrative decisions is generally available to citizens, a Contracting State may therefore be obliged to extend judicial review of an administrative RSD decision to a habitually resident asylum seeker. The relevance of these findings is not limited to RSD proceedings, since the obligations in article 16 are applicable whenever an asylum seeker or refugee seeks access to a court to defend their rights or regulate their affairs. Section 3 concludes.

2. Interpretation of Article 16

The analysis that follows is informed by State practice on the interpretation of article 16. It draws on cases from ultimate[9] and intermediate appellate courts,[10] federal courts,[11] courts specialising in administrative law,[12] and, where particularly

---

[6] See Section 2.3.3.2.

[7] See Section 2.3.3.3, citing Thomas Spijkerboer, 'Higher Judicial Remedies for Asylum Seekers—An International Legal Perspective' in Geoffrey Care and Hugo Storey (eds), *Asylum Law: First International Judicial Conference, London, 1995* (The Steering Committee of the Judicial Conference on Asylum Law 1995) 224.

[8] See Section 2.5.

[9] Such as Australia's High Court, the UK's Supreme Court and, previously, House of Lords, Austria's Supreme Court of Justice, Switzerland's Tribunal fédéral (Supreme Court; referred to in the ILRs as Federal Tribunal), and, on constitutional matters, Germany's Bundesverfassungsgericht (Federal Constitutional Court).

[10] Such as the French Cour d'Appel de Paris; the High Court of Justice of England and Wales (EWHC) and Court of Appeal (EWCA); and the New Zealand High Court.

[11] Such as those in Australia and Canada.

[12] Such as the Council of State (Raad van State), which comprises the highest general administrative court in the Netherlands.

relevant, decisions of lower courts. Regional court jurisprudence is also discussed where it provides useful guidance on State parties' practice or approaches to interpretation. These materials are supplemented by discussion of domestic and regional legislation.[13]

As discussed in Chapter 3, the Vienna Convention on the Law of Treaties permits consideration of 'subsequent practice ... which establishes the agreement of the parties' on the interpretation of the 1951 Convention.[14] Domestic case law is a key source of practice, but one which often lacks the requisite consistency to demonstrate 'agreement'—particularly when one considers the that jurisprudence is often weighted towards common law jurisdictions in the Global North, a tendency that is also evident in the case law gathered for the purposes of this research.[15]

This issue means that it is fundamentally difficult to make definitive conclusions on the consistency of State practice derived from domestic case law. However, the survey of case law uncovered on article 16 for this project itself confirms the existence of different views on the provision's scope across (and sometimes within) jurisdictions.[16] This lack of consensus means that the case law cannot constitute subsequent practice under article 31(3)(b) of the Vienna Convention. Following from the conclusions in Chapter 3, this jurisprudence is nonetheless treated as relevant to interpretation, to the extent that it reveals persuasive arguments on the appropriate scope of article 16. It is not, however, adopted mechanically as evidence of the 'proper' interpretation of the provision. Finally, as argued in Chapter 3, soft law and non-binding sources sit uneasily alongside the rule of treaty interpretation and should be cautiously applied. These sources are, however, mentioned where they are particularly persuasive and may provide guidance.

---

[13] These sources are treated with caution, given that States may not have specifically considered compatibility with article 16 of the 1951 Convention when enacting legislation. The Belgian Court of Arbitration, for example, noted in one case that '[i]t does not appear from the travaux préparatoires of the law of 5 August 2003 that the legislature would have been attentive to the situation of the complainants with refugee status, nor that it ensured the respect of the obligations that flow for them from art 16(2) of the 1951 Convention'—author's translation: Extrait de l'arrêt 104/2006 du 21 juin 2006 (Cour d'Arbitrage), Moniteur Belge (12 July 2006) 35041. This phenomenon is not, of course, unique to article 16 of the 1951 Convention. See also Simon Brown LJ's reference in *R v Uxbridge* to the respondents' acknowledgment that 'until these challenges were brought, no arm of state, neither the Secretary of State, the Director of Public Prosecutions, nor anyone else, had apparently given the least thought to the United Kingdom's obligations arising under article 31 [of the 1951 Convention]': *R v Uxbridge, ex p Adimi* [2001] QB 667, 676.

[14] Vienna Convention on the Law of Treaties, 1155 UNTS 331 (concluded 23 May 1969, entered into force 27 Jan 1980) (Vienna Convention), art 31(3)(b).

[15] See further Chapter 1, section 3.

[16] These inconsistences are due in part to variations in the judicial process in different Contracting States, though in certain cases, it appears that restrictive interpretations of article 16 may be driven by the exigencies of the case at hand and a concern not to 'open the floodgates' to like cases.

2.1 Heading to the Article

The heading 'Access to Courts' has no interpretative value. The Final Act, which can be considered 'context' to the 1951 Convention,[17] states that 'the titles of the chapters and of the articles of the Convention are included for practical purposes and do not constitute an element of interpretation'.[18]

2.2 Article 16(1)

Article 16(1) provides that '[a] refugee shall have free access to the courts of law on the territory of all Contracting States'. This raises four issues, which correspond to the first four issues discussed in Chapter 2. First, does the term 'refugee' encompass the unrecognised asylum seeker? Second, what is the scope of the term 'courts', and what application, if any, does the provision have to administrative or judicial RSD procedures? Third, what is the geographic scope of the provision? Fourth, does 'free access' entail a guarantee of effective access?

2.2.1 Meaning of 'refugee'

Interpreting the term 'refugee' in article 16(1) is deceptively complex. In essence, the question is whether the term should be interpreted as applying only to the recognised refugee, or also to the asylum-seeker, who may meet the refugee definition, but is yet to complete the RSD process. It might be thought that recourse to other provisions in the 1951 Convention that also use the term 'refugee' would resolve the question. However, it is broadly accepted that the term 'refugee' is limited to the recognised refugee in some provisions and extends to the unrecognised asylum seeker in others. Which category article 16 falls into is the focus of this section. In answering this question, the section first examines the various theories that could underpin the categorisation of 1951 Convention provisions, concluding that the best justification for categorisation is that of effectiveness and good faith. As a point of comparison, it then examines the two provisions of the 1951 Convention that are recognised to extend to asylum seekers—article 31 (non-penalisation for illegal entry) and article 33 (*non-refoulement*). After examining the case law on article 16 and finding it to be is inconclusive, the section

---

[17] See art 31(2)(a) ('[a]ny agreement relating to the treaty which was made between all the parties in connexion with the conclusion of the treaty'). It could be argued that the Final Act was only made between those parties that took part in the drafting process, and not therefore between *all* parties to the Convention. However, even on this reading the Final Act could be considered context under art 31(2)(b) (as an instrument 'accepted by the other parties as an instrument related to the treaty').

[18] Final Act of the United Nations Conference of Plenipotentiaries on the Status of Refugees and Stateless Persons, II. For discussion by the Conference of Plenipotentiaries see A/CONF.2/SR.34, 15; A/CONF.2/SR.35, 37-41. See further Chapter 4, Section 4.2.1.

argues that considerations of effectiveness and good faith require that article 16 be extended to asylum seekers.

Article 1A(2) of the 1951 Convention establishes that, '[f]or the purposes of the present Convention', the term refugee shall apply to 'any person who':

> owing to well-founded fear of being persecuted for reasons of race, religion, nationality, membership of a particular social group or political opinion, is outside the country of his nationality and is unable or, owing to such fear, is unwilling to avail himself of the protection of that country; or who, not having a nationality and being outside the country of his former habitual residence as a result of such events, is unable or, owing to such fear, is unwilling to return to it.[19]

On the face of the provision, a person is a refugee once he or she fulfils the criteria listed. In practice, however, some assessment is needed before a State will recognise an individual as a refugee.[20] Until the point of that recognition, an individual is an asylum seeker, even if he or she fulfils the criteria in article 1A(2).[21] It must therefore be determined whether article 16 is limited to the recognised refugee or extends also to the asylum seeker. A third option—extending the scope of the article only to those asylum seekers who *actually* meet the refugee definition—runs into the immediate practical difficulty that it is not possible to assess this without deciding whether or not to recognise an individual as a refugee.

UNHCR asserts that refugee status is 'objective' and crystallises as soon as an individual meets the definition of a refugee.[22] This position is endorsed by many

---

[19] On its face, article 1A(2) limits this grant of refugee status to those who fulfil the definition 'as a result of events occurring before 1 January 1951'. The 1967 Protocol removed this temporal restriction.

[20] See Guy S Goodwin-Gill and Jane McAdam, with Emma Dunlop, *The Refugee in International Law* (4th edn, OUP 2021) 55.

[21] Hathaway and Foster focus instead on the 'declaratory theory', arguing a person who meets the 'well-founded fear' test in article 1A(2) is 'a refugee with rights under international law ... whether or not status has been recognized, or even claimed': James C Hathaway and Michelle Foster, *The Law of Refugee Status* (2nd edn, CUP 2014) 25. But domestic courts do make distinctions between asylum seekers and recognised refugees, at least in respect of certain provisions of the 1951 Convention. Using the language of 'refugee' generally to cover both asylum seekers (who have not yet undergone status assessment) and recognised refugees risks conflating case law on these two categories and overstating the extent to which domestic courts are willing to recognise asylum seekers as rights-bearers. As Hathaway and Foster note, not all asylum seekers will go through a process of status determination: at 26, fn 60. Though in such cases, there are procedures for recognising asylum seekers as 'prima facie' refugees: see UNHCR, 'Guidelines on International Protection No. 11: Prima Facie Recognition of Refugee Status', HCR/GIP/15/11 (24 June 2015), noting that such recognition 'has been a common practice of both States and UNHCR for over 60 years': at 2; UNHCR, *Handbook on Procedures and Criteria for Determining Refugee Status and Guidelines on International Protection under the 1951 Convention and the 1967 Protocol relating to the Status of Refugees* (1979, reissued Feb 2019), HCR/1P/4/ENG/REV.4, para 44.

[22] See UNHCR, *Handbook* (n 21) para 28; UNHCR, 'Note on Determination of Refugee Status under International Instruments', EC/SCP/5 (24 Aug 1977), available via <http://www.refworld.org/docid/3ae68cc04.html>, para 5.

scholars,[23] and has some support in State practice.[24] Within the EU acquis, the preamble to the recast Qualification Directive states that 'the recognition of refugee status is a declaratory act'.[25] However, State practice does not support the general grant of Convention rights to individuals prior to a determination of status.

Hathaway and Foster rely on the declaratory theory as a foundation stone for their argument of 'acquired rights' under the 1951 Convention. Pursuant to this argument, a State is obliged to guarantee an asylum seeker who factually fulfils the definition of refugee in article 1A(2) those rights under the 1951 Convention that are not conditioned on the lawfulness or duration of a refugee's presence in the host State.[26] However the practical effect of the declaratory theory is limited, as many rights in the 1951 Convention will only be granted once recognition has occurred.[27] The rights acquired on a 'provisional basis'[28] prior to status determination under this model are:

> Art. 33 [non-refoulement] ... Arts. 3 (non-discrimination), 4 (religious freedom), 12 (respect for personal status), 13 (preservation of property rights), 16(1) (access to the courts), 20 (access to rationing systems), 22 (primary education), 25

[23] See, eg, Atle Grahl-Madsen, *The Status of Refugees in International Law*, Vol II (A.W. Sijthoff 1972) 224, noting however that 'the enjoyment of certain benefits to be accorded under the Convention is clearly dependent on recognition of the person concerned as a refugee'. Grahl-Madsen gives, as examples, articles 12, 15, and 28 of the 1951 Convention: at 224, fn 87. See also Hathaway and Foster (n 21) 1 and 39–49 (on acquired rights); Björn Elberling, 'Article 16' in Andreas Zimmermann (ed), *The 1951 Convention Relating to the Status of Refugees and its 1967 Protocol* (OUP 2011) 938, 940; and further discussion of the declaratory theory in Chapter 2, Section 2.1.1.

[24] See, eg, *Németh v Canada* [2010] 3 SCR 281, 310 ('Under the Refugee Convention, refugee status depends on the circumstances at the time the inquiry is made; it is not dependent on formal findings. As one author puts it, "it is one's de facto circumstances, not the official validation of those circumstances, that gives rise to Convention refugee status"' [citing James C Hathaway, *The Rights of Refugees under International Law* (1st edn, CUP 2005) 158 and 278]); *R (Hoxha) v Special Adjudicator* [2005] UKHL 19; [2005] 1 WLR 1063, 1082 (Lord Brown) ('[A]s para 28 of the Handbook neatly points out, that someone recognises to be a refugee must by definition have been one before his refugee status had been determined'); *WAGH v Minister for Immigration & Multicultural & Indigenous Affairs* [2003] FCAFC 194, para 25 ('A person does not become a refugee by an act of recognition or grant of status by a Contracting State. A person within the Contracting State who fulfils the Convention definition is, and at all times has been, a refugee.'); see also the Secretary of State's argument in *R (ST) v Secretary of State for the Home Department* [2012] UKSC 12; [2012] 2 AC 135, agreeing that 'the determination that a person is a refugee is declaratory': headnote, argument, 140.

[25] Directive 2011/95/EU of the European Parliament and of the Council of 13 December 2011 on standards for the qualification of third-country nationals or stateless persons as beneficiaries of international protection, and for the content of the protection granted, OJ L 337/9 (recast Qualification Directive), recital 21. See also Council Directive 2004/83/EC of 29 April 2004 on minimum standards for the qualification and status of third country nationals or stateless persons as refugees or as persons who otherwise need international protection and the content of the protection granted, OJ L 304/12 (original Qualification Directive), recital 14.

[26] See Hathaway and Foster (n 21) 26, 39–49.

[27] See Grahl-Madsen, *Status* (n 23) 224; Guy S Goodwin-Gill, 'The International Law of Refugee Protection' in Elena Fiddian-Qasmiyeh, Gil Loescher, Katy Long, and Nando Sigona, (eds), *The Oxford Handbook of Refugee and Forced Migration Studies* (OUP 2014) 40.

[28] See Hathaway and Foster (n 21) 26, citing Hathaway, *Rights* (1st edn) (n 24) 156–60. Hathaway and Foster consider that these 'acquired rights' will cease to apply in the event that an asylum seeker is found not to be a refugee: Hathaway and Foster (n 21) 26, n 54.

(access to administrative assistance), 27 (identity papers), 29 (fiscal equity), 31 (non-penalization for illegal entry and freedom from arbitrary detention) and 34 (consideration for naturalization).[29]

Hathaway's 2021 edition of *The Rights of Refugees under International Law* extends this list to include those rights premised on lawful *or habitual* presence, including articles 14 (intellectual property rights) and 16(2) (same treatment as a national in matters pertaining to access to the Courts).[30]

Goodwin-Gill challenges the position that 'Convention "rights", somehow or other, are applicable prior to recognition, that they "inhere" as a matter of fact alone and without human or State intervention.[31] He nonetheless accepts that States may be obliged to extend certain obligations to asylum seekers by consequence of 'the principles of effectiveness and good faith.[32]

What *is* generally accepted is that States are obliged to afford certain, discrete protections under the Convention both to 'recognised' refugees and to asylum seekers who have not yet had their claim for refugee status determined. This is because such asylum seekers may be refugees. The two articles to which this principle has been applied are article 33 (*non-refoulement*),[33] and article 31 (prohibition of penalisation for unlawful presence).[34]

---

[29] Hathaway and Foster (n 21) 40 (footnotes omitted).

[30] James C Hathaway, *The Rights of Refugees under International Law* (2nd edn, CUP 2021) 180, fn 37; 210–12. Hathaway's comments at 180, fn 37 suggest that rights contingent on 'lawful stay' would not be acquired prior to recognition. This seems in tension with the conclusion at 216 that lawful stay is not contingent upon recognition of refugee status.

[31] Guy S Goodwin-Gill, 'The duty to ensure respect for acquired rights (J. Hathaway & M. Foster, *The Law of Refugee Status, 2nd* edn, 2014, 39–49' (unpublished).

[32] ibid (in reference to the application of *non-refoulement* protection to asylum seekers).

[33] See, eg, UNGA Res 75/163 'Office of the United Nations High Commissioner for Refugees' (16 Dec 2020) ('*Deplores* the refoulement and unlawful expulsion of refugees and asylum seekers, and calls upon all States concerned to respect the relevant principles of refugee protection and human rights'), and to similar effect, UNGA Res 74/130 'Office of the United Nations High Commissioner for Refugees' (18 Dec 2019) para 31; UNGA Res 73/151, 'Office of the United Nations High Commissioner for Refugees' (17 Dec 2018), para 32; UNGA Res 72/150 'Office of the United Nations High Commissioner for Refugees' (19 Dec 2017) para 27; UNGA Res 71/172 'Office of the United Nations High Commissioner for Refugees' (19 Dec 2016) para 25; UNGA Res 70/135 'Office of the United Nations High Commissioner for Refugees' (17 Dec 2015), para 24, amongst others. The 2021 and 2022 Resolutions deplore 'the growing number of incidents of refoulement and unlawful expulsion of refugees and asylum-seekers, as well as practices of denial of access to asylum': UNGA Res 76/143, 'Office of the United Nations High Commissioner for Refugees' (16 December 2021), para 35; UNGA Res 77/198, 'Office of the United Nations High Commissioner for Refugees' (15 December 2022) para 41. See also Advisory Opinion OC-21/14, *Rights and Guarantees of Children in the Context of Migration and/or in need of International Protection* (IACtHR, 19 Aug 2014) para 210; Goodwin-Gill and McAdam (4th edn) (n 20) 244–46, 265; Elihu Lauterpacht and Daniel Bethlehem, 'The scope and content of the principle of *non-refoulement*: Opinion' in Erika Feller, Volker Türk, and Frances Nicholson (eds), *Refugee Protection in International Law: UNHCR's Global Consultations on International Protection* (CUP 2003) 87, 116–18.

[34] See Guy S Goodwin-Gill, 'Article 31 of the 1951 Convention Relating to the Status of Refugees: non-penalization, detention, and protection' in Erika Feller, Volker Türk, and Frances Nicholson (eds) *Refugee Protection in International Law: UNHCR's Global Consultations on International Protection* (CUP 2003) 185, 193, 197ff; *R v Uxbridge, ex p Adimi* [2001] QB 667.

The protection against *non-refoulement* in article 33 'lies at the heart' of the 1951 Convention.[35] Goodwin-Gill and McAdam conclude that article 33 applies both to refugees and asylum seekers, 'at least during an initial period and in appropriate circumstances, for otherwise there would be no effective protection'.[36] There is also judicial support for this position. In *R (ST) v Secretary of State for the Home Department*, Lord Dyson considered, in obiter, that the *non-refoulement* obligation applied to:

> any refugee to whom the Convention applies.... If a refugee *who is claiming asylum* is to be protected from the risk of persecution, she needs the protection afforded by article 33.[37]

Lord Dyson therefore accepts that a person who meets the definition of 'refugee' is entitled to protection against *refoulement* during the RSD process—before recognition as a refugee by a host State. In contrast, the court found that the protection against 'expulsion' in article 32 (the subject of the case) only applied once a refugee has actually been granted asylum.[38] The application of the principle of *non-refoulement* to both asylum seekers and refugees has been consistently recognised by States in the UN General Assembly,[39] and in ExCom Conclusions,[40] which,

---

[35] See *R (ST)* (n 24) 161 (Lord Dyson JSC).

[36] Goodwin-Gill and McAdam (4th edn) (n 20) 265.

[37] *R (ST)* (n 24) 161 (Lord Dyson JSC).

[38] '[Article 32(1)] undoubtedly provides ... additional protection to the refugee who has been granted asylum. Bearing in mind the fundamental object of the Convention, it is not surprising that it was intended by the contracting states that this degree of protection was not to be accorded to a refugee who has been given temporary permission to remain in a territory pending the determination of her claim to asylum.': *R (ST)* (n 24) 161 (Lord Dyson JSC). This distinction is also made in *Szoma v Secretary of State for Work and Pensions* [2006] 1 AC 564, [2005] UKHL 64, para 24 (Lord Brown of Eaton-under-Heywood) ('The term "refugee" in article 32(1) of the Refugee Convention can only mean someone already determined to have satisfied the article 1 definition of that term (as, for example in article 2 although in contrast to its meaning in article 33)'), cited in *R (ST)* (n 24) 144 (Lord Hope of Craighead DPSC).

[39] See n 33; also McAdam and Goodwin-Gill (n 20) 233.

[40] See ExCom, 'Non-Refoulement', Conclusion No 6 (XXVIII) (12 Oct 1977), para (c) (reaffirming that the duty of *non-refoulement* applies 'irrespective of whether or not [persons who may be subjected to persecution if returned to their country of origin] have been formally recognized as refugees'); Executive Committee, 'Protection of Asylum-Seekers in Situations of Large-Scale Influx, Conclusion No 22 (XXXII) (1981), para II.A.2 (noting that the principle of *non-refoulement* includes 'non-rejection at the frontier'); ExCom, 'Identity Documents for Refugees', Conclusion No 35 (XXXV) (18 Oct 1984), para (d) ('Recommended that asylum applicants whose applications cannot be decided without delay be provided with provisional documentation sufficient to ensure that they are protected against expulsion or refoulement until a decision has been taken by the competent authorities with regard to their application'); ExCom, 'General', Conclusion No 41 (XXXVII) (1986), para (j) ('refugees and asylum-seekers have been exposed to physical violence, acts of piracy and forcible return to their country of origin in disregard of the principle of non-refoulement'); ExCom, 'General', Conclusion No 79 (XLVII) (1996), para (i) ('seriously disturbed at reports indicating that large numbers of refugees and asylum-seekers have been refouled'); ExCom, 'General Conclusion on International Protection', Conclusion No 81 (XLVII) (17 Oct 1997), para (i) and ExCom, 'Conclusion on Safeguarding Asylum', Conclusion No 82 (XLVIII) (1997), para d(i) (each noting that *non-refoulement* 'prohibits expulsion and return of refugees ... whether or not they have been formally granted refugee status'; and ExCom, 'Conclusion on

while not in themselves State practice, are considered persuasive by courts.[41] It has also been recognised by the Inter-American Court of Human Rights, which notes that if asylum seekers on the border or illegally on the territory of a State were not protected by *non-refoulement*, 'this right would become illusory and without content'.[42]

A similar approach is taken to article 31 of the 1951 Convention, which prohibits States from penalising refugees on account of their unlawful entry.[43] In *R v Uxbridge*, the High Court Queen's Bench Division found that article 31 applied to asylum seekers. Simon Brown LJ noted: '[t]hat article 31 extends not merely to those ultimately accorded refugee status but also to those claiming asylum in good faith (presumptive refugees) is not in doubt'.[44] The Australian High Court also recognises the application of article 31 to asylum seekers,[45] and the principle of non-penalisation has been incorporated into law in several States.[46]

Like article 16, articles 31 and 33 refer simply to 'refugees'. Article 31 precludes the imposition of penalties 'on account of their illegal entry or presence, on refugees' who meet certain threshold requirements. Article 33 provides that '[n]o Contracting State shall expel or return ("refouler") a refugee in any manner whatsoever to the frontiers of territories where his life or freedom would be threatened' for a Convention reason.[47] But the word 'refugees' is used at many points of the Convention, in situations in which States do not accept the extension of their obligations to asylum seekers. A State is not required, for example, to extend a refugee's right to social security on the same basis as nationals to asylum seekers.[48]

The fact that the word 'refugees' is only accepted to extend to asylum seekers in certain provisions of the Convention suggests that the declaratory theory is not a sufficient basis for arguing that article 16 applies to asylum seekers. Goodwin-Gill's argument based on effectiveness and good faith provides a stronger foundation,

International Protection', Conclusion No 85 (XLIX) (1998), para (aa) (on the need to ensure protection against *non-refoulement* in the case of transfers of asylum seekers to third countries).

[41] On ExCom Conclusions, see discussion in Chapter 3, Section 2.2.3.

[42] Advisory Opinion OC-21/14 (n 33) para 211. On the jurisdictional scope of *non-refoulement* under the American Convention on Human Rights, see also para 219.

[43] Article 31(1) provides: 'The Contracting States shall not impose penalties, on account of their illegal entry or presence, on refugees who, coming directly from a territory where their life or freedom was threatened in the sense of article 1, enter or are present in their territory without authorization, provided they present themselves without delay to the authorities and show good cause for their illegal entry or presence.'

[44] *R v Uxbridge, ex p Adimi* (n 34) 677 (Simon Brown LJ). See also 689 (Newman J): 'No person is within article 31(1) unless he or she is a refugee (which includes presumptive refugees').

[45] *Plaintiff M70/2011 v Minister for Immigration and Citizenship and Another* (2011) 244 CLR 144, 196 (Gummow, Hayne, Crennan, and Bell JJ).

[46] See survey carried out for the 2001 Global Consultations in Goodwin-Gill, 'Article 31' (n 34) 197ff.

[47] 1951 Convention, art 33(1).

[48] See 1951 Convention, art 24(1)(b). Heydon J takes this position in his dissenting judgment in *Plaintiff M70/2011* (n 45) 212, para 167. The obligations in article 24 pertain to refugees 'lawfully staying' in a Contracting State.

and a justification for distinctions in the scope of protection provided by different articles of the Convention.[49] If a State were to *refoule* an asylum seeker without determining whether his or her claim was valid, it would violate its duty to interpret and perform the treaty in good faith.[50] This is not a case of impermissibly relying on good faith to create 'a source of obligation where none would otherwise exist.'[51] If article 33 were interpreted to allow the *refoulement* of an asylum seeker in the process of making his or her claim, but not a recognised refugee, it would render the 1951 Convention's protection nugatory. Similarly, 'avoid[ing] the principle of *non-refoulement* by declining to make a determination of status' would be inconsistent with the obligation of good faith.[52] The core protections of the Refugee Convention would never in fact be engaged. An argument based in a good faith interpretation of article 31 also supports its extension to asylum seekers prior to formal recognition. Article 31 prohibits the imposition of penalties on refugees who have 'come directly' from a place where their life or freedom is threatened and present themselves promptly to authorities 'on account of their illegal entry or presence'. The article contemplates the precise situation in which a refugee approaches a State authority to request asylum. An interpretation of the article that permitted a State to penalise an asylum seeker up until the point of their formal recognition would nullify the protection that the provision is intended to provide.

The question is therefore whether the obligations of good faith and the principle of effectiveness require that the term 'refugee' in article 16 be interpreted, like articles 31 and 33, as extending to asylum seekers. Domestic case law on article 16 is not uniform on this question, and in at least one case, a court has held unequivocally that the obligations in article 16 do not extend to asylum seekers. That case, before the Belgian Court of Arbitration, concerned a law that granted jurisdiction over grave violations of humanitarian law where an action was brought by a national, but denied it in cases where an action was brought by an asylum seeker or a recognised refugee.[53] The court found the law to be inconsistent with article 16(2) insofar as it applied to a recognised refugee, but not insofar as it applied to asylum seekers.[54] Obiter comments in other judgments have also suggested that article 16 is only engaged in the case of recognised refugees: in *Krishnapillai*, the Canadian Federal Court of Appeal appeared to accept that article 16 did not cover

---

[49] See Goodwin-Gill, 'Acquired rights' (n 31); Goodwin-Gill and McAdam (4th edn) (n 20) 244–45.

[50] See Vienna Convention on the Law of Treaties, art 26; art 31; *R v Immigration Officer at Prague Airport and another, ex parte European Roma Rights Centre and Others* [2004] UKHL 55, para 19 (Lord Bingham).

[51] See *Case concerning Border and Transborder Armed Actions (Nicaragua v Honduras), Jurisdiction and Admissibility, Judgment* [1988] ICJ Rep 69, 105; affirmed in *Case concerning the Land and Maritime Boundary between Cameroon and Nigeria (Cameroon v Nigeria), Preliminary Objections, Judgment* [1998] ICJ Rep 275, 297, cited in *Roma Rights* case (n 50) para 19 (Lord Bingham).

[52] Goodwin-Gill and McAdam (4th edn) (n 20) 245.

[53] See further Section 2.3.3.2.2.

[54] Extrait de l'arrêt 68/2005 du 13 avril 2005, 2005/201234 (Cour d'Arbitrage), Moniteur Belge (9 May 2005) 21848, 21850. This case and others in the series are discussed in Section 2.3.3.2.2.

asylum seekers.[55] A passing comment by the High Court of Australia in *NAGV and NAGW* that 'the Convention details the status and civil rights to be afforded within Contracting States *to those accorded the status of* refugee' (mentioning, inter alia, article 16), suggested a similar view.[56] However, in the subsequent case of *Plaintiff M70/2011*, the Australian High Court left open the question of whether obligations beyond articles 31 and 33 were engaged in the case of asylum seekers:

> [t]he extent to which obligations beyond the obligation of non-refoulement (and the obligations under Art 31 of the Refugee Convention concerning refugees unlawfully in the country of refuge) apply to persons who claim to be refugees but whose claims have not been assessed is a question about which opinions may differ. It is not necessary to decide that question.[57]

Courts in New Zealand and the Netherlands have grappled directly with the scope of article 16 of the 1951 Convention and its application to asylum seekers. In *Aivasov*,[58] the Auckland High Court rejected an argument that proceeding with a Refugee Status Appeals Authority (RSAA) hearing without legal aid would breach article 16.[59] The applicant was an asylum seeker who was appealing failed applications for both refugee status and legal aid. The court did not reject the argument on the basis that article 16 was limited to 'refugees', but instead on the basis that the applicant did, in fact, have free access to courts and had been granted 'the same treatment as a national' under article 16(2). The court noted that his 'free access' was 'exemplified by his application to this court', and that he had 'the same treatment as a national in matters concerning access including legal assistance in that the Legal Services Act makes provision for the consideration of legal aid to be granted to a person in the position of the applicant'.[60] The court therefore appeared to accept the potential applicability of article 16 to an asylum seeker.

The Netherlands has taken a more restrictive approach. In some cases, the country's highest general administrative court, the Raad van State, considered it necessary to determine whether the applicant was in fact a refugee before applying

---

[55] *Krishnapillai v The Queen* 2001 FCA 378, para 32 (Décary JA), para 25 ('*Bains* was rendered in a case involving a Convention refugee claimant and not, as in this case, a Convention refugee. The Convention, therefore, did not apply').

[56] *NAGV and NAGW v Minister for Immigration and Multicultural and Indigenous Affairs and Another* (2005) 222 CLR 161, 170, para 19 (Gleeson CJ, McHugh, Gummow, Hayne, Callinan, and Heydon JJ) (emphasis added). A similar implication could be derived from *Minister for Immigration and Multicultural and Indigenous Affairs v QAAH* (2006) 231 CLR 1, 19 (Gummow A-CJ, Callinan, Heydon, and Crennan JJ) (implying that article 16, amongst others, falls within those rights that 'flow from recognition as a refugee').

[57] See n 45 at 196 (Gummow, Hayne, Crennnan, and Bell JJ) (footnotes omitted).

[58] *Aivazov v Refugee Status Appeals Authority* [2005] NZAR 740.

[59] The RSAA was replaced by the Immigration and Protection Tribunal (IPT) in 2010.

[60] *Aivazov v Refugee Status Appeals Authority* (n 58) 744–45.

article 16(2).[61] These cases seem prima facie to support a narrow definition of 'refugee' in article 16 that does not extend to asylum seekers. However, the Dutch jurisprudence is also shaped by the fact that the Raad van State is empowered to determine, in the course of an appeal, whether an individual meets the definition of a refugee. In two cases, the Raad van State undertook its own analysis of to determine if article 16 should be applied. In *KT v State Secretary for Justice*, the Raad van State determined that the applicant 'could be regarded as a refugee within the meaning of the Refugees Convention' and accordingly found article 16 to be engaged.[62] In *KvS v State Secretary for Justice*, it determined that the applicant was not entitled to refugee protection and that, as a result, article 16 was not applicable.[63] Although the Netherlands is not alone in allowing the judicial determination of refugee status,[64] in some jurisdictions, including the UK, courts lack this competence.[65] The fact that not all courts can determine refugee status prior to determining whether article 16 applies may ultimately strengthen the argument that a good faith application of the Convention requires the benefit of this provision to be extended to asylum seekers who may, in time, be found to meet the refugee definition. In a third case, *DG and DD v State Secretary for Justice*, the Raad van State held that since the 1951 Refugee Convention 'does not prescribe that an

---

[61] See, eg, *KT v State Secretary for Justice*, The Netherlands, Council of State (Judicial Division), 10 Apr 1979, 99 ILR 1 ('The question of whether this provision [article 16(2)] is applicable in this case brings with it the need to examine whether the appellant can be regarded as a refugee within the meaning of this Convention); *KvS v State-Secretary of Justice*, Raad van State, Afdeling Rechtspraak, 20 Dec 1977, Rechtspraak Vreemdelingenrecht (1977) No 97, AB (1978) No 188, in LANM Barnhoorn, 'Netherlands Judicial Decisions Involving Questions of Public International Law 1976–1977' (1978) 9 Netherlands Yearbook of International Law 271, 287 ('to answer the question whether the appeal should, nevertheless, be receivable on the basis of [article 16(1)], an investigation is necessary, to see whether the appellant must be regarded as a refugee within the meaning of this Convention'); *A.J. v State-Secretary of Justice,* Council of State, Judicial Division, 13 July 1979, Rechtspraak Vreemdelingenrecht (1979) No 9, Gids Vreemdelingenrecht No. D 12-25, in LANM Barnhoorn, 'Netherlands Judicial Decisions Involving Questions of Public International Law 1979–1980' (1981) 12 Netherlands Yearbook of International Law 322 at 323–24 (finding that while art 34(1)(b) of the Aliens Act 'could well be set aside by Article 16(2) of the Refugees Convention if the appellant could be regarded as a refugee', there was insufficient evidence that the appellant met that description. See also Dana Baldinger, *Vertical Judicial Dialogues in Asylum Cases: Standards on Judicial Scrutiny and Evidence in International and European Asylum Law* (Brill Nijhoff 2015) 28 and Pieter Boeles, 'Effective Legal Remedies for Asylum Seekers according to the Convention of Geneva 1951' (1996) 43 Netherlands International Law Review 291, 305.

[62] *KT* (n 61) 2.

[63] *KvS* (n 61) 288.

[64] See also *Grundul v Bryner & Co G.M.B.H and Richteramt III Bern*, Switzerland, Federal Tribunal, 27 Mar 1957, 24 ILR 483. For an early example of a judicial determination of refugee status, pre-dating the 1951 Convention, see the case history in *Ditte c Joudro, Semaine Juridique*, 1948, 4265, Cass civ, 19 Jan 1948, also cited in Jean-Yves Carlier, *Droit d'asile et des réfugiés: de la protection aux droits (Vol 332)*, Collected Courses of the Hague Academy of International Law (Brill Nijhoff 2008) 320, fn 682.

[65] See *R v Secretary of State for the Home Department, ex parte Jahangeer* [1993] Imm AR 564, available via refworld <https://www.refworld.org/cases,GBR_HC_QB,3ae6b65e2c.html> (noting that '[t]his court is not in general a tribunal of fact and is not in a position to determine status'); *R v Secretary of State for the Home Department, ex parte Sivakumaran* [1988] AC 958, 992 (Lord Keith of Kinkel) (reaffirming that a decision on refugee status was 'one for the Secretary of State alone, not for the court exercising judicial review'); *R v Uxbridge, ex p Adimi* (n 34) 688 (Newman J) (Queen's Bench Division) (citing the principle in *Sivakumaran*).

application for asylum should be decided by a court ... [article 16(1)] does not constitute a basis for a right to judicial review of an asylum decision'.[66] It nonetheless considered that article 16(2) *did* apply to the asylum procedure.[67] The implications of this decision for what constitutes a 'matter pertaining to access to the Courts' are discussed further in Section 2.3.3.2.

In two cases in the UK, the High Court has stated, again in obiter, that article 16 should extend to encompass asylum seekers. In the High Court of England and Wales' 1993 decision of *Jahangeer*, Jowitt J compared article 16 to article 32 (which was in issue in that case), positing that unlike article 32, article 16 covered the 'aspirant refugee'.[68] Justice Jowitt's logic was later considered by the High Court in *Hoxha*.[69] That case dealt with the appropriate scope of article 1C(5), one of the 'cessation' clauses in the 1951 Convention. An argument was made that 'no formal recognition of the claimant's refugee status was required' to trigger the operation of the article 1C(5). In rejecting that argument, Jackson J examined the decision in *Jahangeer*, noting:

> Jowitt J stated that the word 'refugee' is not used in the same meaning throughout the Convention. In some instances it means an aspirant refugee. In other instances it means someone who is established to be a refugee. In the context of Article 16 the word 'refugee' includes an aspirant refugee. For my part, I entirely accept this analysis. Indeed, if one adopts Jowitt J's approach, it is clear that Article 1C(5) refers to a person whose status as refugee has been established.[70]

Appeals of Jackson J's decision to the Court of Appeal and the House of Lords were dismissed. Those judgments did not expressly refer to the comment that refugee 'is not used in the same meaning throughout the Convention', nor to his Honour's obiter statement regarding the scope of 'refugee' in article 16. However, both the Court of Appeal and the House of Lords placed weight on the use of the word 'recognized' in article 1C(5)[71] in concluding that the clause applied only to those who

---

[66] *DG and DD v State Secretary for Justice*, Council of State, Administrative Law Division, 15 Jan 1996, in LANM Barnhoorn, 'Netherlands Judicial Decisions involving questions of public international law, 1995–1996' (1996) 28 Netherlands Yearbook of International Law 325 , 331. See also discussion in Elberling (n 23) 940, Violeta Moreno-Lax, *Accessing Asylum in Europe: Extraterritorial Border Controls and Refugee Rights under EU Law* (OUP 2017) 401; Boeles (n 61) 305, 316–17. Boeles hypothesises that the court's reasoning demonstrates an 'obvious reluctance to recognize any far-reaching consequences of article 16': 317.

[67] *DG and DD* (n 66).

[68] *Jahangeer* (n 65).

[69] *The Queen on the Application of Xhevdet Hoxa v Special Adjudicator* [2001] EWHC Admin 708.

[70] ibid para 47.

[71] Article 1C(5) provides in relevant part that '[t]his Convention shall cease to apply to any person falling under the terms of section A if ... [h]e can no longer, because the circumstances in connexion with which he has been recognized as a refugee have ceased to exist, continue to refuse to avail himself of the protection of the country of his nationality'.

were accepted as refugees following status determination. Keene LJ, in the Court of Appeal, noted:

> [i]t is of some considerable importance that article 1C(5) does not refer to 'cir-cumstances in connection with which he has become a refugee'. It specifically uses the expression 'circumstances in connection with which he has been *recognised* as a refugee' (our emphasis). It is quite clear that the UNHCR Handbook in the passage relied on by the applicants, paragraph 28, distinguishes between being a refugee and being recognised as such ... Article 1C(5) is expressly concerned with those who have been recognised as such, an event of some importance since various rights and benefits have to be accorded to them under the Convention.[72]

In the House of Lords, Lord Brown also placed emphasis on the use of the word 'recognized' in finding that article 1C(5) applied only to refugees who had undergone status determination and not to asylum seekers.[73] Lord Justice Keene and Lord Brown's findings implicitly accept that the term 'refugee' in the 1951 Convention can, in certain circumstances, encompass both refugees and asylum seekers. While article 1C(5), on its terms, relates only to the 'recognized' refugee, their Honours acknowledged that other terms of the Convention may have a broader scope.

Finally, in the EU, both the original and recast Qualification Directive expressly recognise the application of article 16 to asylum seekers.[74] As discussed in Chapter 5, each Directive sets out the circumstances in which Member States may 'revoke, end or refuse to renew the status granted to a refugee' or 'decide not to grant status to a refugee, *where such a decision has not yet been taken*'.[75] Individuals subject to these decisions are entitled to a specified set of rights in the 1951 Convention, including, inter alia, article 16.[76] The reference here to 'refugee' therefore encompasses an asylum seeker who meets refugee definition but has not yet been formally recognised. This aligns with the definition of 'refugee' in each Directive,[77] and the respective preambular statements that '[t]he recognition of refugee status is a declaratory act'.[78]

A counterweight to cases and instruments recognising the potential application of article 16 to asylum seekers is the existence, in many States, of laws and policies that are either expressly designed to limit, or have the practical effect of limiting,

---

[72] *R (Hoxha) v Special Adjudicator* [2002] EWCA Civ 1403, [2003] 1 WLR 241, 249.
[73] *R (Hoxha)* (HoL) (n 24) 1082.
[74] Original Qualification Directive (n 25); Recast Qualification Directive (n 25).
[75] ibid art 14(4)–(5) of each Directive (emphasis added).
[76] '[I]n so far as they are present in the Member State': see original Qualification Directive (n 25) art 14(6); recast Qualification Directive (n 25) art 14(6).
[77] In that it is not contingent on recognition of status: see original Qualification Directive (n 25) art 2(c); recast Qualification Directive (n 25) art 2(d).
[78] Original Qualification Directive, recital 14; recast Qualification Directive (n 25) recital 21.

asylum seekers' access to domestic courts of law. Two examples illustrate this issue. First, in Australia, the Federal Court has referred to 'a legislative intention, evinced repeatedly in the text of various provisions [of the Migration Act], to treat [individuals who arrive by boat] differently, and adversely in a number of different ways: access to the full suite of visas available ... and access to the Courts, being two such ways'.[79] The particular case concerned a privative clause that barred 'certain legal proceedings relating to unauthorised maritime arrivals', including those 'related to the lawfulness of the detention of an unauthorised maritime arrival ... based on the status of the unauthorised maritime arrival as an unlawful non-citizen'.[80] Second, in Hungary, a 2018 amendment to the Criminal Code evinces an intention to limit asylum seekers' access to the asylum system and their capacity to vindicate other legal rights. As discussed in Chapter 1, the amendment criminalised the 'facilitation' of illegal immigration, which extends to '[a]nyone who carries out organizing activities with a view to ... enabling asylum proceedings to be brought in Hungary by a person [who does not meet the definition of a refugee]'.[81] In certain circumstances, the crime carries a term of up to one year's imprisonment.[82] A Venice Commission and Organization for Security and Co-operation in Europe Joint Opinion on the legislative package noted that as the provision 'criminalises the initiation of an asylum procedure or asserting other legal rights on behalf of asylum seekers, it entails a risk of criminal prosecution for individuals and organisations providing lawful assistance to migrants'.[83] In finding the amended law to breach

---

[79] *DBE17 v Commonwealth of Australia* [2018] FCA 1307, para 102 (Mortimer J).

[80] *Migration Act* 1958, s 494AA(1)(c). While the clause purports to prohibit instituting or commencing proceedings in 'any court', it does not oust the High Court's jurisdiction under s 75(v) of the Constitution. See *Plaintiff S157/2002 v Commonwealth* (2003) 211 CLR 476; *Graham v Minister for Immigration and Border Protection* (2017) 263 CLR 1. The applicant argued that this created the 'impracticable consequence' that individuals in the class action could only challenge their detention by 'issuing individual proceedings in the High Court of Australia', and that '[t]he imposition upon the High Court of such a burden would seem an unlikely intention to impute to the legislature': cited in *DBE17 v Commonwealth of Australia* (n 79) para 126. Mortimer J noted that even if the applicant's framing were accepted, '[t]he consequences of compelling litigants to issue proceedings in the High Court is the intended consequence. It is the result of a deliberate policy choice ... to restrict access to Australian courts, and to make it as difficult as constitutionally possible for individuals to litigate over the subject matter categories.': at para 128.

[81] Paragraph 353/A of Law No C of 2012 establishing the Criminal Code (13 July 2012), as excerpted in Case C-821/19, *European Commission v Hungary* (CJEU, Grand Chamber, 16 Nov 2021), para 20. See also Bill No. T/333 amending certain laws relating to measures to combat illegal immigration (May 2018), unofficial translation available via <https://www.helsinki.hu/wp-content/uploads/T333-ENG. pdf>. The new crime is punishable by 'confinement': Paragraph 353/A(1)(b).

[82] Namely, if one conducts such 'organising activities' regularly; for 'financial gain'; to help 'more than one person'; or within 8 kms of the border: see Paragraph 353/A(2)–(3), as excerpted in *European Commission v Hungary* (n 81) para 20.

[83] Venice Commission and OSCE Office for Democratic Institutions and Human Rights, 'Joint opinion on the provisions of the so-called "Stop Soros" draft legislative package which directly affect NGOs (in particular draft article 353A of the Criminal Code on Facilitating Illegal Migration)', CDL-AD(2018)013 (25 June 2018) para 104. See also para 72, noting that it is improper to place criminal sanctions on NGOs for 'getting it wrong'. See further discussion in *European Commission v Hungary* (n 81) paras 61, 65, 90–93.

EU law,[84] the CJEU Grand Chamber noted that it affected an asylum seeker's right to consult a lawyer, since a criminal sanction is 'liable to discourage such persons from providing such services to asylum seekers'.[85]

Although case law and practice do not demonstrate a considered, and consistent, position on whether an asylum seeker is entitled to the protection of article 16, there are persuasive arguments for placing article 16 in the limited category of Convention provisions that are applicable both to refugees and to asylum seekers. For the reasons surveyed in Chapter 1, access to courts is particularly significant for asylum seekers and refugees—critical for their recognition as persons before the law, and essential to the practical exercise of other rights to which they are entitled.[86] It would hardly be acceptable to extend the protections of articles 31 and 33 to the asylum seeker on the basis of the principles of effectiveness and good faith,[87] while simultaneously denying those asylum seekers access to a court in order to enforce those rights, to the extent that they are incorporated into domestic law.[88] Considerations that support this conclusion were well articulated by AG Maduro in Case C-327/02 *Panayotova* [2004], discussing the broader class of third-country nationals:

> [j]udicial protection of fundamental rights is particularly important with regard to the treatment accorded to third country nationals, since the latter constitute 'discrete and insular minorities' ... Aliens, by the very nature of the political community, cannot benefit from all the same rights granted to the citizens of that political communities, but it is precisely for the same reason that they deserve added

---

[84] The amended law was found to breach Hungary's obligations under articles 8(2) and 22(1) of Directive 2013/32/EU of the European Parliament and of the Council of 26 June 2013 on common procedures for granting and withdrawing international protection (recast), OJ L 180/60 (recast Procedures Directive), and under article 10(4) of the Directive 2013/33/EU of the European Parliament and of the Council of 26 June 2013 laying down standards for the reception of applicants for international protection (recast), OJ L 180/96 (recast Reception Directive): *European Commission v Hungary* (n 81) para 144. Article 8(2) of the recast Procedures Directive relates to access to information and counselling in detention facilities and at border crossings, while article 22(1) guarantees applicants 'the opportunity to consult, at their own cost, in an effective manner a legal advisor or other counsellor'. Article 10(4) of the recast Reception Directive guarantees detainees' communication with legal advisers, among others.

[85] ibid para 96. See also paras 98, 108, 131–32.

[86] See Chapter 1, Section 1.1.

[87] See discussion of Goodwin-Gill's argument in this Part.

[88] Such incorporation is not always straightforward, and domestic law may in fact conflict with international obligations—see for example s 197C of Australia's *Migration Act 1958*, which provides that '[f]or the purposes of [removal under] section 198, it is irrelevant whether Australia has non-refoulement obligations in respect of an unlawful non-citizen' and that '[a]n officer's duty to remove as soon as reasonably practicable an unlawful non-citizen ... arises irrespective of whether there has been an assessment ... of Australia's non-refoulement obligations'. The Migration Act 1958 was amended in May 2021 to 'ensure that it *does not* require or authorise the removal' of a person to whom Australia owes protection obligations, except where voluntary removal is requested. See Parliament of the Commonwealth of Australia, Senate, 'Migration Amendment (Clarifying International Obligations for Removal) Bill 2021, Revised Explanatory Memorandum' (2019–2020–2021).

judicial protection where rights granted to them are affected by decisions of the same political community.[89]

The right to access the courts is so fundamental that it should be granted to asylum seekers prior to a formal grant of status. Accepting article 16 into the limited class of obligations that protect both asylum seekers and refugees is ultimately consistent with the 1951 Convention's object and purpose of enhancing and ensuring refugee protection.[90] In many cases, State obligations under article 16 may simply mirror obligations to provide access to courts that protect individuals generally under international human rights law, in those cases where asylum seekers have not been excluded from protection. Rights afforded to asylum seekers and refugees may also provide more robust protection in certain cases, including where positive steps are required to ensure 'effective' access (under article 16(1)) and where an individual has reached the threshold of 'habitual residence' (under article 16(2)).

2.2.2 Courts of law

Although the term 'courts of law' appears relatively straightforward, defining its boundaries can be difficult in practice. This is only exacerbated when one attempts to define the concept across a range of jurisdictions with different institutional frameworks and legal traditions. Most commentators who have addressed the issue consider that the reference to 'courts of law' in article 16 excludes administrative agencies.[91] However the distinction between a court and an administrative agency is not always clean-cut.

In Australia, for example, the High Court has noted that '[i]t is neither possible nor profitable to attempt to make some single all-embracing statement of the defining characteristics of a court,[92] although judicial independence and impartiality are recognised as key components.[93] In *TCL Air Conditioner*, French CJ and

---

[89] Opinion of Advocate General Maduro, Case C-327/02, *Panayotova* (19 Feb 2004), para 47, cited in Cathryn Costello, *The Human Rights of Migrants and Refugees in European Law* (OUP 2016) 9.

[90] See Chapter 3, Section 3.2.2.

[91] See Elberling (n 23) 939; Paul Weis (ed), *The Refugee Convention, 1951* (CUP 1995) 134; Atle Grahl-Madsen, *Commentary on the Refugee Convention 1951, Articles 2–11, 13–37* (Republished by the Division of International Protection of the United Nations High Commissioner for Refugees 1997) art 16, VI.

[92] *Forge v Australian Securities and Investments Commission (ASIC)* (2006) 228 CLR 45, para 64 (Gummow, Hayne, and Crennan JJ).

[93] ibid, noting that '[a]n important element … in the institutional characteristics of courts in Australia is their capacity to administer the common law system of adversarial trial', and the conduct of trial must be 'by an independent and impartial tribunal'. See also para 84 ('History reveals that judicial independence and impartiality may be ensured by a number of different mechanisms, not all of which are seen, or need to be seen, to be applied to every kind of court.'). 'Independence' requires both independence from the executive organs of government and from other actors, including parties to the dispute: See ibid para 74; and also *Cases of De Wilde, Ooms and Versyp ("Vagrancy") v Belgium (Merits)*, App nos 2832/66; 2835/66; 2899/66 (ECtHR, Court (Plenary), 18 Jun 1971), paras 77–78.

Gageler J recalled the 'essential character of a court as an institution that is, and is seen to be, both impartial between the parties and independent of the parties and of other branches of government in the exercise of the decision-making functions conferred on it'.[94] When interpreting the expression 'courts of law', difficulties can be expected to arise at the margins; for example, in drawing the line between a tribunal and a court,[95] or in parsing an institution's functions to determine its ultimate character. Substance, not form, is paramount, and the name of an institution is not definitive.[96] In the US, for example, the immigration court system is staffed by judges under the supervision of the Attorney General who are appointed as 'administrative judge[s] within the Executive Office for Immigration Review' (EOIR).[97]

The difficulties in creating a unitary definition of a court of law across multiple jurisdictions was demonstrated by the European Court of Human Rights (ECtHR) in *X v The United Kingdom*. The Court considered the definition of 'court' in article 5(4) of the European Convention on Human Rights (ECHR),[98] noting that:

> [i]t is not within the province of the Court to inquire into what would be the best or most appropriate system of judicial review in this sphere [namely, judicial review of the detention of a person 'compulsorily confined in a psychiatric institution for an indefinite or lengthy period': see para 52 of the Judgment], for the Contracting States are free to choose different methods of performing their

[94] *TCL Air Conditioner (Zhongshan) Co Ltd v Judges of the Federal Court of Australia* (2013) 251 CLR 533 at 553, para 27 (footnotes omitted).

[95] Craig notes that 'while tribunals may differ from the courts in the way in which they operate, the difference is one of degree rather than kind': Paul Craig, *Administrative Law* (7th edn, Sweet & Maxwell 2012) 233, para 9–003 (footnotes omitted). In *TCL Air Conditioner* (n 94) 565, para 69, the High Court plurality noted that at a State (as opposed to a federal) level, the distinction between a court and an administrative tribunal 'may not always be drawn easily'. For a summary of ECtHR case law on the definition of a tribunal, see ECtHR, 'Guide on Article 6 of the European Convention on Human Rights: Right to a Fair Trial (Civil Limb)' (Council of Europe/European Court of Human Rights, updated 31 August 2022), paras 171–182.

[96] See, eg, *Attorney-General of the Commonwealth of Australia v The Queen (Boilermakers' Case) (Privy Council)* (1957) 95 CLR 529, 539, citing with approval Barton J's statement in *The Waterside Workers' Federation of Australia v J.W. Alexander Ltd (Alexander's Case)* (1918) 25 CLR 434, 451, that 'whether tribunals were Courts, and whether they exercised what is now called judicial power, depended and depends on substance and not on mere name'. This principle is particularly important when interpreting multilateral instruments, given the many names used to describe different institutions worldwide. Barton J continued: '[e]nforceable decision by an authority constituted by law at the suit of a party submitting a case to it for decision is in character a judicial function. "Court" as the name of a place is merely a secondary meaning. "The Court" is the deciding and enforcing authority, even if it sits under a tree, as sometimes it does in parts of the British Empire.': *Alexander's Case*, 451–52.

[97] 8 U.S. Code § 1101(b)(4). See further Amit Jain, 'Bureaucrats in Robes: Immigration "Judges" and the Trappings of "Courts"' (2019) 33 Georgetown Immigration Law Journal 261, 266 (noting that 'a bureaucracy masquerading as a court exacerbates the flaws of both').

[98] Convention for the Protection of Human Rights and Fundamental Freedoms, 213 UNTS 221 (opened for signature 4 Nov 1950, entered into force 3 Sept 1953), as amended by Protocols No 11, ETS No 155 (entered into force 1 Nov 1998), No 14, CETS No 194 (entered into force 1 June 2010) and No 15, CETS No 213 (entered into force 1 August 2021) (ECHR).

obligations. Thus, in Article 5 par. 4 (art. 5-4) the word 'court' is not necessarily to be understood as signifying a court of law of the classic kind, integrated within the standard judicial machinery of the country. This term, as employed in several Articles of the Convention ... serves to denote 'bodies which exhibit not only common fundamental features, of which the most important is independence of the executive and of the parties to the case ... , but also the guarantees'—'appropriate to the kind of deprivation of liberty in question'—'of [a] judicial procedure', the forms of which may vary from one domain to another.[99]

This flexible approach to the definition of 'court' has clear merit when interpreting a multilateral convention. However, there is a distinction between the obligation in article 5(4) of the ECHR (which provides those deprived of liberty by arrest or detention with the right to review the lawfulness of that detention by a court), and article 16(1) of the Refugee Convention (which obliges States to provide 'free access' to courts of law). A broad definition of 'court' in article 5(4) gives a State party greater flexibility, enabling it to fulfil its duties under the Convention through a range of institutions. In contrast, a broad interpretation of article 16(1) may *increase* a State's obligations by requiring it to provide access both to 'courts of law of the classic kind', and other institutions not so classified. In *X v United Kingdom*, the court was prepared, in principle, to characterise bodies like the Mental Health Review Tribunal[100] as courts under article 5(4), provided that they enjoyed 'the necessary independence', guaranteed 'sufficient procedural safeguards appropriate to the category of deprivation of liberty being dealt with', and were competent to order release in the case that detention were found to be unlawful.[101] To take a similar approach to the interpretation of the Refugee Convention could extend the obligations in article 16 to a broad range of administrative bodies that have been empowered to take decisions or hear reviews on refugee status, detention, and other matters.[102]

---

[99] *X v The United Kingdom*, App no 7215/75 (ECtHR, Court (Chamber), 5 Nov 1981), para 53, citing *De Wilde, Ooms and Versyp* (n 93) paras 76 and 78. See also *Weeks v The United Kingdom*, App no 9787/82 (ECtHR, Court (Plenary), Judgment, 2 Mar 1987), para 61.

[100] The Court summarises the nature of this body as consisting of 'a lawyer, a psychiatrist (independent of the detaining authority who examines the patient) and a third member with suitable qualifications'. Its functions include providing periodic advice to the Home Secretary on the condition of a detained patient. See *X v The United Kingdom* (n 99) paras 13–14.

[101] ibid para 61, noting that, if the first two conditions were met, '[t]here is nothing to preclude a specialised body of this kind being considered as a "court" within the meaning of Article 5, par. 4'. The Court ultimately determined that Mental Health Tribunals did not constitute 'courts' within the meaning of the article as they were limited to providing advisory opinions, which the Home Secretary was entitled to reject in certain circumstances: see ibid paras 14, 61. See also *Weeks v The United Kingdom* (n 99) para 61 (noting that a Parole Board may be considered a 'court' under art 5(4) if it meets these conditions).

[102] For an overview of administrative decision-making in three States, see Rebecca Hamlin, *Let Me Be a Refugee: Administrative Justice and the Politics of Asylum in the United States, Canada and Australia* (OUP 2014).

Such an approach may be warranted when it aligns with the context and the object and purpose of a treaty. For example, the Convention on the Rights of the Child (CRC) requires that that the best interests of the child be a primary consideration in 'all actions concerning children, whether undertaken by public or private social welfare institutions, courts of law, administrative authorities or legislative bodies'.[103] The expression 'courts of law' has been interpreted by the Committee on the Rights of the Child as referring to 'all judicial proceedings, in all instances—whether staffed by professional judges *or lay persons*—and all relevant procedures concerning children, without restriction [including] *conciliation, mediation and arbitration*'.[104] Although this is, as commentators have noted, a broad definition, it is arguably justified by both the context of the term (in the treaty's text) and the broader objects of the clause. Article 3 of the CRC clearly intends to capture the full range of administrative and judicial actions that affect children. As Lundy, Tobin and Parkes note, 'formal institutionalized models of decision making in relation to children which involve lay persons' do exist.[105] A technical approach that excluded such proceedings from the scope of article 3 on the grounds that they fell into a grey space between 'judicial' and 'administrative' decision-making would not be in keeping with the clear intent to capture 'all actions' relating to children.

The definition of 'courts of law' in article 16 should similarly be assessed carefully with an eye to its context, object and purpose. While most commentators consider that State obligations under article 16 do not extend to administrative agencies, Boeles is an outlier, arguing that article 16(1) is engaged where 'forms of legal remedies are available to … nationals which do not have a judicial character, such as administrative appeal to a higher administrative body'.[106] The textual context of the 1951 Convention is against Boeles' interpretation of the clause. As Weis, Elberling, and Grahl-Madsen note, other provisions of the 1951 Convention *do* extend to administrative agencies.[107] Article 32 provides that the expulsion of a refugee may only be conducted under a 'decision reached in accordance with due process of law', a term that the *travaux préparatoires* show was intended to cover both administrative and judicial decision-making.[108] Although linguistic differences across the text of ECHR have not prevented the ECtHR from taking a broad and flexible view of 'court' in article 5(4)—article 6, for example, refers not to a court but to an 'independent and impartial tribunal'—an extension of the term

---

[103] 1577 UNTS 3 (adopted 20 Nov 1989, entered into force 2 Sept 1990) art 3.

[104] 'General Comment No. 14 (2013) on the right of the child to have his or her best interests taken as a primary consideration (art. 3, para. 1)', CRC/C/GC/14 (29 May 2013), para 27 (emphasis added).

[105] See Laura Lundy, John Tobin, and Aisling Parkes, 'Article 12 The Right to Respect for the Views of the Child' in John Tobin (ed), The UN Convention on the Rights of the Child: A Commentary (OUP 2019) 421, citing the Scottish child welfare model as an example.

[106] Boeles, 'Effective Legal Remedies' (n 61) 310. See also Pieter Boeles, *Fair Immigration Proceedings in Europe* (Martinus Nijhoff Publishers 1997) 82–83. Boeles considers that this approach 'conforms with the emphasis on the "prevailing system" in [ExCom Conclusion No 8]': ibid (footnotes omitted).

[107] See Elberling (n 23) 939; Weis (n 91) 134; Grahl-Madsen, *Commentary* (n 91) Article 16, VI.

[108] See Chapter 4, Section 5.2.

'court' in article 5(4) has the effect of enhancing Contracting States' flexibility rather than extending their obligations.

Attention to the object and purpose of the 1951 Convention gives some support
to a broad reading of 'courts' in article 16, given the expansive powers granted to
administrative agencies since the adoption of the Convention seventy years ago.
Use of administrative agencies is a means of reducing pressure on the domestic
legal system—funnelling appeals from government decisions into a specialised
tribunal ensures that scarce judicial resources are directed towards other matters. However, in some cases, the administrative bodies tasked with determining
asylum appeals take on the trappings of 'judicial' decision-making. 'Judicialisation'
of a formally administrative entity can serve either the interests of the Executive
(in presenting an administrative agency as having sufficient independence to
guarantee effective appeals, while simultaneously maintaining some control over
decision-making through using the available levers of appointments, funding, and,
in the case of the US, performance targets) or the decision-maker (in bolstering
an argument for greater independence in the face of governmental pressure). It
can also be considered the most efficient route to a final decision, ensuring that review is undertaken by specialist decision-makers while relieving pressures on the
greater court system.[109]

Geoffrey Care's book *Migrants and the Courts*,[110] which examines the asylum
tribunal structure in the UK, notes that while tribunals are 'not courts as lawyers understand them', they have been subject to a 'creeping judicialization'.[111]
The Upper Tribunal in the United Kingdom—staffed by both judges and non-
lawyer members[112]—is invested with statutory powers of 'judicial review'[113]
and is deemed to be a superior court of record under the *Tribunals, Courts and
Enforcement Act 2007* (TCEA).[114] Sir Robert Carnwarth (as he then was), who was
closely involved with the reform of the Tribunals system[115] and appointed the first
Senior President of Tribunals in 2007, notes that the TCEA confirmed 'the place of
tribunals as part of the judicial system, rather than as an appendage of the administration'.[116] These reforms appeared to be intended to insulate certain decisions
of the Upper Tribunal from judicial review in the regular courts.[117] The Supreme

---

[109] See The Rt Hon Lord Robert Carnwath of Notting Hill, 'Where Next for Judicial Review? Some
Lessons from Eight Years in the Supreme Court' (2020) 25 Judicial Review 321,331, paras 46–47.
[110] Geoffrey Care, *Migrants and the Courts: A Century of Trial and Error?* (Routledge Ashgate 2013).
[111] ibid 16, 23.
[112] Tribunals, Courts and Enforcement Act 2007, c 15 (United Kingdom), ss 3(3); 5.
[113] Tribunals, Courts and Enforcement Act 2007, c 15, ss 15–21.
[114] Tribunals, Courts and Enforcement Act 2007, c 15, s 3(5).
[115] Robert Carnwath, 'Tribunal Justice—A New Start' (2009) (Jan) Public Law 48, 49 (noting that
in 2004 he was asked by the Lord Chief Justice to act as 'Shadow' Senior President in relation to the
reforms.
[116] ibid 50.
[117] See Lord Edward Faulks QC (Chair), 'The Independent Review of Administrative Law' (March
2021), para 1.34 (referring to '[a] bona fide attempt to make the Upper Tribunal the final court of appeal
for certain procedural issues'); Carnwath, 'Where Next for Judicial Review? (n 109) 332 (Having been

Court has however confirmed that unappealable decisions of the Upper Tribunal are susceptible to judicial review in certain circumstances.[118] The Faulks review, published in 2021, argues for the abolition of so-called *Cart* judicial review,[119] and the UK government has announced its intention to adopt a narrow ouster clause for that purpose.[120]

There is undoubtedly a distinction between tribunals and courts. However the incremental judicialisation of tribunals—typified by the statutory powers granted to the Upper Tribunal—means that careful analysis may be needed to determine on which side of the line a given institution falls.[121] This characterization is not

closely involved in the preparation of the relevant legislation, I can confirm that our intention was that the Upper Tribunal should … have the status of the High Court and thus be immune from review by the High Court. Our expectation … was that the designation as a Superior Court of Record would have that effect'). But see also Lord Phillips comments in *R (on the application of Cart) v The Upper Tribunal* [2011] UKSC 28, para 86 ('Although the Government argued … this meant that its decisions were not susceptible to judicial review … it does not follow that this was Parliament's intention … What must, I believe, be beyond doubt is that it was Parliament's intention that the two tier structure set up by the TCEA would provide a statutory right of appeal in relation to decisions of tribunals that would, in most cases, provide a satisfactory alternative to judicial review.') In the Divisional Court the government had argued that the deeming provision precluded judicial review; an argument that was, in Lady Hale's words, 'comprehensively demolished': at para 30, referring Laws J's judgment in *R (on the application of Cart) and others v Upper Tribunal and others* [2009] EWHC 3052 (Admin), paras 31–73. The government did not press this argument in the Supreme Court: see para 31 of Lady Hale's judgment.

[118] *Cart* (UKSC) (n 117). *Cart* concerned the specific question of whether a claimant who failed in an appeal to the First-tier Tribunal, and who unsuccessfully applied to the Upper Tribunal for permission to review that decision, could seek judicial review of the Upper Tribunal's refusal: see para 2 (Lady Hale). The Court considered that judicial review should be available on the basis of second-tier appeals criteria: see para 57 (Lady Hale) (noting that 'the adoption of second-tier appeals criteria would be a rational and proportionate restriction on the availability of judicial review of the refusal by the Upper Tribunal of permission to appeal to itself'); also paras 61, 89–95 (Lord Phillips); para 96 (Lord Hope and Lord Rodger); para 97 (Lord Brown); paras 104–105 (Lord Clarke); paras 130–133 (Lord Dyson).

[119] See Lord Edward Faulks QC (Chair), 'The Independent Review of Administrative Law' (March 2021), paras 3.35–3.46 (on the basis that the low success rate of *Cart* judicial review applications did not justify the 'continued expenditure of judicial resources': at 3.46). The methodology in the Faulks review and its finding of a 0.22 per cent success rate were criticized, and the government duly undertook a new analysis, which suggested a success rate of 3.4 per cent, as compared to '40% to 50%' for non-*Cart* judicial review: see Ministry of Justice, 'Judicial Review Reform Consultation: The Government Response' (July 2021), para 35 and Annex E, para 25. However, the Government's methodology has itself been critiqued: see Mikołaj Barczentewicz, '*Cart* Challenges, Empirical Methods, and Effectiveness of Judicial Review' (2021) 84(6) Modern Law Review 1360, 1371, arguing that 'manifest flaws in the Government's paper, likely stemming from inattention to data limitations … render the overall conclusion untrustworthy.' Barczentewicz concludes that '[i]gnoring settlements, the success rates are very close—2.3 per cent (or 3.4 per cent according to the Government) for *Cart* challenges and 3.9 per cent for non-*Cart* cases in the same period. With settlements the comparison could be less favourable to *Cart* cases, but it cannot be simply assumed based on anecdotes that 30–50 per cent of non-*Cart* claims settle favourably to the claimant.': at 1383.

[120] Ministry of Justice (n 119) paras 37–40, 47. The narrow clause will focus on 'removing the route of Cart Judicial Review' (para 47). While review will still be available for excess of jurisdiction or abuse of jurisdiction, the government proposes to oust judicial review over all other errors, including errors of law: see paras 53–54.

[121] See, eg, Mark Elliott and Robert Thomas, 'Tribunal Justice and Proportionate Dispute Resolution' (2012) 71 Cambridge Law Journal 297, 301, noting that the Upper Tribunal has been 'invested with a set of characteristics that set it substantially apart from tribunals as traditionally conceived'.

a matter easily solved by reference to nomenclature, procedure, or membership alone. For those institutions best characterised as courts, the obligations in article 16 will be engaged.

The argument that article 16 obligations should be extended to those institutions best characterised as administrative tribunals is more difficult to sustain. Although the sheer volume of asylum cases currently decided by many tribunals gives some support to a liberal interpretation of 'courts', ultimately, the text and context weighs against this reading.

Furthermore, subsequent practice does not suggest a willingness on the part of States to interpret the provision so broadly. In *R v Hoxha*, Lord Brown suggested that the clearer the 'ordinary meaning' of a term, the greater the weight of 'subsequent practice' that would be necessary to displace it.[122] Applying this dictum in the present case, a high threshold would be necessary to displace the term 'courts of law'. A survey of case law on article 16 has not disclosed any case in which a court has found that a State's obligations under article 16 extend to a guarantee of access to administrative agencies.[123] While, it is difficult to draw definitive conclusions from the survey of the case law, given that its coverage of global practice is not comprehensive,[124] this finding provides provisional support for taking a conservative approach to the definition of 'courts'.

Unless additional practice is uncovered or guidance in this area develops, it is proposed that the term 'courts of law' be interpreted narrowly to only encompass those institutions that substantively meet the criteria of judicial independence and impartiality. It is not proposed, however, to limit article 16(1) to 'civil courts alone', as was done in the case of *Re Colafic*.[125] 'Courts of law' should therefore be construed as applying to all courts that meet the criteria set out here.

---

[122] *R (Hoxha) (HoL)* (n 24) 1085 ('Having regard to the clarity of the "ordinary meaning" born by the proviso to [art] 1C(5), only the most compelling case founded on "subsequent practice" could properly give rise to a different and apparently contradictory interpretation'). In *Hoxha*, Lord Brown noted in obiter that subsequent practice (and UNHCR's interpretation of that practice) was insufficient to displace the clear meaning of art 1C(5), particularly given the 'obvious disagreement of countries as important to the asylum system as Australia, New Zealand, and the UK' (1088). For an early example where State practice was deemed sufficient to displace the clear terms of the Convention, see *Pater v Pater*, Switzerland, Federal Tribunal (Second Civil Division) 13 Oct 1967, 72 ILR 639 (applying the Convention to a Hungarian refugee displaced by the 1956 revolution, despite the Convention's temporal restriction to 'events occurring before 1 January 1951'). The Tribunal noted: '[c]onsiderations which might normally militate against an extensive interpretation of international treaty obligations ... fall away where, as here, the practice of all Contracting States, or at least the practice of those States directly interested in the case being decided, conforms with the interpretation in question.': at 644–45.

[123] At most, the survey has uncovered obiter comments that appear to accept for the purposes of argument that article 16 could potentially be engaged in the context of tribunals. See *Aivazov v Refugee Status Appeals Authority* (n 58) para 26.

[124] See discussion in Chapter 1, section 3.

[125] *Re Colafic and Others,* France, Court of Appeal of Paris (1er Chambre d'accusation), 29 Nov 1961, 44 ILR 187, 189. In terse reasoning criticised by Hathaway in his first edition, the court found that a 'mere reading of [article 16] is sufficient to show that it concerns the civil courts alone'. See further Hathaway, *Rights* (1st edn) (n 24) 646–47, fn 1738.

A consequence of this interpretation of the term 'courts' is that article 16 has no application to administrative RSD procedures. A final question is whether article 16 guarantees any inherent right to judicial review of a negative RSD decision taken by an administrative agency. This question should be answered in the negative. It is well established in case law,[126] commentary,[127] and UNHCR guidance[128] that States retain discretion over precisely how RSD is conducted, a point that has been made expressly in cases addressing the scope and content of article 16.[129] In practice, procedures vary, with some States adopting an administrative system and others relying on executive discretion. Procedures may also change in a single State over time.[130] The non-binding ExCom Conclusion No 8 reflects the general understanding that there is no requirement to adopt a particular model of status determination.[131] Consequently, there is no general obligation to provide judicial review of a decision to deny refugee status under article 16(1). A separate question, discussed in Section 2.3.3, is whether the national treatment requirement in article 16(2) requires a State to provide judicial review of administrative determinations when review of administrative decisions is generally available to citizens of a host State.

2.2.3 On the territory of all Contracting States

Article 16(1) provides that refugees shall have 'free access to the courts of law *on the territory of all Contracting States*' (emphasis added). On its ordinary meaning, the obligation binds all Contracting States, rather than only the State in which a refugee is physically present.[132] A 'refugee' is therefore guaranteed free access to

---

[126] See, in Australia: *Simsek v MacPhee* (1982) 148 CLR 636, 643 (Stephen J); *Minister for Immigration and Ethnic Affairs v Mayer* (1985) 1957 CLR 290, 294 (Gibbs CJ) and 305 (Brennan J); *NAGV and NAGW* (n 56) 170 (Gleeson CJ, McHugh, Gummow, Hayne, Callinan and Heydon JJ); *Plaintiff M70/ 2011* (n 45) 225 (Kiefel J). In Canada: *Németh v Canada* (n 24) 311; in Germany: EZAR 208 No 7, 2 BvR 1938/93; 2 BvR 2315/93 (Federal Constitutional Court), abstracted in (1997) 9 IJRL 292, 294. In the Netherlands: *DG and DD* (n 66) 333; *The Dutch Association of Asylum Lawyers and Jurists (VAJN) and the Dutch Lawyers Committee for Human Rights (NJCM) v Netherlands*, Court of Appeal of the Hague, 31 Oct 2002 in LANM Barnhoorn, 'Netherlands Judicial Decisions involving questions of public international law, 2004–2005' (2006) 37 Netherlands Yearbook of International Law 397, 426. In the UK: *R (Hoxha)* (CA) (n 72) 249.

[127] See, eg, Goodwin-Gill and McAdam (4th edn) (n 20) 56 (noting that the Convention 'says nothing about procedures for determining refugee status and leaves to States the choice of means as to implementation at the national level').

[128] See UNHCR, 'Handbook' (n 21) para 189.

[129] See, eg, *Németh v Canada* (n 24) 311 (noting that while the 1951 Convention 'does provide that refugees shall have free access to the courts … it does not bind the contracting states to any particular process for either granting or withdrawing refugee status.'); *DG and DD* (n 66) 333 ('The Convention does not prescribe that an application for asylum should be decided by a court; in particular, Article 16, paragraph 1, does not contain such a provision').

[130] See, eg, discussion of Australia's introduction, in 1978, of a formal status determination procedure in Claire Higgins, *Asylum by Boat: The Origins of Australia's Refugee Policy* (NewSouth Publishing 2017) 61–77; *Plaintiff M70* (n 45) 225–26 (Kiefel J).

[131] See UNHCR Executive Committee, *Determination of Refugee Status*, No 8 (XXVIII) (12 Oct 1977), para (e)(vi)–(vii).

[132] See *R on the Application of Bisher Al Rawi & Others v SS for Foreign and Commonwealth Affairs and the SS for the Home Department* [2006] EWHC 972 (Supreme Court of Judicature, Queen's Bench

courts of law in Contracting States regardless of where he or she is located,[133] provided that the requisite jurisdictional link exists.[134] The ordinary meaning of the clause also guarantees a refugee access to a Contracting State's courts with respect to conduct that occurs outside of the territory of *any* Contracting State, such as that occurring in a non-Contracting State or on the high seas. Again, there is clearly a need to establish a jurisdictional link under the substantive law of the State in question before a State's obligations in article 16(1) are engaged. This interpretation aligns with the object and purpose of the 1951 Convention proposed in Chapter 3, namely, to enhance and ensure refugee protection.[135] Jurisdiction is not uniquely territorial and to restrict a refugee's 'free access to the courts' would risk a denial of justice.

While this approach to the clause is supported by commentators,[136] Grahl-Madsen adds the caveat that free access is 'subject to the rule … that each Contracting State must determine for its own purposes where a person is to be considered a refugee or not'.[137] For the reasons outlined, it is contended that an asylum seeker is entitled to the benefit of article 16(1) on the basis of a good faith application of the 1951 Convention. This avoids a result that makes a right of access to courts contingent on a separate assessment of refugee status in any jurisdiction in which free access to the courts is sought.

2.2.4 Free access to the courts—is effective access required?

Article 16(1) guarantees free access to courts 'on the territory of all Contracting States'. The ordinary meaning of 'free access' is not immediately clear, given the multiple meanings of the word 'free' (encompassing, amongst others, free from cost and free from conditions). As discussed in Chapter 2, early commentaries on article 16 dealt with 'free access' relatively quickly, noting that that 'free' does not imply a freedom from fees,[138] and, in Grahl-Madsen's case, that 'free access' meant

---

Division Divisional Court), para 61. The question of whether the appellants (who included refugees recognised in the UK) enjoyed 'free access to the courts of law in the territory [of the United States]' was ultimately left undecided by the Court of Appeal: *R (on the application of Al Rawi) v Secretary of State for Foreign and Commonwealth Affairs and Another* [2006] EWCA Civ 1279 (UK) para 129 (Laws LJ). See also Elberling (n 23) 938 (noting that 'obviously, a refugee would not be able to be present on the territory of all contracting States at the same time'), a point affirmed by Moreno-Lax (n 66) 401.

[133] Be that within a Contracting State, a non-Contracting State, or elsewhere.
[134] See, eg, discussion of general jurisdictional principles in Ian Brownlie, *Principles of Public International Law* (7th edn, OUP, 2008) 311–12. See also discussion in Section 2.5.
[135] See discussion in Chapter 3, Section 3.2.2.
[136] See Chapter 2, Section 2.1.3.
[137] Grahl-Madsen, *Commentary* (n 91) Article 16, II.
[138] See Grahl-Madsen, *Commentary* (n 91) Article 16, VI; Weis (n 91) 134. Robinson does not expressly address the scope of the term 'free access': see Nehemiah Robinson, *Convention relating to the status of Refugee: History, Contents and Interpretation: A Commentary* (Institute of Jewish Affairs, World Jewish Congress 1953) 112–13. This interpretation is supported the *travaux préparatoires*. The Ad Hoc Committee adopted an amendment proposed by the UK representative in order to clarify that 'free access' was not misconstrued as freedom from court fees: see Chapter 4, Section 4.2.2.1.

only that 'there should not be any additional obstacles for refugees'.[139] Some recent scholars have proposed that 'free access' entails 'effective access', such that a system that is formally available but practically inaccessible would be inconsistent with the sub-provision.[140] This section examines whether 'free access to the courts of law' in article 16(1) should be interpreted as requiring that a State provide 'effective' access, drawing on case law on the 1951 Convention, and, by analogy, case law on access to courts clauses in other treaties.

Article 16(1) is not subject to any conditions, save that the individual in question be a 'refugee'. In contrast, the protections in article 16(2)—which guarantee 'the same treatment as a national in matters pertaining to access to the courts'—are reserved for those refugees who enjoy 'habitual residence' in a Contracting State, a higher threshold than that provided for in paragraph 1. Logically, the rights set out article 16(2) should therefore be more extensive than those provided by article 16(1). This context supports a narrow reading of the rights guaranteed in article 16(1). For article 16(2) to have meaning, a discriminatory measure that required refugees or asylum seekers to pay higher fees than nationals, excluded them from national legal aid programs, or required the posting of security for costs, would not constitute a breach of article 16(1). Such measures would only breach article 16(2) if the standard of habitual residence were met. Extending this argument further, a requirement that was on its face non-discriminatory between refugees and nationals, but that in practice had discriminatory effects, may also survive challenge under article 16(1).

Is there any place, then, for the argument that 'free' access under article 16(1) requires 'effective' access? Although certain courts have been willing to read an 'effective' requirement into other terms of the Convention,[141] the structure of article 16 at first glance makes the argument a difficult one. A guarantee of 'effective' access—which may require access to legal aid, translators, or other practical necessities, depending on the circumstances of the case[142]—could require even greater

---

[139] Grahl-Madsen, *Commentary* (n 91) Article 16, VI. For a modern example of this principle in action, see Cour constitutionnelle, Arrêt n° 1/2022 (13 January 2022) (Belgium), B.20.2 ('Les dispositions en cause traitent de la même manière toutes les personnes faisant l'objet d'un acte d'exécution d'une demande d'entraide judiciaire, sans établir une distinction selon que celles-ci ont ou non le statut de réfugié'—'The provisions in question treat all people who are the subject of an act of execution of a request for mutual legal assistance equally, without drawing a distinction between those who do or do not have refugee status'—author's translation).

[140] See discussion in Chapter 2, Section 2.1.4.

[141] See *Koe v Minister for Immigration & Multicultural Affairs* (1997) 74 FCR 508 and *Lay Kon Tji v Minister for Immigration & Ethnic Affairs* (1998) 158 ALR 681 (on nationality as 'effective nationality', requiring the beneficiary to receive 'all of the protection and rights to which a national is entitled to receive under customary or conventional international law': *Lay Kon Tji*, 692), noted in Guy S Goodwin-Gill and Jane McAdam, *The Refugee in International Law* (3rd edn, OUP 2007) 67, n 87.

[142] There is scope for further work on defining 'effectiveness' in the context of access to courts. Recent scholarship has drawn on social sciences literature to define 'effectiveness' in other contexts: see Yuval Shany, *Assessing the Effectiveness of International Courts* (OUP 2014), arguing for a goal-based approach to effectiveness, which proposes that 'effective international courts are courts that attain, within a predefined amount of time, the goals set for them by their relevant constituencies.': at 6; and Kirsten Roberts Lyer and Philippa Webb, 'Effective Parliamentary Oversight of Human Rights' in Matthew

accommodations than those guaranteed under the 'national treatment' standard in article 16(2). Would a host State that did not provide free legal aid to its own nationals be bound to do so nonetheless under article 16(1) where necessary for 'effective' access, even if that same State was not required to afford it to a 'habitually resident' refugee claimant under article 16(2)?

No cases were found that engaged directly in with the question of 'effectiveness' in relation to article 16.[143] Guidance can, however, be drawn from ECtHR jurisprudence. As discussed in Chapter 3, both the ECHR and the 1951 Convention call for an 'evolutive' interpretation and a teleological approach that gives particular attention to a treaty's object and purpose. In the case of the 1951 Convention, that object and purpose is directed towards enhancing and ensuring refugee protection. Like the ECHR, it is a rights-based treaty. The ECtHR's approach to its implied 'access to courts' clause in article 6(1) of the ECHR over the past forty-five years[144] is therefore useful guidance in building a reasoned interpretation of article 16(1).

The case of *Golder* provides a clear-cut example of denial of access to a court.[145] Mr Golder was a UK prisoner serving a fifteen-year sentence for a violent robbery. A prison officer, who had been assaulted by several inmates, made an initial statement saying that he thought Golder was one of the attackers.[146] Fearing that the statement and related entries in his prison record had blocked his chances of

Saul, Andreas Follesdal, and Geir Ulfstein (eds), *The International Human Rights Judiciary and National Parliaments: Europe and Beyond* (CUP 2017) 32, drawing on the organisational effectiveness theory goal-based, multiple constituencies, and legitimacy approaches to argue that 'in order to be effective, a parliamentary oversight mechanism should have clear goals and legitimacy in both processes and output and must ensure the appropriate engagement of stakeholders': at 45. An OECD/Open Society Justice Initiative workshop paper notes that '[u]nderstanding effective access to justice requires a focus on outcomes—i.e., the ability of people to address their justice problems in a fair, cost efficient, timely and effective manner': 'Understanding Effective Access to Justice: 3–4 November 2016, OECD Conference Centre, Paris, Workshop Background Paper' (2016), 2. Useful guidance on measuring access to justice is also found in OECD/Open Society Foundations, 'Legal Needs Surveys and Access to Justice' (OECD Publishing, Paris 2019) (see, eg, 24, establishing seven dimensions of access to justice; 143, recalling that vulnerable populations may face specific barriers and that indicators should be designed in a way that is 'responsive to key demographic characteristics'; and Table 4.1 at 146–48, setting out different dimensions of access to justice and appropriate data sources for measuring each). See also European Parliament, Directorate-General for Internal Policies, Policy Department C: Citizens' Rights and Constitutional Affairs, 'Effective Access to Justice: Study for the Peti Committee' (EU 2017), examining petitions to European Parliament on justice and fundamental rights in their context and identifying three main issues that impede effective access to court, namely the organisation of the national justice system; legal and procedural obstacles; and practical obstacles: see Table 1, 24; key findings at 47; and recommendations at 133–34. The report also addresses costs of justice and legal assistance, and access to a fair trial and enforcement of judgments (see, eg, 25–27; key findings at 61 and 78; and recommendations at 135 and 137), issues that may also go to the 'effectiveness' of access.

[143] UNHCR's interventions on *Al-Rawi* raised the issue, but the Court of Appeal did not engage with this argument: see *Al-Rawi* (n 132) paras 121–29 and discussion in Chapter 2, Section 2.2.1.

[144] Since the EctHR found article 6(1) of the ECHR to contain an implied right of access to a court in *Golder v United Kingdom*, App no 4451/70 (ECtHR, Court (Plenary), 21 Feb 1975), paras 36–38.

[145] Ibid. For context on the importance of this case to the development of the Court's jurisprudence, see Ed Bates, *The Evolution of the European Convention on Human Rights: From its Inception to the Creation of a Permanent Court of Human Rights* (OUP 2010) 290–301.

[146] *Golder v United Kingdom* (n 144) paras 11–14.

parole, Golder wrote to the Home Secretary requesting permission to consult a lawyer in order to bring a defamation action against the prison officer.[147] Under the relevant prison rules at the time, permission from the Home Secretary was required for any communication between a prisoner and any outside person, including a legal adviser.[148] Golder's application to the Home Secretary was denied. The Court found it to be 'inconceivable' that article 6(1):

> should describe in detail the procedural guarantees afforded to parties in a pending lawsuit and should not first protect that which alone makes it in fact possible to benefit from such guarantees, that is, access to a court. The fair, public and expeditious characteristics of judicial proceedings are of no value at all if there are no judicial proceedings.[149]

Accordingly, the Court deduced that article 6(1) contained an 'inherent' right of access to the court, which was breached by the Home Secretary's refusal to give Mr Golder leave to consult a solicitor with a view to bringing legal proceedings.[150]

A more complicated situation was presented in the 1979 case of *Airey v Ireland*.[151] Ms Airey, a mother of four children (of whom one was still dependent), with a net weekly wage of less than £40, sought to formalise her separation from her violent and abusive husband. At that time, the Irish Constitution precluded the possibility of divorce.[152] However, spouses were able to enter into a deed of separation as between themselves (which Ms Airey's husband had refused to sign), or to seek a decree of separation from the High Court. Ms Airey's attempts to obtain a decree of separation from the High Court were stymied by her inability to find a solicitor willing to take on her case—no legal aid was available, and she lacked the funds to pay.[153] The evidence showed that obtaining a decree of separation was not straightforward—Ms Airey would have had to furnish evidence of adultery, cruelty, or unnatural practices, and in all 255 judicial separation proceedings that had been conducted in the previous six years, the petitioner had been legally represented.[154] In these circumstances, the Court was willing to find a breach of the inherent right of access to courts under article 6(1). Finding that the Convention was 'intended to guarantee not rights that are theoretical or illusory but rights that are practical and effective', a principle that applied 'particularly' to the right of access to the courts 'in view of the prominent place held in a democratic society by the

---

[147]   Ibid para 16.
[148]   See ibid para 17, citing rules 33(2), 34(8) and 37 of the Prison Rules 1964.
[149]   Ibid para 35.
[150]   Ibid paras 36, 39.
[151]   *Airey v Ireland*, App no 6289/73 (ECtHR, Chamber, 9 Oct 1979).
[152]   See then article 41.3.2° of the Irish Constitution, cited in ibid at para 10. The constitutional prohibition on laws granting divorce in Ireland was lifted in 1995.
[153]   The costs involved in bringing proceedings were estimated to be £500–£700 in the case of an uncontested action, and £800–£1200 if contested: ibid para 11.
[154]   Ibid paras 10–11.

right to a fair trial',[155] the Court considered that the relevant question was whether the alternative proposed by Ireland, that Mrs Airey appear unrepresented, 'would be *effective*, in the sense of whether she would be able to present her case properly and satisfactorily'.[156] In light of the complexity of the proceedings, the Court considered it 'most improbable that a person in Mrs Airey's position … can effectively present his or her own case'.[157] The Court emphasised that article 6(1) did not 'guarantee any right to free legal aid as such' (a contention that would have been difficult to support given that article 6(3)(c) of the ECHR provides specific guarantees in relation to *criminal* legal aid, but the article is silent on civil legal aid). It nonetheless considered that article 6(1) 'may sometimes compel the State to provide for the assistance of a lawyer when such assistance proves indispensable for an *effective* access to court either because legal representation is rendered compulsory … or by reason of the complexity of the procedure or of the case'.[158] Since *Airey*, the ECtHR has found a breach of access to a court in analogous situations,[159] including the imposition of excessive court fees,[160] impractical time limits,[161] and 'procedural rules barring certain subjects of law' from instituting proceedings.[162]

The Court's general approach to the inherent right of access to the courts was reaffirmed by the Grand Chamber in *Zubac v Croatia*.[163] It affirmed that article 6(1) 'secures to everyone the right to have a claim relating to his civil rights and obligations brought before a court', that this right must be 'practical and effective', and that, while a State may set limitations on the exercise of the right, those limitations 'must not restrict the access left to the individual in such a way or to such an extent that the very essence of the right is impaired'.[164]

For its part, the Inter-American Court of Human Rights (IACtHR) has affirmed a 'general obligation to respect and ensure the exercise of rights'[165] that is rooted in the principle of effectiveness:

> the absence of an effective remedy to violations of the rights recognized by the [American] Convention is itself a violation of the Convention … for such a

---

[155] Ibid para 24.
[156] Ibid (emphasis added).
[157] Ibid.
[158] Ibid para 26 (emphasis added).
[159] Cases cited in this sentence are drawn from ECtHR, 'Guide on Article 6' (n 95) para 120.
[160] See eg *Kreuz v Poland*, App no 28249/95 (1st Section, 19 June 2001) paras 66–67 (where the court fee sought was 'equal to the average annual salary in Poland': para 62); *Podbielski and PPU Polpure v Poland*, App no 39199/98 (4th Section, 26 July 2005) paras 64–70.
[161] *Ivanova et Ivashova c Russie*, Req no 797/14 and 67755/14 (ECtHR, 3rd Section, 26 Jan 2017), paras 57–58.
[162] ECtHR, 'Guide on Article 6' (n 95) para 120, citing eg *The Holy Monasteries v Greece*, App nos 13092/87 and 13984/88 (ECtHR, Chamber, 9 Dec 1994) para 83.
[163] *Zubac v Croatia*, App no 40160/12 (ECtHR, Grand Chamber, 5 Apr 2018).
[164] ibid paras 76–79.
[165] Advisory Opinion OC-18/03, *Juridical Condition and Rights of Undocumented Migrants* (IACtHR, 17 Sept 2003) para 109. See also para 101, finding the principle of 'equality before the law, equal protection before the law and non-discrimination' to be *jus cogens*.

remedy to exist, it is not sufficient that it be provided for by the Constitution or by law or that it be formally recognized, but rather it must be truly effective in establishing whether there has been a violation of human rights and in providing redress. A remedy which proves illusory because of the general conditions prevailing in the country, or even in the particular circumstances of a given case, cannot be considered effective.[166]

Referring to '[t]he right to judicial protection and judicial guarantees', the Court further noted:

[the right] is violated for several reasons: owing to the risk a person runs, when he resorts to the administrative or judicial instances, of being deported, expelled or deprived of his freedom, and by the negative to provide him with a free public legal aid service, which prevents him from asserting the rights in question. In this respect, the State must guarantee that access to justice is genuine and not merely formal.[167]

In the specific context of legal representation, the IACtHR also considered the circumstances of the case and the context of the legal system as factors when considering if 'legal representation is or is not necessary for a fair hearing'.[168] The nature of the applicant is also clearly significant; the Court has determined that States are obliged to ensure that any child in immigration proceedings is able to exercise their right to legal counsel through 'the offer of free State legal representation services'.[169]

The willingness of the ECtHR and the IACtHR to expand the substantive content of rights by reference to the principle of effectiveness reflects a general concern to ensure that those rights are not reduced to abstractions. Providing the necessary scaffolding to give these rights practical effect is ultimately consistent with the underlying object and purpose of the ECHR and American Convention respectively. As argued in Chapter 3, although the 1951 Convention is an agreement between States, its object and purpose is directed towards enhancing and ensuring refugee protection. Applying the interpretative model adopted by the ECtHR and the IACtHR to the 1951 Refugee Convention is consistent with its object and purpose of assuring 'refugees the widest possible exercise of ... fundamental rights and freedoms'.[170]

---

[166] ibid para 108, citing previous jurisprudence including *Case of the 'Five Pensioners' v Peru* (IACtHR, Merits, Reparations and Costs, 28 Feb 2003) para 136.

[167] ibid para 126.

[168] Advisory Opinion OC-11/90, *Exceptions to the Exhaustion of Domestic Remedies (Arts 46.1, 46.2.a and 46.2.b of the American Convention on Human Rights)* (IACtHR, 10 Aug 1990), available via <http://hrlibrary.umn.edu/iachr/b_11_4k.htm>, para 28, cited in Advisory Opinion OC-21/14 (n 33) para 129.

[169] Advisory Opinion OC-21/14 (n 33) para 131.

[170] 1951 Convention, preamble. See further discussion in Chapter 3, Section 3.2.2.

What, then, does it mean to interpret a State's obligation to provide 'free access to the courts of law' in accordance with the principle of effectiveness? Drawing from the ECtHR and IACtHR jurisprudence, it can be deduced that an examination of context and individual circumstances is needed to determine what positive steps are required to render a right of access to courts 'effective'. In some cases, there may be no need for any action over and above that which a State generally provides to applicants, for example where a relatively simple matter is contested by a litigant who is fluent in the language of the jurisdiction and has the funds to procure a lawyer. In others, consideration of the nature of the rights at issue, and the litigant's personal circumstances (including age, language skills, financial situation, familiarity with the jurisdiction, detention status, and any other specific indications of vulnerability, including past trauma) may result in a conclusion that specific steps are needed to safeguard the right of access to the courts. This reading of article 16(1) is not inconsistent with the presence of specific guarantees in article 16(2) for the habitually resident refugee, since it does not create a *general* entitlement to, for example, legal aid or translation. It is only when such measures are necessary to ensure effective access to a court that the State's obligations are engaged.[171] It is, however, difficult to conceive of an effective judicial review of a negative RSD decision that lacked suspensive effect.

Where the State places limitations on the right of access to courts, the *Zubac* test—whether those limitations impair 'the very essence of the right'—is helpful guidance that can be applied on a case-by-case basis.[172] A similar approach seems to underlie the Human Rights Committee (HRC) finding in *A v Australia* that the applicant's repeated movement between detention centres and need to change legal advisers did not breach his right to bring proceedings before a court under the ICCPR.[173] The Committee noted that the applicant 'retained access to legal advisers; that this access was inconvenient, notably because the remote location of Port Hedland [in Australia] does not ... raise an issue under article 9, paragraph 4 [granting the right of anyone deprived of liberty by arrest or detention to bring proceedings before a court]'.[174] Assistance can also be sought from domestic courts' analysis of access to courts as a constitutional right.[175] For example, in *UNISON*, the UK Supreme Court considered that 'impediments to the right

---

[171] A similar approach was taken by the ECtHR in *Airey* (n 151). There, 'effective access' under the implied right in article 6(1) of the ECHR was found to require civil legal aid despite the presence of express guarantees in relation to criminal legal aid (but not civil legal aid) in article 6(3)(c).

[172] *Zubac v Croatia* (n 163) para 78.

[173] *A v Australia*, Comm no 560/1993, CCPR/C/59/D/560/1993 (30 Apr 1997), para 9.6 (referring to rights under art 9(4) ICCPR).

[174] ibid.

[175] See, eg, *R (UNISON) v Lord Chancellor (Equality and Human Rights Commission and another intervening) (Nos 1 and 2)* [2017] UKSC 51 para 66, discussed in Guy S Goodwin-Gill, 'The Office of the United Nations High Commissioner for Refugees and the Sources of International Refugee Law' (2020) 69 International and Comparative Law Quarterly 1, 28.

of access to the courts can constitute a serious hindrance even if they do not make access completely impossible.[176] It ultimately held that an impugned order increasing fees for access to employment tribunals and employment appeals tribunals rendered rights nugatory insofar as it had 'the practical effect of making it unaffordable for persons to exercise rights conferred on them by Parliament, or of rendering the bringing of claims to enforce such rights a futile or irrational exercise.[177]

Interpreting article 16(1) of the 1951 Convention as requiring 'effective' access to the courts expands the scope of a Contracting State's obligations. Generally, States are required to ensure that asylum seekers and refugees possess practical and effective rights to access the courts to regulate their affairs and defend their rights. In the RSD context, article 16(1) does not require a Contracting State to institute judicial review of a negative administrative RSD decision where no such review exists.[178] However, where judicial review is provided, Contracting States are under an obligation to ensure that asylum seekers have effective access to that review, in the circumstances of the case. The question of whether article 16(2) may require a State to institute judicial review of administrative RSD decisions in order to guarantee a habitually resident asylum seeker the same treatment as a national is addressed in Section 2.5.

2.3 Article 16(2)

Article 16(2) provides that '[a] refugee shall enjoy in the Contracting State in which he has his habitual residence the same treatment as a national in matters pertaining to access to the Courts, including legal assistance and exemption from *cautio judicatum solvi*'.

---

[176] *UNISON* (n 175) para 78. See also *R v Secretary of State for Social Security, ex parte Joint Council for the Welfare of Immigrants* [1996] 4 All ER 385, in which it was held that rights afforded to asylum seekers by domestic Statute were impermissibly rendered nugatory by subordinate legislation under a different Act. The court noted that 'the 1993 Act confers on asylum seekers fuller rights than they had ever previously enjoyed, the right of appeal in particular. And yet these regulations for some genuine asylum seekers at least, must now be regarded as rendering these rights nugatory. Either that, or the 1996 regulations necessarily contemplate for some a life so destitute that, to my mind, no civilised nation can tolerate it.': at 401 (Simon Brown LJ). The court considered it 'unlawful to alter the benefit regime so drastically as must inevitably not merely prejudice, but on occasion defeat, the statutory right of asylum seekers to claim refugee status': ibid.

[177] ibid para 104. The evidence on the record showed a 'dramatic and persistent fall in the number' of claims brought' in Employment Tribunals since the Fees Order came into force, with a 'long-term reduction in claims accepted … of the order of 66-70%': ibid para 39. Statistics also showed a marked decrease in successful claims seeking small awards: para 42.

[178] The position is similar to that taken by the ECtHR in *Zubac v Croatia* (n 163) para 80, where the Court noted: 'Article 6 of the Convention does not compel the Contracting States to set up courts of appeal or of cassation. However, where such courts do exist, the guarantees of Article 6 must be complied with.'

This sub-provision raises three main interpretative questions, which correspond to the next three issues examined in Chapter 2. These issues are the appropriate definition of 'habitual residence', and whether legal residence is a pre-requisite; the scope of the term 'matters pertaining to access to the Courts'; and the appropriate comparator for whether a 'refugee' is afforded 'the same treatment as a national'. The question of whether the term 'refugee' in article 16(2) has the same scope as in article 16(1) is also addressed.

2.3.1 Refugee

For the reasons set out in Section 2.2.1, the term 'refugee' in article 16(2) should be construed to cover both recognised refugees and asylum seekers, on the basis of a good faith reading of the 1951 Convention and the principle of effectiveness. While it is recognised that the term 'refugee' may have different meanings in different clauses of the 1951 Convention, it is unlikely to possess two different meanings within a single clause. In practice, however, the application of article 16(2) to asylum seekers will be limited in many cases by the threshold requirement of 'habitual residence'. When an asylum seeker does meet the test of habitual residence, he or she should be entitled to the benefit of article 16(2).

2.3.2 Habitual residence

In 1951, the Convention's drafters gave little thought to the process by which asylum seekers would be recognised as refugees.[179] It is unlikely that they anticipated the lengthy, complex process that status determination can now entail. In some cases, asylum seekers have been required to wait years before being deemed eligible even to make a protection claim.[180] Some asylum seekers are detained while awaiting the initial outcome of their claim, and, if rejected, throughout the review process.[181] Even if released into the community, asylum seekers may spend significant periods on temporary visas as they work their way through appeals processes.[182] In *NHV*,

---

[179] See further Chapter 4, Section 5.1.

[180] See discussion of the Australian fast-track assessment model in Jane McAdam and Fiona Chong, *Refugee Rights and Policy Wrongs: A frank, up-to-date guide by experts* (New South 2019) 43. On delays in RSD processing in Nauru, see UNHCR, 'UNHCR monitoring visit to the Republic of Nauru 7–9 October 2013' (26 Nov 2013), available via <https://www.unhcr.org/en-au/58117b931.pdf> noting that 'there remain long delays in the processing of claims, with only one claim for refugee status having been finally determined and handed down in the 14-month period since the transfer of asylum-seekers from Australia to Nauru commenced in September 2012'): at 1. As of 28 February 2023, 10 asylum seekers on Nauru were still yet to have their status determined: see 'Offshore processing statistics' (Refugee Council of Australia, 7 March 2023) <https://www.refugeecouncil.org.au/operation-sovereign-borders-offshore-detention-statistics/2/>.

[181] See the mandatory detention regime in Australia, discussed in McAdam and Chong (n 180) 94–113.

[182] Again in Australia, the Minister may exercise his or her discretion to release an asylum seeker from detention on a bridging visa: Migration Act 1958, s 195A(2). Those who arrived without a visa were previously barred from receiving a permanent visa even if their asylum claim is successful, and subjected to periodic reassessment of their need for protection: see ibid 18–26, 97. A 'Resolution of Status' visa is now available.

the Supreme Court of Ireland considered the case of a Burmese asylum seeker who applied for asylum in July 2008, one day after his arrival in Ireland.[183] After a convoluted process,[184] he was eventually granted refugee status sometime after 27 April 2016.[185] In the interim, he was barred from seeking employment and was required to live in State housing while being provided with an allowance of €19 per week.[186] In *R(ST)*, the UK Supreme Court considered the case of a woman who had spent more than thirteen years classed as a temporary entrant pending determination of her status, and liable to detention.[187] The proper interpretation of 'habitual residence' takes on a particular salience in light of such cases.[188] Is there a point at which an asylum seeker, living either on a series of temporary visas, or irregularly, in a State, will nonetheless be considered a 'habitual resident' of that State? Is there therefore a point at which a State is required to grant to an asylum seeker 'the same treatment as a national in matters pertaining to access to the courts' under article 16(2) of the 1951 Convention?

The 1951 Convention conditions the exercise of rights on habitual residence in two provisions: article 16(2)–(3), and article 14 (which guarantees a refugee the same rights as a national with respect to trademarks and rights in literary, artistic, and scientific works). Commentators on the Convention offer broad formulas as to what is necessary to satisfy the test of 'habitual residence'. For example, Weis argues that 'habitual residence' was intended to be distinguished from 'purely temporary residence'.[189] Relying on Weis, Elberling considers that habitual residence 'does not require a permanent stay or even a plan to make one's stay permanent',

---

[183]   *NHV v Minister for Justice & Equality* [2017] IESC 35.

[184]   See ibid para 2.

[185]   ibid para 4 (the Court notes that|the appellant was granted refugee status after the Court granted leave to appeal on 27 April 2016). Counsel for the respondent had argued that this situation was 'highly unusual' and 'exceptional': see ibid para 7.

[186]   By operation of s 9(4) of the Refugee Act 1996: see ibid paras 1, 3. The High Court found in principle that 'in circumstances where there is no temporal limit on the asylum process, then the absolute prohibition on seeking of employment contained in s 9(4) (and re-enacted in s 16(3)(b) of the 2015 Act) is contrary to the constitutional right to seek employment', but adjourned consideration of the court's order for six months to enable further submissions to be made: para 21. It noted that in the present case, 'the point has been reached when it cannot be said that the legitimate differences between an asylum seeker and a citizen can continue to justify the exclusion of an asylum seeker from the possibility of employment': para 20.

[187]   *R (ST)* (n 24) 142, para 5 (Lord Hope). Her temporary admission was 'extended from time to time'. The complicated developments throughout that period are set out at 142–45, paras 6–12. The appellant argued, inter alia, that she was entitled to the protection against expulsion under article 32 as a refugee 'lawfully in [the UK's] territory'. The Court ultimately found that the appellant's presence in the United Kingdom did not amount to 'lawful presence' for the purposes of art 32 of the 1951 Convention: para 66.

[188]   It could be argued that these cases are, conversely, examples of situations in which applicants were given unfettered access to the courts, with the result that they were able to access every possible avenue of appeal. However, the question of whether an asylum seeker is entitled to, for example, legal aid on the same basis as nationals under article 16(2) of the Refugee Convention remains an important issue, even where it appears that general access to courts is granted.

[189]   Weis (n 91) 123.

though 'something more than mere presence' is required.[190] Hathaway considers that habitual residence requires simply that 'a refugee's presence ... be ongoing in practical terms'.[191] However, as discussed in Chapter 2, his view of the position of 'habitual residence' within the hierarchy of his 'attachment theory' has changed between the first and second editions of his seminal text, *The Rights of Refugees under International Law*.[192] In the first edition (published in 2005), 'habitual residence' was at the apex of the hierarchy of attachment, above 'lawful presence'. On this view, it would not be possible to be habitually resident in a State in which one is not lawfully present.[193] The view that 'lawful' presence is a necessary element of habitual residence divided later commentators.[194] However, in his second edition (published in 2021), habitual residence was moved to the middle of the hierarchy, below both 'lawfully staying' and 'durable residence'.[195] Accordingly, Hathaway now accepts that, in principle, it is possible to be habitually, but not lawfully, present.[196]

However, Hathaway's original characterisation of habitual residence—as at the apex of the hierarchy of attachment—has received obiter support from the UK Supreme Court. In *R(ST) v Secretary of State for the Home Department*,[197] the Court was called on to consider the meaning of the word 'lawfully' in article 32 of the Convention. Lord Hope of Craighead noted that '[a]n examination of the Convention shows that it contemplates five levels of attachment to the contracting states', with 'habitual residence' being the strongest link.[198] The appellant was ultimately found not to be 'lawfully' present in the United Kingdom despite more than thirteen years spent on temporary admission arrangements. This seemingly contradictory conclusion derives from section 11(1) of the UK Immigration Act

---

[190]   See Elberling (n 23) 940, citing Weis (n 91) and Robinson (n 138). Elberling also comments on the position that habitual residence requires a grant of refugee status, finding that '[t]his interpretation does not accord with the wording, system, or drafting history of Art. 16': (n 23) 941.

[191]   Hathaway, *Rights* (1st edn) (n 24) 909; *Rights* (2nd edn) (n 30) 214.

[192]   See Chapter 2, Section 2.1.5.

[193]   Hathaway here notes that this 'most demanding' level of attachment 'requires only a period of de facto continuous and *legally sanctioned residence*' (emphasis added): Hathaway, *Rights* (1st edn) (n 24) 192. See also 909–10 (footnotes omitted).

[194]   Compare, in favour of this position, Weis (n 91) 123 (noting that in cases where refugees are 'illegally in the country, they would be only receive the treatment accorded to aliens generally under Article 7, paragraph 1'); Robinson (n 138) 108; Grahl-Madsen, *Commentary* (n 91) Article 14; Grahl-Madsen, *Status* (n 23) 340, fn 29 ('It seems that the term "ordinarily residence" may best be compared with the term "lawfully staying"'); Goodwin-Gill and McAdam (4th edn) (n 20) 597 ('In order to obtain the benefit of the articles cited above [including article 16(2)], the refugee must show something more than mere lawful presence' (footnotes omitted)). But see contra, Axel Metzger, 'Article 14 (Artistic Rights and Industrial Property/Propriété Intellectuelle et Industrielle)' in Zimmermann (n 23) 905 (arguing that the drafting history does not indicate that illegal refugees should be deprived for the protection of their intellectual property' and that this protection is available 'both to legal and illegal refugees' (footnotes omitted)); Spijkerboer (n 7) 221; Elberling (n 23) 940.

[195]   Hathaway, *Rights* (1st edn) (n 24).

[196]   Hathaway, *Rights* (2nd edn) (n 30) 211 (footnotes omitted). See further Chapter 2, Section 2.1.5.

[197]   *R (ST)* (n 24).

[198]   ibid 147 (Lord Hope of Craighead, with whom Baroness Hale of Richmond, Lord Brown of Eaton-under-Heywood, Lord Mance, Lord Kerr of Tonaghmore, and Lord Clarke of Stone-Cum-Ebony JJSC agreed), citing Hathaway's analysis of attachment to the asylum state.

1971, which, at that time, deemed a person 'who has not otherwise entered the United Kingdom' not to have done so, 'so long as he is detained, or temporarily admitted, or released while liable to detention, under the powers conferred by Schedule 2'.[199] If habitual residence is accepted to be a higher threshold than lawful presence, then an asylum seeker in the appellant's position would equally fail to meet the test of habitual residence under article 16(2) of the Convention.

But are the different standards of presence in the Convention necessarily arranged in a hierarchy at all? In his first edition, Hathaway argued that the 'short list of rights subject to the fifth level of attachment' (habitual residence) shows the drafters' lack of appetite for 'the conditioning of access to refugee rights on the satisfaction of a durable residence requirement'.[200] But why then choose national treatment as regards access to the courts and 'artistic rights' as the two most demanding rights? A better theory may be that the drafters were influenced by past iterations of rights in deciding on the level of attachment to import, without too much attention as to how those rights might fit hierarchically into the Convention.[201] Carlier notes:

> [i]l serait excessif de considérer que les rédacteurs ont construit un système cohérent et réfléchi de droits au regard de la proximité entre le réfugié et l'Etat d'accueil, même si la conférence des plénipotentiaires l'évoque. Il convient de reconnaître, avec Guy Goodwin-Gill, qu'il y a peu de cohérence.[202]

Rather than accepting the recalibration of Hathaway's hierarchy, this book rejects the premise that the Convention creates a 'hierarchy' of attachment at all. If the different iterations of 'residence' in the 1951 Convention are not, in fact, organised in a hierarchy, the proper interpretation of 'habitual residence' must be determined independently, without attention to 'lawful' status. Case law on the interpretation of habitual residence in the context of the 1951 Convention does not provide a great deal of guidance on the appropriate scope of the provision. Beyond the obiter statements of the UK Supreme Court, the notion of habitual residence been discussed in relatively few cases.[203] In the Dutch case *KT v State Secretary for Justice*,

---

[199] The section as it then stood clarified that these actions must be 'under the powers conferred by Schedule 2' of the Act: see ibid 145, para 14 (Lord Hope). The words 'or temporarily admitted, or released while liable to detention' were omitted from s 11 by operation of the Immigration Act 2016 (c. 19): see sch. 10, para 15(a). These changes were in force as of 21 November 2021.

[200] Hathaway, *Rights* (1st edn) (n 24) 190.

[201] Carlier notes that 'the question of whether or not to use the terms 'presence', regular residence' or habitual residence' was the subject of extensive discussions for some provisions and no discussion at all for others'—author's translation: Carlier (n 64) 288.

[202] 'It would be excessive to consider that the drafters had built a consistent system and reflected the rights therein with regard to the level of connection between the refugee and the host State, even if that is mentioned by the Conference of Plenipotentiaries. It is preferable to recognise, with Guy Goodwin-Gill, that there is little consistency.'—author's translation: Carlier (n 64) 288–289, referring to Guy S Goodwin-Gill, *The Refugee in International Law* (2nd edn, Clarendon Press 1996) 307. See also Goodwin-Gill and McAdam (4th edn) (n 20) 595.

[203] Weis cites Ev. Bl.Nr. 357/57, which appears to refer to 3 Ob 359/57 (24 July 1957) Oberster Gerichtshof (Supreme Court of Justice, Austria) (via Austrian Rechtsinformationssystem (RIS)—summary only): (n 91)

the court found that a law barring judicial review of a negative status determination made within one year of the asylum seeker's arrival in the Netherlands was incompatible with article 16(2).[204] In that case, the applicant had been present in the Netherlands for less than twelve months at the time the initial decision was made, and approximately three years at the time of the Raad van State's decision. The court noted that '[a]s the appellant has been a resident of this country without interruption since entry on 31 January 1976, [article 16(2)] is applicable to this case, *if* the appellant can be regarded as a refugee within the meaning of Article 1 of the Convention'.[205] As discussed, the court was empowered in that case to determine, on its own authority, that the appellant did, in fact, meet the definition of a refugee, and on that basis accorded him the benefit of article 16(2).[206]

Given the paucity of case law directly related to the 1951 Convention, it is helpful to consider the appropriate definition of 'habitual residence' more broadly, and as a matter of principle. The term 'habitual residence' is a common term in private international law—Dicey, Morris and Collins note that it is the preferred formula for conflict of laws problems',[207] and there is a wealth of commentary on its interpretation.[208] Different jurisdictions may take different approaches,[209] and even within a single jurisdiction, the term can be applied flexibly. In the UK, for example, Baroness Hale considered in *Mark v Mark* that 'habitual residence may have a different meaning in different statutes according to their context and purpose'.[210]

135, noting that the court held habitual residence to be 'the place in which a person uses [*sic*] to sojourn during some time even if not uninterruptedly. The intention to remain permanently is not relevant but only whether a person makes, in fact, a place the centre of their life, their economic existence and their social relations. This is also the case of the refugee who establishes residence in a place in order to clarify his or her future fate'. See also *Compagnie des Phosphates et du Chemin de Fer de Gafsa v Wechsler*, France, Court of Appeal of Paris, 12 Dec 1967, 48 ILR 171, 172 in which the court considered the habitual residence of a recognised refugee to be 'indisputable', but provide no further explanation of this conclusion; and *KT* (n 61).

[204] *KT* (n 61). See also the earlier case *KvS* (n 61) (finding art 16(1) not to apply to a case where the court determined the appellant not to be a refugee). Boeles notes that in later jurisprudence, the Raad van State considered that article 16 only prevented a refugee being 'subject to a provision which denied him the right of appeal on account of the length of his stay in the Netherlands' and on that basis found that a bar on a refugee requesting an 'expeditious appeal' was consistent with article 16: see Boeles (n 61) 305.

[205] *KT* (n 61) 3 (emphasis added).

[206] Although arguably, by engaging in the process of determining whether the appellant was a refugee, the Court was in fact allowing an 'appeal' of the initial rejection.

[207] Lord Collins of Mapesbury (ed) with specialist editors, *Dicey, Morris and Collins on Conflict of Laws* (15th edn, Sweet & Maxwell 2012), 176, para 6–118.

[208] See, for example, ibid 176–193, paras 6–118 to 6–156; HCCH, 'Note on Habitual Residence and the Scope of the 1993 Hague Convention' (Mar 2018). Guidance can also be taken with due caution from approaches to the interpretation of similar terms: see e.g. *Al-Juffali v Estrada and another* [2016] EWCA Civ 176, paras 54–92 (Lord Dyson MR, King, Hamblen LJJ agreeing), finding that 'permanent residence' may indeed be inferred in circumstances where an individual lacks a permanent right to reside in the United Kingdom and has no intention to obtain such a right).

[209] Compare *Dicey, Morris and Collins* (n 207) Rules 17 and 18, covering the traditional English interpretation and the EU law respectively: 177, 6R–122; 187, 6R–145; 193, 6–155.

[210] *Mark v Mark* [2005] UKHL 42.

In that case, the Court accepted that the applicant's illegal presence in the United Kingdom did not prevent her from meeting the test of 'habitual residence' in order to bring divorce proceedings.[211] This outcome followed from the purpose of the legislation, namely, to determine when two parties' connection with the United K was sufficiently close to justify granting jurisdiction to its courts to dissolve their marriage.[212] However, Baroness Hale noted that in other contexts, particularly those 'conferring entitlement to some benefit from the state … it would be proper to imply a requirement that residence be lawful'.[213] This adaptable approach would appear to leave open the potential for asylum seekers who are illegally present or deemed not to be present to nonetheless be considered habitually resident for certain purposes under UK law.[214] However, in *R (on the application of YA) v Secretary of State for Health*,[215] Ward LJ challenged the view that an asylum seeker could ever be considered 'ordinarily resident' (a term considered to be synonymous with 'habitually resident' under UK law).[216] His Honour stated:

> [a]sylum seekers are clearly resident here but is the manner in which they have acquired and enjoy that residence ordinary or extraordinary? Normal or abnormal? Were they detained, then no one would suggest they were ordinarily resident in the place of their detention. While they are here under sufferance pending investigation of their claim they are not, in my judgment, ordinarily resident here. Residence by grace and favour is not ordinary.[217]

Ward LJ's characterisation of the asylum seeker's position as 'extraordinary', and hence incapable of meeting the threshold of 'ordinary' residence, sits uncomfortably

---

[211] Section 5(2) of the Domicile and Matrimonial Proceedings Act 1973 provided that the court only had jurisdiction to hear divorce proceedings if either of the parties to the marriage is domiciled in England and Wales at the commencement of proceedings or 'was habitually resident … throughout the period of one year ending with that date': see *Mark v Mark* (n 210) para 26 (Baroness Hale). See further Pippa Rogerson, 'Illegal Overstayers Can Acquire a Domicile of Choice or Habitual Residence in England' (2006) 65 *Cambridge Law Journal* 35. See also the case of *R v Barnet London Borough Council, ex p Nilish Shah* [1983] 2 AC 309, 343–44, setting out the general domestic test applied to 'ordinary residence', and an exception (in obiter) for those who are in a country unlawfully.

[212] *Mark v Mark* (n 210) para 33 ('The purpose of the 1973 Act was to provide an answer to the question "when is the connection with this country of the parties and their marriage sufficiently close to make it desirable that our courts should have jurisdiction to dissolve the marriage?" ').

[213] ibid para 36 (Baroness Hale). The approach in *Mark v Mark* (n 210) is therefore squared with Lord Scarman's test for 'ordinary residence' set out in *R v Barnet London Borough Council* (n 211). Lord Scarman considered, in obiter, that '[i]f a man's presence in a particular place or country is unlawful, eg, in breach of immigration laws, he cannot rely on his unlawful residence as constituting ordinary residence (even though in a tax case the Crown may be able to do so)'. See further Baroness Hale's discussion of *Shah* at paras 31–32, 36.

[214] Under Baroness Hale's approach, it may, hypothetically, be easier to mount a claim that a court should have jurisdiction over a claim involving an asylum seeker than a claim to legal aid on the same basis as a national, which could be considered more akin to a 'benefit'.

[215] [2009] EWCA Civ 225.

[216] *Mark v Mark* (n 210) para 33 (Baroness Hale), citing *Ikimi v Ikimi* [2001] EWCA Civ 873.

[217] *R (on the application of YA)* (n 215) para 61.

with the Supreme Court's findings *Mark v Mark*.[218] Particularly when asylum applications take many years to resolve, lives continue; relationships form; employment is taken up, whether legally or illegally. Conflicts may arise, independently of the asylum process, that call for resolution in the courts. Rather than focusing on the 'extraordinary' nature of the asylum seeker's plight, the very ordinariness of life under conditions of temporary or illegal residence should be recognised. As Waller LJ noted in the Court of Appeal, 'there must be a very large number of extremely longstanding but unlawful residents in this and other countries whose only real links are with their adopted country and whose personal affairs should properly be governed by the laws of that country, whether to their advantage or to their disadvantage'.[219]

Some guidance can also be drawn from approaches to 'habitual residence' in other multilateral conventions. The term 'habitual residence' appears in numerous conventions concluded by the Hague Conference on Private International Law.[220] It has traditionally been left undefined, so as to 'leave the notion free from technical rules'.[221] However, a 2018 Note on habitual residence under the 1993 Hague Convention on Inter-Country Adoption did elaborate on the term's meaning.[222] It noted that habitual residence is an 'autonomous concept', determined 'on the facts of each particular case, and in light of the objectives of the particular Hague Convention rather than each State's domestic law constraints'.[223] Habitual residence is considered a 'question of fact' for the appropriate State authorities to determine, though generally treated as 'denoting the country which has become the focus of the individual's domestic and professional life'.[224] A non-exhaustive list of factors that can be considered when determining habitual residence is included,

---

[218] It can also be contrasted with Baroness Hale's hypothetical account of the asylum seeker's position, in the context of domicile: 'A further problem in regarding legality as an essential element [of domicile] … is the shifting nature of immigration status. An asylum seeker, for example, may commit a criminal offence by entering this country illegally. But on making his claim to the authorities, he may be granted temporary admission. His presence is no longer illegal, but under section 11(1) of the Immigration Act 1971 he is deemed not to be here at all. Is he then to be prevented from acquiring a domicile of choice here, although he undoubtedly has no intention of returning to his country of origin?': *Mark v Mark* (n 210) para 48.

[219] *Mark v Mark* [2004] EWCA Civ 168, para 57, cited by Baroness Hale in *Mark v Mark* (n 210) para 34.

[220] Habitual residence has been called 'the main connecting factor used in all the modern Hague Conventions': HCCH (n 208), para 5. See, eg, Convention relating to Civil Procedure, 286 UNTS 265 (signed 1 Mar 1954, entered into force 12 Apr 1957) art 32; Convention concerning the Powers of Authorities and the Law Applicable in Respect of the Protection of Infants, 658 UNTS 143 (signed 5 Oct 1961, entered into force 4 Feb 1969), arts 1, 4–6, 8, 11–13; Convention on the Recognition of Divorces and Legal Separations, 978 UNTS 393 (signed 1 June 1970, entered into force 24 Aug 1975), arts 2–3; Convention on Protection of Children and Cooperation in Respect of Intercountry Adoption, 1870 UNTS 182 (signed 29 May 1993, entered into force 1 May 1995), art 14. See also *Dicey, Morris and Collins* (n 207) 177, 6–123.

[221] *Dicey, Morris and Collins* (n 207) 177, 6–123, noting that this lack of definition is a 'matter of deliberate policy'.

[222] HCCH (n 208).

[223] ibid para 5 (footnotes omitted).

[224] ibid para 7 (footnotes omitted).

with the provisos that 'no single factor is determinative'; that the weighting of the factors may vary depending on the circumstances; and that 'greater caution is necessary where the amount of time spent in the country is relatively short'.[225] These factors include the length of time a person has been living in a State and the conditions of his or her stay (including immigration status), as well as his or her reasons for moving to and living in a State, intentions, place of work, and ties to the purported State of habitual residence and any other relevant State.[226]

Although formulated in the context of a specific treaty, these principles are helpful guidance when interpreting the term 'habitual residence' in the 1951 Convention. They support the view that 'habitual residence' should be interpreted autonomously in the Convention, rather than in accordance with each State's domestic understanding of the term.[227] The consequence of treating habitual residence as an autonomous term is that domestic laws which 'deem' asylum seekers not to be habitually resident, or create presumptions against such recognition, would not be decisive in determining an individual's residence status. This would have the effect of promoting consistency in the interpretation of the Convention. Second, an approach based on the object and purpose of the 1951 Convention aligns with the rule of treaty interpretation in article 31 of the Vienna Convention on the Law of Treaties by providing a means of enhancing and ensuring refugee protection.[228] The fact-based approach advocated for in the 2018 Note seems appropriate given the varied circumstances of asylum seekers worldwide. Applying this approach, temporary or irregular residence in a host country would be a 'factor' to be considered when determining whether an asylum seeker was habitually resident, though not necessarily determinative. Some caution would be called for before concluding that an asylum seeker attained habitual residence immediately upon entering the territory of a host State, particularly since it is entirely possible to have no habitual residence at all.[229] However, with the passage of time, an individual's claim for habitual residence might be strengthened. The intention of an asylum seeker to establish himself or herself in the host State would also be relevant

---

[225] ibid paras 69–70.

[226] For a detailed list, with examples, see ibid para 70.

[227] The alternate approach was adopted, for example, in the interpretation of the term 'lawful presence' by the UK Supreme Court in *R (ST)* (n 24). Lord Hope noted that 'there is no consensus among the commentators that lawful presence should be given an autonomous meaning or what that meaning should be': para 34 (see also Lord Dyson, para 63). Lord Dyson further noted that 'if it had been intended to restrict the power of the contracting states to decide whether a refugee is lawfully present in its territory, this would surely have been stated explicitly': para 64. The word 'lawfully' is arguably more susceptible to a domestic interpretation than 'habitually resident'. The Hague Conference's strong statements on the autonomous nature of the term 'habitually resident' also speaks in favour of a unified approach.

[228] See further Chapter 3, Section 3.2.2.

[229] In the context of the 1951 Convention, see Grahl-Madsen, *Commentary* (n 91) Article 16, VIII ('This implies that refugees who have not established habitual residence in any country will not benefit from the provisions of paragraphs 2 and 3'); Weis (n 91) 134; Hathaway, *Rights* (2nd edn) (n 30) 920; Robinson (n 138) 107, fn 151 ('it is difficult to envisage a refugee having no habitual residence except new refugees who did not yet succeed in establishing "habitual residence" anywhere').

and weighed against his or her actual immigration status. This graduated approach has the benefit of flexibility and practicality. It is responsive to the Convention's purpose of assuring to refugees 'the widest possible exercise of ... fundamental rights and freedoms', while maintaining the textual integrity of article 16. Under this approach, 'habitual residence' remains a functional threshold that individuals must cross in order to access the broader set of rights afforded by article 16(2) of the 1951 Convention. An assessment of individual circumstances appears to be the clearest means of fairly establishing whether that threshold is met.

2.3.3 Same treatment as a national in matters pertaining to access to the Courts

Article 16(2) obliges the State to provide a refugee with the 'same treatment as a national' as regards 'matters pertaining to access to the Courts, including legal assistance and *exemption from cautio judicatum solvi*'. This section briefly addresses the scope of the two specific examples highlighted in article 16(2), before analysing the general scope of the clause and the appropriate comparator for determining whether a 'refugee' has received the 'same treatment as a national'.

2.3.3.1 Legal assistance and exemption from cautio judicatum solvi

Article 16(2) provides for two express cases in which a habitually resident 'refugee' is entitled to the same treatment as a national—legal assistance, and exemption from *cautio judicatum solvi*.

The ordinary meaning of 'legal assistance' is somewhat ambiguous, but commentators typically consider it to be synonymous with legal aid.[230] This approach was also taken by the New Zealand High Court in *Aivasov*,[231] and, in obiter, by the Canadian Federal Court of Appeal in *Krishnapillai*.[232]

These two cases provide additional guidance on how 'same treatment' should be understood. In *Aivasov*, Venning J noted that the applicant had been granted:

> the same treatment as a national in matters concerning access including legal assistance in that the Legal Services Act makes provision for the consideration of legal aid to be granted to a person in the position of the applicant.[233]

---

[230] See Grahl-Madsen, *Commentary* (n 91) Article 16, VII (referring to 'legal aid or legal assistance'); Robinson (n 138) 113 (referring to 'free legal assistance' in order to relieve the burden on indigent claimants); Hathaway, *Rights* (2nd edn) (n 30) 922. This also appears to be the implication of Weis' comment (echoing Grahl-Madsen) that the provision applies 'only in so far as legal assistance is provided for by the State or under a State support scheme' (rather than by bar associations): Weis (n 91) 134.

[231] (n 58). See Elberling (n 23) 945.

[232] *Krishnapillai v the Queen* 2001 FCA 378, para 32 (Décary JA) ('No suggestions were made that in Canada refugees do not have free access to the leave requirement procedure ... counsel did not argue that legal aid ... services were not available').

[233] *Aivazov* (n 58), rejecting an argument that proceeding with a Refugee Status Appeals Authority hearing without legal aid would breach article 16.

A similar approach was taken by Décary JA in *Krishnapillai*, rejecting an argument that article 16(2) was inconsistent with the existence of a (general) leave requirement before a right to appeal could be exercised:[234]

> [a]rticle 16 does not define a special procedure nor does it provide for special procedures for refugees. Quite to the contrary: in granting refugees the right to equal treatment before the courts, it implicitly recognizes that refugees are subject to the procedures available in the country in which they have their habitual residence. Article 16 does not impose on the state the obligation to make available to refugees because they are refugees the most favourable procedures that can be put in place.[235]

As these statements suggest, the ordinary meaning of 'same treatment' should be interpreted as requiring a State to guarantee an eligible person the right to *apply*, on an equal basis to nationals, for any benefits, rights, or other matters that relate to access to the courts. An absolute bar on access to legal aid based on citizenship or status would fall foul of the sub-provision. Making that access subject to general conditions would not.

Finally, a habitually resident 'refugee' is entitled to an exemption from posting security for costs. This right has been recognised in a handful of cases—some extending it to an asylum seeker.[236] The more complex question of whether an eligible person is entitled to seek security for costs from another party to litigation is addressed in section 2.3.3.2.

---

[234] The applicant was a recognised refugee who sought to challenge a deportation decision which had been taken on the grounds that he was a danger to the public. The court noted, in the course of its judgment, that '[l]eave requirement is a usual procedure in Canadian law and is, in Canadian terms, an accepted form of access to the courts of the country. No suggestions were made that in Canada refugees do not have free access to the leave requirement procedure': *Krishnapillai* (n 232) para 32.

[235] ibid para 31.

[236] See *Grundul v Bryner* (n 64) (applying article 16(3)); *Loprato v Zickman*, France, Court of Cassation (First Civil Chamber) 30 Mar 1971, 72 ILR 586 (in obiter, finding that the right only applied to plaintiffs and did not extend to a right to demand *cautio judicatum solvi* from the other party); *K c Etat belge*, Bruxelles (21e ch) (20 January 2006), in *Journal des Tribunaux*, 2006, 373 (applying the principle to an asylum seeker appealing a refusal to grant refugee status). See further Carlier (n 64) 325 (referring to the latter case; noting that the same approach has been taken to stateless persons; and also citing Belgian cases relating to 'certain social rights' ('certains droits sociaux') in which the right has been recognised). For a case addressing this issue without reference to article 16, see *Jannatu Alam v Minister of Home Affairs*, Case no 3414/2010 (High Court of South Africa, 16 Feb 2012) (considering whether an asylum seeker should be required to furnish security for costs in an action for unlawful arrest and detention and finding that '[s]uch an order ... would have the effect of precluding [the] plaintiff from proceeding with this action'). Cited in Fatima Khan and Ncumisa Willie, 'Strengthening Access to Justice for Women Refugees and Asylum Seekers in South Africa' in David Lawson, Adam Dubin, and Lea Mwambene (eds), *Gender, Poverty and Access to Justice: Policy Implementation in Sub-Saharan Africa* (Routledge 2020) 186.

2.3.3.2 Matters pertaining to access to the Courts

Article 16(2) provides that a refugee 'shall enjoy … the same treatment as a national *in matters pertaining to access to the Courts*, including legal assistance and exemption from *cautio judicatum solvi*.'[237] As Lord Berwick noted in *Adan v Secretary of State for the Home Department*, 'the starting point must be the language itself'.[238] The subject of the equal treatment is therefore 'matters pertaining to access to the Courts'. Use of the word 'including' indicates that legal assistance and exemption from security for costs are two examples of a broader category. The phrase 'matters pertaining to access to the Courts' is therefore best construed as a self-standing source of rights, which includes, but is not limited to, 'legal assistance' and an exemption from security for costs.

This construction opens the more difficult question of the scope of 'matters pertaining to access to the Courts'. Case law on issues found to fall within and outside the scope of 'matters pertaining to access to the Courts' is surveyed in the sections that follow. Perhaps unsurprisingly, this survey does not reveal any consistent approach. The matters found to fall within the scope of the clause reflect the legal issues faced by individual claimants, and it is difficult to discern any coherent, underlying rationale for inclusion or exclusion. A possible typology of issues falling within the scope of 'matters pertaining to access' is then proposed.

2.3.3.2.1 Case law on issues found to constitute matters pertaining to access to the Courts Decisions in France and Switzerland have found that 'matters pertaining to access to the Courts' extend to an exemption from requirements that would otherwise apply to non-citizens under private law in divorce proceedings.[239] These decisions effectively treat the refugee as if he or she were a national for the purposes of determining jurisdiction in disputes involving conflict of laws issues. In *Pater v Pater*, the Swiss Federal Tribunal found that a Hungarian refugee living in Switzerland was entitled to petition for a divorce in the same manner as a Swiss national, without the need to prove that the basis of his divorce petition was recognised in Hungary.[240] In *Eglin v Marculeta*, the Tribunal de grande instance of Paris applied article 16(2) to grant France jurisdictional competence over a refugee

---

[237] First emphasis added.

[238] [1999] 1 AC 293, 305.

[239] See *Pater v Pater* (n 122) 642; *Eglin v Marculeta*, France, Tribunal de grande instance of Paris (Chambre du Conseil) 17 Apr 1970, 70 ILR 356 (granting France jurisdictional competence over refugees under a bilateral treaty establishing the appropriate fora for disputes).

[240] The Tribunal noted that article 16(2) 'takes precedence in its sphere of application over [article 7 h (1) of the Federal Law on the civil law relations of persons established or resident in Switzerland (NAG)] … A refugee within the meaning of the Convention who, like the plaintiff, lives in Switzerland, can therefore petition for divorce in his place of residence … based on substantive Swiss law': *Pater v Pater* (n 122) 642.

under a bilateral treaty with Switzerland. It found that: 'in the application of Article 1 of the Franco-Swiss Treaty ... defining the division of competence between the two national jurisdictions, a refugee domiciled or resident in France is to be assimilated to a French national'.[241] Taking a robust view of the scope of the clause, the Tribunal held:

> [t]he purpose of this provision is to integrate a refugee into the community of the country in which he has taken refuge, in the field of access to courts which includes, in the broad sense, the rules of jurisdictional competence.[242]

While Carlier refers to *Eglin v Marculeta* as an 'isolated decision' in French jurisprudence,[243] a similar approach was taken in the earlier case of *Wechsler* before the Court of Appeal of Paris. The case concerned a Roumanian refugee who was attempting to sue a Tunisian company in the French courts.[244] The court held that a habitually resident refugee was entitled under article 14 of the Civil Code to bring a case without the condition of reciprocity, noting:

> the term 'access to the courts' in the sense of Article 16 of the Convention of 1951 must, in order that its purposes may be fully realized, be interpreted broadly, to include *the application of rules of jurisdiction reserved to French nationals*.[245]

Other issues that have been considered to be 'matters pertaining to access to the Courts' for the purpose of article 16(2) include the grant of national treatment to a deceased refugee's estate in probate (in Austria);[246] a bar on access to an appellate court to bring interim injunction proceedings (Belgium);[247] and a bar on judicial

---

[241] *Eglin v Marculeta* (n 239) 357.

[242] ibid.

[243] Carlier (n 64) 327 ('une décision isolée de la jurisprudence française'). Carlier notes that '[l]'assimilation du réfugié au national est ici parfaite' ('here, there is perfect assimilation of the refugee to the citizen'—author's translation).

[244] See ILR headnote, *Compagnie des Phosphates et du Chemin de Fer de Gafsa v Wechsler* (n 203).

[245] *Compagnie des Phosphates et du Chemin de Fer de Gafsa v Wechsler* (n 203) 174 (emphasis added). The court also made reference to Mr Wechsler's wish to 'enjoy the benefit of assimilation into the body of this country effected in his regard by the Convention of 1951 (and more particularly in the field of access to the courts by Article 16 of that Convention)', which France 'can only fully realise ... through its courts': at 173.

[246] Per the summary on RIS, the court found that the estate of a deceased refugee should be treated in the same manner as the estate of an Austrian citizen: see <https://www.ris.bka.gv.at/Dokumente/Jus tiz/JJR_19910227_OGH0002_0020OB00641_9000000_001/JJR_19910227_OGH0002_0020OB00 641_9000000_001.pdf>, summarising 2Ob641/90 (27 Feb 1991) Oberster Gerichtshof (Supreme Court of Justice, Austria) (via RIS—summary only (German)). I am grateful to Gesa Bent for assisting with this translation. Elberling cites this case, together with IVb 626/80 (10 June 1982) (1982) *Neue Juristische Wochenschrift* 2732, for the principle that art 16(2) 'bestows on courts in cases involving refugees the same international competence as they would have in cases involving their nationals': (n 23) 942, fn 86.

[247] See Boeles (n 61) 305, referring to *Cour d'Appel Bruxelles* (29 June 1989) (1989) 54 *Revue du droit des étrangers* 153. Boeles notes that the Tribunal Civil (Ref.) Bruxelles has also found article 16 to be applicable in the case of 'threatened expulsion of an applicant whose application for asylum was declared to be "fraudulent or manifestly unfounded"': ibid.

appeal of any decision on refugee status taken within one year of a refugee's[248] arrival (in the Netherlands).[249] Commenting in obiter, the Canadian Federal Court of Appeal has also opined that the reference to 'including' brings within the scope of the obligation 'items such as free assistance of an interpreter'.[250]

2.3.3.2.2 Case law on issues and matters excluded from matters pertaining to access to the Courts Issues that have been found *not* to constitute 'matters pertaining to access to the Courts' include, first, a right to be granted security for costs from another party;[251] second, immunity from extradition;[252] and, third (and surprisingly), 'judicial review in the form of an appeal'.[253] Finally, there is also inconsistent jurisprudence on the question of whether a refugee is entitled to bring a case under universal jurisdiction provisions that are otherwise only available to nationals, in Belgium and the ECtHR respectively.[254] The reasoning behind the restrictive application of article 16(2) in these four sets of cases is analysed in turn.

The decision to deny a refugee the right to be granted security for costs suggests a far more restrictive approach to article 16(2) than that taken in *Eglin v Marculeta* or *Wechsler*, despite the fact that all three cases were decided in France. In *Loprato v Zickman*,[255] the Court of Cassation held:

> the right to require payment of a *cautio judicatum solvi* is reserved to nationals and certain foreigners to whom it has been formally granted by treaty, which is not the case here since the [1951 Convention] only exempts a refugee from the obligation to pay the *cautio*.[256]

---

[248] The applicant was not recognised as a refugee at the time that he brought the case. The court made a determination that the applicant was a refugee under the 1951 Convention as an interim step in deciding that he was entitled to the benefit of article 16(2). See *KT* (n 61) 3. Courts in other jurisdictions may not be empowered to make such a determination.

[249] See *KT* (n 61). Article 34 of the Judicial Review and Administrative Decisions Act 'had the effect of denying an alien the right of appeal against any decision concerning his application for refugee status if that decision had been taken within twelve months of his arrival in the Netherlands': 1–2. See also, in obiter, *DG and DD* (n 66) 334.

[250] *Krishnapillai* (n 232) para 30.

[251] *Loprato v Zickman* (n 236).

[252] See *Re Colafic* (n 125); *T v Swiss Federal Prosecutor's Office,* Switzerland, Federal Tribunal, 28 Sept 1966, 72 ILR 632. Although it did not specifically engage with the scope of article 16(2), the Canadian Supreme Court's finding that 'Canada's obligations under the Refugee Convention do not require an earlier formal determination of refugee status to be binding on the extradition authorities' also bolsters this position: see *Németh v Canada* (n 24) 312, para 52.

[253] *DG and DD* (n 66) 334.

[254] See *Naït-Liman v Switzerland*, App no 51357/07 (Grand Chamber, 15 Mar 2018) and the line of Belgian cases in the Court of Cassation and Court of Arbitration discussed in Part.2.3.3.2.2.

[255] *Loprato v Zickman* (n 236).

[256] ibid 587. For the original judgment via legifrance, see <https://www.legifrance.gouv.fr/affichJuriJ udi.do?idTexte=JURITEXT000006985016>. See further Carlier (n 64) 326, discussing commentators on the case.

The Court did not appear to countenance the possibility that a right to require payment of the security could fall within the general scope of 'matters pertaining to access to the Courts' in article 16(2). A similar result was reached in *Fligelman v Pinsley and Others*,[257] which concerned article 16 of the 1954 Convention on Statelessness (framed in largely similar terms to article 16 of the 1951 Convention).[258] There, the Court of Appeal of Paris argued that the right to demand security for costs could not be characterised as a restriction on access to the courts:

> it would be impossible, without giving this provision an extension which neither the letter nor its spirit justifies, to grant a stateless person a right which is traditionally reserved to nationals and, exceptionally, as a special favour, to specified foreigners … To deny a stateless person the right to require his foreign opponent to furnish security is not, as was contended, a restriction on his freedom to sue or be sued, but is only the refusal of a privilege of nationality to which *no legal provision*, as it stands, intended to entitle him.[259]

These two cases can be compared with an earlier decision of the Court of Appeal of Paris in relation to the 1933 Convention,[260] which had a similar, but not identical, sub-provision to article 16(2).[261] The court held that Russian refugees in France were entitled to the benefit of security for costs under the 1933 Convention, noting:

> [i]f the text in question means that Russian refugees enjoy the same rights and privileges as nationals, then they ought not only to be exempt from furnishing security for costs in actions brought by them against French subjects but also have the right to require it from foreigners who sue them.[262]

Carlier notes that this approach has been taken in Belgian jurisprudence on the 1951 Convention.[263]

---

[257] *Fligelman v Pinsley and others*, France, Court of Appeal of Paris (1st Chamber), 2 Oct 1962, 44 ILR 143. Cited in Elberling (n 23) 942; Hathaway, *Rights* (1st edn) (n 24) 911; Carlier (n 64) 326.

[258] Article 16 of the 1954 Convention relating to the Status of Stateless Persons is identical to article 16 of the 1951 Refugee Convention in all respects save its subject (a 'stateless person' rather than a refugee): Convention relating to the Status of Stateless Persons (adopted 28 Sept 1954, entered into force 6 June 1960) 360 UNTS 117. It is not clear if the court expressly considered the phrase 'other matters' however.

[259] *Fligelman v Pinsley* (n 257) 144 (emphasis added).

[260] Convention Relating to the International Status of Refugees, No 3663 [1935] LNTSer 91; 159 LNTS 199 (signed 28 Oct 1933, entered into force 13 June 1935) (1933 Convention).

[261] ibid. The relevant section of article 6 read: 'In the countries in which they have their domicile or regular residence, [refugees] shall enjoy, in this respect, the same rights and privileges as nationals; they shall, on the same conditions as the latter, enjoy the benefit of legal assistance and shall be exempt from *cautio judicatum solvi*.' See further Chapter 4, Section 2.2.

[262] *Ivanoff v Fondation Bélaïeff*, France, Court of Appeal of Paris, 25 Mar 1937, 8 ILR 310, 310. The International Law Reports note that these comments were in obiter, as the defendants raised their request for security for costs out of time: ibid 311.

[263] See Carlier (n 64) 326.

The two judgments which held that refugees were not entitled to immunity from extradition were grounded in quite different reasoning. In *T v Swiss Federal Prosecutor's Office*,[264] the Swiss Federal Tribunal considered the different levels of treatment granted to refugees across the 1951 Refugee Convention (which included, together with article 16(2), 'numerous other provisions prescribing only equality with other foreigners'). It concluded that a refugee was 'treated equally with nationals of the host country only to a limited extent', and, as a result, 'it cannot be inferred from the Convention that his status is equal to that of a Swiss national for the purposes of the law of extradition'.[265] In contrast, the Court of Appeal of Paris in *Re Colafic* argued that a 'mere reading' of article 16 'is sufficient to show that it concerns the civil courts alone', and that therefore it had no application in the case of extradition. A concern for public policy implications is also suggested in the court's statement that '[i]f the contention of the defence were accepted, no action could be taken on any request for the extradition of foreigners who had taken refuge in France'.[266] The argument that article 16 only extends to civil matters should be rejected. However, the finding that article 16(2) does not grant a refugee immunity from extradition seems intuitively correct.[267] Immunity from extradition does not answer the description of a matter 'pertaining to access to the Courts'. It is a rather a question of substantive law. Granting a refugee (or asylum seeker) a general entitlement to national treatment under substantive law would conflict with the clear differentiations laid out elsewhere in the Convention (with regards, for example, to rights of association in article 15).[268]

The surprising finding that 'judicial review in the form of an appeal' is not a 'matter pertaining to access to the Courts' in the case *DG and DD* is more difficult to rationalise,[269] and has been criticised by commentators.[270] In that case, the appellants were denied refugee status by the Dutch State Secretary for Justice and unsuccessfully appealed that decision to the President of the District Court in the Hague. The appellants subsequently sought to appeal the District Court's decision to the Raad van State.[271] Under Dutch law, decisions made under the Aliens Act were excluded from general rights of appeal.[272] The appellants argued that this

---

[264] (n 252).

[265] ibid 635.

[266] *Re Colafic* (n 125) 189.

[267] Hathaway takes the same view, considering the extradition argument to have been 'sensibly reject[ed]': *Rights* (1st edn) (n 24) 646–47, fn 1738.

[268] For which the standard is 'the most favourable treatment accorded to nationals of a foreign country, in the same circumstances'.

[269] *DG and DD* (n 66) 334.

[270] See Boeles (n 61) 317 (considering the finding 'highly disputable, if not evidently incorrect'). Elberling's interpretation of article 16(2) also runs counter to this finding: see Elberling (n 23) 945–46.

[271] This background is set out in the summary provided by the Netherlands Yearbook of International Law (n 66) 332.

[272] Under the Council of State Act. See summary provided by the Netherlands Yearbook of International Law (n 66) 332.

exclusion was incompatible with article 16(2) of the 1951 Convention,[273] which has direct effect in the Dutch legal system and is binding. The court noted that the Convention 'does not prescribe that an application for asylum should be decided by a court', and, accordingly, held that article 16(1) 'does not constitute a basis for a right to judicial review of an asylum decision'.[274] However, in line with previous case law, it held that article 16(2) *did* apply to the asylum procedure.[275] The court considered the scope of 'matters pertaining to access to the Courts', finding that while it extended to the two examples of legal assistance and an exemption from security for costs, as well as a requirement that 'aliens wishing to appeal to the administrative courts should have had their principal residence in the Netherlands for at least one year',[276] it did not extend to judicial review. The court reasoned:

[t]he common feature of these examples is that they make access to the courts more difficult. The purpose of the institution of appeal is, by contrast, to provide the edifice of legal protection with an extra floor ... the States that are parties to the Convention are free to organise the asylum procedure as they see fit, in other words with or without the involvement of the courts of law and with or without provision for judicial assessment at two instances. In addition, it should be pointed out that the Convention merely lays down a minimum standard. In view of all of this, it is hard to regard appeal as a 'matter pertaining to access to the courts' within the meaning of Article 16(2). It is true that the Article guarantees a refugee the same treatment as a national. And it is also true that Dutch nationals may in general appeal against a decision of a court on an application challenging a decision of a government authority. It follows, however, from the previous paragraph that this guarantee does not oblige the Netherlands as a Contracting Party to organise the asylum procedure in such a way that decisions on refugee status are subject to judicial review in the form of appeal.[277]

This reasoning provides an unsatisfactory basis for the distinction between a residency bar on appeal (which the court recognises as prohibited under article 16(2)), and a total bar on appeal (which is considered acceptable). Two points help to explain the court's decision. First, the court's finding had the effect of denying the appellants a *second* level of judicial review, rather than a complete denial of access to the courts.[278] Second, the court appears to have felt constrained by article 94 of the Constitution of the Netherlands, which provides that '[s]tatutory regulations

---

[273] *DG and DD* (n 66) 333.
[274] ibid.
[275] ibid, see also *KT* (n 61).
[276] As considered in the earlier case *KT* (n 61).
[277] *DG and DD* (n 66) 333.
[278] See also, in this regard, the finding of the Cour Administrative of the Grand-Duche de Luxembourg that it was not inconsistent with article 16 to limit review to what was in essence judicial review rather than an appeal on the merits: Cour administrative - Arrêt n° 22646C du 10 juillet 2007.

in force within the Kingdom *shall not be applicable* if such application is in conflict with provisions of treaties or of resolutions by international institutions that are binding on all persons'.[279] The court characterised the residency bar as an 'admissibility' requirement which was capable of 'non-application'.[280] In contrast, the bar on appeals was characterised as 'a power expressly withheld from the Division by the legislature'. The Court noted:

[a]rticle 94 does not have such a wide scope that it empowers the courts to bring a given area of law within their jurisdiction of their own volition (in which connection they would then have to make up for any procedural gaps by drawing up their own rules).[281]

The court's finding on the objective scope of 'matters pertaining to access to the Courts' may therefore have been affected by the Netherlands' particular constitutional framework for the incorporation of international law.

Finally, the 'universal jurisdiction' cases address a delicate issue with significant policy ramifications. Universal jurisdiction generally refers to a State's capacity to criminalise conduct, or provide for civil remedies, in the absence of traditional jurisdictional connecting factors. Accordingly, a State may seek to exercise jurisdiction 'regarding a crime committed by a foreign national against another foreign national outside its territory'.[282] In practice, a State may moderate its exercise of jurisdiction over international crimes by requiring some connection with the forum State. It is in this context that the question whether a recognised refugee—or an asylum seeker—can bring a civil action in relation to international crimes has been raised.

In *Naït-Liman v Switzerland*,[283] the ECtHR considered the case of a refugee living in Switzerland (the applicant) who claimed to have been tortured in Tunisia on the orders of the then Minister of the Interior. The applicant's attempt to bring a civil claim for compensation against his alleged abuser was barred by the Swiss courts for lack of jurisdiction. Under the Swiss *Loi fédérale sur le droit international privé* (LDIP), a 'safety valve' clause 'intended to avoid denials of justice'[284] granted jurisdiction to 'the Swiss judicial or administrative authorities of the locality with which the case has a sufficient connection' if the LDIP did not otherwise provide for a forum and proceedings abroad were impossible or it was unreasonable to require

---

[279] Constitution of the Kingdom of the Netherlands 2018, Published by the Ministry of the Interior and Kingdom Relations, available via <https://www.government.nl/documents/reports/2019/02/28/the-constitution-of-the-kingdom-of-the-netherlands>.

[280] *DG and DD* (n 66) 334.

[281] ibid.

[282] Mr. Charles Chernor Jalloh, 'Universal Criminal Jurisdiction', in *Report of the International Law Commission*, A/73/10 (70th sess, 2018), Annex A, 307.

[283] (n 254).

[284] Judgment of the Federal Supreme Court, para 3.4, as excerpted in ibid 7, para 30.

them to be brought.[285] The Swiss Federal Supreme Court, dismissing the applicant's appeal, held that the clause required 'a sufficient connection with Switzerland':[286]

> the claimant complains of acts of torture that were allegedly committed in Tunisia, by Tunisians resident in Tunisia, against a Tunisian residing in Italy. All of the specific features of the case come back to Tunisia, except for the fact of residence in Italy at the relevant time. The facts of the case thus have no connection with Switzerland.[287]

The ECtHR case focused on the applicant's claim that the Swiss courts had violated article 6(1) of the ECHR in denying jurisdiction. However, the applicant also raised article 16 of the 1951 Convention in support of his case.[288] Switzerland challenged his reliance on article 16, arguing that 'none of the international instruments invoked by the applicant recognised [universal civil jurisdiction], particularly Article 16 [of the 1951 Convention], and that no rule of customary international law provided for it.'[289] The Court addressed and rejected the applicant's argument briefly. It noted that the applicant had only made a general reference to article 16 in his action between the Swiss Federal Supreme Court and had failed to articulate the relevance of article 16 to the complaint.[290] Nonetheless, the Court noted:

> the text of Article 16 refers in general terms to the right of refugees to have access to a court, but does not guarantee as such the right to bring proceedings against a foreign State or one of its officials for acts of torture committed abroad. In consequence, even supposing that the applicant had duly raised this complaint before the domestic courts, he cannot extract an additional argument from it in support of his application.[291]

The Court's finding could be construed in two ways. First, it could be considered to reflect the basic proposition that article 16(2) does not grant an automatic right to bring a claim, but merely that one's application must be assessed in the same manner as a national's application would. Article 16 cannot create a 'right' to bring a claim where no such automatic right exists under domestic law. Second, it could be construed as a restrictive reading of article 16(2) that limits the potential scope of 'other matters'. However, it appears that no argument based on the scope of 'matters pertaining to access to the Courts' was expressly put to the Court, and that the

---

[285] *Loi fédérale sur le droit international privé*, s 3, cited in *Naït-Liman* (n 254) 10, para 37. For a summary of similar laws in other jurisdictions, see ibid 29–30, paras 88–89.

[286] Judgment of the Federal Supreme Court, para 3.3, as excerpted in *Naït-Liman* (n 254) 7, para 30.

[287] ibid para 3.5, as excerpted in *Naït-Liman* (n 254) 7, para 30.

[288] See *Naït-Liman* (n 254) 41, para 136.

[289] ibid 44, para 148.

[290] ibid 54–55, para 197.

[291] ibid 55, para 197, emphasis added. Compare Dissenting Opinion of Judge Serghides at para 86.

applicant failed to mount an argument on the appropriate scope of the provision. The Court does not appear to have examined whether the Swiss Courts would have considered a similar claim brought by a citizen would meet the 'sufficient connection' standard under article 3 of the LDIP. In other words, the Court did not identify an appropriate comparator for determining whether the applicant received the same treatment as a national.

Belgium, which gives direct effect to article 16(2),[292] has generated a second line of case law on the capacity of a refugee or asylum seeker to bring a 'universal jurisdiction' claim.[293] Carlier provides detailed commentary and context to these cases, which concerned a conflict between the Belgian Court of Cassation and Court of Arbitration.[294] The cases involved four Burmese refugees (one recognised in Belgium, the others elsewhere) who brought a case against the oil and gas company Total Fina Elf, alleging violations of their human rights in connection its operations in Myanmar.[295] At the time the initial case was brought, Belgian law granted universal jurisdiction for grave violations of humanitarian law.[296] Subsequently, the law was abrogated and replaced, with jurisdiction limited to those cases where the complainant was a Belgian national or had been principally resident in Belgium for at least three years when the action was commenced, or where an alleged perpetrator was Belgian or principally resident in Belgium as at the date that the law entered into force.[297] The purpose of this amendment was, apparently, to put an end to the 'manifestly abusive political use' of the 1993 law.[298] In two separate cases, the Court of Cassation posed questions to the Court of Arbitration (Cour d'Arbitrage) on whether the divestment of jurisdiction over cases brought by (i) a recognised refugee in Belgium, and (ii) an asylum seeker legally staying in Belgium, would be contrary to the Belgian Constitution.[299] The Court of Arbitration held that the law violated article 16(2) of the 1951 Convention insofar as it applied to a recognised refugee,[300] but not in its application to asylum seekers.[301] The Court of Cassation,

---

[292] See Extrait de l'arrêt 104/2006 (n 13) 35042.
[293] On these cases and the underlying legislation, see Carlier (n 64) 327–36.
[294] See Carlier (n 64) 327–333.
[295] ibid 328–29.
[296] ibid 329.
[297] ibid.
[298] '[U]tilisation politique manifestement abusive'—author's translation. *Doc parl,* Chambre, S.E. DOC 51-0103/001, 3, cited in Extrait de l'arrêt 68/2005 (n 54) 21850.
[299] See Cour de Cassation de Belgique, Arrêt, No P.04.0482.F (5 May 2004); Cour de Cassation de Belgique, Arrêt, No P.04.0352.F (19 May 2004) (Question 1).
[300] See Extrait de l'arrêt 68/2005 (n 54) 21850 ('Elle est ... disproportionnée en ce que, en contradiction avec l'article 16.3 de la Convention du 28 juillet 1951 relative du statut des réfugies, elle exclut également le réfugié reconnu en Belgique'—'It is disproportionate in that, contrary to article 16(3) of the [1951 Convention], it also excludes recognised refugees in Belgium'—author's translation).
[301] ibid ('[e]n revanche, dès lors que cette disposition [l'article 16(2)] s'applique pas aux candidats réfugiés, le législateur a pu traiter ceux-ci autrement que les Belges'—'On the other hand, since this provision [article 16(2)] is not applicable to asylum seekers, the legislator has been able to treat them differently from Belgians'—author's translation).

however, declined to give effect to the Court of Arbitration's decision. It held that the unconstitutionality identified by the Court of Arbitration could not be remedied without prejudicing the rights of the accused.[302] This was challenged in the Court of Arbitration, which annulled the relevant provision of the 2003 law in a subsequent decision. The Court of Arbitration characterised the annulled provision as jurisdictional rather than substantive:

[l]a disposition annulée ne crée aucune incrimination et ne commine aucune peine, son objet étant uniquement de déterminer la compétence des juridictions belges ... L'annulation porte en effet que sur la compétence des juridictions belges.[303]

The Court of Cassation held firm however, refusing to retract its earlier decision relinquishing jurisdiction despite the annulation.[304]

2.3.3.2.3 Case law on differential regimes Finally, these cases must be weighed against those in which different regimes for asylum seekers and nationals are upheld without any reference to article 16. Although the judges in these cases may not have turned their minds to the application of article 16,[305] the prevalence of different regimes for asylum seekers and nationals indicates States' understanding of their own obligations under the 1951 Convention. For example, the recast Procedures Directive,[306] which is part of the CEAS and binding on EU Member States,[307] affirms and regulates the use of several mechanisms to expedite asylum applications, including accelerated procedures[308] and safe country of origin designations. If it is accepted that the Procedures Directive, like other elements of the CEAS, constitutes State Practice under the 1951 Convention, then its provisions are relevant for determining Contracting States' own understanding of the scope of their obligations under the 1951 Convention.[309] In *R(G) v Immigration Appeal Tribunal*,[310] the Court of Appeal upheld a system that provided discriminatory

---

[302] Cour de Cassation de Belgique, Arrêt, No P.04.0482.F (29 June 2005) ('Attendu que la Cour ne pourrait remédier à l'inconstitutionnalité dont la Cour d'arbitrage a déclaré ledit article 29, § 3, alinéa 2, entaché, qu'au prix d'une application analogique de cette disposition légale au préjudice des personnes poursuivies').

[303] Extrait de l'arrêt 104/2006 (n 13) 35043, B.16 ('the annulled provision creates neither incrimination nor punishment, its object being solely to determine the competence of Belgian courts ... The annulation relates solely to the competence of the Belgian courts'– author's translation).

[304] Cour de Cassation de Belgique, Arrêt, No P.07.0031.F (28 Mar 2007).

[305] See comment in n 13.

[306] Recast Procedures Directive (n 84).

[307] Excepting Ireland and Denmark: see recitals 58–59.

[308] See recast Procedures Directive (n 84) art 31(8).

[309] But see, eg, the note of caution expressed by Hathaway and Foster (n 21) 12.

[310] *R(G) v Immigration Appeal Tribunal* [2004] EWCA Civ 1731; [2005] 1 WLR 1445.

appeal rights to asylum seekers (as compared to nationals) without any consideration of article 16, noting:

> we do not consider that those seeking immigration decisions are in a position that is necessarily analogous to those seeking other forms of relief under procedures which involve tribunals ... as article 5(1)(f) of the ECHR recognises, non-nationals seeking entry or asylum stand in a fundamentally different legal situation from those who can enter or remain by right. The courts will so far as possible ensure due process for them, but *due process does not necessarily mean the same process for all*.[311]

In a similar vein, countries have adopted accelerated procedures for the review of negative RSD decisions,[312] including the introduction of stringent time limits for applying for judicial review.[313] UNHCR considers that 'an asylum-seeker's failure to submit a request within a certain time limit or the non-fulfilment of other formal requirements should not in itself lead to an asylum request being excluded from consideration'.[314] However, it does not suggest that this principle derives from article 16(2), and accepts the application of 'special procedural devices for dealing in an expeditious manner with applications which are obviously without foundation'.[315] There is scant discussion in the case law as to whether article 16(2) is engaged by the application of short time limits for judicial or administrative

---

[311] ibid 1459 (Lord Phillips) (emphasis added). The approach in *R(G)* was confirmed in relation to an updated statutory review scheme in *R (F (Mongolia)) v Asylum and Immigration Tribunal* [2007] 1 WLR 2523. See also Lord Phillips' comment in *R (on the application of Cart) v The Upper Tribunal* [2011] UKSC 28, paras 93 that it would be 'totally disproportionate' for judicial supervision of the Upper Tribunal to 'extend to the four stage system of paper and oral applications first to the Administrative Court and then, by way of appeal, to the Court of Appeal, to which the ordinary judicial review procedure is subject' (Lord Clarke agreeing at para 106).

[312] See, eg, the new 'fast-track' administrative review system applicable to a particular group of asylum seekers in Australia: Migration Act, Pt 7AA; discussed in Emma Dunlop, Jane McAdam, and Greg Weeks, 'A Search for Rights: Judicial and Administrative Responses to Migration and Refugee Cases' in Matthew Groves, Janina Boughey, and Dan Meagher, *The Legal Protection of Rights in Australia* (Hart 2019) 335, 345–46. More generally, see UNHCR, 'Global Consultations on International Protection, Asylum Processes (Fair and Efficient Asylum Procedures)', EC/GC/01/12 (31 May 2001), paras 12, 42.

[313] Although Australian law now allows for an extension of time limits on applications to the Federal Court and the Federal Circuit Court respectively, this has not always been the case. See, ss 477–477A Migration Act 1958, and an example of the effect of the previous s 478(1) of the Act in *Sahak v Minister for Immigration and Multicultural Affairs* [2002] FCAFC 215.

[314] UNHCR, 'Global Consultations' (n 312) para 19.

[315] See 'UNHCR Statement on the right to an effective remedy in relation to accelerated asylum procedures issued in the context of the preliminary ruling reference to the Court of Justice of the European Union from the Luxembourg Administrative Tribunal regarding the interpretation of Article 39, Asylum Procedures Directive (APD); and Articles 6 and 13 ECHR' (21 May 2010), para 5 (noting however that the goal of swift and efficient examination cannot trump the 'effective exercise of the prohibition of refoulement' (footnotes omitted)).

review,[316] although this has been posed as an example of a 'matter' covered by article 16(2).[317]

2.3.3.2.4 Conclusions on matters pertaining to access to the Courts

This survey of case law highlights three points relevant to the interpretation of article 16(2). First, the case law is too scarce and inconsistent to constitute 'subsequent practice' relevant to the interpretation of the provision under article 31(3)(b) of the Vienna Convention. Second, analysis of article 16(2) in cases is often limited. This appears in some cases to be due to limited submissions on its scope and content. For instance, in *Naït-Liman v Switzerland,* the Court noted that the applicant 'simply referred, in very general terms' to article 16 before the Federal Supreme Court, 'without explaining for what reason and in what respect it could have been relevant to the complaint'.[318] The lack of analysis in many judgments—and complete silence on the potential application of article 16 in others—limits their potential to guide the interpreter in the development of a systematic and logical approach to the clause. Third, the political and domestic context in which article 16(2) is applied should be considered. Even when article 16(2) is given direct effect, decisions may be influenced by the domestic constitutional structure and the political context in which they are made. In the Netherlands, the extension of article 16(2) to asylum proceedings is affected by the fact that the courts are empowered to conduct status determination in the course of a judgment. Conversely, the Court's hesitance to extend the scope of article 16(2) to encompass appeal rights seems to have been influenced by the Dutch constitutional framework. In Belgium, it is an open question whether the court's finding that article 16(2) did not extend to asylum seekers was conditioned by the political context—namely, the concern not to create a 'pull factor' for asylum seekers who wished to bring an action under the universal jurisdiction laws. The court gave no indication that this was the case, but reasoning elsewhere in the judgment referred to the context of the 2003 amendments, and the legislator's objective of preventing individuals from moving to Belgium for the purpose of bringing complaints under the law.[319]

---

[316] Whether a twenty-eight-day time limit for appealing a negative decision to an administrative tribunal was inconsistent with article 16 was however considered and rejected in obiter by Justice Heerey in *Fernando v Minister for Immigration and Multicultural Affairs* [2000] FCA 324 (Australia). His Honour dismissed the argument primarily on the grounds that international obligations have no direct force of law in Australia, but also noted that even if that were not the case, the 1951 Convention 'establishes no particular procedural process for the purpose of determining whether any individual is in fact entitled to refugee status.': para 36 (see also Finkelstein J, para 53).

[317] See Baldinger (n 61) 29.

[318] *Naït-Liman* (n 254) 55, para 197.

[319] See discussion of the second question raised in case no. 3008 ('la différence de traitement n'est pas manifestement disproportionnée par rapport à l'objectif poursuivi d'éviter des plaintes déposées par des personnes qui s'installent en Belgique pour la seule raison d'y trouver ... la possibilité de rendre les juridictions belges compétentes pour les infractions dont ces personnes se prétendent être victimes.'— 'The difference in treatment is not manifestly disproportionate to the object pursued of avoiding cases

What guidance can these decisions provide, then, for the interpretation of article 16(2)? On its ordinary meaning, 'matters pertaining to access to the Courts' must have a broader application than the two examples cited in article 16(2).[320] When determining the parameters of such 'matters', however, some underlying logic or principle is required beyond a simple tally of what matters domestic courts have, or have not, deemed to be covered by the phrase.[321] The typology proposed attempts to categorise the types of 'matters' engaged by article 16(2).

2.3.3.2.5 A typology of matters covered by article 16(2)   The phrase 'matters pertaining to access to the Courts' potentially has a wide scope. As Spijkerboer notes, there is no rationale for limiting its scope to ' "normal" legal problems such as divorce, labour relations, contracts, etc.', to the exclusion of asylum procedures.[322] The word 'including' demonstrates that the phrase is non-exhaustive[323] and extends to matters beyond 'legal assistance' and exemption from security for costs. Those two examples are however indicative of class of matters that fall within the category 'matters pertaining to access to the Courts'. They demonstrate, at the least, that those matters extend to practical, facilitative matters, and to procedural matters pertaining to access to the Courts.

One possible approach to interpreting the phrase would be to draw on a distinction between practical and procedural matters that pertain to access to the courts, on the one hand, and matters of substantive law, on the other.[324] In private international law, much attention has been paid to the question of which matters fall

---

lodged by those who settle in Belgium for the sole purpose of finding there the possibility of making the Belgian courts competent to hear the offences of which those persons claim to be victims'—author's translation): Extrait de l'arrêt 68/2005 (n 54) 21850.

[320] This view receives some, though not unequivocal, support from the comments made by the Belgian representative in the course of the drafting process: See Chapter 4, Section 4.2.3.3. For similar views in the literature, see, eg, Robinson (n 138) 113 ('par. 2 explicitly assimilates refugees ... to nationals *insofar as access to the court in general and* the requirement of *cautio judicatum solvi* and free legal assistance in particular are concerned' (first emphasis added)); Grahl-Madsen, *Commentary* (n 91) Article 16, VII (noting that the national treatment rule 'has, therefore, *mostly* bearing on their eligibility for legal assistance and exemption from *cautio judicatum solvi*') (emphasis added); Carlier (n 64) 321–22 ('*Parmi* les droits relatifs au libre accès aux tribunaux, sont *expressément visées* l'assistance judiciaire et l'exemption de caution *judicatum solvi*' (first emphasis added)). No analysis of the scope of 'matters pertaining to access' is made by Weis at all, who focuses solely on the two examples given: see Weis (n 91) 134. Moreno-Lax focuses her analysis on article 16(1) rather than 16(2)–(3): see (n 66) 400–402.

[321] Elberling argues, for example, that 'matters pertaining to access to the Courts' covers 'requirements to be fulfilled by claimants in order for their claims to be decided by the courts', but also relies on examples from the case law (denying, for example, that article 16(2) extends to an entitlement to be granted the benefit of a *caution judicatum solvi*: (n 23) 942.

[322] Spijkerboer (n 7) 221.

[323] See Perry Herzfeld and Thomas Prince, *Interpretation* (2nd edn, Thomson Reuters 2020) 50–52.

[324] Though 'procedural matters' is a wider field than 'matters relating to access to the courts'. For article 16(2) to be engaged, it must also be shown that a matter of procedure is also linked to issues of access.

on each side of the substance/procedure distinction.[325] However Garnett notes a general trend towards adopting a narrow view of procedure, which aligns with the underlying aims of discouraging forum shopping and promoting consistent outcomes across different national courts.[326] The narrow ambit of 'procedure' for the purposes of the private international law substance/procedure distinction reflects policy imperatives that are simply not relevant to article 16(2). A more liberal approach to the scope of 'matters pertaining to access to the courts' is likely to afford greater rights to the asylum seeker or refugee, better aligning with the object and purpose of the 1951 Convention.[327]

While a focus on procedure may therefore be helpful in conceptualising which matters pertain to 'access to the Courts', the boundaries that apply in the private international law context are not definitive. The ultimate question is whether a given matter can be characterised as 'pertaining to access to the Courts'. It is not possible to answer this question exhaustively for every conceivable "matter" that could arise and much will depend on the facts and legislation at issue in the individual case.

While recognising that each matter must be examined individually, it is proposed that article 16(2) cover two classes of matters:

- Practical matters, such as the availability of translation or legal aid;
- Procedural matters that pertain to access to the courts.[328]

The first limb of this typology recognises that there may be matters pertaining to access that are not necessarily within the remit of the court system. It captures matters that are integral to access but may be controlled by actors and institutions other than the courts themselves, such as publicly funded legal assistance.[329]

The second limb covers procedural matters that pertain to access to the courts. However, the scope of this limb is not necessarily confined to the boundaries of what is considered 'procedural' for the purposes of private international law.

---

[325] See Richard Garnett, *Substance and Procedure in Private International Law* (OUP 2012); Richard Garnett, 'Substance and Procedure' in Jürgen Basedow, Giesela Rühl, Franco Ferrari, and Pedro de Miguel Asensio (eds), *Encyclopedia of Private International Law*, Vol 2 (Edward Elgar 2017) 1667–75.

[326] See Garnett, *Substance and Procedure in Private International Law* (n 325) 2 (identifying these aims and noting that they are 'compromised when national systems of choice of law allow too wide a scope for the operation of forum law at the expense of foreign rules'); and Garnett, 'Substance and Procedure' (n 325) 1668 (noting signs of a breakdown of the traditional divide between the approach taken in common and civil law countries, with Australia and Canada now also taking a narrower view of procedure).

[327] See Chapter 3, Section 3.2.2.

[328] See also 1951 Convention, art 25(1), (4).

[329] See, eg, UNGA, 'Report of the Special Rapporteur on the human rights of migrants on his mission to Australia and the regional processing centres in Nauru', A/HRC/35/25/Add.3 (24 April 2017), paras 91 (noting that '[t]here can be no effective access to justice ... adequate legal representation and sufficient legal aid funding') and 126 (calling on the Australian government to '[e]nsure that migrants, asylum seekers and refugees, whatever their status, have easy access to competent lawyers, free of charge when needed, in order to challenge any decision made that threatens their rights and freedoms, especially in expulsion, detention and asylum procedures').

A third possible class of matter, raised in the case law, is that of jurisdictional competence—the obligation to treat an asylum seeker or refugee as if they were a national when applying jurisdictional rules.[330] This reflects an expansive interpretation of the phrase 'same treatment as a national in matters pertaining to access to the Courts'. The interpretation aligns with the 1951 Convention's object and purpose and is directed towards enhancing and ensuring refugee protection. However, is does seem to strain the ordinary meaning of 'matters pertaining to access to the courts'. The case law suggests that there is some appetite to expand a State's duty under article 16(2) to encompass jurisdictional competence. While I do not propose to include this category in the typology, I note it as an area of evolving practice.

This typology is not intended to supplant the question of whether a matter 'pertain[s] to access'. It is that question that the decision maker must ultimately decide when determining if article 16(2) applies.

2.3.3.3 Same treatment as a national: the appropriate comparator

When article 16(2) is engaged, some form of comparator is required to determine if an asylum seeker or refugee is receiving the 'same treatment as a national'.

As noted in Chapter 3, 'same treatment as a national' is framed in a manner that allows adaptation and change over time.[331] The appropriate standard, therefore, should be measured by a national's current treatment, rather than any historical assessment.

Finding an appropriate 'comparator' raises more difficult issues. Two positions proposed by commentators are, first, that of a citizen's right to appeal administrative decisions,[332] and second, that of 'substantively equal' procedural treatment.[333] A third approach, proposed in relation to an asylum seeker's entitlement to legal aid, involves identifying the 'underlying factual predicate' for assisting a national and applying that premise to an asylum seeker.[334] Pursuant to this approach, 'If nationals would receive legal aid when faced with a risk of comparable gravity, then so too should habitually present refugees'.[335]

As noted in Chapter 2,[336] the first approach seems difficult to apply if, as is commonly the case, a State allows appeals from some administrative decisions

---

[330] See Section 2.3.3.2.1 above.
[331] See Chapter 3 Section 3.1.2.
[332] See Boeles, 'Effective Legal Remedies' (n 61) 308 (considering that 'refugees acquire from Article 16 a right of access to the courts for appeal against administrative decisions in disputes about questions of law raised by the Convention, in those cases where the national law of the State of habitual residence *provides for its own nationals an appeal to the courts against administrative decisions*' (emphasis added). See also Boeles, *Fair Immigration Proceedings in Europe* (n 106) 81; and Baldinger (n 61) 29 (considering 'shorter time limits' to be 'more stringent admissibility conditions which do not apply to nationals in administrative court proceedings').
[333] Spijkerboer (n 7) 224. See also Elberling (n 23) 945, proposing '"procedurally" equal treatment'.
[334] Hathaway, *Rights* (2nd edn) (n 30) 924 (footnotes omitted).
[335] ibid.
[336] See further Chapter 2, Section 2.1.7.

but not others; or sets different procedural barriers (such as time limits) in rela-tion to different classes of decision.[337] The second offers more flexibility, though perhaps at the expense of clarity. The third is, at first glance, more tailored, but ultimately replaces one ambiguous comparator with another. What is a risk of 'comparable gravity'? This question could be answered by looking at the terms of article 1A(2)—namely, a risk of being persecuted for a Convention reason. However, the 'risk' could also be characterised as one of expulsion (using similar logic to that underlying the ECtHR's jurisprudence and the HRC's conclusions on asylum applications). This view could underpin a much more restrictive approach.

Despite the difficulties in pinning down its precise content, the approach of 'substantively equal' procedural treatment seems to be the most appropriate com-parator when applying article 16. It is sufficiently linked to the text of the provision (in its reference to 'same treatment'), while also drawing attention to the need to avoid discriminatory approaches. The question of precisely what constitutes 'sub-stantively equal' procedural treatment may ultimately be impossible to determine in the abstract. It calls for a fact-based approach comparing the impugned measure with the specific legal system in which it is found.[338]

Finally, there is the challenge of UNHCR's view that while '[a]ll applicants should have the right to an independent appeal or review against a negative de-cision', whether administrative or judicial, 'this may be more simplified in the case of admissibility decisions or decisions made under accelerated procedures'.[339] This view, expressed in the context of the 2000 Global Consultations, should not be treated as persuasive guidance on the scope (or limitations) of article 16(2). UNHCR's treatment of article 16(2) remains limited, and the organisation does not seem to have grappled with the potential implications of article 16 for asylum seekers undergoing a status determination review process. While a clear state-ment from UNHCR on the scope of article 16 would provide persuasive guidance, its comments here should not be considered determinative of its views on the matter.

---

[337] In *DG and DD* (n 66) 35, for example, the court dismissed an alternative argument based on anti-discrimination by noting that '[t]he exclusion of appeal in proceedings under the Aliens Act is justified on the grounds of the need to reach a final decision as quickly as possible', and 'other admin-istrative law disputes in which a need for rapid decision-making plays a role are also excluded from judicial review'. See also *Fernando v Minister for Immigration and Multicultural Affairs* (n 316) para 20 (Heerey J), detailing the disparate approaches to statutory time limits providing for administrative or judicial review in Australian domestic law. Heerey J considered, in obiter, rejecting an argument based on discrimination under the ICCPR, that 'it is impossible to say that there is a general legal norm in Australia that time limits can always be extended and that the appellant has been deprived of that right': para 37.

[338] See also Elberling (n 23) 945, noting that the extent to which article 16(2) protects asylum seekers in the context of status determination 'may well depend on the peculiarities of the legal system of the State of refuge'.

[339] UNHCR, 'Global Consultations' (n 312) para 50(p).

2.4 Article 16(3)

Article 16(3) provides that 'a refugee shall be accorded in the matters referred to in paragraph 2 in countries other than that in which he has his habitual residence the treatment granted to a national of the country of his habitual residence'. In essence, article 16(3) grants a 'refugee' the benefit of reciprocity under any bilateral arrangements between his or her host State and a third State in relation to 'matters pertaining to access to the Courts'.[340] He or she will be treated equally to a national of the country of habitual residence in actions before the courts of third States.

2.4.1 Meaning of 'refugee' and 'habitual residence' in article 16(3)

In line with the interpretation of 'refugee' and 'habitual residence' set out for article 16(1) and 16(2), it is argued that the protection guaranteed in article 16(3) extends both to refugees and to asylum seekers who fulfil the test of 'habitual residence' (be it lawful or unlawful under domestic law).[341]

In practice, article 16(3) is unlikely to be engaged by an asylum seeker who is unlawfully (albeit habitually) present in a host State. There may be practical or legal restrictions on an asylum seeker's ability to travel while his or her application is pending,[342] limiting the likelihood of cases brought under the territorial jurisdiction of a third State. While an asylum seeker could arguably find himself or herself engaged in court proceedings in a third State on the basis of non-territorial jurisdiction, the more likely scenario in which article 16(3) would apply involves a recognised, mobile refugee with dealings across multiple jurisdictions. The very unlikelihood of the application of article 16(3) to an unlawfully present asylum seeker poses a challenge to the proposed interpretation of 'refugee' and 'habitual residence'. While it is generally accepted that the meaning of the term 'refugee' may have a different scope in different articles of the 1951 Convention, it would be quite

---

[340] This reciprocity could go therefore beyond that granted in article 7 of the 1951 Convention, which provides that '[e]xcept where this Convention contains more favourable provisions, a Contracting State shall accord to refugees the same treatment as is accorded to aliens generally' (emphasis added).

[341] For a different view (based on the declaratory theory) with largely similar consequences, see Elberling (n 23) 942: 'Like the other two paragraphs of Art. 16, this paragraph too lays down a subjective right granted to refugees regardless of whether they have been accepted as such by the State concerned or any other State'.

[342] In the UK, for example, r 333C of the *Immigration Rules* provides that '[a]n application may be treated as impliedly withdrawn if an applicant leaves the United Kingdom without authorisation at any time prior to the conclusion of their asylum claim'. The websites of two US immigration law bodies counsel against leaving the country while an asylum application is pending, even if 'advance parole' is granted: see 'Can I travel while my asylum case is pending?' (*Hacking Immigration Law, LLC*, undated) <https://hackinglawpractice.com/faqs/can-i-travel-while-my-asylum-case-is-pending/>; 'Work and travel while pending' (Immigration Equality, 3 June 2020) <https://immigrationequality.org/legal/legal-help/asylum/work-and-travel-while-pending/>. In Australia, risks remain even after a grant of refugee status: The Refugee Council of Australia noted in 2019 that it was 'increasingly hearing of refugees who have had their Protection visa cancelled while overseas': 'Travel warning for refugees with pending citizenship or visa applications' (Refugee Council of Australia, 3 June 2019) <https://www.refugeecouncil.org.au/travel-warning/>.

another matter to defend a position that a term had a variable meaning *within* a single provision of the Convention. A survey of the case law reveals no cases in which a court has applied the benefit of article 16(3) to an asylum seeker (and only four cases that address the provision at all).[343]

This lack of jurisprudence is not altogether surprising given that article 16(3) is engaged only where specific conditions are met (and would also cease to have any application upon the naturalisation of a recognised refugee).[344] However, it speaks against placing too much weight on article 16(3) as a tool in the interpretation of articles 16(1) and (2) of the Convention. Rather than treating the practical unlikelihood of the application of article 16(3) as grounds for limiting the scope of those provisions, it is contended that article 16(3) should simply be recognised as being likely to have limited applicability on the facts. Furthermore, if the object and purpose of the Convention is considered—namely, to enhance and ensure refugee protection[345]—the fact that a provision may only apply in a limited set of circumstances is not a ground for a denial of its application in such circumstances altogether. As noted in Section 2.3.2, the complex and protracted processes of RSD seen in many jurisdictions would not have been conceived of by the Convention's drafters. In *Sepet*, Lord Bingham stated that to call the 1951 Convention a 'living instrument' meant that 'while its meaning does not change over time its application will'.[346] The application of article 16(3) may be unlikely, but that unlikelihood is not a rationale for restricting the scope of the provision as a whole when the rule of treaty interpretation in article 31 of the Vienna Convention supports a broader interpretation.

2.4.2 Use of the term 'countries'

Article 16(3) uses the term 'countries' rather than 'Contracting States' to describe both the refugee's place of habitual residence and the place in which he or she seeks to exercise rights of access to the courts. On this basis, several commentators have argued that a refugee who is the habitual resident of a non-Contracting State is entitled to the benefit of article 16(3).[347] This interpretation would imply, inversely,

---

[343] See Section 2.4.

[344] See 1951 Convention, art 34 ('The Contracting States shall as far as possible facilitate the assimilation and naturalization of refugees').

[345] See Chapter 3, Section 3.2.2.

[346] in *Sepet v Secretary of State for the Home Department* [2003] UKHL 15, para 6 (Bingham LJ).

[347] Elberling (n 23) 943, citing Grahl-Madsen, *Commentary* (n 91) Article 16, II (who finds that art 16(3) applies to 'refugees residing in non-Contracting States') and Hathaway, *Rights* (2nd edn) (n 30) 921. See also Weis (n 91) 134 and Robinson (n 138) 113 ('In other Contracting Countries refugees are assimilated to nationals of the *country* of their habitual residence, under par. 3'). But see, conversely, Carlier (n 64) 321 ('les paragraphes 2 et 3 introduisent le principe d'égalité entre le réfugié et le national de son pays de résidence, auquel il est assimilé tant dans son pays de résidence (par. 2) que dans un autre *Etat contractant* (par. 3)'—'paragraphs 2 and 3 introduce the principle of equality between the refugee and the national of his country of residence, to which he is assimilated both in his country of residence (para 2) and in another *contracting state* (para 3)'—author's translation) (emphasis added).

that non-Contracting States are obliged to grant national treatment to refugees, a reading that cannot be sustained. It is therefore an open question whether the reference to 'countries' and 'country' should be read as synonymous with 'Contracting States'.

2.4.3 Case law on article 16(3) and UNHCR guidance

The case law on article 16(3) is limited and adds little to the discussion of article 16(2). Of the four cases found in the survey, three consider whether a refugee who would otherwise be liable to post security for costs is entitled to an exemption on the basis of article 16(3). In the first case, the Swiss Commercial Court for Zurich[348] found that the applicant was not exempt from posting security for costs, since the 1951 Convention had not yet entered into force in Switzerland.[349] In the second,[350] a recognised refugee in Norway sued a company in Switzerland. After a lower court judgment ordered that he pay security for costs, the complainant appealed to the Federal Tribunal. The International Law Reports note that the key question before the court was whether the complainant was in fact a refugee.[351] Having decided that he was, the court stated that:

> [a]ccording to Article 16(3) of the Geneva Convention, a refugee must be treated in States parties to that Convention in which he is not habitually resident on the same footing as a national of the State in which he is resident with respect to access to the courts, judicial assistance, and *cautio judicatum solvi*. The complainant has been resident in Norway since 1955. He must therefore be treated in Switzerland as though he was a Norwegian national.[352]

In the third, the District Court of Amsterdam considered article 16(3).[353] It found that the Fargion heirs, who held refugee status and had settled in Italy, were not required to post security for costs in a counterclaim before the Dutch courts, since an Italian national would not be required to do so under Dutch domestic law.[354] These three cases are a straightforward application of article 16(3),

---

[348] *Security for Costs (Statelessness) Case*, Switzerland, Commercial Court for Zurich, 1 Apr 1954, 21 ILR 303.

[349] The court noted: 'The legal position will change only when the Agreement concerning the Legal Status of Refugees signed on June 28, 1951, enters into force in Switzerland; in conformity with Article 16, para. 3, of that Agreement a refugee resident in France will be assimilated to French nationals resident in France for the purposes of exemption from giving security for costs in proceedings before Swiss courts': ibid 304.

[350] *Grundul v Bryner* (n 64). Cited by Weis (n 92) 135.

[351] *Grundul v Bryner* (n 64) 484.

[352] ibid 485.

[353] *Huijing's Handelmaatschappij NV v Fargion Heirs*, The Netherlands, District Court of Amsterdam, 13 Dec 1972, 73 ILR 676.

[354] In this case, article 152 of the Code of Civil Procedure: see ibid 677.

since they each focused on a matter expressly singled out in article 16(2) for equal protection.

A fourth case engaged with the broader question of which unenumerated rights may fall within the category of 'matters pertaining to access to the Courts' under article 16(2). In *Eglin v Marculeta*,[355] the Tribunal de grande instance of Paris interpreted a Franco–Swiss Treaty as applying equally to French citizens and to refugees domiciled or resident in France. The case stemmed from an application for exequatur of a Swiss judgment concerning divorce and custody after the applicant's relationship with her husband, a Spanish refugee living in France, broke down. Her husband argued that under the Franco–Swiss Treaty, the application should have been instituted in the French courts. Applying article 16(3) of the 1951 Convention, the court rejected the exequatur application, essentially finding that a Swiss national was not entitled to commence divorce proceedings in Switzerland against a refugee resident in France, due to the division of competences between France and Switzerland under the Franco–Swiss Treaty. The court noted that 'in the application of Article 1 of the Franco–Swiss Treaty ... defining the division of competence between the two national jurisdictions, a refugee domiciled or resident in France is to be *assimilated to a French national*'.[356] The case law demonstrates the practical protection afforded by article 16(3) under private law and also emphasises the extent to which article 16 is concerned with granting a refugee the conditions necessary to conduct a full civil life.

Finally, UNHCR's persuasive position that a refugee seeking to exercise rights in a foreign Contracting State is not required to undergo a second RSD process should be accepted.[357] As UNHCR suggests, requiring a 'fresh determination' before granting rights under article 16(3) would be contrary to the principle of effectiveness.[358]

2.5 Subject-matter Jurisdiction

A final note is needed on the question of 'subject-matter jurisdiction'—the eighth issue examined in Chapter 2.[359] As a general rule, this book argues that article 16 does not oblige a Contracting State to 'create' jurisdiction to hear a dispute where no such jurisdiction otherwise exists.[360] It does not accept that article 16 provides

---

[355] *Eglin v Marculeta* (n 239).
[356] ibid 357 (emphasis added).
[357] UNHCR, 'Note on the Extraterritorial Effect of the Determination of Refugee Status under the 1951 Convention and the 1967 Protocol Relating to the Status of Refugees', EC/SCP/9 (24 Aug 1978) available via <https://www.refworld.org/docid/3ae68cccc.html>, para 15, discussed in Chapter 2, Section 2.2.
[358] ibid.
[359] See Chapter 2, Section 2.1.8.
[360] Compare Boeles (n 61) 301.

a basis for vindicating a Convention right that is neither self-executing[361] nor enshrined in domestic legislation. Although an argument can be made that the drafters expected that refugees would be in a position to claim their Convention entitlements on the domestic level, this does not extend to an obligation upon States to incorporate Convention rights into domestic legislation. A Party's obligation to perform a treaty in good faith does not impose a requirement that it be performed through legislative amendment, and article 16 does nothing to alter that position. Neither is there any basis under article 16 for arguing that judicial review of RSD is required as a general rule.[362]

Different considerations are at play where a State enables one class of individuals to bring a claim but not another. In such a case, article 16 *may* be engaged if the asylum seeker or refugee in question is habitually resident in the host State. Discriminatory access to redress may breach a State's article 16(2)–(3) obligations to provide 'the same treatment as a national'. Much will turn in practice on how to apply the comparator in these cases. Consider, for example, the Australian bar on asylum seekers bringing a claim for damages for unlawful imprisonment.[363] If the comparator of 'substantively equal' procedural treatment is applied, the appropriate question is whether an Australian national who was unlawfully detained by the Commonwealth would be entitled to redress. Discriminatory treatment will constitute a breach of article 16(2).

Likewise, while a State is not obliged to guarantee judicial review of negative RSD decisions, a discriminatory bar on appeals may breach the obligation to guarantee the 'same treatment as a national'. If review of administrative decisions is generally available to citizens, a Contracting State may therefore be obliged to extend judicial review of an administrative RSD decision to a habitually resident asylum seeker.

3. Conclusion

The conclusions reached here suggest that article 16 of the 1951 Convention has a broad scope. Its application to asylum seekers and refugees expands the scope of protection to encompass individuals seeking review of negative RSD decisions in domestic courts. The need to ensure 'effective' access to courts may require a State to provide positive assistance—in the form of legal aid, translation, or other

---

[361] See for example the Netherlands Constitution (n 279) art 93 ('Provisions of treaties and of resolutions by international institutions which may be binding on all persons by virtue of their contents shall become binding after they have been published').

[362] Where the asylum seeker has reached the standard of habitual residence, article 16(2)'s potential application should however be considered.

[363] See *Migration Act 1958* s 494AA(1)(c): 'Bar on certain legal proceedings relating to unauthorised maritime arrivals'; *DBE17 v Commonwealth* (n 79).

measures—to ensure that the right of access to courts is guaranteed in the circumstances of the case. Under the flexible, fact-based approach to 'habitual residence' taken here, an asylum seeker may reach the status of 'habitual residence' despite having a precarious legal status, and become entitled to the more robust set of rights in article 16(2). These rights, in line with the proposed approach to 'matters pertaining to access to the Courts', extend to practical facilitative matters, including interpretation and legal aid; and to procedural matters that pertain to access to the courts. While article 16 does not provide a general basis for the creation of jurisdiction where it does not otherwise exist, discriminatory access to remedies may involve a breach of article 16(2)–(3). It is hoped that this analysis encourages greater attention to article 16 and its capacity to safeguard the rights of asylum seekers and refugees more generally.

7

Conclusion

This book has sought, through doctrinal legal analysis, to interrogate the scope and content of article 16 of the 1951 Convention, and to determine whether its obligations extend beyond those that otherwise bind States under international human rights treaties, customary law, and general principles of law. Answering this question has required sustained analysis not only of article 16, but also of broader obligations under international, specialised, and regional treaty regimes, as well as under general international law. The book concludes that article 16 remains a robust and relevant source of protection that, in certain circumstances, guarantees greater protection than international human rights law and general international law. Far from being a dead letter, subsumed by developments in international human rights law, article 16 is a critical guarantee for refugees and asylum seekers that warrants closer attention from States, UNHCR, and scholars.

Chapter 1 presented the research question and contextualised the analysis through an examination of current protection challenges. Chapter 2 then surveyed eight issues on which views on article 16 had developed in the seventy years since the 1951 Convention was adopted, and the range of scholarly approaches on each. Chapter 3 turned to the rule of treaty interpretation, arguing for an evolutionary, teleological approach to the interpretation of the 1951 Convention. However, it also drew a distinction between the interpretative choices open to the scholars and judges, arguing that scholars should take a more cautious approach that does not place undue reliance on soft law or treat case law as declarative of 'subsequent practice' absent a clear consensus across jurisdictions. Having established the parameters of the interpretative process, the book then mapped the arc of article 16's development, beginning with its origins in Chapter 4. A close examination of access to courts clauses in early treaties and the *travaux préparatoires* to the 1951 Convention suggested that access to courts clauses were narrowly understood, and that article 16 was drafted in order to provide more expansive rights than were typically afforded to aliens, in view of their special vulnerabilities. It was stressed, however, that the purpose of the analysis was to situate article 16 in its historical context and to identify preoccupations of the drafters, rather than to uncover their subjective intention and to use that intention as indicative of the scope of article 16. Chapter 5 addressed a key question—whether the rapid development of international human rights law, and concomitant developments in customary international law and general principles of law, had subsumed the protections afforded by article 16. Building on the work of previous scholars, the chapter argued that

Access to Courts for Asylum Seekers and Refugees. Emma Dunlop, Oxford University Press. © Emma Dunlop, 2024.
DOI: 10.1093/oso/9780198885597.003.0007

international human rights law consists of an uneven patchwork of protections, with variation across regional regimes and additional protections available under specialised treaties. Critically, this survey also demonstrated certain commonalities in the interpretative process, particularly attention to the need to ensure the effectiveness of human rights protections.

Against this background, Chapter 6 then presented an argument on the scope and content of article 16, responding to each of the eight issues set out in Chapter 2. It concluded that article 16 guarantees significant protections both to refugees and asylum seekers. Binding on the 149 Contracting States to the 1951 Convention and its Protocol, it falls within the limited category of Convention rights which are attracted prior to status determination. It requires that access to courts be 'effective', an obligation that may require States to take positive steps, such as the provision of legal aid (in both civil and criminal matters, as appropriate), translation, and legal information in order to enable asylum seekers and refugees to regulate their affairs and defend their rights. As a provision premised on a jurisdictional link rather than a territorial one, it binds States that engage in offshore processing, or intercept asylum seekers on the high seas. Furthermore, lawful presence is not a pre-requisite for the engagement of the higher protections in article 16(2), which may be engaged by the unlawful, albeit habitually resident, asylum seeker. As a result, States are obliged to ensure that asylum seekers who reach the threshold of habitual residence (through a delay on processing their asylum claim, for example) are granted the same treatment as a national citizen in matters pertaining to access to the Courts. This obligation covers two classes of matters: (i) practical facilitative matters and (ii) procedural matters that pertain to access to the courts. Such treatment must be 'substantively equal' to that afforded to the host country's citizens.

The book also identified limitations on the scope of article 16. First, its protections are limited to the court system, and do not extend to guaranteeing access to administrative agencies that undertake RSD. It is supplemented, therefore, by regional and specialised treaties that guarantee access to administrative procedures; by soft law standards and guidance, including ExCom Conclusions;[1] and by principles of domestic law. Second, except where a right to a judicial review is mandated because of the existence of comparative rights for nationals under article 16(2), the provision does not guarantee a right to judicial review where it is not recognised under municipal law. Obligations to ensure the maintenance of judicial review of administrative action may however exist under domestic law, as evidenced by decisions in the Australian High Court and the UK Supreme Court respectively.[2] And

---

[1] See, eg, Guy S Goodwin-Gill and Jane McAdam, with Emma Dunlop, *The Refugee in International Law* (4th edn, OUP 2021) 602–604.

[2] In Australia, see the High Court's interpretation of the privative clause at issue in *S157/2002 v Commonwealth* (2003) 211 CLR 476, which was found not to bar judicial review of administrative decisions affected by jurisdictional error. The majority noted that the Court's constitutional role as the 'ultimate decision-maker in all matters where there is a contest' limited the capacity of Parliament or

a State that does provide judicial review of RSD will be bound by the terms of article 16. As argued in Chapter 6, this requires Contracting States to ensure effective access in the circumstances of the case. Effectiveness calls for attention to the individual in his or her context—to particular vulnerabilities or hindrances, the counteraction of which may require positive accommodations on the part of the State. Article 16 is therefore only part of the complex puzzle of obligations that regulates State action. However, its concreteness and its broad scope—binding three-quarters of the world's States—warrant giving it greater attention when analysing the consistency of State actions with international refugee law.

Although this book has sought to emphasise the importance of article 16 as a source of asylum seeker and refugee rights, several obstacles stand in the way of its implementation. First, the obligations in article 16 are not easily generalisable across jurisdictions. Article 16(2) of the 1951 Convention measures refugee rights by reference to rights held by nationals in each Contracting State. The shifting standard means that the obligations owed to a refugee cannot be assessed independently of a careful assessment of the national legal system and domestic rights.[3] The general doctrinal analysis presented here can potentially assist the careful country-by-country work that is needed to ascertain the precise scope of each State's obligations under article 16. Implementation of State obligations may differ in the case of a sudden influx of refugees; the encampment of refugees in a remote location; or the use of 'offshore' RSD processes. Studies of individual States also have the potential to illustrate variances in what Gammeltoft-Hansen has termed the 'quality of protection' available under the 1951 Convention.[4] An in-depth examination of protection provided in Contracting States with different institutional capacities, affording different levels of rights protection, could provide insights into this broader issue. In conducting such research, scholars must also

---

the Executive to 'avoid, or confine, judicial review': at 514 (Gaudron, McHugh, Gummow, Kirby and Hayne JJ). The majority interpreted the expression 'decision … made … under this Act' in s 474(2) of the Migration Act as encompassing only those decisions 'which involve neither a failure to exercise jurisdiction nor an excess of the jurisdiction conferred by the Act'. at 506. See also the reasoning of Gleeson CJ at 494 (finding that Parliament had not, in this case, evinced an intention to preclude judicial review of a decision made in good faith that nonetheless involved a breach of natural justice). In the UK, see the Supreme Court's decision in *R (on the application of Cart) v Upper Tribunal* [2011] UKSC 28, discussed in Chapter 6, Section 2.2.2.

3 This was one of the factors that led Elberling to comment on the impossibility of 'sweeping statements' on domestic regimes' compatibility with the obligations in article 16: Björn Elberling, 'Article 16' in Andreas Zimmermann (ed), *The 1951 Convention Relating to the Status of Refugees and its 1967 Protocol* (OUP 2011) 945. Elberling does make several 'general statements' on the legality of certain restrictive measures: see Chapter 1, Section 1.2.

4 Thomas Gammeltoft-Hansen, *Access to Asylum: International Refugee Law and the Globalisation of Migration Control* (CUP 2011) 29. Gammeltoft-Hansen identifies three ways in which protection standards vary across Contracting States: first, differences in actual implementation, second, differences due to the use of reservations to the 1951 Convention, and third, differences where 'rights pertaining to refugees are specifically granted at a level relative to how each country treats different categories of people'. He considers this third category 'perhaps the most important': at 28–29.

consider activities beyond the border, given that article 16(1) applies to refugees both within and outside the territory of a Contracting State. Naturally, rights afforded to nationals should be examined, since article 16(2) calls for an analysis of citizens' rights before the rights held by refugees can be identified. This should extend to a consideration of the categories of matters identified in Chapter 6, namely, (i) practical matters and (ii) procedural matters that pertain to access to the courts.

Second, promoting a consistent approach to the interpretation of article 16 is challenged by the lack of a mechanism under the 1951 Convention by which asylum seekers and refugees can obtain an authoritative finding on the scope of rights and obligations. States' reluctance to bring actions in the International Court of Justice to confirm the interpretation or application of the 1951 Convention,[5] and the limitations of UNHCR's role as an interpreter of the Convention,[6] has led to a situation in which domestic courts and scholars play a central role in interpretative questions. There have been proposals over the years to create a centralised body capable of answering questions on the scope of the 1951 Convention; one suggestion is the establishment of an 'International Judicial Commission for Refugees' to deliver non-binding opinions on the interpretation of the 1951 Convention.[7] In 2012, an expert roundtable on the supervision of the 1951 Convention concluded that there was 'real value in considering' the establishment of a committee of experts within UNHCR to issue Advisory Opinions on the interpretation and application of the 1951 Convention.[8] It remains to be seen whether such a body will be developed to further the goal of ascribing an autonomous meaning to the 1951 Convention's terms.

The analysis conducted here and the conclusions reached suggest that article 16 deserves increased attention to ensure that asylum seeker and refugee rights are guaranteed more broadly. A robust and concrete obligation to ensure effective access to courts is key to unlocking the full gamut of rights to which asylum seekers and refugees are entitled, under both international and domestic law.

---

[5] See article 38 of the 1951 Convention, which had never been invoked at the time of writing.

[6] As noted in Chapter 3, UNHCR's duty of supervising the application of the Convention under article 35 of the 1951 Convention 'does not extend to a mandate to provide authoritative rulings or opinions on the meaning of particular treaty terms': McAdam, 'Interpretation' (n 1) 79.

[7] See Anthony M North and Joyce Chia, 'Towards Convergence in the Interpretation of the Refugee Convention: A Proposal for the Establishment of an International Judicial Commission for Refugees' in Jane McAdam (ed), *Forced Migration, Human Rights and Security* (Hart Publishing 2008).

[8] See Summary Conclusions of the 'Roundtable on the Future of Refugee Convention Supervision' (2013) 26 Journal of Refugee Studies 327, 328.

Bibliography

Books and Monographs

American Law Institute, *Restatement of the Law Third: The Foreign Relations Law of the United States* (Vol 2, 1987)

Baldinger, D., *Vertical Judicial Dialogues in Asylum Cases: Standards on Judicial Scrutiny and Evidence in International and European Asylum Law* (Brill Nijhoff 2015)

Bates, E., *The Evolution of the European Convention on Human Rights: From its Inception to the Creation of a Permanent Court of Human Rights* (OUP 2010)

Battjes, H., *European Asylum Law and International Law* (Martinus Nijhoff Publishers 2006)

Baxter, R.R., *Treaties and Custom (Vol 129)*, Collected Courses of the Hague Academy of International Law (Brill Nijhoff 1970)

Bingham, T., *The Rule of Law* (Allen Lane, Penguin Books 2010)

Boeles, P., *Fair Immigration Proceedings in Europe* (Martinus Nijhoff Publishers 1997)

Borchard, E.M., *The Diplomatic Protection of Citizens Abroad or the Law of International Claims* (The Banks Law Publishing Co. 1928)

Brownlie, I., *Principles of Public International Law* (7th edn, OUP 2008)

Brownlie, I. and Goodwin-Gill, G.S., (eds), *Brownlie's Documents on Human Rights* (6th edn, OUP 2010)

Care, G., *Migrants and the Courts: A Century of Trial and Error?* (Routledge Ashgate 2013)

Carlier, J.Y., *Droit d'asile et des réfugiés: de la protection aux droits (Vol. 332)*, Collected Courses of the Hague Academy of International Law (Brill Nijhoff 2008)

Clooney, A. and Webb, P., *The Right to a Fair Trial in International Law* (OUP 2020)

Costello, C., *The Human Rights of Migrants and Refugees in European Law* (OUP 2016)

Crawford, J., *Brownlie's Principles of Public International Law* (9th edn, OUP 2019)

Crawford, J.R., *Chance, Order, Change: The Course of International Law (Vol 365)*, Collected Courses of the Hague Academy of International Law (Brill Nijhoff 2013)

Craig, P., *Administrative Law* (7th edn, Sweet & Maxwell 2012)

Dastyari, A., *United States Migrant Interdiction and the Detention of Refugees in Guantánamo Bay* (CUP 2015)

Dembour, M., *When Humans Become Migrants: Study of the European Court of Human Rights with an Inter-American Counterpoint* (OUP 2015)

Foster, M., *International Refugee Law and Socio-Economic Rights: Refuge from Deprivation* (CUP 2007)

Francioni, F., (ed), *Access to Justice as a Human Right* (OUP 2007)

Gammeltoft-Hansen, T., *Access to Asylum: International Refugee Law and the Globalisation of Migration Control* (CUP 2011)

Gardiner, R.K., *Treaty Interpretation* (2nd edn, OUP 2015)

Garnett, R., *Substance and Procedure in Private International Law* (OUP 2012)

Gleeson, M., *Offshore: Behind the Wire on Manus and Nauru* (NewSouth Publishing 2016)

Goodwin-Gill, G.S., *International Law and the Movement of Persons between States* (Clarendon Press, OUP 1978)

Goodwin-Gill, G.S., *The Refugee in International Law* (2nd edn, Clarendon Press 1996)

Goodwin-Gill, G.S. and McAdam, J., *The Refugee in International Law* (3rd edn, OUP 2007)

Goodwin-Gill, G.S. and McAdam, J., with Dunlop, E., *The Refugee in International Law* (4th edn, OUP 2021)

Grabenwarter, C., *European Convention on Human Rights – Commentary* (C.H. Beck, Hart, Nomos 2014)

Grahl-Madsen, A., *Commentary on the Refugee Convention 1951, Articles 2–11, 13–37* (Republished by the Division of International Protection of the United Nations High Commissioner for Refugees 1997)

Grahl-Madsen, A., *The Status of Refugees in International Law* (Vol II, A.W. Sijthoff 1972)

Hamlin, R., *Let Me Be a Refugee: Administrative Justice and the Politics of Asylum in the United States, Canada and Australia* (OUP 2014)

Hathaway, J.C., *The Rights of Refugees under International Law* (2nd edn, CUP 2021)

Hathaway, J.C., *The Rights of Refugees under International Law* (1st edn, CUP 2005)

Hathaway, J.C. and Foster, M., *The Law of Refugee Status* (2nd edn, CUP 2014)

Herzfeld, P. and Prince, T., *Interpretation* (2nd edn, Thomson Reuters 2020)

Higgins, C., *Asylum by Boat: The Origins of Australia's Refugee Policy* (NewSouth Publishing 2017)

Higgins, R., *Problems & Process: International Law and How We Use it* (Clarendon Press 1994, reprinted 2010)

Hill, J., *Aust's Modern Treaty Law and Practice* (4th edn, CUP 2023)

Holborn, L.W., *Refugees: A Problem of Our Time: The Work of the United Nations High Commissioner for Refugees, 1951–1972* (The Scarecrow Press, Inc 1975)

Jayawickrama, N., *The Judicial Application of Human Rights Law* (CUP 2002)

Joseph, S. and Castan, M., *The International Covenant on Civil and Political Rights: Cases, Materials and Commentary* (3rd edn, OUP 2013)

Linderfalk, U., *On the Interpretation of Treaties: The Modern International Law as Expressed in the 1969 Vienna Convention on the Law of Treaties* (Springer 2007)

McAdam, J. and Chong, F., *Refugee Rights and Policy Wrongs: A Frank, Up-to-Date Guide by Experts* (New South 2019)

Meron, T., *Human Rights and Humanitarian Norms as Customary Law* (OUP 1989)

Moreno-Lax, V., *Accessing Asylum in Europe: Extraterritorial Border Controls and Refugee Rights under EU Law* (OUP 2017)

Murray, R., *The African Charter on Human and Peoples' Rights: A Commentary* (OUP 2019)

Nowak, M., *U.N. Covenant on Civil and Political Rights: CCPR Commentary* (N.P. Engel 1993)

Paulsson, J., *Denial of Justice in International Law* (CUP 2005)

Pobjoy, J.M., *The Child in International Refugee Law* (OUP 2017)

Roberts, A., *Is International Law International?* (OUP 2017)

Robinson, N., *Convention Relating to the Status of Refugee: History, Contents and Interpretation: A Commentary* (Institute of Jewish Affairs, World Jewish Congress 1953)

Schoenholtz, A.I., Ramji-Nogales, J., and Schrag, P.G., *The End of Asylum* (Georgetown University Press 2021)

Shany, Y., *Assessing the Effectiveness of International Courts* (OUP 2014)

Sinclair, I., *The Vienna Convention on the Law of Treaties* (2nd edn, Manchester University Press 1984)

Venzke, I., *How Interpretation Makes International Law: On Semantic Change and Normative Twists* (OUP 2012)

Villiger, M.E., *Commentary on the 1969 Vienna Convention on the Law of Treaties* (Martinus Nijhoff Publishers 2009)

Weis, P., (ed), *The Refugee Convention, 1951* (CUP 1995)

Chapters

Boza Martínez, D., 'Procedural Rights Protecting Immigrants Right to a Fair Trial (Article 6) and Right to an Effective Remedy (Article 13)' in Moya, D. and Milios, G. (eds), *Aliens before the European Court of Human Rights: Ensuring Minimum Standards of Human Rights Protection* (Koninklijke Brill 2021)

Burgorgue-Larsen, L., 'The Right to an Effective Remedy', in Burgorgue-Larsen, L. and Úbeda de Torres, A., *The Inter-American Court of Human Rights – Case Law and Commentary* (Greenstein, R. tr, OUP 2011)

Cantor, D.J. and Barichello, S., 'Protection of Asylum Seekers under the Inter-American Human Rights System' in Abass, A. and Ippolito, F. (eds), *Regional Approaches to the Protection of Asylum Seekers: An International Legal Perspective* (Ashgate 2014)

Chetail, V., 'Moving Towards an Integrated Approach of Refugee Law and Human Rights Law' in Costello, C., Foster, M., and McAdam, J. (eds), *The Oxford Handbook of International Refugee Law* (OUP 2021)

Chetail, V., 'Are Refugee Rights Human Rights? An Unorthodox Questioning of the Relations between Refugee Law and Human Rights Law' in Rubio-Marin, R. (ed), *Human Rights and Immigration* (OUP 2014)

Chetail, V., 'The Transnational Movement of Persons under General International Law – Mapping the Customary Law Foundations of International Migration Law' in Chetail, V. and Bauloz, C. (eds), *Research Handbook on International Law and Migration* (Edward Elgar 2014)

Dunlop, E., McAdam, J. and Weeks, G., 'A Search for Rights: Judicial and Administrative Responses to Migration and Refugee Cases', in Groves, M., Boughey, J., and Meagher, D. (eds), *The Legal Protection of Rights in Australia* (Hart Publishing 2019)

Einarsen, T., 'Drafting History of the 1951 Convention and the 1967 Protocol' in Zimmermann, A. (ed), *The 1951 Convention Relating to the Status of Refugees and its 1967 Protocol* (OUP 2011)

Elberling, B., 'Article 16' in Zimmermann, A. (ed), *The 1951 Convention Relating to the Status of Refugees and its 1967 Protocol* (OUP 2011)

Feller, E., 'Preface' in Feller, E., Türk, V., and Nicholson, F., (eds), *Refugee Protection in International Law: UNHCR's Global Consultations on International Protection* (CUP 2003)

Flynn, E., 'Article 13 [Access to Justice]' in Della Fina, V., Cera, R., and Palmisano, G. (eds), *The United Nations Convention on the Rights of Persons with Disabilities: A Commentary* (Springer 2017)

Flynn, E., 'Article 13 Access to Justice' in Bantekas, I., Ashley Stein, M., and Anastasiou, D. (eds), *The UN Convention on the Rights of Persons with Disabilities: A Commentary* (OUP 2018)

Francioni, F., 'The Rights of Access to Justice under Customary International Law' in Francioni, F. (ed), *Access to Justice as a Human Right* (OUP 2007)

Garnett, R., 'Substance and Procedure' in Basedow, J., Rühl, G., Ferrari, F., and de Miguel Asensio, P. (eds), *Encyclopedia of Private International Law*, Vol 2 (Edward Elgar 2017)

Gibney, M.J., 'The State of Asylum: Democratisation, Judicialisation and Evolution of Refugee Policy' in Kneebone, S. (ed) *The Refugee Convention 50 Years On: Globalisation and International Law* (Ashgate Publishing Limited 2003)

Goodwin-Gill, G.S., 'The International Law of Refugee Protection' in Fiddian-Qasmiyeh, E., Loescher, G., Long, K., and Sigona N. (eds), *The Oxford Handbook of Refugee and Forced Migration Studies* (OUP 2014)

Goodwin-Gill, G.S., 'The Search for the One, True Meaning ...' in Goodwin-Gill, G.S. and Lambert, H. (eds), *The Limits of Transnational Law: Refugee Law, Policy Harmonization and Judicial Dialogue in the European Union* (CUP 2010)

Goodwin-Gill, G.S., 'Article 31 of the 1951 Convention Relating to the Status of Refugees: Non-penalization, Detention, and Protection' in Feller, E., Türk, V., and Nicholson, F. (eds), *Refugee Protection in International Law: UNHCR's Global Consultations on International Protection* (CUP 2003)

Iván, J., 'Where do State Responsibilities Begin and End: Border Exclusions and State Responsibility' in O'Sullivan, M. and Stevens, D. (eds), *States, the Law and Access to Refugee Protection: Fortresses and Fairness* (Hart Publishing 2017)

Khan, F. and Willie, N., 'Strengthening Access to Justice for Women Refugees and Asylum Seekers in South Africa' in Lawson, D., Dubin, A., and Mwambene, L. (eds), *Gender, Poverty and Access to Justice: Policy Implementation in Sub-Saharan Africa* (Routledge 2020)

Lauterpacht, E. and Bethlehem, D., 'The Scope and Content of the Principle of *Non-Refoulement*: Opinion' in Feller, E., Türk, V., and Nicholson, F. (eds), *Refugee Protection in International Law: UNHCR's Global Consultations on International Protection* (CUP 2003)

Lundy, L., Tobin J., and Parkes, A., 'Article 12: The Right to Respect for the Views of the Child' in Tobin, J. (ed), *The UN Convention on the Rights of the Child: A Commentary* (OUP 2019)

McAdam, J., 'The Refugee Convention as a Rights Blueprint' in McAdam, J. (ed), *Forced Migration and Global Security* (Hart Publishing 2008)

McAdam, J., 'Interpretation of the 1951 Convention' in Zimmermann, A. (ed), *The 1951 Convention Relating to the Status of Refugees and its 1967 Protocol* (OUP 2011)

Metzger, A., 'Article 14 (Artistic Rights and Industrial Property/Propriété Intellectuelle et Industrielle)' in Zimmermann, A. (ed), *The 1951 Convention Relating to the Status of Refugees and its 1967 Protocol* (OUP 2011)

Naldi, G.J. and d'Orsi, C., 'The Role of the African Human Rights System with Reference to Asylum Seekers' in Abass, A. and Ippolito, F. (eds), *Regional Approaches to the Protection of Asylum Seekers: An International Legal Perspective* (Ashgate 2014)

O'Sullivan, M., 'Interdiction and Screening of Asylum Seekers at Sea: Implications for Asylum Justice' in O'Sullivan, M. and Stevens, D. (eds), *States, the Law and Access to Refugee Protection: Fortresses and Fairness* (Hart Publishing 2017)

O'Sullivan, M. and Stevens, D., 'Access to Refugee Protection: Key Concepts and Contemporary Challenges', in O'Sullivan, M. and Stevens, D. (eds), *States, the Law and Access to Refugee Protection* (Hart Publishing 2017)

Pellet, A., 'Article 42' in Zimmermann, A. (ed), *The 1951 Convention Relating to the Status of Refugees and its 1967 Protocol* (OUP 2011)

Pobjoy, J.M., 'Article 22: Refugee Children' in Tobin, J. (ed), *The UN Convention on the Rights of the Child: A Commentary* (OUP 2019)

Roberts Lyer, K. and Webb, P., 'Effective Parliamentary Oversight of Human Rights' in Saul, M., Follesdal, A., and Ulfstein, G. (eds), *The International Human Rights Judiciary and National Parliaments: Europe and Beyond* (CUP 2017)

Sachs, A. (Justice), 'From Refugee to Judge of Refugee Law' in Simeon, J.C. (ed), *Critical Issues in International Refugee Law: Strategies Toward Interpretative Harmony* (CUP 2010)

Schultz, J. and Einarsen, T., 'The Right to Refugee Status and the Internal Protection Alternative: What Does the Law Say?' in Burson, B. and Cantor, D.J. (eds), *Human Rights and the Refugee Definition: Comparative Legal Practice and Theory* (Brill Nijhoff 2016)

Skordas, A., 'Article 7' in Zimmermann, A. (ed), *The 1951 Convention Relating to the Status of Refugees and its 1967 Protocol: A Commentary* (OUP 2011)

Spijkerboer, T., 'Higher Judicial Remedies for Asylum Seekers – An International Legal Perspective' in Care, G. and Storey, H. (eds), *Asylum Law: First International Judicial Conference, London, 1995* (The Steering Committee of the Judicial Conference on Asylum Law 1995)

Tobin, J. with Read, C., 'Article 40: The Rights of the Child in the Juvenile Justice System' in Tobin, J. (ed), *The UN Convention on the Rights of the Child: A Commentary* (OUP 2019)

Úbeda de Torres, A., 'The Right to Due Process', in Burgorgue-Larsen, L. and Úbeda de Torres, A. (eds), *The Inter-American Court of Human Rights – Case Law and Commentary* (Greenstein, R., tr, OUP 2011)

Wouters, J. and Ryngaert, C., 'Impact on the Process of Formation of Customary International Law' in Kamminga M.T. and Scheinin, M. (eds), *The Impact of Human Rights Law on General International Law* (OUP 2009)

Journal articles

Almutawa, A., 'The Arab Court of Human Rights and the Enforcement of the Arab Charter on Human Rights' (2021) 21 Human Rights Law Review 506

de Andrade, M., 'The Two-Step Methodology for the Identification of General Principles of Law' (2022) 71 International and Comparative Law Quarterly 983

Baillet, C.M., 'National Case Law as a Generator of International Refugee Law: Rectifying an Imbalance within UNHCR Guidelines on International Protection' (2015) Emory International Law Journal 2059

Barczentewicz, M., '*Cart* Challenges, Empirical Methods, and Effectiveness of Judicial Review' (2021) 84(6) Modern Law Review 1360

Barnhoorn, L.A.N.M, 'Netherlands Judicial Decisions Involving Questions of Public International Law, 2004–2005' (2006) 37 Netherlands Yearbook of International Law 397

Barnhoorn, L.A.N.M, 'Netherlands Judicial Decisions Involving Questions of Public International Law, 1995–1996' (1996) 28 Netherlands Yearbook of International Law 325

Barnhoorn, L.A.N.M, 'Netherlands Judicial Decisions involving Questions of Public International Law, 1976–1977' (1978) 9 Netherlands Yearbook of International Law 271

Boeles, P., 'Effective Legal Remedies for Asylum Seekers according to the Convention of Geneva 1951' (1996) 43 Netherlands International Law Review 291

Byrnes, A., 'Kirby Lecture in International Law 2014: The Meaning of International Law: Government Monopoly, Expert Precinct, or the People's Law?' (2014) 32 Australian Year Book of International Law 11

Cantor, D. et al, 'Externalisation, Access to Territorial Asylum, and International Law' (2022) 34 International Journal of Refugee Law 120

Cantor, D.J. and Chikwanha, F., 'Reconsidering African Refugee Law' (2019) 31 International Journal of Refugee Law 182

Cantor, D.J., 'Reframing Relationships: Revisiting the Procedural Standards for Refugee Status Determination in Light of Recent Human Rights Treaty Body Jurisprudence' (2015) 34 Refugee Survey Quarterly 79

Carnwath, R., 'Tribunal Justice – A New Start' (Jan 2009) Public Law 48

Cerna, C.M., 'Reflections on the Normative Status of the American Declaration of the Rights and Duties of Man' (2009) University of Pennsylvania Journal of International Law 1211

Chiusssi, L., 'Remarks on the ILC Work on the Identification of Customary Law and Human Rights: Curbing "Droit de l'Hommisme"?' (2018) 27 Italian Yearbook of International Law 163

Critchfield, R., 'Toni Sender: Feminist, Socialist, Internationalist' (1992) 15 History of European Ideas 701

Dugard, J., 'The Future of International Law: A Human Rights Perspective – With Some Comments on the Leiden School of International Law' (2007) 20 Leiden Journal of International Law 729

Dugard, J., 'The Opinion on South-West Africa (Namibia): The Teleologists Triumph' (1971) 88 The South African Law Journal 460

'Editorial: Paul Weis 1907–1991' (1991) 3 International Journal of Refugee Law 183

Elliott, M. and Thomas, R., 'Tribunal Justice and Proportionate Dispute Resolution' (2012) 71 Cambridge Law Journal 297

Fitzmaurice, G.G., 'The Meaning of the Term "Denial of Justice"' (1932) 13 British Yearbook of International Law 93

Fitzpatrick, J., 'Book reviews and notes: *The Refugee Convention, 1951, The Travaux Préparatoires Analysed with a Commentary*. Edited by Paul Weis. New York: Cambridge University Press, 1995' (1996) 90 American Journal of International Law 175

Francis, A., 'Bringing Protection Home: Healing the Schism Between International Obligations and National Safeguards Created by Extraterritorial Processing' (2008) 20 International Journal of Refugee Law 273

Gageler, S. (SC), 'Impact of Migration Law on the Development of Australian Administrative Law' (2010) 17 Australian Journal of Administrative Law 92

Gammeltoft-Hansen, T. and Hathaway, J.C., '*Non-Refoulement* in a World of Cooperative Deterrence' (2015) 53 Columbia Journal of Transnational Law 235

Garner, J.W., 'International Responsibility of States for Judgments of Courts and Verdicts of Juries amounting to Denial of Justice' (1929) 10 British Yearbook of International Law 181

Gilbert, G., 'UNHCR and Courts: *Amicus curiae … sed curia amica est?*' (2016) 28 International Journal of Refugee Law 623

Goodwin-Gill, G.S., 'The Office of the United Nations High Commissioner for Refugees and the Sources of International Refugee Law' (2020) 69 International and Comparative Law Quarterly 1

Goodwin-Gill, G.S., 'Book Review, "The Refugee Convention, 1951. The *Travaux Préparatoires* analysed, with a Commentary by the late Dr Paul Weis"' (1996) 9 Journal of Refugee Studies 103

Hathaway, J., 'Reconceiving Refugee Law as Human Rights Protection' (1991) 4 Journal of Refugee Studies 113

Hyndman, P., 'The 1951 Convention and Its Implications for Procedural Questions' (1994) 6 International Journal of Refugee Law 245

Jain, A., 'Bureaucrats in Robes: Immigration "Judges" and the Trappings of "Courts"' (2019) 33 Georgetown Immigration Law Journal 261

Johnston, K.A., 'The Nature and Context of Rules and the Identification of Customary International Law' (2021) 32(4) European Journal of International Law 1167

Kidane, W., 'Missed Opportunities in the International Law Commission's Draft Articles on the Expulsion of Aliens' (2017) 30 Harvard Human Rights Journal 77

Kosař, D. and Lixinski, L., 'Domestic Judicial Design by International Human Rights Courts' (2015) 109 American Journal of International Law 713

Marceau, G., 'WTO Dispute Settlement and Human Rights' (2002) 13 European Journal of International Law 757

Moreno-Lax, V., 'Seeking Asylum in the Mediterranean: Against a Fragmentary Reading of EU Member States' Obligations Accruing at Sea' (2011) 23 International Journal of Refugee Law 174

Murphy, S.D., 'The Expulsion of Aliens (Revisited) and Other Topics: The Sixty-Sixth Session of the International Law Commission' (2015) 109 American Journal of International Law 125

Ramji-Nogales, J., 'Undocumented Migrants and the Failures of Universal Individualism' (2014) 47 Vanderbilt Journal of Transnational Law 699

Peters, A., 'Humanity as the A and Ω of Sovereignty' (2009) 20 European Journal of International Law 513

Rodrik, D., 'Rights Not Recognized: Applying the Right to Recognition as a Person before the Law to Pushbacks at International Borders' (2021) 33 International Journal of Refugee Law 541

Rogerson, P., 'Illegal Overstayers Can Acquire a Domicile of Choice or Habitual Residence in England' (2006) 65 Cambridge Law Journal 35

Roht-Arriaza, N., 'State Responsibility to Investigate and Prosecute Grave Human Rights Violations in International Law' (1990) 78 California Law Review 449

Rubenstein, J.L. (Maître), 'The Refugee Problem' (September 1936) 15 International Affairs 716

Sackville, R. (Justice), 'Some Thoughts on Access to Justice' (FCA) (2003) Federal Judicial Scholarship 22

Satterthwaite, M.L. and Dhital, S., 'Measuring Access to Justice: Transformation and Technicality in SDG 16.3' (Jan 2019) 10 Global Policy 96

Sherman, J., 'The Right to an Interpreter under Customary International Law' (2017) Columbia Human Rights Law Review 257

Simma, B. and Alston P., 'The Sources of Human Rights Law: Custom, Jus Cogens, and General Principles' (1988–1989) 12 Australian Year Book of International Law 82

Sivakumaran, S., 'The Influence of Teachings of Publicists on the Development of International Law' (2017) 66 International and Comparative Law Quarterly 1

Spiegel, H.W., 'Origin and Development of Denial of Justice' (1938) 32 American Journal of International Law 63

Sztucki, J., 'The Conclusions on the International Protection of Refugees Adopted by the Executive Committee of the UNHCR Programme' (1989) 1 International Journal of Refugee Law 285

Thirlway, H., 'Human Rights in Customary Law: An Attempt to Define Some of the Issues' (2015) 28 Leiden Journal of International Law 495

Wilson, R.R., 'Access-to-Courts Provisions in United States Commercial Treaties' (1953) 47 American Journal of International Law 20

Reports, Media, Occasional Papers, Miscellaneous

Annuaire de l'Institut de Droit International, *Travaux préparatoires de la Session de Lausanne, Septembre 1927, Tome I* (Goemaere 1927)

Council of Europe, 'Explanatory Report to the Protocol No. 7 to the Convention for the Protection of Human Rights and Fundamental Freedoms' (Strasbourg, 22 November 1984)

Doherty, B. and Saba Vasefi, S., 'Asylum seeker boy on Nauru pleads for medical help for his mother' (*The Guardian*, 26 April 2018) <https://www.theguardian.com/australia-news/2018/apr/25/asylum-seeker-boy-on-nauru-pleads-for-medical-help-for-his-mother>

Durieux, J.F., 'Salah Sheekh is a Refugee: New Insights into Primary and Subsidiary Forms of Protection', Refugee Studies Centre, Working Paper Series No 49 (October 2008) 8

Eberechi, O.E., 'A Comparative Analysis of the Application of the 1951 Refugee Convention to Victims of Sexual Violence in South Africa, Tanzania and Uganda' (2020) 23 PER/PELJ <https://perjournal.co.za/article/view/6225/10396>

ECtHR, 'Guide on Article 13 of the European Convention on Human Rights: Right to an effective remedy' (updated 31 August 2022)

ECtHR, 'Guide on Article 6 of the European Convention on Human Rights: Right to a Fair Trial (Civil Limb)' (Council of Europe/European Court of Human Rights, updated 31 August 2022)

ECtHR, 'Guide to Article 1 of Protocol No. 7 to the European Convention on Human Rights: Procedural safeguards relating to expulsion of aliens' (Council of Europe, updated 31 August 2022)

Faulks, E (Lord, QC) (Chair), 'The Independent Review of Administrative Law' (March 2021)

Forteau, M., 'A New "Baxter Paradox"? Does the Work of the ILC on Matters Already Governed by Multilateral Treaties Necessarily Constitute a Dead End? Some Observations on the ILC Draft Articles on the Expulsion of Aliens', available via <https://harvardhrj.com/wp-content/uploads/sites/14/2016/06/Forteau.pdf>

'Further Written Submissions on Behalf of the Intervener (UNHCR)' in Goodwin-Gill, G.S., 'The Queen (Al-Rawi and others) v Secretary of State for Foreign and Commonwealth Affairs and another (United Nations High Commissioner for Refugees intervening)' (2008) 20 International Journal of Refugee Law 675

European Commission, Amended proposal for a Regulation of the European Parliament and of the Council establishing a common procedure for international protection in the Union and repealing Directive 2013/32/EU, COM(2020) 611 final (23 September 2020)

European Commission, 'Proposal for a Regulation of the European Parliament and of the Council establishing a common procedure for international protection in the Union and repealing Directive 2013/32/EU', COM(2016) 467 final (13 July 2016)

European Commission, 'Proposal for a Regulation of the European Parliament and of the Council on standards for the qualification of third-country nationals or stateless persons as beneficiaries of international protection, for a uniform status for refugees or for persons eligible for subsidiary protection and for the content of the protection granted and amending Council Directive 2003/109/EC of 25 November 2003 concerning the status of third-country nationals who are long-term residents', COM(2016) 466 final (13 July 2016)

European Parliament, Directorate-General for Internal Policies, Policy Department C: Citizens' Rights and Constitutional Affairs, 'Effective Access to Justice: Study for the Peti Committee' (EU 2017)

'Explanations relating to the Charter of Fundamental Rights', 2007/C 303/02 (14 December 2007)

Federal Court of Australia, Annual Report 2020–2021, available via <https://www.fedcourt.gov.au/digital-law-library/annual-reports/2020-21>

Federal Court of Australia, Annual Report 2021-2022, available via <https://www.fedcourt.gov.au/digital-law-library/annual-reports/2021-22>

Gaja, G., 'General Principles of Law' in Max Planck Encyclopedia of International Law [MPIL] (updated April 2020), <https://opil-ouplaw-com.wwwproxy1.library.unsw.edu.au/view/10.1093/law:epil/9780199231690/law-9780199231690-e1410?print=pdf>

'Global Consultations on International Protection, Update 1 August 2002' (UNHCR) available via <http://www.unhcr.org/3d4928164.html>

Goodwin-Gill, G.S., 'Introductory Note', Audiovisual Library of International Law, available via <http://legal.un.org/avl/ha/prsr/prsr.html>

Goodwin-Gill, G.S., 'Procedural History', Audiovisual Library of International Law, available via <http://legal.un.org/avl/ha/prsr/prsr.html>

Goodwin-Gill, G.S., 'The duty to ensure respect for acquired rights (Hathaway, J. and Foster, M. *The Law of Refugee Status*, 2nd edn, 2014, 39–49)' (unpublished)

HCCH, 'Note on Habitual Residence and the Scope of the 1993 Hague Convention' (March 2018)

Inter-American Commission on Human Rights, 'Report on Terrorism and Human Rights', OEA/Ser.L/V/II.116, Doc. 5 rev. 1 corr. (11 October 2002), available via <http://www.cidh.org/terrorism/eng/toc.htm>

International Commission of Jurists, 'The Arab Court of Human Rights: A Flawed Statute for an Ineffective Court' (2015), available via <https://www.icj.org/wp-content/uploads/2015/04/MENA-Arab-Court-of-Human-Rights-Publications-Report-2015-ENG.pdf>

International Commission of Jurists, 'Principles on the Role of Judges and Lawyers in Relation to Refugees and Migrants' (May 2017) available via <https://www.icj.org/wp-content/uploads/2017/07/Universal-Refugees-Migrants-Principles-Publications-Report-Thematic-Report-2017-ENG.pdf>

Kaldor Centre, 'Factsheet: Do People Seeking Asylum Receive Legal Assistance?' (updated May 2020), available via <https://www.kaldorcentre.unsw.edu.au/publication/legal-assistance-asylum-seekers>

Kaldor Centre, 'Research Brief: "Fast track" Refugee Status Determination' (updated June 2022)

Keith, K.J., 'Interpreting Treaties, Statutes and Contracts', New Zealand Centre for Public Law, Occasional Paper No 19 (May 2009)

Law Council of Australia, 'The Justice Project: Final Report – Part 1: Asylum Seekers' (August 2018)

Ministry of Justice, 'Judicial Review Reform Consultation: The Government Response' (July 2021)

OECD/Open Society Foundations, 'Legal Needs Surveys and Access to Justice' (OECD Publishing 2019)

OECD/Open Society Justice Initiative, 'Understanding Effective Access to Justice: 3–4 November 2016, OECD Conference Centre, Paris, Workshop Background Paper' (2016), available via <https://www.oecd.org/gov/Understanding-effective-access-justice-workshop-paper-final.pdf>

Parliament of the Commonwealth of Australia, Senate, 'Migration Amendment (Clarifying International Obligations for Removal) Bill 2021, Revised Explanatory Memorandum' (2019–2020–2021)

Refugee Advice & Casework Service (RACS), 'Submission no 108' (9 October 2017) available via <https://www.lawcouncil.asn.au/justice-project/justice-project-submissions>

Rishmawi, M., 'Arab Charter on Human Rights (2004)', Max Planck Encyclopaedia of Public International Law (June 2008)

Rishmawi, M., 'The League of Arab States: Human Rights Standards and Mechanisms: Towards Further Civil Society Engagement: A Manual for Practitioners' (Open Society Foundations/Cairo Institute for Human Rights Studies, n.d.) available via <https://www.cihrs.org/wp-content/uploads/2015/12/league-arab-states-manual-en-20151125.pdf>

Thirlway, H., 'Professor Baxter's Legacy: Still Paradoxical?' (2017) 6(3) ESIL Reflections available via <https://esil-sedi.eu/wp-content/uploads/2017/03/ESIL-Reflection-Thirlway_0.pdf>

'Roundtable on the Future of Refugee Convention Supervision' (2013) 26 Journal of Refugee Studies 327

'Rules of Procedure of the African Commission on Human and Peoples' Rights' (adopted by the Commission during its 27th Extra-ordinary session on 19 February–4 March 2020)

'Toni Sender, 76, Socialist Leader – Reichstag Foe of Nazis Dies – Aided Labor at U.N.' (*New York Times*, 27 June 1964) 25

'Written submissions on behalf of the Office of the United Nations High Commissioner for Refugees, Intervener', in Goodwin-Gill, G.S., '*The Queen (Al-Rawi and others) v Secretary of State for Foreign and Commonwealth Affairs and another* (United Nations High Commissioner for Refugees intervening)' (2008) 20 International Journal of Refugee Law 675

Venice Commission and OSCE Office for Democratic Institutions and Human Rights, 'Joint Opinion on the rovisions of the So-called "Stop Soros" Draft Legislative Package which Directly Affect NGOs (In Particular Draft Article 353A of the Criminal Code on Facilitating Illegal Migration)', CDL-AD (2018) 013 (25 June 2018)

UN and related documents

'Annex to Questionnaire No. 4, Report of the Sub-Committee' (Guerrero Report), in League of Nations, Committee of Experts for the Progressive Codification of International Law, 'Report of the Council of the League of Nations on the Questions which appear Ripe for International Regulation (Questionnaires No 1 to 7)', C.196.M.70.1927.V (20 April 1927)

Committee on the Elimination of Discrimination against Women, 'General recommendation No. 33 on women's access to justice', CEDAW/C/GC/33 (3 August 2015)

Committee on the Protection of the Rights of All Migrant Workers and Members of Their Families and Committee on the Rights of the Child, 'Joint General Comment No. 4 (2017) of the Committee on the Protection of the Rights of All Migrant Workers and Members of Their Families and No. 23 (2017) of the Committee on the Rights of the Child on State Obligations regarding the Human Rights of Children in the context of International Migration in Countries of Origin, Transit, Destination and Return', CMW/C/GC/4-CRC/C/GC/23 (16 November 2017)

Committee on the Rights of the Child, 'General Comment No. 24 (2019) on children's rights in the child justice system' CRC/C/GC/24 (18 September 2019)

Committee on the Rights of the Child, 'General comment No. 14 (2013) on the right of the child to have his or her best interests taken as a primary consideration (art. 3, para. 1)', CRC/C/GC/14 (29 May 2013)

Committee on the Rights of the Child, 'General Comment No. 12 (2009): The right of the child to be heard', CRC/C/GC/12 (20 July 2009)

Committee on the Rights of the Child, 'General Comment No. 10 (2007) Children's rights in juvenile justice', CRC/C/GC/10 (25 April 2007)

Committee on the Rights of the Child, 'General Comment No. 6: Treatment of Unaccompanied and Separated Children outside their Country of Origin', CRC/GC/2005/6 (1 September 2005)

Committee on the Rights of Persons with Disabilities (CRPD Cttee), Concluding observations on the combined second and third periodic reports of Hungary', CRPD/C/HUN/CO/2-3 (20 May 2022)

CRPD Cttee, 'Concluding observations on the combined second and third periodic reports of Mexico', CRPD/C/MEX/CO/2-3 (20 April 2022)

CRPD Cttee, 'Concluding observations on the initial report of Estonia', CRPD/C/EST/CO/1 (5 May 2021)

CRPD Cttee, 'Concluding observations on the initial report of Greece', CRPD/C/GRC/CO/ 1 (29 October 2019)

CRPD Cttee, 'Concluding observations on the initial report of India', CRPD/C/IND/CO/1 (29 October 2019)

CRPD Cttee, 'Concluding observations on the initial report of Iraq', CRPD/C/IRQ/CO/1 (23 October 2019)

CRPD Cttee, 'Concluding observations on the initial report of Kuwait', CRPD/C/KWT/CO/ 1 (18 October 2019)

CRPD Cttee, 'Concluding observations on the initial report of Albania', CRPD/C/ALB/CO/ 1 (14 October 2019)

CRPD Cttee, 'Concluding observations on the initial report of Myanmar', CRPD/C/MMR/ CO/1 (22 October 2019)

CRPD Cttee, 'Concluding observations on the combined second and third periodic reports of Ecuador', CRPD/C/ECU/CO/2-3 (21 October 2019)

CRPD Cttee, 'Concluding observations on the initial report of Turkey', CRPD/C/TUR/CO/ 1 (1 October 2019)

CRPD Cttee, 'Concluding observations on the initial report of New Zealand', CRPD/C/ NZL/CO/1 (31 October 2014)

CRPD Cttee, 'General comment No. 2 (2014): Article 9: Accessibility', CRPD/C/GC/2 (22 May 2014)

CRPD Cttee, 'General Comment No. 1 (2014): Article 12: Equal recognition before the law', CRPD/C/GC/1 (19 May 2014)

CRPD Cttee, 'Guidelines on article 14 of the Convention on the Rights of Persons with Disabilities: The right to liberty and security of persons with disabilities' (adopted 14th sess, September 2015)

United Nations Economic and Social Council (ECOSOC), 11th sess, 407th meeting, E/ SR.407 (11 August 1950)

ECOSOC, 11th sess, 406th meeting, E/SR.406 (11 August 1950)

ECOSOC, 11th sess, 399th meeting, E/SR.399 (2 August 1950)

ECOSOC, 11th sess, 'Refugees and Stateless Persons, Resolutions adopted by the Economic and Social Council on 11 August 1950', E/1818 (12 August 1950)

ECOSOC, 11th sess, Social Committee, 156th meeting, E/AC.7/SR.156 (14 August 1950)

ECOSOC, 11th sess, Social Committee, 166th meeting, E/AC.7/SR.166 (7 August 1950)

ECOSOC, 'Ad Hoc Committee on Statelessness and Related Problems: Denmark-United Kingdom: Proposed Text for Article 36', E/AC.32/L.33 and its Corr 1 (10 February 1950)

ECOSOC, 'Ad Hoc Committee on Statelessness and Related Problems: Status of refugees and stateless persons – Memorandum by the Secretary-General', E/AC.32/2 (3 January 1950)

ECOSOC, 'Ad Hoc Committee on Refugees and Stateless Persons: Refugees and Stateless Persons: Compilation of the Comments of Governments and Specialized Agencies on the Report of the Ad Hoc Committee on Statelessness and Related Problems (Document E/ 1618) (Memorandum by the Secretary-General)', E/AC.32/L.40 (10 August 1950)

ECOSOC, 'Ad Hoc Committee on Statelessness: Draft Convention Relating to the Status of Refugees: Decisions of the Working Group taken on 9 February 1950', E/AC.32/L.32 (9 February 1950)

ECOSOC, 'Ad Hoc Committee on Statelessness and Related Problems: Decisions of the Committee on Statelessness and Related Problems taken at the afternoon meeting of 1 February 1950', E/AC.32/L.22 (1 February 1950)

ECOSOC, 'Ad Hoc Committee on Statelessness and Related Problems: Preliminary draft Convention relating to the Status of Refugees (and Stateless Persons): Communication from the International Labour Organisation', E/AC.32/L.9 (26 January 1950)

ECOSOC, 'Ad Hoc Committee on Statelessness and Related Problems: France: Proposal for a draft Convention', E/AC.32/L.3 (17 January 1950), and its CORR.1 (18 January 1950) and CORR.2 (25 January 1950)

ECOSOC, 'Ad Hoc Committee on Statelessness and Related Problems: Summary Record of the First Meeting', E/AC.32/SR.1 (23 January 1950)

ECOSOC, 'Council Committee on Non-Governmental Organizations: Communication from the Agudas Israel World Organization distributed to the Ad Hoc Committee on Statelessness and Related Problems in Accordance with Article 81 of the Rules of Procedure, in Full, at the Request of a Member of the Council: Proposed Text of Art 24 of the Proposed Draft Convention on Refugees', E/C.2/242 (1 February 1950)

ECOSOC, Official Records, Third Year, 6th sess, Supp 1 (New York 1948)

ECOSOC, 'Report of the Ad Hoc Committee on Refugees and Stateless Persons: Second Session' E/1850; E/AC.32/8 (25 August 1950)

ECOSOC, 'Report of the Ad Hoc Committee on Refugees and Stateless Persons', E/1618, E/AC.32/5 (17 February 1950) and its Corr.1

ECOSOC, Resolution 672 (XXV), 'Establishment of the Executive Committee of the Programme of the United Nations High Commissioner for Refugees' E/RES/672 (30 April 1958)

ECOSOC, Resolution 18(III) 'Refugees and displaced persons' (3 October 1946)

ECOSOC, Resolution 116(VI)D, Resolutions of 1-2 March 1948

ECOSOC, Resolution 248(IX)A (6 August 1949)

ECOSOC, Resolution 248(IX)B (8 August 1949)

ECOSOC, Resolution 319(XI) (Resolutions of 11 and 16 August 1950)

UNHCR Executive Committee (ExCom), 'Conclusion No. 116 (LXXIII) on mental health and psychosocial support' (2022)

ExCom, 'Conclusion on refugees with disabilities and other persons with disabilities protected and assisted by UNHCR', Conclusion No 110 (LXI) (12 October 2010)

ExCom, 'Conclusion on International Protection', Conclusion No 85 (XLIX) (1998)

ExCom, 'Conclusion on Safeguarding Asylum', Conclusion No 82 (XLVIII) (1997)

ExCom, 'General Conclusion on International Protection', Conclusion No 81 (XLVIII) (17 October 1997)

ExCom, 'General', Conclusion No 79 (XLVII) (1996)

ExCom, 'Problem of Refugees and Asylum-Seekers Who Move in an Irregular Manner from a Country in Which They Had Already Found Protection', Conclusion No 58 (XL) (13 October 1989)

ExCom, 'Detention of Refugees and Asylum-Seekers', Conclusion No 44 (XXXVII) (13 October 1986)

ExCom, 'General', Conclusion No 41 (XXXVII) (1986)

ExCom, 'Identity Documents for Refugees', Conclusion No 35 (XXXV) (18 Oct 1984)

ExCom, 'The Problem of Manifestly Unfounded or Abusive Applications for Refugee Status or Asylum', Conclusion No 30 (XXXIV) (20 October 1983)

ExCom, 'Protection of Asylum-Seekers in Situations of Large-Scale Influx', Conclusion No 22 (XXXII) (21 October 1981)

ExCom, 'Determination of Refugee Status', Conclusion No 8 (XXVIII) (12 October 1977)

ExCom, 'Non-Refoulement', Conclusion No 6 (XXVIII) (12 October 1977)

Final Act of the United Nations Conference of Plenipotentiaries on the Status of Refugees and Stateless Persons, II, available via <http://www.unhcr.org/protect/PROTECTION/3b66c2aa10.pdf>.

Human Rights Committee (HRC), 'Concluding observations on the fourth periodic report of the Plurinational State of Bolivia', CCPR/C/BOL/CO/4 (2 June 2022)

HRC, 'Concluding observations on the fifth periodic report of Israel', CCPR/C/ISR/CO/5 (5 May 2022)

HRC, 'Concluding observations on the eighth periodic report of Ukraine', CCPR/C/UKR/CO/8 (9 February 2022)

HRC, 'Concluding observations on the sixth periodic report of Mexico', CCPR/C/MEX/CO/6 (4 December 2019)

HRC, 'Concluding observations on the fourth periodic report of Estonia', CCPR/C/EST/CO/4 (18 April 2019)

HRC, 'Concluding observations on the fourth periodic report of Bulgaria', CCPR/C/BGR/CO/4 (1 November 2018)

HRC, 'Concluding observations on the sixth periodic report of Hungary', CCPR/C/HUN/CO/6 (9 May 2018)

HRC, 'Concluding observations on the sixth periodic report of Australia', CCPR/C/AUS/CO/6 (1 December 2017)

HRC, 'Concluding observations on the initial report of South Africa', CCPR/C/ZAF/CO/1 (27 April 2016)

HRC, 'Concluding observations on the second periodic report of Greece', CCPR/C/GRC/CO/2 (3 December 2015)

HRC, 'Concluding observations on the sixth periodic report of Canada', CCPR/C/CAN/CO/6 (13 August 2015)

HRC, 'Concluding observations of the Human Rights Committee', CCPR/C/CHE/CO/3 (3 November 2009)

HRC, 'General Comment No. 35: Article 9 (Liberty and security of person)' CCPR/C/GC/35 (16 December 2014)

HRC, 'General Comment No. 32: Article 14 Right to Equality before courts and tribunals and to a fair trial', CCPR/C/GC/32 (23 August 2007)

HRC, 'General Comment No. 31', CCPR/C/21/Rev.1/Add.13 (26 May 2004)

HRC, 'General Comment No. 29: State of Emergency (Article 4)', CCPR/C/21/Rev.1/Add.11 (32 August 2001)

HRC, General Comment No. 15, 'The Position of Aliens Under the Covenant', HRI/GEN/1/Rev.1 at 18 (1986)

Human Rights Council, 'Equality and non-discrimination under article 5 of the Convention on the Rights of Persons with Disabilities: Report of the Office of the United Nations High Commissioner for Human Rights', A/HRC/34/26 (9 December 2016)

Human Rights Council, 'Report of the Working Group on Arbitrary Detention', A/HRC/13/30 (18 January 2010)

International Law Commission (ILC), Draft articles on diplomatic protection' in Report of the International Law Commission, Vol II, A/61/10 (58th sess, 2006)

ILC, 'Draft articles on the expulsion of aliens', in Report of the International Law Commission, A/69/10 (66th sess, 2014)

ILC, 'Draft conclusions on identification of customary international law', in Report of the International Law Commission, A/73/10 (70th sess, 2018)

ILC, 'Draft conclusions on subsequent agreements and subsequent practice in relation to the interpretation of treaties' in Report of the International Law Commission, A/73/10 (70th sess, 2018)

ILC, 'Fragmentation of International Law: Difficulties arising from the Diversification and Expansion of International Law: Report of the Study Group of the International Law Commission, Finalized by Martti Koskenniemi', A/CN.4/L.682 (13 April 2006)

ILC, 'Provisional summary record of the 3493rd meeting', A/CN.4/SR.3493 (71st sess, 29 July 2019)

ILC, 'Provisional summary record of the 3490th meeting', A/CN.4/SR.3490 (71st sess, 25 July 2019)

ILC, 'Provisional summary record of the 3489th meeting', A/CN.4/SR.3489 (71st sess, 24 July 2019)

ILC, 'Third report on general principles of law by Marcelo Vázquez-Bermúdez, Special Rapporteur', A/CN.4/753 (73rd sess, 2022)

ILC, 'Second report on general principles of law by Marcelo Vázquez-Bermúdez, Special Rapporteur', A/CN.4/741 (72nd sess, 2020)

ILC, 'First report on general principles of law by Marcelo Vázquez-Bermúdez, Special Rapporteur', A/CN.4/732 (71st sess, 2019)

ILC, 'Fourth report on identification of customary international law by Michael Wood, Special Rapporteur', A/CN.4/695/Add.1 (68th sess, 2016)

ILC, 'Second report on identification of customary international law by Michael Wood, Special Rapporteur', A/CN.4/672 (66th sess, 2014)

ILC, 'Ninth Report on the expulsion of aliens, Submitted by Mr. Maurice Kamto, Special Rapporteur', A/CN.4/670 (66th sess, 2014)

ILC, 'Sixth report on the expulsion of aliens, by Mr. Maurice Kamto, Special Rapporteur', A/CN.4/625 and Add 1–2 (62nd sess, 2010)

ILC, 'First report on diplomatic protection, by Mr. John R. Dugard. Special Rapporteur', A/CN.4/506 and Add 1 (52nd sess, 2000)

ILC, 'Report of the International Law Commission on the work of its eighteenth session', in Yearbook of the International Law Commission 1966, Volume II

ILC, 'Third report on the law of treaties, by Sir Humphrey Waldock, Special Rapporteur', in Yearbook of the International Law Commission 1964, Volume II

Inter-Parliamentary Union (IPU)/UNHCR, 'A guide to international refugee protection and building state asylum systems Handbook for Parliamentarians N° 27, 2017' (2017) available via <https://www.refworld.org/docid/5a9d57554.html>

'International Principles and Guidelines on Access to Justice for Persons with Disabilities' (August 2020), available via <https://www.ohchr.org/Documents/Issues/Disability/SR_Disability/GoodPractices/Access-to-Justice-EN.pdf>

Jalloh, C.C., 'Universal criminal jurisdiction', in Report of the International Law Commission, A/73/10 (70th sess, 2018), Annex A

League of Nations, 'Conference for the Codification of International Law: Bases of Discussion for the Conference drawn up by the Preparatory Committee: Volume III. Responsibility of States for Damage caused in their Territory to the Person or Property of Foreigners', C.75.M.69.1929.V et Erratum et Supplément (a) (15 May 1929)

League of Nations, 'Inter-Governmental Conference on the Legal Status of Refugees coming from Germany: Provisional minutes, Fourth meeting', Conf. S.R.A./1st Session/P.V.4 (16 July 1936), United Nations Archives at Geneva (digital), Ref Code R5761/50/24919/24499

League of Nations, 'Inter-Governmental Conference on the Legal Status of Refugees coming from Germany: Provisional minutes, Sixth meeting', Conf. S.R.A./1st Session/P.V.6 (16 July 1936), United Nations Archives at Geneva (digital), Ref Code R5761/50/24919/24499

League of Nations, 'International Conference for the Adoption of a Convention concerning the Status of Refugees coming from Germany: Provisional Minutes, Fifth meeting', Conf. C.S.R.A/P.V.5 (9 Feb 1938), United Nations Archives at Geneva (digital), Ref Code 5793/50/32794/32089

League of Nations, Nansen International Office for Refugees (under the Authority of the League of Nations), 'Report of the Governing Body for the Year ending June 30th, 1937 on the Russian, Armenian, Assyrian, Assyro-Chaldean, Saar and Turkish Refugee problems', A.21.1937.XII (20 August 1937)

League of Nations, 'Report of the Inter-Governmental Advisory Commission for Refugees on the Work of its Fifth Session and Communication from the International Nansen Office for Refugees', C.266.M.136.1933 (18 May 1933)

Procés-Verbaux de la Conférence Intergouvernementale pour les Réfugies. Tenue à Genève du 26 au 28 octobre 1933', C.113.M.41.1934 (1 March 1934), Annex I

UN Ad Hoc Committee on Refugees and Stateless Persons, 'A Study of Statelessness, United Nations, August 1949, Lake Success - New York' (1 August 1949) E/1112; E/1112/Add.1, available via <http://www.refworld.org/docid/3ae68c2d0.html>

United Nations Counter-Terrorism Implementation Task Force, Working Group on protecting human rights while countering terrorism, 'Basic Human Rights Reference Guide: Right to a Fair Trial and Due Process in the Context of Countering Terrorism' (United Nations, October 2014)

United Nations Development Programme (UNDP), 'Access to Justice: Practice Note' (9 March 2004)

UN General Assembly (UNGA), 69th sess, Sixth Committee, 'Summary record of the 19th meeting', A/C.6/69/SR.19 (17 November 2014)

UNGA, 5th sess, Third Committee, 337th–338th meeting, A/C.3/SR.337–338 (6 December 1950)

UNGA, 5th sess, Third Committee, 332nd meeting, A/C.3/SR.332 (1 December 1950)

UNGA, 5th sess, Third Committee, 324th–330th meetings A/C.3/SR.324–330 (22 November 1950–30 November 1950)

UNGA, Conference of Plenipotentiaries on the Status of Refugees and Stateless Persons, 'Draft Convention Relating to the Status of Refugees: Report of the Style Committee', A/CONF.2/102 (24 July 1951)

UNGA, Conference of Plenipotentiaries on the Status of Refugees and Stateless Persons, 'Draft Convention Relating to the Status of Refugees: France – Amendment to Article 26', A/CONF.2/62 (10 July 1951)

UNGA, Conference of Plenipotentiaries on the Status of Refugees and Stateless Persons, 'Draft Convention Relating to the Status of Refugees: UK Amendment to Article 27', A/CONF.2/60 (9 July 1951)

UNGA, Conference of Plenipotentiaries on the Status of Refugees and Stateless Persons, 'Draft Convention Relating to the Status of Refugees: Style Committee: Text of Articles Adopted', A/CONF.2/AC.1/R.2 (18 July 1951)

UNGA, Conference of Plenipotentiaries on the Status of Refugees and Stateless Persons, 'Draft Convention Relating to the Status of Refugees, Israel:UK: Note on Article 3 (B)', A/CONF.2/84 (17 July 1951)

UNGA, Conference of Plenipotentiaries on the Status of Refugees and Stateless Persons, 'Draft Convention relating to the Status of Refugees: Federal Peoples' Republic of Yugoslavia: Amendments to the draft Convention', A/CONF.2/31 (4 July 1951)

UNGA, Conference of Plenipotentiaries on the Status of Refugees and Stateless Persons, 'Texts of the Draft Convention and the Draft Protocol to Be Considered by the Conference: Note by the Secretary-General', A/CONF.2/1 (12 March 1951), available via <https://www.refworld.org/docid/3ae68ce944.html>

UNGA, Conference of Plenipotentiaries on the Status of Refugees and Stateless Persons, 'Text of Articles adopted by the Conference on 4 and 5 July 1951', A.CONF.2/L.1 (5 July 1951)

UNGA, ExCom, Summary Record of the 621st meeting on 7 October 2008, A/AC.96/SR.621

UNGA, ExCom, Summary Record of the 558th meeting on 4 October 2001, A/AC.96/SR.558

UNGA, ExCom, Summary Record of the 442nd meeting held on 9 October 1989, A/AC.96/SR.442

UNGA Res 73/203, 'Identification of Customary International Law' (20 December 2018)

UNGA Res 77/198, 'Office of the United Nations High Commissioner for Refugees' (15 December 2022)

UNGA Res 76/143, 'Office of the United Nations High Commissioner for Refugees' (16 December 2021)

UNGA Res 75/163, 'Office of the United Nations High Commissioner for Refugees' (16 December 2020)

UNGA Res 74/130, 'Office of the United Nations High Commissioner for Refugees' (18 December 2019)

UNGA Res 73/151, 'Office of the United Nations High Commissioner for Refugees' (17 December 2018)

UNGA Res 72/150, 'Office of the United Nations High Commissioner for Refugees' (19 December 2017)

UNGA Res 72/117, 'Expulsion of Aliens' (7 December 2017)

UNGA Res 71/172, 'Office of the United Nations High Commissioner for Refugees' (19 December 2016)

UNGA Res 70/135 'Office of the United Nations High Commissioner for Refugees' (17 December 2015)

UNGA Res 70/1, 'Transforming Our World: The 2030 Agenda for Sustainable Development' (25 September 2015)

UNGA Res 69/119, 'Expulsion of Aliens' (10 December 2014)

UNGA Res 67/187, 'United Nations Principles and Guidelines on Access to Legal Aid in Criminal Justice Systems' (20 December 2012)

UNGA Res 429(V), 'Draft Convention relating to the Status of Refugees' (14 December 1950)

UNGA Res 428(V) (14 December 1950)

UNGA Res 8(I), 'Question of Refugees' (12 February 1946)

UNGA Res 62(I), 'Refugees and Displaced Persons' (15 December 1946)

'United Nations Principles and Guidelines on Access to Legal Aid in Criminal Justice Systems', annexed to UNGA Res 67/187 (20 December 2012)

UNGA, 'Executive Committee of the Programme of the United Nations High Commissioner for Refugees', 72nd sess, summary record of the 742nd meeting, A/AC.96/SR.742 (15 October 2021)

UNGA, 'Note on International Protection', A/AC.96.1222 (19 July 2022)

UNGA, 'Note on International Protection', A/AC.96/1211/Rev.1 (1 October 2021)

UNGA, 'Note on International Protection: Report of the High Commissioner', A/AC.96/1156 (12 July 2016)

UNGA, 'Note on International Protection: Report of the High Commissioner', A/AC.96/1053 (30 June 2008)

UNGA, 'Note on International Protection', A/AC.96/951 (13 September 2001)

UNGA, 'Note on International Protection (submitted by the High Commissioner)', A/AC.96/830 (7 September 1994)

UNGA, 'Refugees and Stateless Persons: Report of the Secretary-General', A/C.3/527 (26 October 1949), available via <http://www.refworld.org/docid/3ae68bf00.html#_edn15>

UNGA, 'Report of the Special Rapporteur on the Promotion and Protection of Human Rights and Fundamental Freedoms while Countering Terrorism', A/63/223 (6 August 2008)

UNGA, 'Report of the United Nations High Commissioner for Refugees', A/32/12 (2 September 1977)

UNGA, 'Report of the United Nations High Commissioner for Refugees', A/31/12 (1 January 1976)

UNGA, 'Right to Access to Justice under Article 13 of the Convention on the Rights of Persons with Disabilities: Report of the Office of the United Nations High Commissioner for Human Rights', A/HRC/37/25 (27 December 2017)

United Nations High Commissioner for Refugees (UNHCR), 'Analytical Report: On the Legislation and Practice of the Republic of Uzbekistan in the Context of Prospects for the Accession to the 1951 Convention relating to the Status of Refugees and its 1967 Protocol' (2022)

UNHCR, 'Comments of the United Nations High Commissioner for Refugees on Proposed Rules from U.S. Citizenship and Immigration Services (U.S. Department of Homeland Security): "Procedures for Asylum and Bars to Asylum Eligibility", "Fee Schedule and Changes to Certain Other Immigration Benefit Request Requirements", and "Asylum Application, Interview, and Employment Authorization for Applicants"' (21 Feb 2020) available via <https://www.refworld.org/docid/60f845f14.html>

UNHCR, 'Conclusion of the Executive Committee on International Protection and Durable Solutions in the Context of a Public Health Emergency' (October 2021)

UNHCR, 'Conclusions on International Protection adopted by the Executive Committee of the UNHCR Programme: 1975–2017 (Conclusion No. 1–114)' (October 2017)

UNHCR, 'Detention Guidelines: Guidelines on the Applicable Criteria and Standards relating to the Detention of Asylum-Seekers and Alternatives to Detention' (2012) available via <http://www.unhcr.org/en-au/publications/legal/505b10ee9/unhcr-detention-guidelines.html>

UNHCR, 'Expert Meeting: The Concept of Stateless Persons under International Law: Summary Conclusions' (2010), available via <https://www.unhcr.org/4cb2fe326.pdf>

UNHCR, Handbook on Procedures and Criteria for Determining Refugee Status and Guidelines on International Protection, HCR/1P/4/ENG/REV.4 (1979, reissued February 2019)

UNHCR, Global Trends: Forced Displacement in 2021 (UNHCR 2022)

UNHCR, 'Guidelines on International Protection No 13: Applicability of Article 1D of the 1951 Convention relating to the Status of Refugees to Palestinian Refugees', HCR/GIP/17/13 (December 2017)

UNHCR, 'Guidelines on International Protection No. 12, Claims for Refugee Status Related to Situations of Armed Conflict and Violence under Article 1A(2) of the 1951 Convention and/or 1967 Protocol Relating to the Status of Refugees and the Regional Refugee Definitions', HCR/GIP/16/12 (2 December 2016)

UNHCR, 'Guidelines on International Protection No. 11: Prima Facie Recognition of Refugee Status', HCR/GIP/15/11 (24 June 2015)

UNHCR, 'Guidelines on International Protection: Child Asylum Claims under Articles 1A(2) and 1(F) of the 1951 Convention and/or the 1967 Protocol Relating to the Status of Refugees', HCR/GIP/09/08 (22 December 2009)

UNHCR, 'Guidelines on International Protection: "Internal Flight or Relocation Alternative" within the Context of Article 1A(2) of the 1951 Convention and/or the 1967 Protocol Relating to the Status of Refugees', HCR/GIP/03/04 (23 July 2003)

UNHCR, 'Guidelines on International Protection: Cessation of Refugee Status under Article 1C(5) and (6) of the 1951 Convention relating to the Status of Refugees (the "Ceased Circumstances" Clauses)', HCR/GIP/03/03 (10 February 2003)

UNHCR, 'Guidelines on International Protection: "Membership of a Particular Social Group" within the Context of Article 1A(2) of the 1951 Convention and/or its 1967 Protocol Relating to the Status of Refugees', HCR/GIP/02/02 (7 May 2002)

UNHCR, 'Legal Considerations on the Roles and Responsibilities of States in Relation to Rescue at Sea, Non-refoulement, and Access to Asylum' (1 December 2022)

UNHCR, 'Mapping Statelessness in the Republic of Korea' (December 2021)

UNHCR, 'Mapping Statelessness in Slovakia' (2022)

UNHCR, 'Note on the Extraterritorial Effect of the Determination of Refugee Status under the 1951 Convention and the 1967 Protocol Relating to the Status of Refugees', EC/SCP/9 (24 August 1978), available via <https://www.refworld.org/docid/3ae68cccc.html>

UNHCR, 'Note on Determination of Refugee Status under International Instruments', EC/SCP/5 (24 August 1977), available via <http://www.refworld.org/docid/3ae68cc04.html>

UNHCR, 'UNHCR Comments on the European Commission's Proposal for a Directive of the European Parliament and of the Council on Minimum Standards for the Qualification and Status of Third Country Nationals or Stateless Persons as Beneficiaries of International Protection and the Content of the Protection Granted (COM(2009)551, 21 October 2009)', (UNHCR, July 2010)

UNHCR, 'UNHCR Comments on the European Commission Proposal for an Asylum Procedures Regulation – COM(2016)467' (April 2019)

UNHCR, 'UNHCR Guidelines on International Legal Standards Relating to Decent Work for Refugees' (July 2021) available via <https://www.refworld.org/docid/60e5cfd74.html>

UNHCR, 'UNHCR Intervention before the Court of Appeal of England and Wales in the Case of the European Roma Rights Center and Others (Appellants) v. (1) The Immigration Officer at Prague Airport, (2) The Secretary of State for the Home Department (Respondents)' (30 Jan 2003), available via <https://www.refworld.org/docid/3e5ba6d45.html>.

UNHCR, 'UNHCR Legal Observations on the Illegal Migration Bill' (2 May 2023 (updated))

UNHCR, 'UNHCR Monitoring Visit to the Republic of Nauru 7–9 October 2013' (26 November 2013) available via <https://www.unhcr.org/en-au/58117b931.pdf>

UNHCR, 'UNHCR Recommendations on the Implementation of the Illegal Migration Act 2023' (6 October 2023)

UNHCR, 'UNHCR Statement on the Right to an Effective Remedy in Relation to Accelerated Asylum Procedures Issued in the Context of the Preliminary Ruling Reference to the Court of Justice of the European Union from the Luxembourg Administrative Tribunal regarding the interpretation of Article 39, Asylum Procedures Directive (APD); and Articles 6 and 13 ECHR' (21 May 2010)

UNHCR, 'States Parties to the 1951 Convention relating to the Status of Refugees and the 1967 Protocol' (as of April 2015) <http://www.unhcr.org/en-au/protection/basic/3b73b0 d63/states-parties-1951-convention-its-1967-protocol.html>

Document Series

ExCom Summary Records: A/AC.96/SR.304 to A/AC.96/SR.754 (1979 to 2022)

Conference of Plenipotentiaries Summary Records: Documents A/CONF.2/SR.1 to A/CONF.2/SR.35 (19 July 1951 to 3 December 1951)

Ad Hoc Committee on Statelessness and Related Problems Summary Records (First Session): Documents E/AC.32/SR.1 to E/AC.32/SR.32 (23 January 1950 to 24 February 1950)

Ad Hoc Committee on Statelessness and Related Problems Summary Records (Second Session): E/AC.32/SR.33 to E/AC.32/SR.43 (20 to 28 September 1950)

Online Materials

'African Human Rights System' (International Justice Resource Center (IJRC), undated) <https://ijrcenter.org/regional/african/#African_Court_on_Human_and_Peoples8217_Rights>

'Arab League Secretary General Welcomes Saudi Arabia's Ratification on the Statute of Arab Court for Human Rights (Saudi Press Agency, 24 June 2016) <https://www.spa.gov.sa/viewfullstory.php?lang=en&newsid=1513644>

'Arab Rights Charter Deviates from International Standards, says UN official' (UN News, Press Release, 30 January 2008)

'Bill No T/333 Amending Certain Laws Relating to Measures to Combat Illegal Immigration' (May 2018), unofficial translation, available via <https://www.helsinki.hu/wp-content/uploads/T333-ENG.pdf>

'Chart of Signatures and Ratifications of Treaty 005' (Council of Europe, status as of 11 April 2023) <https://www.coe.int/en/web/conventions/full-list/-/conventions/treaty/005/signatures?p_auth=Lv2PfBpi/>

'The Executive Committee's Origins and Mandate' (UNHCR, undated) <http://www.unhcr.org/en-au/executive-committee.html>

'English Version of the Statute of the Arab Court of Human Rights' (tr. Mohammed Amin Al-Midani, non-official translation) (Arab Center for International Humanitarian Law and Human Rights Education (ACIHL), undated) <https://acihl.org/texts.htm?article_id=44>

'UNHCR Executive Committee of the High Commissioner's Programme Composition for the period October 2022-October 2023' (UNHCR, undated), available via <https://www.unhcr.org/en-au/excom/scaf/5bbc66644/excom-composition-period-october-2022-october-2023.html>

'Fact Sheet: Metering and Pushbacks' (American Immigration Council, 8 March 2021) <https://www.americanimmigrationcouncil.org/research/metering-and-asylum-turnbacks>.

'Growth in United Nations Membership, 1945–Present' (United Nations, undated) <https://www.un.org/en/about-us/growth-in-un-membership>

ICRC, 'IHL Database', 'Rule 100. Fair Trial Guarantees' available via <https://ihl-databases.icrc.org/customary-ihl/eng/docindex/v1_rul_rule100>

ICRC, 'IHL Database', 'Practice Relating to Rule 100. Fair Trial Guarantees', available via <https://ihl-databases.icrc.org/customary-ihl/eng/docindex/v2_rul_rule10>.

ILC, 'Analytical Guide on the Work of the International Law Commission: Expulsion of Aliens', available via <https://legal.un.org/ilc/guide/9_12.shtml>

'Inter-American Human Rights System' (Inter-American Court of Human Rights, undated) <https://www.corteidh.or.cr/que_es_la_corte.cfm?lang=en>

'International Principles and Guidelines on Access to Justice for Persons with Disabilities' (Office of the High Commissioner for Human Rights, undated) <https://www.ohchr.org/EN/Issues/Disability/SRDisabilities/Pages/GoodPracticesEffectiveAccessJusticePersonsDisabilities.aspx>

'List of Countries which have Signed, Ratified/Acceded to the Protocol to the African Charter on Human and Peoples' Rights on the Establishment of an African Court on Human and Peoples' Rights' (African Union, 14 February 2023) <https://au.int/sites/default/files/treaties/36393-sl-PROTOCOL_TO_THE_AFRICAN_CHARTER_ON_HUMAN_AND_PEOPLESRIGHTS_ON_THE_ESTABLISHMENT_OF_AN_AFRICAN_COURT_ON_HUMAN_AND_PEOPLES_RIGHTS_0.pdf>

'List of Countries which have Signed, Ratified/Acceded to the African Charter on Human and Peoples' Rights' (African Union, 15 June 2017) <https://au.int/sites/default/files/treaties/36390-sl-african_charter_on_human_and_peoples_rights_2.pdf>

'List of Countries which have Signed, Ratified/Acceded to the Protocol on the Statute of the African Court of Justice and Human Rights' (African Union, 18 June 2020) <https://au.int/sites/default/files/treaties/36396-sl-PROTOCOL%20ON%20THE%20STATUTE%20OF%20THE%20AFRICAN%20COURT%20OF%20JUSTICE%20AND%20HUMAN%20RIGHTS.pdf>

'Medical Transfer Proceedings' (Kaldor Centre, undated) <https://www.kaldorcentre.unsw.edu.au/medical-transfer-proceedings>

'Middle East and North Africa' (IJRC, undated) <https://ijrcenter.org/regional/middle-east-and-north-africa/>

'Offshore Processing Statistics' (Refugee Council of Australia, 7 March 2023) <https://www.refugeecouncil.org.au/operation-sovereign-borders-offshore-detention-statistics/2/>

'People-centred Measurement of Access to Civil Justice: The New Global SDG Indicator 16.3.3' (OECD, undated) <https://www.oecd.org/governance/global-roundtables-access-to-justice/people-centredmeasurementofaccesstociviljusticethenewglobalsdgindicator1633.htm>

'The Republic of Guinea Bissau becomes the Eighth Country to Deposit a Declaration under Article 34(6) of the Protocol establishing the Court' (ACtHPR, Press Release, 3 November 2021) <https://www.african-court.org/wpafc/the-republic-of-guinea-bissau-becomes-the-eighth-country-to-deposit-a-declaration-under-article-346-of-the-protocol-establishing-the-court/>

Stork, J., 'New Arab Human Rights Court is doomed from the Start' (HRW, 26 November 2014) <https://www.hrw.org/news/2014/11/26/new-arab-human-rights-court-doomed-start>

'Targets and Indicators' (United Nations, Department of Economic and Social Affairs, undated) <https://sdgs.un.org/goals/goal16>

'Travel Warning for Refugees with Pending Citizenship or Visa Applications' (Refugee Council of Australia, 3 June 2019) <https://www.refugeecouncil.org.au/travel-warning/>

'Work and Travel While Pending' (Immigration Equality, 3 June 2020) <https://immigrationequality.org/legal/legal-help/asylum/work-and-travel-while-pending/>

Index